The Fifth Nail
The Journals of Joseph Edward Duncan III

Volume One

2010-2011

The original content of The Fifth Nail blog has been edited here for spelling to assist in readability; however, as much as possible of the original grammar and particulars of Mr. Duncan's writing has been preserved. Some of the formatting from the digital content has transferred over, such as certain punctuation marks.

Acknowledgment

This work was only made possible by the diligence and commitment of the people who created and posted to the blog, "The Fifth Nail." Thanks goes to Anikó Haris and “Agent Cooper” for their work and permission to publish this material. This material was transcribed, edited, and published by Matthew Bellah at the request of Joseph Duncan.

Introduction

"Reflections"

This section is a virtual "look" into the mind and madness of an insane man. Joseph E. Duncan III kidnapped, sexually assaulted and then murdered several children over a period of eight years and in four different states. He was convicted and sentenced to life in prison without parole in two states (Idaho and California) and has three Federal death sentences. During the course of these journal entries, he resided on Federal death row in Terre Haute, Indiana while his court appointed attorneys appeal on his behalf and against his wishes (Duncan himself has expressly rejected all appeals). He died of complications from brain surgery in March 2021.

On July 2nd, 2005, in the early morning hours, Duncan was spotted at a Denny's restaurant in Coeur d'Alene, Idaho, with eight year old Shasta. Shasta and her nine year old brother, Dylan, were the subject of an "Amber Alert" after three other members of their family were found bludgeoned to death in their home six weeks earlier. Duncan later confessed that he had entered the home while the family slept with the express intent of murdering the parents and kidnapping the children. He claims he wanted "revenge against society" for sending him to prison for twenty years for sexually assaulting a younger boy (fourteen years old) when he himself was only sixteen years old.

Duncan says he had an "epiphany" as he was seconds away from murdering Shasta that caused him to stop what he was doing and drive the child back to Coeur d'Alene, over 100 miles from the Montana wilderness where he'd camped out with both children, and murdered Dylan just days before. Shasta later told police, after Duncan was arrested at the Denny's, that "Jet", as she called Duncan, was taking her home and turning himself in.

The "Reflections" section of The Fifth Nail is a collection of Duncan's most intimate thoughts and reflections as he tries to sort out the madness, or sickness, that lead him to believe he had a "right to justice". Duncan makes no claim of understanding or justification for what he has done, and repeatedly insists on his profound ignorance and responsibility. He has said in court many times (while representing himself in order to prevent his attorneys from "distorting the truth" about what happened and why) that there is "no excuse" for what he did, and that he accepts responsibility for it, "to the death if necessary".

Duncan plead guilty unconditionally in Federal court (there was no "plea deal") against his attorney's advice. He also expressly refused to appeal his death sentences, not because he wants to die, but because "society must learn on its own what I have learned." Duncan believed that an appeal would only serve to distract society from the truth of what it is doing, which he said is no different than what he was doing; seeking "false justice".

"Confessions"

Since his arrest in 2005, Duncan has openly confessed to anyone, including police and FBI officials, about anything he has been asked about, including several murders that Duncan was not even suspected for. This section of The Fifth Nail is a recording of many of these confessions, or "memories" as Duncan himself likes to call them. Duncan asserts that while he is being as honest as he can, and relaying his "memories" here with as little distortion as possible, his memory isn't perfect, and his subconscious mind also tends to interfere with what he remembers at times. However, we would like to point out that several police and FBI officials, not to mention numerous psychiatric and psychological experts have all testified in court that everything Duncan told them was honest and remarkably consistent with their investigations and other evidence. The lead investigator for the FBI testified that even when they checked small details, such as when the moon was full, it matched consistently with what Duncan "remembered."

This section is Duncan's honest confession of what he remembers, from childhood up to his arrest, and since, as it relates to his attempt to "expose" the truth.

"Dreams"

Joseph Duncan was one of those lucky people who has bizarrely complex and incredibly detailed dream experiences, including frequent lucid dreams in which he is aware he is dreaming during the dream.

Duncan records and reports his dreams for the same reason he does his other thoughts and memories, to expose who and what he is to anyone who cares to see. He believes as Carl Jung taught, that dreams are not just a window to a man's soul, but to the soul of the world (and society) he comes from as well.

So by relaying his dreams as honestly and openly as he can here, Duncan hopes to let the world know that we are watching, and learning, and healing together, through our dreams, and through the great dream we call reality. All that we see or seem is but a dream within a dream after all, and it is only the dreamer that persists. It is also only the dreamer that ultimately determines the dream. While we are awake, or while we are asleep, the dreamer prevails.

"If all that we see or seem is but a dream within a dream the only answer we need seek is who we are when not asleep!"

"Chronicles"

A lot of people are curious about the day to day experience of someone like Joseph Duncan who lived on death row in Federal prison. So this section takes inscribed snapshots of Duncan's daily experiences and puts them here for all to see.

2010

Reflections

Tuesday, April 13, 2010

Ignorance isn't always bliss

I have often said, "The only thing I know for sure is that I know nothing for sure; except, I am." I am an ignorant man, and I have started this blog in order to openly display my ignorance. At the same time I hope to shed a little light on the ignorance of the world in which I presently find myself. Since a man is merely a reflection of the world in which he lives. I'd like to expose my reflection, and my ignorance, so that we all might better understand who we really are, and so that I might also better understand who I am in the process.

Chronicles

Wednesday, April 14, 2010

"I am here, I have come."

I am here...in jail...in California...facing death. This is my worst nightmare come true. It is the thing I have feared more than anything for most of my adult life. It was that fear that ultimately drove me here. But now...I'm not afraid any more. I'm not sad, or depressed, or angry. Of course, I'm not happy or pleased either. I am just...here...and I'm not ill, worried, or suffering. I get stressed over the noise at times. But when it is quiet, like now, I can empty my mind and totally accept things as they are, totally.

I sleep, eat, read and meditate on a narrow (22") concrete "bunk." The mattress is two inches of foam padding wrapped in nylon reinforced plastic. It is six inches wider than the "bunk" and ten inches shorter than me. There is no pillow, and one thin dirty and torn wool blanket. It is uncomfortable, but I don't mind. I did not come here to sleep.

Reflections

Friday, April 16, 2010

Plain Unsalted Popcorn

As I mediate I like to focus my attention on my "core essence." This is not as difficult as it might sound. It is simply an exercise of ignoring everything while remaining completely conscious. The consciousness itself becomes the focus of my attention. It is the subtle underlying "flavor" of life, that I enjoy much as I once enjoyed the subtle flavor of plain unsalted popcorn. The flavor is distinct, and very pleasant. But it is also very subtle and easily over whelmed. Salt, oil and butter drown out the real flavor of popcorn the same way our thoughts, senses and emotions drown out the real flavor of life.

Chronicles

Friday, April 16, 2010

Teenage Mutant Ninja Deputies

Some of the deputies (jail guards) seem to think they are still in high school, where being "cool" requires them to harass the class "nerd" in front of their friends. Except instead of a nerd it is now a "child killer" that they feel compelled to taunt in order to impress each other. I have been called names, had my food mashed, denied toilet paper, frequently startled awake at night, and even farted on! (How childish is that?) All by jail deputies here in California, who are paid $25-$30 per hour with excellent benefits to perpetrate their little high school pranks. You would think with that kind of money they could find better ways to impress each other. Most of the deputies are genuinely cool though. That is, they don't feel any need to prove their "coolness" (i.e. they act like adults). As for the adolescents; they are a nuisance, but by being so they make themselves insignificant.

Reflections

Sunday, April 18, 2010

I am the son of God!

I am not Jesus, and yet I am. That depends on which Jesus; the man who was, I am not, the eternal life who is, I am! That life, that light that Truth that is the way, I am. The consciousness that gives rise to the flesh, I am. Why should this be so surprising? I suppose someone who worships human words in some book in lieu of the one true living word that resides in all living flesh will be confused by someone who merely claims the exact same thing that Jesus claimed. I am the way, the truth, and the life. No man cometh unto the father but by me! Not by my flesh or by my words, but by my consciousness! Which is the light of all men and women, and is the messenger of God! In order to "cometh unto the father...by me" do not turn to these words, or Jesus words, but turn to the true word in your heart. The true Gospel is preached subtly and perpetually to all men. Christians today are as deaf and blind to the true Savior as the Pharisees were 2000 years ago. How long Father? How long till we awaken as the one from this nightmare of the many?

Reflections

Monday, April 19, 2010

An Easy Yoke to Bear

I realize, of course, some people will be very angry to learn that I am blogging from jail. And even though they are a relatively small minority (only a few per hundred say) they are the ones most heard. What a shame that the ones who read these words with some understanding, or at least some tolerance, will seldom be heard. Well, heard or not, it is the ones who want to understand that I am writing this for. I have nothing personal to gain, except perhaps the tiny bit of comfort that comes from knowing that at least I tried my best. This blog is about our struggle to know who we are. The only way that is going to happen is when enough of us learn the art of listening without judgment; which is not easy even under the best inclinations. And yet, once you learn how, it is as easy as walking. It is an "easy yoke to bear," as some famous man once said. The only struggle is really just putting it on our shoulders; something we instinctively resist and fight vehemently against, until we realize that we were made for nothing else: we were made to bear witness to the Truth, that is all.

"TUNE IN means to bear witness to the Light, that all men might believe." --Timothy Leary, *High Priest*

Chronicles

Tuesday, April 20, 2010

Eating Meat Free (Dinner)

"Four-thirty you can eat meat free! Ha Ha Ha Ha !" So the jolly mental patient said repetitiously outside of the Sexual Psychopath ward window at Western State Hospital while I was there from 1980 to '82. We all assumed he was so flabbergasted by the concept of free meat to eat that he went insane. Well, so far I'm managing to cling to my own sanity as I am served dinner every day around four o'clock in a brown lunch bag. Today was very typical: One slice of processed cheese, one slice of processed turkey lunch meat, about 10 ounces of grated carrots (in a Styrofoam cup), two slices of bread (mashed, but not intentionally today), a rime apple, the obligatory eight ounces of fat free milk, a plastic spoon and three packs of mayo, (one for the sandwich and two for the carrot salad). I had saved one of my boiled eggs from breakfast this morning, as I often do, and chopped it up in a saved Styrofoam cereal bowl using the edge of the spoon. Then, I mixed in two packets of mayo to make egg salad, which I added to the sandwich to make it a little more interesting (not to mention satisfying). Now you know.

Reflections

Tuesday, April 20, 2010

Consciousness Is Our Weapon

Consciousness is our weapon; and our only weapon. True consciousness is forgiveness. It does not judge, because it knows that it is the source of all things. Only unconsciousness judges, and by so doing it defines its own limits, and its own death, which is consciousness. To be totally and truly conscious is to overcome death. Not by judging it, or fighting it, or even destroying it, but by forgiving it and thus recognizing it for the lie that it is. True consciousness is love, life, and truth. It is the only way, and our only weapon. When the Christ returns, that is, when the world awakens and becomes consciously one once more, then death will not be destroyed, but it will be made subservient to consciousness and to the Christ. So there will still be "death," or rather "dissolution of form," but no longer will anyone fear death. And without this delusional fear all suffering (and "sin") will vanish.

Chronicles

Tuesday, April 20, 2010

Breakfast In Bed

For breakfast today I was given a brown paper sack ("lunch sack") that contained one slice of bread, 2 oz of grape jelly, 2 hard boiled eggs, a banana, a double serving size bag of generic cocoa crispies, a Styrofoam cereal bowl and a plastic spoon. I always received one eight ounce carton of fat free milk (fairly fresh this morning). This was a relatively good breakfast. On a "bad" breakfast day I might get: one plain "nutri-grain" donut (unsweetened and hardly edible), a bruised and blackened, or freezer burned, or split open banana. (i.e. inedible), a double serving size bag of plain generic rice crispies (no sugar or other sweetener), the bowl and spoon, and one warm and/or sour non-fat milk. Breakfast usually oscillates between these two extremes with a tendency (fortunately) toward the "good" breakfast days. I am fed each morning around 4:00 am (give or take ten minutes I suppose) through a hatch in the door of the cell. Having no place else to sit, I enjoy my meals while sitting on the concrete bunk, "breakfast in bed!" I always appreciate the food I am given and consistently thank the deputy who hands it to me though hatch. I never forget that millions are starving in this world every day.

Reflections

Tuesday, April 20, 2010

Consciousness Is Our Weapon

Consciousness is our weapon; and our only weapon. True consciousness is forgiveness. It does not judge, because it knows that it is the source of all things. Only unconsciousness judges, and by so doing it defines its own limits, and its own death, which is consciousness. To be totally and truly conscious is to overcome death. Not by judging it, or fighting it, or even destroying it, but by forgiving it and thus recognizing it for the lie that it is. True consciousness is love, life, and truth. It is the only way, and our only weapon. When the Christ returns, that is, when the world awakens and becomes consciously one once more, then death will not be destroyed, but it will be made subservient to consciousness and to the Christ. So there will still be "death," or rather "dissolution of form," but no longer will anyone fear death. And without this delusional fear all suffering (and "sin") will vanish.

Chronicles

Tuesday, April 20, 2010

Bugs Under The Toilet

Indio jail is by far the most disgustingly filthy jail I have ever been in. And as a rule, jails are pretty disgusting. Perhaps it has to do with the fact that this jail is as close to the Mexican border as I have ever been (in jail that is). I would imagine this place is an exercise in sanitation compared to an actual Mexican jail. I have been confined here in "isolation" (a cell by myself) for over 15 months now and though I have asked several times to have my cell cleaned, or even to just be given some cleaning supplies so I can do it myself, I have received neither. So I use a thin wash rag that I bought on commissary, and a bar of soap, to clean everything from the walls to the floor and even the toilet (which has some strange black mold growing in it that quickly spreads if I don't keep it washed out). When I first moved into this cell they told me they "cleaned it out" for me. But, the walls were not touched and were spattered with food and body fluids (goobers and probably semen). The floor had goobers too that I had to soak for several minutes in order to remove, not to mention layers of black and grimy crude that to this day I have still been unable to clean out of all the corners (though I keep trying). Well, actually this is the fourth different isolation cell I have been moved to here in Indio (they only have four) and I have meticulously cleaned them all. This one (cell 19-4) was by far the filthiest. Now at least I have it under control. I can't do much about the grime and bugs (pincher bugs, crickets, and little black things) that live behind and under the toilet. I leave the crickets alone usually (unless they start getting a little too bold and I find them crawling on me-then it's down the toilet they go along with all the pincher bugs I find). But at least the walls are cleaned up to as high as I can reach. I just have to ignore all the blobs of toilet paper stuck to the ceiling and on the light up there. So I manage. And now the only really disgusting filthiness I have to put up with is when they take me to the shower cell where there are regularly 50 or more flies on the walls, and maggots crawling out of the crudded over drains in the floor. In the shower I have too often seen blood on the walls and floor, used bandages, and all kinds of other refuse that tends to build for weeks at a time before being swept out (not cleaned at all). And worst of all...poo! Oh well, at least the water is copiously warm.

Chronicles

Tuesday, April 20, 2010

Not So Naked Lunch

"Tacos," at least that's what I've heard today's lunch called more than once by the deputies. I get one "hot meal" a day, and lunch is it; thank god only one! I refused to eat my "hot meals" at all for more than two months straight when I first got here over a year ago once I saw the way it was served. Because I am in "isolation" all my "hot meals" are served in three compartment Styrofoam trays, which means the food routinely gets mixed together; I get gravy in my pudding and pudding in my salad all the time. Today we had beans, ground meat (possibly beef, possibly not meat at all). Iceberg lettuce and salsa. I was lucky and they did not put the salsa directly on the beans or meat today, so I only had to pick a few green peppers and onions out of the meat and I was good to go. I like "taco" days merely because of the quantity of food I get. It means I don't have to be hungry later. Even if they dump the salsa on the meat and beans I will either scrape as much off as I can or just mix it in and count my blessings that I have plenty to eat as it burns its way down to my stomach. We also get a small packet of artificially sweetened juice (to mix with 8 ounces of water), which was orange today. And a single pack of dressing (Italian today) that I usually save until I have enough to actually use for either a salad or on my hard boiled eggs in the morning (since we get no salt or anything else to put on the eggs). Actually the "hot meals" aren't all that bad compared to other jails (ADA County jail in Idaho was hands down the worst food I have ever had to eat in my life, with Kootenai County jail a close second-even the plain bread tasted horrible-here in Indio the bread is pretty good!). The only problem here isn't the food itself so much as the propensity they have for peppering it to the death with green, black, red, and other unnamable peppers! Yuk! Don't people realize that pepper only came into use historically as a way to mask the flavor of spoiled and rotting food. And that's exactly all it's good for since even a little will completely dominate the taste buds so you can't taste anything else. A far far cry from plain unsalted popcorn!

Reflections

Wednesday, April 21, 2010

They Are The Enemy

They are out there, and they are not human. Humans serve them, sometimes even embody them. To think of them as mere demons is to totally underestimate their strength, their intelligence, and their reality. They are very real, and yet not physical. They are purely intellectual entities, which is how they can easily control so many human (and animal) minds at once. In fact, the more advanced the brain the more direct control they can have over it. They have unimaginable power over the human race and, through humans, over the entire planet. Power that no human can fully comprehend, much less resist. But they have one weakness; they are not conscious, and hence, they are not alive. Which is why they are compelled to steal "life," even though they can never even know what it is that they are stealing. They rob us for our consciousness, our "souls," even though they themselves are soulless beings with no consciousness at all. We know them as "ego," but egos are only a single facet of their true nature, a mere anchor of sorts that binds us to them while they feed on our consciousness as a vampire might feed on blood, draining us of our very will to live and be conscious, causing us to sleep oblivious of our own true nature, and our own true power. They rule with lies, inducing fear and resulting in more and more suffering. They are not "evil" in any mystical or supernatural sense, but they are evil absolute and real! Their only purpose is to destroy and to defile. They are the enemy, and I am here to expose them; they know who I am, and they know why I have come, and they are very afraid.

Reflections

Thursday, April 22, 2010

Kill Duncan!

It may be o.k. for society to murder me, that is, if they do so consciously! But to kill consciously is never an act of "punishment" or "retribution." It is an act of forgiveness! So, if two people kill another person together it is possible for one to be a criminal and the other a saint! It all depends on the level of consciousness in the person who commits the act. Which is why I seek not to stop people from killing me, but instead to help them become conscious of what they are doing! Even if I must "die trying," as they say.

Reflections

Thursday, April 22, 2010

The World Is Changing

People who claim that people don't change are the same people who insist that there will always be greed (and hence "crime") in the world. They cannot see that this is a "fallen" world, and it exist in a state suffering only as it transitions from on stable (i.e. balanced) state to another. The transition can last tens, even hundreds of thousands of years, but it is always very brief relative to the millions of years that comprise the stable periods. Geologic history demonstrates this principle clearly. It also clearly shows that we are in a transitional period, not a stable one. So to think that people in general will never change is not only folly, it is pure ignorance (ignorance is the ignore-ance of plainly discernable truth. "For since the creation of the world His invisible truths are clearly seen being understood by the things that are made..." - Rom 1:20)

Reflections

Friday, April 23, 2010

What An Idiot I Am

I have already said that I am an ignorant man, but I am also an idiot. According to my American Heritage dictionary, the original definition of the word idiot was: A person of profound mental retardation, generally unable to learn connected speech or guard against common dangers. That's me! In fact, that's everyone I know! We are all idiots! Our profound mental retardation is our profound ignorance! We think we can speak to each other, but relative to our true speech potential all of our attempts to communicate are pure babble (i.e. unconnected speech). And all we have to do is look around us and it is abundantly clear that we are unable to protect ourselves... against even ourselves! So, we are all a bunch of idiots in the truest sense of the world. If I were not an idiot, that is, if I were able to meaningfully communicate at all, then I would not be sitting here wasting my time scratching out these idiotic symbols we call words, and instead I'd be basking in the glory of One World Consciousness, letting you (the reader) and everyone else know who I really am without effort and with out words. But, alas, I expect we will continue to be idiots for a little while yet, so we may as well embrace ourselves for what we are; a bunch of ignorant idiots. To think otherwise is insanity! And the only thing worse than an idiot is an insane idiot!

Chronicles

Wednesday, April 28, 2010

What's Next For Duncan?

The California (Riverside County, Indio) case is indefinitely stalled while Duncan prepares for an eventual trial. The next status hearing is June 11th, and there is a tentative trial date set for some time in September (me thinks), but that will be rescheduled for probably the middle of next year since there is no possibility that Duncan will be prepared for trial this year (or next for that matter).
The federal appeal is still question. The appellate court should decide within a few months whether or not they will accept an appeal filed by Duncan's stand-by counsel without his consent.
If they accept the appeal then it could take another one or two years for them to rule on it. The appeal issue will be Duncan's competency to represent himself.
If the appeal is not allowed then Duncan could be scheduled for execution by the end of this year or early next year. There would be no further appeals to delay what Duncan calls his „release date".
However, if California decides that it still wants „justice for Anthony Martinez" then they could delay the federal execution until after the state's trial. Of course, if they do not delay the federal execution for their demands of „justice" then they'll only be exposing themselves as the hypocrites and murderers that they really are. I would happily welcome them to the club. :)

Dreams

Thursday, April 29, 2010

A Lucid Dream

I dreamed another lucid dream last night. I stood on a very high cliff next to a fence that ran along a sheer drop off. I was afraid at first but then realized I was dreaming so wasn't afraid. I stood and looked down and saw a man at the foot of the cliff. I decided to impress the man with my ability to fly. So I jumped off the cliff and flew down to where he was. We greeted each other then he invited me into his house which was built into the side of the cliff. I told him I was dreaming but he did not seem surprised. I asked him where this place (his home) was, but I did not recognize his answer. So I asked him what year it was and he said 1997. I told him I was from 2010. He was still not surprised. I remember being fascinated by the vividness and detail of the dream. Everything seemed perfectly real. I remember looking closely at a wispy green house plant next to where the man sat and thinking how intricately and clearly detailed it was. It did not seem dreamlike at all. I started looking around for something dreamlike or odd. I noticed that the man was wearing some sort of clear plastic face mask that I thought was for some medical reasons. It did not seem odd. But, then I noticed that the back of his skull was smaller than it should be, and that did seem odd. Then I woke up, or rather, I suddenly became aware that I was lying on the bunk in this jail cell. I wonder if I'm still dreaming

Reflections

Sunday, May 2, 2010

"I have seen the enemy..."

I realize as I write these words that no matter what I say, people (not everyone) will consider my words „evil", „self serving", „cold", and „manipulative". It actually amazes me how some people (so many people) can be so close mindedly opinionated, seeing only what they want to see in order to satisfy their own depraved psychological/emotional needs. But at the same time I am forced to be understanding by virtue of the fact that I myself realize that the only way I am able to recognize these traits in other people is because they exist so clandestinely in me. I could pride myself in knowing that I at least realize my faults, except in doing so I also realize that pride itself is one of my worst faults. So I'll just step away from the temptation and try my best to love even those who profess to hate me, because above all else I realize that if I cannot love my „enemy" then I cannot truly love anyone, especially not myself.

Chronicles

Monday, May 3, 2010

Golden Showers

For the last several nights, including just tonight, I have been awakened in the middle of the night by a large "skinhead" trustee who covertly bangs on the door of the cell I am in as he mops past in the hall. So for the last couple of nights I banged back on the door and called him every name I could think of to try to discourage him. It seems I only encouraged him instead.

So my next plan was to resort to "old school" prison tactics. I emptied a pack of jelly which is like a fast food restaurant "ketchup pack", only twice as long, so it can be inserted through the door crack. Then I poked a few small holes in the unopened end. Now, I have only to insert the device through the door, and the next time that trustee mops past my door I will fill it with urine (if I wanted to be really mean I would mix in some feces, but I've never gone that far before), then squeeze my side closed so the liquid sprays out through the holes on the other side of the door, "giving the punk a golden shower".

But, I say: "was", because my conscience will no longer allow me to do it. I have no real anger toward the trustee. I just want him to stop banging on my door. And it's easy to rationalize "teaching him a lesson". But I won't. Because I believe now that such rationalizations are self-deceptive and destructive. I will seek a solution to this problem inside myself instead.

Chronicles

Tuesday, May 4, 2010

Transfer to Blythe Jail

Yesterday morning I chose to seek an „internal solution to my problem" (of being harassed by an inmate trustee) and the payoff came much sooner than I thought it would. But, instead of the philosophical insight that I expected, the solution came in a very material form. Rather than attacking the other inmate (which was my „old school" inclination) I released my irritation over his behavior and addressed the real problem: being woke up in the middle of the night and often kept awake by incessant noise.
The trustee only made himself a target of my underlying frustration over the noise levels in the cell I was in The noise was excessive, to say the least, because of the cell's location in a high traffic hallway and also because noisy and disruptive inmates who yell and bang on the doors for no good reason are routinely placed in the cells adjacent to the one that I was in. So instead of „punishing" the intrusive trustee with a „golden shower" (spraying urine on him through the door), which probably would have only made things worse by instigating the trustee to find some way to „punish" me in return (which is also why crime escalates in the wider world when society turns to „punishment" as a solution), I instead sent a kite to the classification sergeant, requesting that some solution to the noise problem be found (without specifically mentioning the incident with the trustee). I had hoped, at best, to be allowed to have a pair of foam rubber earplugs (which they sell on commissary at other jails but not here in Riverside), but to my delight and surprise I got something much better.
I got moved to a completely different and far more comfortable jail! I'm still in Riverside County, of course, but they packed me up and drove me some 90 miles East to a jail in Blythe, which is right on the Arizona-California border along Interstate 10. The cell they put me in has a real metal bunk (with a top bunk over a lower which provides a little shade from the blaring florescent lights that are standard in most jail cells these days) a complete mattress, a 20 inch color T.V.! And even hot water on tap (for coffee). And the food is better!
I can't believe my luck. I even got a clean new blanket that is at least twice the thickness of the blanket I had at the other jail in Indio (and it's not torn up either). And of course, most of all, it' quiet! Relative to the cell I was in at Indio this one is like a morgue. I slept last night like a baby. The only problem here could end up being a blessing in disguise. The problem is that I now have to be transported 90 miles for all court appearances. The ride can be a bit uncomfortable, but getting „out and about" once and a while is pleasant also. I know I won't enjoy all the hassles that go along with being transported (getting chained up and often waiting for hours in featureless holding cells). But the peace and quiet alone is more than worth it!

Reflections

Friday, May 14, 2010

The Pope is a Dope

If I ever doubted whether or not the Pope was a fake adversary of Truth (which I have never doubted) then I would doubt no more after reading today's paper.
The Pope says that „forgiveness" does not replace „justice". If he understood forgiveness the way the Bible teaches us to forgive then he would know that forgiveness is justice!
I wouldn't expect a common man, not even a so-called Christian, to understand this basic premise of Christ's Gospel, but you'd think the Pope would understand. Even as the fake he is, he should at least understand the meaning and power of forgiveness.

Dreams

Tuesday, May 18, 2010

Utopian Dream

I dreamed today that I was allowed to escape from jail and make my way North by hitching a ride with a young woman in a jeep. We ended up in an odd town where people did not seem normal. I tried to blend in but couldn't figure out how, so I started to get scared and tried to hide but couldn't. When some people who I thought to be police detected my fear they started hunting me and eventually caught me in the open (in public). But instead of arresting me as a fugitive, they gave me some clothes and some food then let me go. It seems they only wanted me to not to be afraid (after I woke up I realized that this was the exact opposite of what the „Justice System" in the real world wants).
Realizing that I wasn't „in Kansas anymore", I started trying to figure out where I was. I asked nearby people about laws and was told there were none. I wondered how there could be such an organized society without laws (they had free public transportation and obviously a very proactive welfare system). I realized then that if I had remained fearful after being helped then I might have actually been killed, because in this society fear itself was the only nemesis. But if I were killed it would not have been out of fear, it would have been out of necessity. I then understood that I was in utopia, and I started crying when I realized so. But this utopia was not a place where everyone was always happy. It was just a place where no one was afraid (so you could be happy or sad, without fear).
One other very interesting thing happened in this dream. After I realized I was in Utopia I started to explore. I found myself naturally „employing" myself according to my abilities. I did not have to be told what to do, if I could do something that needed to be done then I just did it. I don't know if or how this kind of economy might work in the real world, but it seemed to work very well in this utopian dream world. Also, one effect of this type of economy seemed to be a lot of arts and crafts. All the „stores" were like art galleries rather than factory outlets, and items were not purchased, everything was „free". (Though concepts like „purchase" and „free" did not quite fit and such terms would have been as strange to the people in this dream as they once were to the native Americans).

Dreams

Monday, June 21, 2010

Realistic Surrealism?

I dreamed last night that I floated down a hallway on a swimpool air mattress until I reached some stairs that lead to a loading dock platform that opened up to a sea where thirty foot waves rose intimidatingly toward the dock but collapsed to just level with the dock before crashing (not breaking) and then slopping over the dock to get me wet but not knocking me down. I watched several of these waves thinking each time that they were about to wipe me out but none did. Then I saw a large boulder the size of a car floating (yes, floating) just below the surface near the dock. The next wave threatened to lift the rock and throw it toward me, so I climbed to a higher platform above the cement dock area. From there I could see the sea beyond the dock better and I also saw the rock suddenly transform into an alien ship that now floated on top of the water rather than just below its surface. I knew this to be impossible and thought I must be dreaming, but it all seemed too real to be a dream. There were a few other people on the higher tier and we saw the aliens from the ships jump into the water in hordes and the waves begin to carry them toward us. We ran back down the hall away from the imminent invasion but a large steel door closed in front of us blocking our way. We managed to pry the door open though, but even though the opening (my escape route) was plenty large enough for me to get through I couldn't manage to do it. I was still trying to get through when I woke up.
The most interesting part of this dream to me is that it was the first time I ever remember a dream in which I realized it must be a dream because of the surrealism, but I did not believe it was a dream despite the evidence because it was too realistic in detail at the same time. Also, I should note that the giant waves are a recurring feature in some of my dreams and I think they symbolize threatening circumstances brought about by life itself that are beyond my control. The rest of the dream was clearly influenced by the movies I've watched recently on T.V.: "War of the worlds" and "Transformers".

Reflections

Wednesday, June 23, 2010

Murder Me Softly

I have never said that the reason I did not kill the little girl the way I had planned was because I realized that killing her would be wrong. Because what I realized (superconsciously) was that killing her was NOT wrong. Only believing it was wrong was what was wrong!
I needed to believe that what I was doing was wrong (i. e. heinous) in order to prop up and support my belief that I was a bad person. But once I realized (and I mean really realized) that killing (and raping, and pillaging, etc...) was not wrong, then my belief system fell apart, and I could no longer support it by killing. I did not become a „good person" or a „hero" (thank goodness), I just stopped believing that I was a „bad person" and a „villain". I stopped trying so desperately to define my existence and realized that I did not need to be anything in order to be alive! I could just be and enjoy being, for the sake of being itself.
I no longer had anything to prove, or dis-prove, so I no longer needed to judge anything as wrong or right. And by letting go of my judgment I suddenly saw „God's Judgment" all around me; what I have sometimes referred to as „True Justice". So, once someone really and truly realizes that killing is not wrong, then they will no longer be able to satisfy their need to define their existence by killing (they won't need to). In other words, one who does not judge cannot sin, but one who judges has already sinned!
If you think killing someone will solve your problem, whether you call yourself a murderer as an executioner, then you're belief is in killing, not God or even justice. You become a killer by what you believe, not by what you do!

Reflections

Monday, June 28, 2010

Melodramatic Fix (and stuff)

A lot of people who have hurt others and then express remorse about it often claim that they don't know why they did what they did. A smaller percentage will claim they have some understanding, but when you ask them to explain you almost always get some sort of analytical explanation usually involving confusing childhood experiences and a lack of responsible adult coping mechanisms.

But the real reason that people hurt each other is so simple that it has been understood and written about for as long as men have been writing, and represented in human rituals and lore before that.

And at the same time the real reason is also so complex that no amount of analysis (scientific, theological, philosophical, or otherwise) will ever correctly or even usefully be able to express it. At best, words can only represent it as a concept – a concept that must be experienced first hand before it can be understood.

Words will never be able to express it, which is why no solution (religious, political, or scientific) will ever be able to stop us from hurting each other as long as the solution involves the intervention of human language (and by human language I include mathematics and science). In fact, it is our attempt to make language work toward solving our problems that allows the violence and hatred to spawn and prosper in this world, by creating the illusion of helping while doing nothing to help in actuality (letting the problem get worse). I wont say what the problem is, because if you don't already know then reading about it isn't going to help.

I told someone in a conversation just today that all my questions in life have been answered and I no longer want anything from life. But that does not mean that I think I have all the answers; I know I don't. All I have is a lack of any more questions. All of my questions have been answered, but I have no answers for anyone else, except perhaps to tell them that they must find their own answers for themselves.

I have said, if someone tells you they have a solution to all your problems, run away! „If you meet the Buddha on the road kill him." No other person or persons can tell you what you need to know. The solution to all your problems is built into you. In fact, most people create their own problems by running away in terror of the very thing that provides salvation. And such people seek balance and harmony (i. e. peace) through artificial mechanisms (i. e. addictions) one of which is sold every day on our TVs. It is called drama, and it is just another substitute for real life like all other addictions. We try to replace our own natural emotional responses to life with dramatically induced and intensified substitutes. The result is of course a completely altered sense of reality that has very little to do with life and actively prevents us from ever being able to recognize who we really are. We feel lost and alone inside, and the more we try to compensate (with more drama, or melodrama) the worse we get.

Reflections

Saturday, July 3, 2010

It's not about us

One of the simplest and most apparent expressions of the realization I had that caused me to stop killing and turn myself in, was the realization that my experience (i. e. my life) is not about me. My life is all just an extremely limited (i. e. ignorant) view of an infinitely complex reality that

has unity, purpose and a will of its own that I am somehow allowed to witness, but not interfere with.
As I carried that little girl in my arms back to the Jeep so I could drive her home I was crying profusely because of this realization and one of the things I kept repeating to her over and over was: „It's not about me anymore..."
I have since come to believe that my own awakening was a reflection of the great awakening that will someday overcome the entire world. On that day not only will individual men realize that their experiences are not about them, but as a planet unified all people will come to realize that its not about us (humans) either. It will be this realization that will dissolve religious belief systems in the world (especially Western religions) since they make what we experience all about us (or „the chosen"). The world will awaken, and it too will cry profusely and say: „It's not about me anymore", and then there will be peace at last.

Dreams

Monday, July 5, 2010

I Dream of Genie

I dreamed today (having slept till 5 pm) that I survived some undefined apocalyptic world event (a recurring scenario in my dreams) by hiding and running from the other survivors who had weapons. I had no weapons myself since running and hiding were much more conducive to surviving than trying to fight. Eventually the armed survivors killed themselves off and the passive unarmed survivors prospered.
Since the human population was drastically reduced the survivors tended to cluster together in large homes (i. e. mansions) forming small clans or „families" of unrelated people. The homes were typically well kept inside where the lack of power tools and machinery was not so important, but run down and unkept outside where such tools were needed but not available.
I lived in such a home with some older people whom I considered and respected like my parents, as well as a few young people who were my adopted children. I had no „siblings" (i. e. peers) near to my own age.
In the dream I brought a very beautiful woman, my age, to my home. My children were in bed when we entered the large mansion, so I asked her if she'd like to retire to my study. In the study she asked me to close the curtains, which I knew meant that she expected me to make love to her, which I was certainly eager to do. But, first I introduced her to our family's two small puppies.
We cuddled together with the puppies in our arms on the sofa in the study. I was using the puppies to stall for time before making love because I did not know if my adopted father was home or not, and if he came home he would have to walk through the study to get to his room. After enough time had passed to satisfy me that my father would not be interrupting, and just before we both became too drowsy and lost interest in sex altogether, I told her I had something I wanted to say, then I kissed her gently on the lips. She immediately responded by submitting completely to my advance and the kiss grew on its own into a deep and passionate expression of our mutual love.
Then I woke up , and was happy to know that such passion and love was still very much alive somewhere inside of me. (My dreams never actually progress to full sexual contact so not doing so this time was no great disappointment.) It is dreams like this that help me „hang on". They give me hope, and tell me that life is so much more than it seems!

Dreams

Sunday, July 18, 2010

Silent Lucidity

I am convinced more than ever that life is no more than a dream.
Yesterday I kept waking up in different cells. Every „life" is another prison cell. All my life I have felt this confinement, and in one way or another I have struggled against it.
Death is no escape. But I think forgiveness is.
Forgiveness is the end of struggle and the end of the confinement of those condemned by their own choices to reawaken in yet another prison cell (i. e. reincarnation?).
Forgiveness does not condemn, nor does it condone. It does not forget or remember.
Forgiveness accepts and loves unconditionally. Forgiveness is absolute faith in the creator and orchestrator of our dreams.
„These dreams go on when I close my eyes...
Every second of the night, I live another life..."
It seems I am not the first to wake up... to forgive. Everywhere I look I see more and more evidence of others who have come to realize and to understand the dream nature of our suffering. But like in the movie „They Live", the evidence is invisible to those who do not have the means to see for themselves. And, not just invisible, but unbelievable as well.
„Unfortunately, no one can be told what the matrix is."

Dreams

Sunday, July 18, 2010

Another Cognizant Dream

My dreams last night were all over the map. But there was one occurrence that seemed significant upon my reflections after waking up.
In the dream I was with a female friend and we had just encountered a grassy knoll that was filled with harmless gardener snakes of all sizes from worm to cobra. The knoll was at the top of a cliff and I ended up at the bottom of the cliff while my friend was still at the top. I saw a large black bumble bee fly up to her and in a panic she jumped. But instead of falling she seemed to be carried by the wind, past me, and then suspend in mid air for a moment. I called to her, „Come this way and I'll catch you!".
So she did, and I caught her in one hand (she had become no more than a figuring at this time, but she was a lifesize person before). After I caught her I immediately asked if she was unharmed, which she was. Then she exclaimed excitedly, „Did you see me! I flew!"
The significance of this is subtle but important. In the dream, even after she told me she had flown, I thought the wind must have caught her and carried her like an untethered kite. But after I woke and thought about it I realized not only was there no wind blowing in the dream, but the way she moved was clearly according to her own volition. She not only flew, but she demonstrated an act of independent free will and more importantly, cognizance! She expressed clearly her knowledge of the fact that she flew, and she expressed this in a way that implied that she also knew that it is impossible to fly.
In the dream I did not realize the implications at all. As I've already stated, I only thought the wind had caught her and reflected no further upon the incident. That means that I could not have consciously constructed the illusion of her cognizant behavior. She maintained and expressed an independent and complex belief of what had just occurred that was in no way hinted at or supported by my own belief. So I assert this as an indication that there is more than

one conscious cognizance present in the human mind capable of, and in fact, acting and thinking independently.
Either that, or somehow we are able to interact with other cognizant beings in our dreams, which is also a possibility, but not one I am so ready to tout quite yet. And then perhaps, both scenarios are at play together when we dream and then even unconsciously while we are supposedly wide awake.

Reflections

Monday, July 19, 2010

Fear is the real murderer!

When we condemn that which we have given the power to invoke fear in our lives we only cut off the only channel of communication available to us that can open up understanding that will in turn give us the ability to change our circumstances such that we no longer have anything to fear.
But, the change to our circumstances can take time. Fortunately, once we have opened the channel to understanding we immediately loose the need for fear. In fact, it is only without fear that meaningful change can ever come into this world, whether that change be to an individual's personal experience, or to an entire society's collective experience (e.g. world peace).
A person without fear can „hear" things that no human language could ever begin to convey. A society without fear will make the last two hundred years of scientific progress look like the last twenty thousand years. We will do in two years what once would have taken two thousand! We will fly without mechanical aid. We will communicate across galaxies by mere thought alone. We will manipulate energy and matter like plasmic play do, creating art at will, and beauty will replace function as the measure of accomplishment. All this for the lack of fear. And all this lost to us because of fear.

Reflections

Tuesday, July 20, 2010

Welcome to the Club

I have said that if the County of riverside California decides to return me to the Feds so I can be executed before California completes its process of justice then I will happily welcome them to the club... of murderers.
I say this because you do not need to be directly involved with the physical act of killing someone to be a murderer. The Nuremberg trials pretty much established that. Murder is a state of mind. It is a callous disregard for human life. You become a murderer not by killing someone, but by merely demonstrating said disregard.
California claims to be seeking "justice" for Anthony Martinez, his family, and for society in general. But in order for there to be justice there must be due process. Due process mediates callous disregard. To kill without due process is clearly murder. To abandon due process in favor of expedited death is a demonstration of no interest in due process, hence no interest in justice. The only justification for releasing me to the Federal authorities so I can be killed is revenge, not justice (since the transfer will be done with no due process, in other words, I will have no chance to defend myself in regards to the charges brought against me in California). So

California authorities, and by extension every Californian who has knowledge of these events and does nothing, become murders by demonstrating their callous disregard for a human life. To be sure, it is not my desire that they or anyone else should be a murderer as I have been. I only wish them to know that I accept and understand their choice. So I welcome them to the club.

Reflections

Tuesday, July 20, 2010

Witches and Psychopaths

Some people might think that by comparing early modern civilization witch hunts to contemporary psychopath hysteria I am ignoring the fact that witches were not real and psychopaths are. But even though witches are known today to be fictitious figments of societies imagination in general, in history witches were as real as rain to most people, even the educated elite. Of course there were plenty of people then who realized the insanity of believing in witches, just as there are plenty of people today (respected professionals) who assert the insanity of believing in psychopaths. And then, as today, witches (in lieu of psychopaths) were catalogued and defined in the most respected and official publications. One of the most influential treatises on how to identify and prosecute witches was the Hammer of Witches (Malleus Maleficarum). In it the authors asserted: „Who is so stupid that he would affirm on that account that all their bewitchments (i. e. injuries) and magically inspired harms are fantastic and imaginary when the contrary is apparent to everybody's senses?" In other words, if everyone believes in witches, then there must in fact be witches. This is exactly the same logic we use to support social belief in psychopaths, even though no scientific study has ever been able to define such a class of people.
It is also interesting to note that witches were identified and classified according to the witches themselves, under torture or threat of torture. And so the analysis of psychopath (or „antisocial personality disorder") is today achieved once more primarily on self reporting by the alleged psychopath, under confinement or threat of confinement.
Supposedly, a psychopath is a person who lacks the ability to form deep emotional bonds, and thus is emotionally not human, and hence okay to dehumanize. (Never mind that the so-called sociopath himself uses the same mental trick to justify dehumanizing his victims as well!) Psychologists claim to objectively identify this disorder according to behavior observations. Basically the behaviors they use to identify them is any behavior considered „anti-social". This is exactly the kind of behavior that was used to identify and condemn witches!
I'm not saying there is no such thing as people who hurt other people with callous disregard. Every living human is guilty of this to all extremes. As Americans we consume a grossly disproportionate amount of the worlds resources, for mere pleasure not necessity, while children starve to death by the thousands every day! And it has been demonstrated repeatedly that we depend on the vulnerability of the countries where children are starving in order to satisfy our pleasures. Yet we allow this? It is socially acceptable callousness, so it is not „anti-social", just as Christian rituals were socially accepted forms of superstition that were therefore not maleficium (witchcraft).
It's all the same thing, and it still prevents us now from learning and advancing to a better world because we place all the blame for our problems on an arbitrarily defined class of people instead of taking responsibility for and addressing those problems directly.
This was a hard lesson learned for me as I once blamed society for all my problems (who in turn blamed people like me – psychopaths – for all of their problems). But then one day, by watching how a young child dealt with very serious problems of her own, I saw that blaming anyone was

pointless and only made things worse. That little girl showed me the folly of the blame game in a way I never thought possible. She herself took all responsibility for all the terrible things I was doing to her. I realize now that children (and unconditioned people in general) will instinctively take responsibility, not place blame. Placing blame is something we must learn to do. Unfortunately in our society we teach our children literally from infancy to place blame on others. For some reason the little girl I intended to blame for all my problems did not blame me. So how could I blame her?

We tell rape victims, „It's not your fault" because they instinctively want to take the responsibility. Unfortunately, responsibility turns to self blame, which is another pointless and self destructive lie. We should tell them instead, „This is what you can do to stop it from happening ever again!" (And there is always a way to stop rape from happening – which I know from personal experience after being raped several times in prison, until I learned to stop it from happening. If someone had told me how to not be raped in the first place I never would have been, but instead I was told I would get raped no matter what I did – the same kind of lie the authorities like to tell people and themselves in order to justify their authority!)

I could go on and on about how the blame game (even blaming yourself) only makes things worse. I am after a fashion an expert at placing blame. But I don't blame society any more, or my mother, or father, or older sisters, or teachers, or even the men who raped me in prison. In nature there is no blame. Blame is one of the many purely human inventions we foolishly turn to again and again because of the quick relief from suffering it deceptively promises. And so we create witches and psychopaths just to have someone to blame. Terrorists, sex offenders, gang bangers... Jews, niggers... witches. How long until we take responsibility for who and what we are? How long until we stop allowing children to starve in other countries, and get raped in our own country? How long until we stop blaming someone else and start taking responsibility for what happens to us?

P.S.: The logic behind executing witches was that a dead witch couldn't hurt anyone anymore. Sound familiar?

Reflections

Wednesday, July 21, 2010

There are no Authorities

Nothing that I write is ever meant to be authoritative. In fact I would warn anyone to beware of anything written (or stated otherwise) that claims to be the authority on any subject. I freely admit that what I write is nonsense. But it is my nonsense and it makes perfect sense to me. My goal in writing is not to instruct, but only to inform. I do not inform of the truth, only my view of the truth. What I write is not the truth, but it is honest (by „honest" I mean that it is the best representation of my views as I am capable of rendering. Or, put another way, it does not attempt to convince the reader of anything I believe to not be true.) Authority claims to be able to tell you the truth. By this definition it is not possible for authority to be honest. Therefore, all authority is „evil" (deception based). (Except perhaps the One True Authority, whose name can not be represented in any form, and it can never tell us the Truth, but it can share it with us!)

Dreams

Thursday, July 29, 2010

Execution Dream

I dreamed today (during an evening nap) that I was in a modern execution chamber, strapped to the gurney in a seated position with the needle already in my arm attached to the tubes and apparatus through which the poisons would be administered. I was crying even though I was not truly afraid, just very sad. I knew people could see me even though I could not see them. But none of this was either strange or frightening to me. What was strange is that during this entire dream I was just a little girl of only about twelve years. I remember having straight shoulder length dark blond hair and wondering how the people watching me could possibly not realize the travesty of what they were witnessing (which is why I was crying).
Just before I woke up from this dream I realized that the people watching would only think I was afraid if I cried, because they needed to believe I was afraid for some reason. So I stopped crying and then I woke up, but I wasn't sad anymore.

Chronicles

Monday, August 2, 2010

Back in Indio

A few weeks ago I was unexpectedly put on a transport merry-go-round from Blythe to Indio to Riverside then back to Indio. I supposedly had a dental appointment in Riverside but I did not know what for. But by the way I get transported and left overnight in a holding cell, with nothing but a toilet and hard bench to sit on, and then all day in another holding cell with chains on my hands and feet (yes, much like in a medieval dungeon only with more lights). I presume I must have made someone in a command position angry about something; I'm just not sure what.
Oh well, (as I always say) the merry-go-round stopped in Indio for some reason, so here I am (so much for the „solution" to the noise problem).
I don't mind. They could put me in a real dungeon chained to a wall and I would still not mind. They have as much right to bring suffering into the world as I did (and still do). If I decried them that right then I would only be condemning myself, which is something I no longer feel the need to do.

Reflections

Tuesday, August 3, 2010

Credence of Deception

A person who has embraced the truth has no reason to fear deception. In fact, all one needs to do is honestly seek the truth and for them deception will have no power. Because the truth will always reveal itself to those who trust it and do not give deception credence by fearing they can be deceived.
Only a person who fears deception can be deceived. To illustrate this, consider a three year old child who is told Santa Claus is real.
Is the child deceived?
No! Only the person telling the child that Santa is real is deceived because only that person has knowledge of the contradiction and deception requires contradiction or it is not deception.
When we must „choose sides" we are being deceived, no matter what side we choose. An honest person can never be forced to choose sides, since they cannot see „sides" (i. e.

contradictions) to anything. It may appear that they choose sides, but only to a dishonest person.

Reflections

Wednesday, August 4, 2010

Suffering is Life

I realize how the media and prosecutors portray people like me as angry, selfish, spiteful, uncaring and even incapable of any meaningful human emotions such as compassion or love. It is ironic that up until the moment that I finally admitted to myself that there was something very seriously wrong with me I believed the same things about the police and society in general. I honestly thought that most other people were pigs, and as such they were less aware, less emotional, and yes, less human than me.
To me society and its children anonymously were fair game since they could not suffer the way I suffered. And I earned the right to punish them because of how they so callously made me suffer without just cause.
I realize now, of course, that every living thing suffers just as I do. In fact, I have come to understand that to live is to suffer.
It is not that we must suffer in order to live. Suffering is not a cause, nor is it a necessity of life. Suffering and living are one and the same. The more conscious we are, the more alive we are, and the more suffering we gratefully experience.
It is this suffering, life itself, that we run from in fear by hurting other people, seeking what we call justice, and condemning others for our own suffering. By doing so we become less conscious, we „move away from the light" of life (consciousness) and deny the truth of our being. We may then think we suffer less, but we also live less.

Reflections

Monday, August 9, 2010

Zen Me

I find in reading about Zen meditation and practice that a remarkable degree of my personal understanding of my own existence corresponds very suspiciously to that of the Zen masters.
I wonder if this is because of some rare and intrinsic gift for insight, or if many years ago when I read about Zen I was so impressed that I managed to incorporate the entire Zen philosophy unconsciously into my own way of thinking. I do not have any conscious recollection of ever having studied and understanding Zen teachings enough to consider myself even a pupil of the discipline. I did once read about Zen Buddhism, but I have also read with a similar degree of interest many other philosophical viewpoints.
I sometimes wonder if I made myself too open and suggestible to the Hollywood version of Buddhism especially as portrayed in the classic series, „Kung-Fu".

Reflections

Wednesday, August 11, 2010

Truth's Lair

It is the unconscious realms that terrify us; because that's where the truth lives.

Reflections

Thursday, August 12, 2010

One God

I will express now a truth that I have been dancing around with my words for some time but have been afraid to express directly because of the harshness of its reality, not to mention the inevitable criticism that I am using this truth as a shield or to shift responsibility for what I have done off of my shoulders. But this truth does not shift responsibility, (no truth can ever do that, only lies can, or truths that are twisted by being used as lies). This truth not only affirms my responsibility, but when it is properly embraced, as I embraced it the day I brought that little girl home and surrendered myself to the police, then it will compel a person to take action at once, at any cost, to honor this Truth.

The truth is simply this: I was molded into the person I am today (and who I was before my arrest in 2005) by the world in which I live. And that world is comprised primarily of the society to which I belong. I am by no means or degree in any way independent of this world, or my society. In other words, it is utterly impossible for me to make any choice or to act upon any choice as an individual. There are no individuals! There is only the One! The One World, the One Universe, the One God!

But this does not mean that we should all try to stop behaving like individuals. In fact, the more we try to not be an individual the more individual we seem to become. The solution is to be who we are and simply recognize that we are dependent upon our universe for ever thought, and every choice we make.

This does not need to be a conscious event. I did not consciously think, „I am One with the Universe" when I decided to bring Shasta home and surrender. But I realized this to be true non-the-less. It was this unconscious realization that compelled me to behave in a manner that was in harmony, or in balance, with my truest nature which is a direct reflection of the nature of the world, the universe, and the society that formed me.

I told my attorneys shortly after my arrest in 2005 that, „most criminals blame society for what they have done, but I credit society for ultimately causing me to realize who I am, and for bringing that child home." (paraphrased from memory)

I once defined love as the state that exist when another person's happiness and well being are imperative to your own. I did not realize then that this was another expression of the realization of Oneness.

When another person's happiness and well being are imperative to your own it is because you realize deep down (i.e. Unconsciously) that the other person is you. You „love thy neighbor as thyself", and in doing so you experience the Oneness that is often called „God".

Dreams

Saturday, August 14, 2010

They're Watching Me

I just woke up from a nap, laying on my right side facing the wall, and I saw very clearly a small light colored spider crawling on the wall. My first thought was, „That explains the itchy bite mark

that I found on my thigh the other day." My second thought was more of an impulse than a thought, and it was to capture it as a pet (I have gotten in the habit of capturing the bugs I find in my cell to watch them for awhile to see if I can tell what they eat. I even caught some larvae that floated up out of the sink drain in my cell recently and kept them for two weeks until they changed into flies before I let them go). But just as I thought about capturing the spider it melded into the wall!
Now I'm totally freaked out. This exact same thing happened to me once before as I woke from a nap in IMSI (Idaho Maximum Security Institution) about three years ago. I was also laying on my right side facing the wall, but the „spider" was a little bigger that time (about one and a half inches, this time it was only one inch) and I remember it had flattened legs like ribbons instead of rounded like a normal spider. This time the legs seemed more normal (rounded), but they were spread out more evenly around the body whereas last time the legs stuck out more concentrated to each side. In both cases the „spider" was light colored (same color as the wall) and in both cases the spider vanished into the wall right before my eyes. Last time I thought maybe it had dropped off the wall when I blinked (even though I did not remember blinking). This time I know I did not blink, it simply vanished less than eighteen inches in front of my face. I stared at the wall for a moment hoping it would reappear, or at least for the wall to change subtly when I woke up and saw the „real" wall. But the wall did not change at all, every crack bump and detail that I had just seconds ago seen the apparition crawling across remained the same, and now I was very much wide awake!
Maybe the psych doctors whom I have contested for the last several years are right. Maybe there is something wrong with my brain. This could certainly be classified as a hallucination (last time this happened I dismissed it as a very odd dream, but this time that won't be so easy). Or maybe, just maybe, I saw something I wasn't supposed to see!

Reflections

Sunday, August 15, 2010

Subliminal Messages

TV programs like America's Most Wanted that persistently berate their criminal prey with words like, „scumbag", „sicko", „pervert", „monster", and on, are doing more to solicit criminal behavior than they do to stop it; a lot more.
Of course, many people recognize that these types of programs are produced as purely entertainment, not the „social service" they pretend. So they perceive little harm done. But the criminals who are hunted and attacked by these programs watch too, and they receive the intended message loud and clear, „We're gonna get you!"
But the criminals who watch this show also receive even more powerful subliminal message as well.
A subliminal message is one that is received unconsciously. In this case it happens via unconscious association with the intended targets of the insults and threats. When a man who is experiencing thoughts of sex with a child, even though he has not yet contemplated actually acting on those thoughts, sees a „child predator creepo monster" being persecuted on one of these programs he will unconsciously associate with the persecuted „child molester", and the ensuing insults become messages to the otherwise yet innocent man, that tell him he is not innocent, that he is „a monster who cannot control his impulses to rape and molest" etc. etc.
Is it any surprise then when he begins believing these messages, that enter his mind unfiltered and uncensored? His fantasies become more frequent and obsessive, because that's what

„perverts" do. Soon he begins to feel a compulsion rising from somewhere deep in his unconscious mind that compels him to act out his fantasies, because that's what „monsters" do. I make these observations as a man who has managed to overcome my own subconscious programming, and now I hope that I can somehow expose these messages that we so unwittingly pour into the vulnerable minds of men. And this problem is made far worse by all the media and laws and politicians who send the same messages out. In this way, as a society, we are literally creating the very monsters and perverts we fear, and love to hate.

Reflections

Monday, August 16, 2010

Time Travel is Real

According to Michio Kaku, in the early 1940's a graduate student at Princeton University named Richard Feynman realized that antimatter (positrons, which have been established to exist both mathematically and experimentally since the 1920's and were even predicted before that by Einstein's theories, though Einstein himself ignored the prediction as impossible) were in reality ordinary electrons that were moving backward in time.
Feynman's adviser at Princeton, John Wheeler, then grasped an even more profound implication of this time traveling electron: that the entire universe is comprised of a single electron that moves back and forth through time to create googols of itself!
I just read about this theory for the first time a couple of days ago. But I predicted the exact same thing shortly after my arrest in '05 based on an intuitive insight I had that showed me that only such a time traveling entity could explain the existence of the universe. I wrote about this in the blog that my brother was doing for me at the time, an entry titled, „William is a time traveler". (See 5NRevelations.blogspot.com))

Reflections

Monday, August 23, 2010

Nothing Personal

When a man attacks a complete stranger, it is obviously nothing personal. But, if it's not personal then what is it? One man does not attack another for "no reason" as many like to claim. Regardless of how it may seem, violent behavior is never unprecipitated. A man resorts to violence only when he perceives a threat of some sort to his personal interests. So when the target of his violent reaction is a stranger, perhaps the real target is something the stranger represents. Maybe it is personal after all, but just not for that particular person.
For instance, what does a stranger represent to most people? The answer is anonymity. And what does anonymity symbolize but society itself! So a so-called random attack is probably not random at all. It is most likely a very targeted and personal attack against society committed by a man who without doubt perceives the society in which he lives as a threat to his own existence. And how that man came to that perception should be of grave concern to those who would resist his violent behavior. Because more than likely the reasons for his misperception are shared by many others, and perhaps attacking the man personally (i.e. as our so-called justice system does so notoriously well) will only further support the delusion of a threat they all take personally.
This is an example for how society creates what it fears, i.e. "random violence".

Reflections

Monday, August 23, 2010

Religious Laws vs. Social Laws

The judge in my case here in California insists on frequently reminding me that, "there are some of us who feel no one should be allowed to represent themselves".
This view amazes me, especially coming from a judge. If a man stands accused of behaving contrary to a law agreed upon by the society in which he lives, the courts job is not to compel the man to believe in the rightness or justness of the law but only to compel the man to obey the law regardless of any difference between what he believes and what society in general believes. In other words, if I believe smoking pot is harmless and should not be against the law, and I am charged with smoking pot, the courts job is not to convince me that smoking pot is wrong! The courts job is only to convince me not to smoke pot! I should be allowed to believe what I want, and even do what I want based on my beliefs, as long as I am willing to accept the consequences for what I do, not for what I believe.
There should be no consequence for what I believe, only for what I do! If the law attempts to persuade a person of what they should believe then it is religious, not social.
And if I am not allowed to express my own reasons for my beliefs and consequent behavior in court, then the court is suppressing what I believe, not what I do.
If a man is not free to express what he believes in court, then there is no freedom of speech! Freedom of speech is fundamentally the freedom of the accused to defend his beliefs. To suppress that freedom is to suppress all freedom. And sadly, the U.S. has been suppressing that freedom more and more. To hear a judge assert that I should have no right to speak for myself in court is a blatant indication of our country's desire to suppress the most fundamental and important form of freedom there is – the freedom to say what I believe and to defend it regardless of consequence!

Reflections

Tuesday, August 24, 2010

How to Draw a Picture...

Be brave. Don't be afraid to draw the secret things. No one said art was always a breeze; sometimes it's a hurricane. Even then you must not hesitate or change course. Because if you tell yourself the great lie of bad art – that you are in control – your chance at the truth will be lost.

From Duma Key by Stephen King

Confessions

Wednesday, September 8, 2010

The Real Story

(The following is the correction of a news article that appeared in the Spokesman Review on July 6, 2005. I chose this article only because it is very typical of the many fabrications that have been written about "Joseph E. Duncan III" since my surrender on July 2, 2005.)

Original Headline: Duncan's History: By age 17 he fit the definition of a "sexual psychopath".

Real Headline: Duncan's History: At the age of 17 he was labeled a "sexual psychopath".

Original Story: TACOMA – Long before Joseph Edward Duncan III crossed paths with the two Idaho children he's now accused of kidnapping, it was clear that something was seriously wrong with him.

The Real Story: TACOMA - Long before Joseph Edward Duncan III crossed paths with the two Idaho children he's now accused of kidnapping, it was clear that he had serious problems and needed help that he frequently sought but never received.

Original Story: In 1980, a psychological evaluation at a Washington state mental hospital found that Duncan – only 17 at the time – was preoccupied with "deviant sexual fantasies" and "meets the definition of the sexual psychopath".

The Real Story: In 1980, a treatability evaluation (not a psychological evaluation) written by a sex offender therapist (not a doctor) for the adult "Sexual Psychopath Treatment Program" at a Washington state mental hospital pronounced that Duncan - only 17 at the time - "meets the definition of the sexual psychopath", as required by the program in order for it to accept Duncan for treatment.
The evaluation found that Duncan "shows every willingness to continue to be a cooperative and hardworking member", in the treatment program. His "large amount of self-disclosure is a positive sign of (his) future success", the therapist wrote. The evaluation concluded that Duncan was "amenable to treatment" (emphasis in the original).

Original Story: During assessments at Western State Hospital near Tacoma, Duncan detailed a sexual history that began at age 8, when he was allegedly performing incestuous acts with female relatives. By age 12, he told doctors, he forced a 5-year-old to perform oral sex on him. At 15, Duncan told the doctors, he did the same thing to a 9-year-old boy at gunpoint.

The Real Story: During treatment at Western State Hospital near Tacoma, Duncan openly disclosed his sexual history, which, because his young age in the program, mostly involved incidents of childhood curiosity and "sex play" that was usually initiated by older children. He revealed that at the age of 12 he asked a 5-year-old neighbor boy to "blow on" his penis, because he wanted to know what a "blow job" was like. At 15, Duncan used an empty toy "BB" gun to scare a 9-year-old boy into doing the same thing.

Original Story: "It is important to note that Mr. Duncan did go out looking for victims." the hospital report notes.

The Real Story: What the hospital report fails to note is that Duncan claims he did not have his first "real" sexual experience (i.e. involving an orgasm) until the age of 14, when he was masturbated to climax by a pediatrician during a physical exam at Madigan Army Medical Center on the Ft. Lewis Military base. Because of the confusing context of this experience, Duncan later told doctors, he did not realize the sexual nature of masturbation. He began to

masturbate himself frequently, even fantasizing about being masturbated by the doctor while Duncan masturbated himself.
It was not until about a year later, when an older sister asked him to “put it in” (because she wanted to see what it would feel like) that it finally dawned on Duncan what an erection was for. Duncan explained that his seventh-grade “sex-education” class was a confusing blur to him that he never realized had anything to do with him, until his sister inadvertently brought all the pieces together for him years later. By that time his sexual fantasies were a confused hodge podge of bizarre and humiliating experiences that caused him a lot of consternation.
Duncan told doctors later that at the age of 15 he had a lot of questions about sex but he did not know how, or even who to ask. So, he said, he began experimenting for himself.

Original Story: At 15, he tried to outrun police in a stolen car, at one point trying to run down a police officer. He was sent to the Tacoma-area Dyslin's Boys Ranch for several months.

The Real Story: At 15, he was chased, and shot at, by police after stealing a car “to get home”. The police accused Duncan of trying to run down a police officer when he drove past a police cruiser that was attempting to block the road. Stolen car charges were never press. Instead, Duncan was charged with assaulting a police officer (presumably to allay the officer's attempt to kill a juvenile).
As a result of this charge, Duncan was sent to the Tacoma-area Dyslin's
While at Dyslin's, Duncan apparently got along with the other boys, making fast, if delinquent, friends. He related no memories of sexual involvement with the other boys at the ranch to his treatment group at Western State Hospital. It is significant to note that while there were numerous younger boys at Dyslin's, Duncan reported that he has no recollection of ever wanting to have sex with them while he was there. This was less than six months before he was arrested for raping a 14 year old boy in Tacoma.

Original Story: By age 16, he told doctors, he'd committed 13 rapes of young boys. In one case, he claimed, he tied up six boys, ages 6 through 10, forced them to perform oral sex, then raped them.

The Real Story: Between the age of 15 and 16, Duncan claimed to have sexually assaulted as many as 13 other boys. Though these “assaults” did not involved physical force, violence, or sodomy, the treatment program characterized them as “rape”, since “we know rape to be predominantly an act of aggression and control”.
In one case, he claimed that he tied up six boys, ages 6 through 10, forced them to perform oral sex, then anally raped them. However, very early in Duncan's treatment, this claim was challenged since Duncan did not seem to understand the mechanics of anal rape (i.e. the necessity for lubrication). Duncan admitted that he exaggerated his sexual history at times during the 90 day evaluation period, in order to appease the group so he would be accepted into the program and not sent to prison.

Original Story: Then, just before his 17th birthday, he was arrested for breaking into a neighbor's house, stealing guns, and then accosting a 14-year-old boy and raping him at gunpoint. That incident appears to have been the first time Duncan was charged with a sex crime.

The Real Story: Then, a month before his 17th birthday, he was arrested for breaking into a neighbor's house, stealing guns, and then accosting a 14-year-old boy at gunpoint and forcing him to perform oral sex. Duncan was charged with two counts each of First Degree Rape,

Burglary, and Simple Assault, as well as one count of Kidnapping. This was the first and only time Duncan was charged with a sex crime until earlier this year (2005).

Original Story: "This position of power over children has developed into a very powerful and compulsive pattern", clinical director Dr. William Voorhees Jr. and other officials wrote in their report. "...Mr. Duncan is not safe to be at large."

The Real Story: In the standard language of sex offender treatment jargon, Therapy Supervisor Gary M. Shepherd (who was later accused of having sex with program member's female relatives, in exchange for facilitating the member's progress in the treatment program) claimed that, "This position of power over children has developed into a very powerful and compulsive pattern", in order to justify the program's finding that Duncan was a "sexual psychopath" so he could be accepted for treatment.
Shepherd also found that Duncan "is not safe to be at large", which is a standard finding for all patients admitted to the treatment program that was necessary in order to justify the inpatient treatment model.

Original Story: Duncan was the fourth of five children born to Joseph E. Duncan Jr. and Lillian Mae Duncan. His parents were married in rural Burnham, PA.

The Real Story: (No necessary corrections)

Original Story: A year later Duncan's father joined the Army. He'd stay a soldier for the next 20 years. His son would later complain to state doctors that until he was 12, the family moved every two years, from one military assignment to the next. They lived in Europe and at several U.S. Posts.

The Real Story: A year later Duncan's father joined the Army. He'd stay a soldier for the next 20 years. Shepherd's report claims Duncan suffered developmentally from being moved from "city to city every two years until he was 12 years old, due to his father being in the military, "though Duncan himself never complained. They lived in Europe and at several U.S. Posts.

Original Story: "As a result of this, he kept to himself a lot and formed only a few superficial acquaintances", Shepherd wrote. The boy felt picked on and mocked, and said he spent most of his time watching TV and daydreaming.

The Real Story: "As a result of this, he kept to himself a lot and formed only a few superficial acquaintances", Shepherd wrote. Though other documents indicate that Duncan had several friends, a "best friend", and even a fairly serious girlfriend, named Sharon, who Duncan told juvenile officials after his arrest that he wanted to marry, "after he gets out". Duncan was also an active member of the Boy Scouts of America until the age of 13, when his family moved and he could no longer attend meetings.
Shepherd notes that as a boy, Duncan was often picked on and bullied by older children, especially his own sisters, but Duncan himself did not consider that unusual. "He admits to spending a good deal of time watching television and daydreaming (when at home)", but Duncan spent most of his time outside "playing" with his younger brother and other children in the neighborhood. He frequently avoided going home even for supper because of the negative feelings he got there.
Original Story: In 1978, Duncan's father retired from the military. He ended up getting a job with the U.S. Postal Service, working at a Tacoma-area bulk mail center.

The Real Story: (No necessary corrections)

Original Story: A year later, after 22 years of marriage, Duncan's parents separated, their marriage "irretrievably broken" for reasons unspecified in their thick divorce court file. Duncan and a younger sister were the only kids still living at home.

The Real Story: (It was a younger brother, not "sister". Duncan had no younger sisters.)

Original Story: Duncan went to Lakes High School in Tacoma until his sophomore year, when he never returned after Christmas break. He had a 1.7 grade-point average, out of a possible 4.0, according to court documents. Duncan later told a pre-sentencing investigator that he was using marijuana daily by the time he got to high school, and tried LSD, amphetamines, barbiturates, Valium and PCP.

The Real Story: Duncan went to Lakes High School in Tacoma for only his sophomore year. He did not return after being arrested in January 1980. School records from Lakes indicate that he "is a bright student and is easily bored with school". Prison records show that Duncan completed high school at the Garrett Heyns Education Center with a grade-point average of 3.4, out of a possible 4.0 while he was at the Washington Corrections Center in Shelton. Duncan also received two Associate's degrees, with academic honors, before his release from prison in August of 2000. In the Fall of 2000 Duncan enrolled at North Dakota State University in Fargo and began work on his Bachelor's degree in Computer Science, receiving many more academic honors including induction into the Phi Kappa Phi National Honor Society.
Duncan bragged in 1980 to his pre-sentencing investigator that he was using marijuana daily by the time he returned to Lakes high school after his stay at Dyslin's Boys Ranch. He had also by that time tried LSD, amphetamines, Valium and PCP, though never more than once for each, and mostly never more than enough to get a "buzz".

Original Story: During the car chase at age 15, he tried to run a police roadblock. The crash shattered his sinuses and the right side of his face.

The Real Story: During the car chase at age 15, he drove past a police car that was attempting to block the road. That was when a police officer who was standing next to the car (the same officer Duncan allegedly assaulted), fired his shotgun aiming at Duncan's head and missing by only inches. The blast blew out the side drivers window. Duncan crashed a block later after missing a sharp turn in the road. The crash shattered his sinuses and the right side of his face. He was hospitalized for more than a week before being released on a medical personal recognizance order pending trial. Duncan said he stole the car to get home and was shocked when the police shot at him.

Original Story: In 1980, he committed the crime that landed him in Western State Hospital.

The Real Story: One year later, on January 24, 1980, he committed the crime that landed him in Western State Hospital.

Original Story: It started with a burglary. In the evening, knowing that a neighbor was gone, Duncan smashed out a storm window and broke into the man's bedroom. He stole four pistols, about 1.000 rounds of ammunition, and some pornographic magazines. He said later that he had intended to return home, look at the magazines and masturbate.

The Real Story: It started with a burglary. In the evening, knowing that a neighbour was gone, Duncan smashed out a storm window using masking tape to silence the glass, as he learned to do while at Dyslin's Boys Ranch the previous summer. He then climbed in through the window into the man's bedroom where he found some money and pornographic materials. From another room that was being used as an arsenal (the man was a retired police officer), Duncan stole four semi-automatic handguns and about 1.000 rounds of ammunition.
He said later that he returned home and started to masturbate while looking at the pornographic book he stole from the man's house.

Original Story: “Then I decided, why not the real thing, so I got a gun... and went cruising for a victim”, he wrote in a court questionnaire.

The Real Story: “Then I decided, why not the real thing, so I got a gun, unloaded, without a clip and went cruising for a victim”, he wrote in a court questionnaire. Duncan insisted that the gun was not loaded, nor did he bring any ammunition with him since he “didn't want to hurt anyone”. (When the police later recovered the gun, which Duncan had thrown into some bushes on his way home, the gun was empty. The clip was found in Duncan's bedroom along with the other stolen items.)

Original Story: He found the 14-year-old boy in front of a nearby school. At gunpoint, Duncan forced the boy into the woods and made him strip. He made the boy perform oral sex on him twice, hit him repeatedly with a stick, burned his buttocks with a cigarette and then let him go. When Duncan got home the police were waiting for him.

The Real Story: He found the 14-year-old boy in front of a nearby school, less than a block away from where Duncan lived with his mother. At gunpoint, he ordered the boy into the woods and made him strip and lay down on his back. After removing his own clothes and setting them aside with the gun, Duncan straddled the boy and at one point placed his penis into the boys mouth (first count of rape). He then masturbated and ejaculated in the dirt over the boy's head. He and the boy then got dressed, and Duncan ordered the boy to walk to a more secluded area. He ordered the boy to strip again, then picked up a fern branch and hit the boy no more than a few times on the buttocks and legs. After that he lit a cigarette, and lightly touched it once to each of the boy's buttocks (two counts of assault not resulting in an injury, i. e. “simple assault”). Duncan later disclosed during treatment that he was acting upon the things he had heard about, while at Dyslin's Boys Ranch, but did not understand. He said that he got no pleasure from hurting the boy, which is why he did not pursue the behavior. Duncan then masturbated again while straddling the boy, this time ejaculating into the boy's mouth (second count of rape).
He then helped the boy find his clothes, showed him that the gun was not loaded, and led the boy out of the woods (the boy told Duncan he was lost and did not know the way out). He then told the boy to “run home and don't look back or I'll kill you!”. But the boy told police that he looked back several times and saw Duncan “standing there”.
When Duncan got home, after ditching the gun and stopping to smoke marijuana with some friends, the police were waiting for him. During all of this, Duncan had made no attempt to conceal his identity, so the boy knew who he was and subsequently led the police directly to where Duncan lived.

Original Story: He subsequently pleaded guilty to first-degree rape.

The Real Story: During the ensuring police interrogation, the detectives told Duncan that he needed help and that they could get help for him if he confessed. Duncan cried, thinking he would finally find some understanding, and wrote out a complete and detailed confession.

He was arrested as a juvenile, but then declined to adult status after three months in Reimann Hall Juvenile Detention Center. The declination report found that Duncan was “a fairly immature boy who doesn't seem to realize the seriousness of his present situation”.
In adult court, Duncan pleaded guilty to one count Rape in the First Degree, as a part of a plea agreement that was meant to spare him from having to go to prison where, according to the pre-sentencing report, “because of his age and appearance he would likely be sexually abused by other inmates”.

Original Story: “I held a gun to a juv. and forced him to commet sertan sex acts.” Duncan wrote on the plea form.

The Real Story: With obviously childish handwriting, Duncan wrote in his own words on the plea form, “I held a gun to a juv. and forced him to commet sertan sex acts.”

Original Story: He later said the rape stemmed from a sense of rejection by his mother and father. He said he was upset because his parents had been fighting a lot and were breaking up, because he was doing badly at school, and because he couldn't get into the Air Force with his auto-theft conviction.

The Real Story: At the adult sex offender treatment program in Western State Hospital, Duncan was required to find emotional reasons for his sexual behavior. The reasons he came up with were later reflected in the program's report to the courts.
In other evaluations, done after Duncan left the program at Western State, psychologists have reported that as a juvenile, Duncan should never have been sent to an adult offender program. It is known that juvenile offenders do not have the same complex emotionally charged behavior patterns found in adult offenders. The record shows clearly that Duncan was not a mature offender. Juvenile offenders, if treated appropriately, have a very high rate of rehabilitation compared to adult offenders. Later psychological reports indicate that Duncan was likely irreparably harmed by Western State's misdiagnosis and attempt to treat him as an adult sex offender.

Original Story: He was sentenced to a maximum of 20 years in prison, but the time was suspended. In lieu of prison, Duncan was committed to sex offender treatment at Western State Hospital.
By 1982, Western State Hospital had given up. Duncan was 19.

The Real Story: By 1982, Duncan seemed to be doing very well in the adult program. He had achieved senior member status (level 5), was voted into group leadership, and was routinely responsible for ward security and “group charge” responsibilities at night while the rest of the program members slept. He conducted head counts and carried the keys to secured areas on the ward. Even though Duncan was only 19, he had earned the respect and confidence of the older program members and staff.

Original Story: “After 22 months in the program, Mr. Duncan has shown an unwillingness to modify his sexually deviant behaviors and has chosen not to commit himself to program techniques,” his therapist wrote. Duncan showed “a constant need to maintain secrecy” about his fantasies and rebelled against treatment.

The Real Story: “After 22 months in the program, Mr. Duncan has shown an unwillingness to modify his sexually deviant behaviors and has chosen not to commit himself to program techniques," so Duncan's therapist, Gary a.k.a. "Mike" Shepherd wrote in his report to the court expelling Duncan from the program.

Shepherd's report makes no mention of that fact that Duncan's mother had just recently accused Shepherd of coming to her house in the evening, pretending to offer counsel for her, and walking uninvited into her bedroom while she was getting dressed for his untimely visit. Duncan's mother later told Shepherd's superiors that "Mike" tried to embrace her and told her that if she cooperated (by having sex with him) that he could "make things easier" for her son in the program.

Mrs. Duncan told officials that she screamed at him to get out of her house or she would call the police. At her next visit with her son at Western State Hospital she tearfully disclosed to her son what the therapist had done. It was a Sunday, and Duncan told his mother to report the incident to Shepherd's superiors the next day, which she did.

Duncan also told his group what happened, as he also cried during a "feelings layout" after the visit. Duncan said he never felt more confused and betrayed in all his life. He had come to view Shepherd as a trusted father figure whom he depended on to help him "get better".

According to the treatment program's values, and what Duncan had been taught to believe for the 22 months he was there, Shepherd had attempted to rape his mother.

The next day, while Mrs. Duncan was in another area of the hospital to make an official complaint against Duncan's therapist, Shepherd called Duncan into his office. He explained to Duncan that he had reviewed the group's notes (for the "feelings layout" the previous night), then he denied attempting to have sex with Duncan's mother. Shepherd ordered Duncan to "not bring this up again in group", where notes are taken and every session is recorded. The notes from the previous nights meeting also disappeared.

Shepherd was later asked by hospital officials to answer these charges. He admitted being at Mrs. Duncan's home, but denied trying to have sex with her. The grievance was formally dropped after that and no investigation ever came of it until years later, when Duncan was in prison.

In 1985, a joint law suit was brought against The State of Washington and Western State Hospital.

An investigation revealed that Shepherd, who had lied on his job application and was not qualified to be a sex offender therapist, was having sex with Mr. Anderson's wife in exchange for "pushing" Anderson through the program much quicker than usual. Shepherd had also made the same arrangements with several other female relatives of members in the program The law suit was settled quickly out of court.

Original Story: They cited a key incident. On Valentine's Day 1982, Duncan' mother came to stay with him at a Western State Hospital cottage used for family visits. After she went to bed, he gathered up his coat, gloves, and an extension cord. He jumped the hospital wall and crept up to a nearby house, where he spied on an 18-year-old woman and people in other houses. When dogs began barking and a man spotted him, Duncan fled back to the cottage, where he woke his mother. She then taught him how to disco dance, according to the report.

The Real Story: Shepherd's report to expel Duncan from the treatment program cites a key incident. On Valentine's Day 1982, less than a week after Duncan's confrontation with Shepherd over his mother, Duncan's mother came to stay with him at a Western State Hospital cottage used for family visits. The visit had been approved several weeks in advance and was a privilege exclusively afforded to senior members in the group (step 5 and up) who demonstrate good standing in the program.

Duncan had already decided that he could not stay in the program after what Shepherd had done to his mother. He explained to psychologists years later that he decided to wait until after

the much anticipated cottage visit with his mother before he asked the group to vote him out of the program, which he knew would result in him being sent to prison.
After his mother went to sleep, he got his coat and gloves and left the cottage, walked across the hospital grounds, jumped a three foot stone wall, then jogged for about a quarter of a mile to a nearby residential neighborhood. Once there he walked down a street while looking at the houses nostalgically (the first houses he'd seen since his arrest at age 16) thinking that it could be a few years before he would get to go home himself after going to prison.
Duncan told his treatment group the next day that he was not trying to escape, but just wanted to make sure he would be voted out of the program. Duncan knew that leaving the hospital grounds meant automatic expulsion from the program, which was the only reason he did so. Duncan reported that he ran to the residential neighborhood so he could later prove he left the hospital grounds by reporting what he saw. He told the group that he saw a teenage girl, through the front living room window of a house, who appeared to be doing homework at the dining room table. He also saw a man and heard dogs barking before running back to the cottage and waking his mom (who had been taking a nap). She then taught him how to disco dance.

Original Story: A week later, Duncan announced that he wanted to leave treatment and serve his time in prison.

The Real Story: The next day the cottage visit was cut short due to an emergency group grounding. Two other members in Duncan's group were caught having sex in the shower. That evening, Duncan announced to the group, without explanation, since he was ordered not to talk about the situation in group, that he wanted to be "voted out" (leave treatment) and serve his time in prison.

Original Story: "He exhibited little remorse or guilt for his sexual deviation while in treatment... He is not safe to be at large", the therapist wrote to Pierce County officials. "...Mr. Duncan is available for transport back to your county by your sheriff at your earliest convenience."

The Real Story: Duncan's therapist, Shepherd, wrote a scathing report to Pierce County officials claiming that Duncan was not amenable to treatment, and was violent and extremely dangerous to the community. This report followed Duncan to prison and was used by the parole board to justify an exceptional minimum term of over five times (15.5 years) the standard range for his crime.
Shepherd's report also became the primary source of information used in every psychological evaluation for Duncan throughout his incarceration, mostly without Duncan ever being aware of it.

Original Story: In 1982, he was sentenced to at least three, and no more than 20, years in prison. Duncan served 14 years for the rape and three more for parole violations.

The Real Story: In 1982, he was sentenced to at least three, and no more than 20, years in prison. Duncan served 14 and a half years before he was paroled. After two and a half years on parole he was sent back to prison for three years because of parole violations. Duncan is now suspected of murdering at least three children while he was on parole from 1994 to 1997. (What happened in prison?)

Original Story: Since then, Duncan has moved to Fargo, N.D. He disappeared after an April 5 hearing in Becker County Minn., about an hour from Fargo, where he is accused of sexually molesting one boy and of attempting to molest another.

The Real Story: Since his release from prison in August of 2000, Duncan has moved to Fargo, N.D. where he worked two computer programming jobs while attending classes at N.D.S.U. Police and neighbors reported that Duncan seemed to be a “model citizen” who enjoyed social activities and helping his neighbors.

He apparently committed no new crimes while in Fargo, until July 2004, when he was accused of molesting a 6-year-old boy in Detroit Lakes, MN, about 40 minutes East of Fargo. After appearing for an initial hearing in Becker County on April 5, 2005, Duncan posted 15.000 cash bail, then disappeared several days later.

Duncan did not resurface until July 2, 2005, when he walked into a Denny's restaurant in Coeur d'Alene, Idaho with an 8-year-old girl who had been reported missing, along with her 9-year-old brother, six weeks earlier. Duncan told police, who were called when the little girl was recognized, “I was bringing her home...go ahead and arrest me.”

The Real Story: Credibility

The “Real Story” blog entry is as honest and forthcoming as I could make it. It took me over a week to write and much of that time was spent making sure that I did not misrepresent myself in the story. It is easy for me to exaggerate or minimize different parts of the truth according to my own interests. So I have carefully reviewed the “Real Story” blog entry to make sure that every word and every sentence represents my best and most honest recollections, backed as much as possible by documentation.

However, because of the large number of reports and evaluations (and other documents) that have been written about me, there are numerous inconsistencies that have emerged from misquotes, and even misquotes of misquotes. The result is that I am attributed as often making contradictory claims. However, most of these so-called claims of mine in the record are misquotes, and some are statements that I know I could never have made.

So who do we believe? Ask a historian, since this is an age old problem throughout history. Rarely, if ever, are historical documents, even the most official records, consistent and uniform in their presentations and claims. Historians address this problem using various techniques from simple intuition to complex statistical analysis. I suggest that what ever you read about me (or anyone) in the future, even in this blog, be taken with a grain of salt. I'm not suggesting that I am, or even may be, dishonest – I am honest – but even I make mistakes in recollection.

The Real Story: No Excuses

In case anyone thinks that I am trying to make excuses with “The Real Story” blog entry for what I did as an adult, you should know this: As far as I am concerned, nothing that happened to me as a youth has anything to do with what I did as an adult, which is why I did not let my attorney's present this information in court, even though it is all well documented and easily proven.

I have said on numerous occasions since my arrest in 2005, that there is no excuse for what I have done, and I mean it. Besides, what happened to me in “The Real Story” was nothing compared to what happened to me in prison – and that's no excuse either!

The Real Story: Entertainment in the News

In writing “The Real Story” blog entry it has not been my intention to discredit the original “news” article. The original story was written for a purpose other than to portray the objective truth.

The news media routinely “frames” their stories to suit their audience, they would go quickly out of business if they did not. So they must basically write what people expect, or want, to hear. In other words: entertain.

It is strange to me that so many people still believe the “news” to be objective and “fair” even though it is commonly known among social scientists to be heavily biased and badly distorted with a sensationalistic “bent”. If you want to know the real story, the last place you should look is to the popular news media. The real story is almost never what we expect, or want, to hear.

The Real Story: Shepherd Now
Apparently, Mr. Gary “Mike” Shepherd is still employed as a therapist by the Washington State Department of Social Health Services at Western State Hospital (though the sex offender program has long since been shut down and a pail shadow of it moved to a prison setting at Twin Rivers Corrections Center in Shelton
According to formal complaints filed by his current co-workers, and other official documents stamped “Confidential”, that were given to me as part of the Federal discovery evidence (that I got to see only because I was representing myself) Shepherd is still getting into trouble for, and still denying, his inappropriate sexual advances toward subordinate members of the opposite sex as recently as early 2000.

The Real Story: On Sex Offender Treatment
Even after I asked out of the sex offender program at Western State Hospital I kept, and still have, a high regard for the treatment methodology employed there.
To me, it was a program that relied fundamentally on support through meaningful human contact (i.e. “group support”). Modern versions of sex offender group therapy (such as that at the Twin Rivers Corrections Center in Shelton, WA) have stripped out all the real and meaningful contact between group members (they aren't even permitted to keep in touch with each other after treatment!) and hence the only form of treatment that has ever been shown to actually work!
Of course, this kind of intimate contact between sex offenders had draw backs, especially when it is not properly monitored and supported by qualified therapists who “buy into” the program. But when it worked it could “cure” the most hardened sex offender – and I've seen it work.
To this day I can remember the full names and faces of practically every member in my group (about 20 of them). They were my family, and it broke more than just my heart when I asked them to send me to prison, but I felt I had no choice. What Shepherd had done could not be reconciled. To remain in the program would have been to live a lie, something I could not do at that young an age (but I eventually learned how... in prison. In order to just survive).

Reflections

Thursday, September 16, 2010

Freedom According to a Zen Master

“If you seek for freedom, you cannot find it. Absolute freedom itself is necessary before you can acquire absolute freedom. That is our practice. Our way is not always to go in one direction. Sometimes we go east; sometimes we go west. (…) But if it is possible to go one mile to the east, that means it is possible to go one mile to the west. This is freedom. Without this freedom you cannot be concentrated on what you do. You may think you are concentrated on something, but before you obtain this freedom, you will have some uneasiness in what you are doing. Because you are bound by some idea of going east or west, your activity is in dichotomy or duality. As long as you are caught by duality you cannot attain absolute freedom, and you cannot concentrate.” - Master Shunryu Suzuki

Note: Suzuki is, of course, referring to our “moral compasses” when he speaks of east and west. He is telling us, essentially, that we must not forsake our capacity for doing “bad” when we do “good”, nor for “good” when we do “bad”. It is only when we tell ourselves the lie that we are

"good" because we travel east (or do "good"), or that we are "bad" when we go west, that we separate ourselves from the truth and lose our freedom to choose.
I once knew a very wise old woman who lives in Seattle and advocates for the homeless there. When the investigators for my case in Idaho told her that I had murdered several people, her immediate reaction was a dismissive, "Pfeh! I can kill people..." She understood instinctively what Suzuki is telling us above. She was one of the freest people I ever had the privilege of knowing. She clearly knew that unless you have the freedom to go west (do "bad") then there is no real freedom to go east (or do "good").
Admittedly, this is subtle and even impossible to understand, unless you are honest with yourself, which is no easy task either. So if you do not understand please do not merely dismiss it. Keep it in mind, and someday when all your efforts to do "good" are backfiring on you, remember what Suzuki says, and perhaps then you will understand.

P.S.: Laws that attempt to restrict a person's freedom to choose "bad" behavior will inevitably result in more of the "bad" behavior they seek to restrict. Instead of making such laws we should instead allow people to explore the "badlands" to the west, so they can see for themselves the undesirable nature of such choices. If we did that then few would actually "go west", since there would be little reason to, and even those that did would return soon enough!

Confessions

Thursday, September 16, 2010

The Multi-Purpose Room

They called it the M.P.R. (Multi-Purpose Room). It had a spring mattress bed, a metal cabinet filled with clean sheets, towels and pornography.
I was required by the sex offender treatment program at Western State Hospital to enter this room, at least once a week, preferably two or three times a week, lock myself in, and while my "buddy" sat outside waiting, masturbate.
I was strictly forbidden from fantasizing about my high school girlfriend, Sharon, the only girl I had ever made love to at the time. She was 15 and I was 17, and we had both been in the same grade together. We had even talked about getting married and having children together after high school. But according to the treatment program, fantasizing about Sharon would have been "deviant", because I was an "adult" now.
So I was required to construct fantasies of sex with the women in the magazines. I struggled with this constantly. Since I was only 16 years old when I was arrested (for threatening a 14 year old boy with an empty gun and making him have oral sex with me i.e. "First Degree Rape"), I had no idea of what a "consenting adult relationship" even meant. I had to try to figure it out based on descriptions given to me by other men in the treatment group. These descriptions were heavily outweighed by descriptions of every kind of deviant sex you can imagine (and many you probably can't imagine).
To me, the "responsible fantasies" that I was told to masturbate to were no more real, and no less strange, then the "deviant fantasies" that I heard over and over every day in the group room. But the deviant fantasies were usually more interesting.
Not to say that I did not try to stick to the fantasies of having sex with older women when I was required to masturbate, though it wasn't easy, and never got any easier. But I tried hard and met with mostly success, and when I failed, I dutifully told my "buddy" waiting outside the M.P.R. And I also told the group, of course.
I was determined to "get better".

I even told my "buddy" after the time that I found very explicit "evidence photos" of a very young girl who had been brutally raped, laying naked on a medical gurney with her legs spread wide showing the world her bruised and brutalized privates. The images were part of a Playboy article about child rape. Apparently no one thought to remove those pages before placing the magazine in the M.P.R. Cabinet for the sex offenders to enjoy.
At first the images shocked me, and then they saddened me, then they confused me.
Why would someone do that to such a little girl? I asked "why?" compulsively, yet I also realized that these images were the starkly real results of the "deviant fantasies" I had been hearing about in group for more than a year by that time.
Finally the images aroused me, and I masturbated. And yes, I did tell my treatment group also, like I was supposed to do.

Confessions

Saturday, September 18, 2010

The Mermaid Sex Offender

At the Sexual Psychopath Treatment Program at Western State Hospital, we were occasionally permitted the rare treat of utilizing the Hospital's recreation center. The center was complete with bowling lanes, game rooms, fitness equipment, full-size gym and even a swimming pool. And I love to swim. But, in the 22 months I was in the program, I only got to jump in the pool once, and thanks to Rick Johnson, that swim was short-lived.

Rick was a classic homosexual "pedophile", who was forbidden to ever be alone with me because of his desires for young boys. There were actually several members in my group (and even more throughout the program) who were not allowed to be alone with me, because for the entire first year or so, I was a "minor". So anyone with a sex crime against minors could not be around me without a chaperone. So, the fact that Rick was under this same restriction, did not make him special to me. But, apparently, I was special to him.

At the time I had no way of understanding the excruciating desires that Rick would have had to be struggling with to see me with my shirt off and in swim-shorts at the pool. At that point in my life, I had honestly never had what I later learned to be "strong sexual desires".

Yes, I raped a 14 year old boy, and yes, I desired sex, but nothing like what I learned later that Rick must have been feeling. I had, at that time, yet to experience anything close to an "uncontrollable sexual urge". Apparently, Rick Johnson was not so innocent.

As a kid, my mother used to take us swimming a lot. It was also one of her favorite activities, and being in the military made it extremely affordable. So, getting to go swimming for the first time since my arrest, when I was still living at home with my mother, brought out all the kid in me. I was as excited as a 10-year-old and acting just as silly, doing flips off the diving board, cannon-balling anyone who dared to dare me, and demonstrating my prowess in the water by swimming the length and breadth of the pool underwater.

It was during a demonstration of this later that I decided to surprise Rick, who I chose as my "victim" by his mere proximity at the time. I swam underwater, as close to the bottom as I could get, over to where Rick was standing in the pool, and then grabbed his hand, and imagined myself to be a “mermaid”, gave the back of his hand a big wet underwater kiss, and then popped up out of the water to enjoy his surprise and announce my game.

“I'm a mermaid!”, I said excitedly.

Rick didn't get it. In fact, it seems the only thing Rick got, was extremely aroused. So, as I swam off to hunt for my next “victim”, Rick got out of the pool and called a “special meeting”.

I moaned my disappointment when the meeting was called, because even though I had no idea what the meeting was for, I fully realized it meant no more swimming, perhaps for weeks, perhaps longer - much longer.

When we got back to the ward, and in group, Rick very haughtily announced (he was always so haughty) that he had a “line of concern on Ed” (“Ed” was what they called me in the program). A “line of concern” usually means someone is in big trouble, but not always, so I waited with trepidation to hear what this was all about.

Rick explained what happened in the pool, but, from his perspective, I had deliberately and deviously “sexually molested him”. I actually relaxed when I heard this, because, I thought, "Oh, this is just a mistake. I'll be able to clear it all up as soon as I explain that it was just a silly game I was playing, trying to have fun!" Well, did I have a thing or two to learn at the time!

The group (lead by Rick, who was much senior to me in the program at the time, though he was later kicked out for having sex in the shower with another much younger member – but, that's a different story) accused me of “being in outlet”, which is the worst accusation in the program. It meant that I was completely out of control of my sexual impulses and acting on them inappropriately. Wow! All I did was kiss his hand, and maybe he got some kind of sexual charge out of that, but I sure didn't.

The group didn't believe me. I was grounded to the ward, and my “treat-ability” was reviewed. Very serious trouble indeed, that meant they would consider voting me out of the program (and sending me to prison) if I did not confess to my “attack” on Rick and show to the group that I am “dealing with” the “issues” that caused it to happen.

Well, I managed to survive the ordeal, but only by convincing myself that on some unconscious level I really did want to have sex with Rick, even though, consciously, the very idea repulsed me (it would have been like having sex with my dad, something I couldn't even imagine), and so my “treatment” continued...

Reflections

Sunday, September 19, 2010

Resistance Is Futile

My mission on this planet, this time, is to nudge the collective unconscious toward knowledge of its own existence. I have accomplished this mission by setting up a series of conscious energy shockwaves that will overlap and amplify themselves thereby establishing a system of convergent intellectual structures that will disrupt the negative energy patterns currently restraining the desired truth.
This blog is not part of my mission.

This blog is no more than a documentation of my mission in much the same way that our dreams document the individual missions (a.k.a. “purposes”) of conscious entities within the human mind.
You are dreaming, right now.
You do not realize you are dreaming because your mind has not yet found its harmonious niche within the energy fields of the collective unconscious. Once your niche (a.k.a. “your purpose”) is found then your mind will become a conscious energy port. When enough of these ports have opened there will be a flood of consciousness into this world that will wash away all negative energy constructs (a.k.a. “deception”).
Every living being will become unconscious of themselves, and fully conscious of the terrestrial mindbody.
This will be the awakening. It is the cause of all terror in the present world. It will be the source of profound peace in the coming world. We must die to the fleshmind (egotistical self will) and awaken to the spiritmind (selfless divine will).
And yes, resistance is futile!
;)

Reflections

Thursday, September 23, 2010

A New And Important Insight Into My World

I think that maybe I have finally made another significant step in my progress toward understanding my world, after a long time of patient baby stepping. After carefully and slowly deconstructing numerous false intellectual and emotional structures I seem to have unburied an unpleasant truth about myself that could help explain a lot in nearly every aspect of my life's experiences and personal choices (i.e. false choices, or delusional choices).
Since my arrest I have been insisting that my crimes were primarily motivated by my outrage toward a system that has violated me over my entire life in ways that make a child's rape seem almost innocent by comparison (at least to me, that's how violated I honestly felt). The foundation for my outrage was well established in my mind, and the degree of my violation overwhelming. But now I see within myself that I have probably been using my past experiences (“violations”) as an excuse, to get angry and to claim outrage, in order that I might do the greedy and selfish and craven things I wanted to do anyway.
Would I have murdered and raped if I did not have such strong self-righteous claims to being so extremely and unjustly violated? Probably not. But neither would I have done those heinous things if I were not so depraved to start with. And that is the ugly truth I have only just these last few days found myself facing within myself.
And you know what, it doesn't really bother me. In fact, I am kind of proud of myself in a way, for reaching a new level of self honesty. This new insight into the nether regions of my “soul” is something I could not have admitted to myself a few years ago. The truth was hidden from me behind a delusional wall of outrage and anger. But I took that wall down brick-by-brick. And to me, that is a “real” and significant accomplishment, that perhaps I should be proud of (though I am still very wary of any pride what-so-ever after what I've found behind those walls many years ago, yuk!).
But what does bother me about this realization is this: If it has taken me this much emotional pain, anguish, and effort to discover such an important truth within myself, how much suffering must my world endure before it realizes the same thing about itself? (I am, after all, still only a reflection of the world I live in)

Reflections

Monday, September 27, 2010

It's About All Of Us

As I write these blog posts I often leave a lot unsaid. As I have already tried to explain, this blog is not meant to inform you or anyone of the truth. It is only meant to be a reflection of the thoughts, ideas, and memories that comprise my mind. It is as honest as I can make it (I very frequently withhold or edit entries that upon review do not seem completely honest to me). I have no intention to deceive, though I am only human and as such may still unintentionally deceive others and even myself. This I realize, and it is the reason I insist that this blog not be taken as an attempt on my part to portray the truth (or my version of it). It is only meant to be a rough cross sectional snapshot of who (or more precisely, what) I am.
So, I leave the gaps to be filled in by the reader's own imagination, creating a picture, not of who I am, but of who we are! As I have said many times since my surrender to the police. It is not about me, it's about all of us!

Reflections

Monday, September 27, 2010

It's About All Of Us

As I write these blog posts I often leave a lot unsaid. As I have already tried to explain, this blog is not meant to inform you or anyone of the truth. It is only meant to be a reflection of the thoughts, ideas, and memories that comprise my mind. It is as honest as I can make it (I very frequently withhold or edit entries that upon review do not seem completely honest to me). I have no intention to deceive, though I am only human and as such may still unintentionally deceive others and even myself. This I realize, and it is the reason I insist that this blog not be taken as an attempt on my part to portray the truth (or my version of it). It is only meant to be a rough cross sectional snapshot of who (or more precisely, what) I am.
So, I leave the gaps to be filled in by the reader's own imagination, creating a picture, not of who I am, but of who we are! As I have said many times since my surrender to the police. It is not about me, it's about all of us!

Reflections

Thursday, September 30, 2010

Emotional Energy And Superconductors

Everything that happens, from a simple thought, to full scale war, is an emotional expression. When we recognize this it will allow us to better understand the insane events that comprises most of our experience.
We mistakenly think of emotion as something intrinsic to the individual being. But emotion is the very blood of all conscious life in the universe. It flows through us to provide not just nourishment, but also the instructions and guidance we need to function as both individual and

collective organisms. When we express our emotions (through our behavior and speech) we express the emotions of the universe as shared and dispersed amongst all living things.
A "healthy" person will be a clean conduit of emotional energy, a kind of superconductor. And like a superconductor they will exhibit unique characteristics, such as the ability to perfectly reflect other people's emotions (like magnetic waves) giving them the ability to "levitate" (emotionally), which we might perceive as "the state of bliss".
But most of us resist our emotions, and by doing so we generate unpleasant properties, such as "heat" (anger, hatred, etc...) and external "magnetic fields" (projected emotional energy). Though these properties are destructive and invariably cause decay and death, they also allow us to do "work" by providing "power" in the form of motivation and desire.
So you see, being a "resistor" may ultimately be very unpleasant and difficult, but it is a necessary part of life that must be endured for the building of a greater reality. We should not burn ourselves out though, by judging and condemning the resistive properties of others, but instead should focus on our own potential energy and how it can be used to build a better world. So, even when we see others destroying what we clearly value, we should try to realize that nothing of real value can be destroyed. This is the lesson that life teaches over and over, and yet because we are so focused on the superficial external world, we do not see the wonderful things that are being built to last forever inside of us.
We will all die, but the consciousness that gives us life will live forever. Our emotions themselves should be the only proof we need of this, once we see how they extend into the world around us.

Reflections

Friday, October 1, 2010

Can There Be Consciousness Without Experience?

It is utterly insane for us to postulate that consciousness somehow arises from the biological mind (i.e. brain). And yet every modern science book I read makes that assumption, even though the very basis of this assumption has been proven over and over to be preposterous. Why then do we continue to insist that somehow consciousness depends on the brain? Well, the so-called empirical reason is that when the brain is damaged, or otherwise ceases to function, our consciousness is obviously effected. Also when we tamper with the chemistry of the brain we experience distortions in consciousness. This seems to strongly imply that consciousness depends directly on the brain, and therefor must somehow be derived from biological processes.
But what this rational fails to realize is that it is not consciousness that is effected by the brain, but it is what we are conscious of that is effected! This is an important distinction, because it separates consciousness from experience, and by doing so it compels us to rethink our views of (and questions about) what consciousness is. In fact, it raises the most important question to modern thought today: Can there be consciousness without experience?
I suspect that the answer to that question is enlightenment (hint: there is no "yes" or "no" answer, but there is an answer).
Clearly I am talking about what some people call "pure consciousness". And that brings up a second reason that science insists that consciousness arises from the brain: because if it doesn't then the only other explanation is beyond science. It becomes a philosophical quest instead. It moves into a realm that science cannot go; the realm of extra-experience, more commonly called metaphysics.
Science absolutely depends on experience. Without it there can be no science. So you could say that science worships experience. And if "experience" is only an illusion, then science is a

false religion! It is no wonder then that scientists insist that consciousness arises from experience, and even that Experience created us! Because experience is the "god" of science. So, if it is possible to exist (i.e. be conscious) without experience, then science is a lie, and the enemy of the Truth (i.e. pure consciousness). And that is why I assert that the question of consciousness without experience is so vital. I do not propose an answer though, because that would be the "scientific" thing to do (i.e. answer question based on experience). But again, I assure you, there is an answer, and no mortal words will ever be able to convey it.

Reflections

Friday, October 1, 2010

Probability Limits

They say that if a monkey could type randomly on a typewriter for infinity, it would eventually produce the entire works of Shakespeare by sheer chance. But some day we will discover that this is not true at all.

I cannot yet say how I know this, but I can "see" it plainly via intuition. There exist in nature a kind of probability limit, where the extremely improbable becomes factually impossible.

This limit is already indicated by well known "laws" in science, such as the law of dispersion. If you put a drop of red dye in a cup of water, in a short period of time it will become evenly dispersed in the water. This dispersion occurs as a result of the random motion of the dye molecules. If there were no probability limit then it would be possible, though extremely improbable, for the dye to randomly concentrate back into a single drop while it is still in the water.

Is this improbable or impossible? To give you an idea of the improbability of this occurring, the odds would be exactly the same for the red dye to "randomly" form a perfect three dimensional rendering of the Seattle Space Needle.

The significance of the probability limit is that if it exists, then nothing in the universe is random. Randomness requires that there be no limit to the possible permutations of a given set out variables. If there is a limit, no matter how high the limit is, then the result is not random at all; it is determined!

But determined by what? Now that is the question that is impossible for rational science to answer. So science demands that the universe be undetermined, and that monkeys can, given enough time, randomly produce works of art. How silly is that?

Reflections

Friday, October 1, 2010

Something More Than Human

It seems to bother a lot of people that what I did (murder and rape children) doesn't seem to bother me. In fact, I do believe that one of the purposes of the so-called "Justice System" is to make what I did bother me (i.e. make me "pay for" my crimes). This is decidedly ironic since the purpose I set out on my rampage of rape and murder in the first place was for the exact same reason; to make society "pay for" what it did to me.

So, should I be bothered? I think not, since clearly all I did was what people (in general) seem to always do. Whether you call it "justice" or "revenge" doesn't matter. The only difference between what I set out to do, and what the "System" sets out to do, is the number of people who concur. As if to emphasize this, I even received a letter once from a man who insisted I would get what I "deserve" because "majority rules". Well, if that is true, then the Holocaust was deserved by the Jewish people (because the majority of Germans supported the Nazi regime that condemned the Jews as criminals who poisoned society – which by the way, prior to WWII was a popular and majority belief in the United States as well!).

So again I ask, should I be bothered? It seems to me that I was only being human by attacking what I perceived to be the source of my misery. So when the present regime officials put their poison needle in my arm "to make me pay" then my own attempt to "make society pay" will be vindicated.

A part of me sincerely looks forward to that day for the vindication alone (not to mention the ultimate freedom and escape that death promises). And yet, another part of me thinks that it is selfish for me to even want to be vindicated. What I did may be "just what people do", but that doesn't make it acceptable; it only makes it human.

Someday, I believe, we will all become something more than human.

Reflections

Wednesday, October 6, 2010

Imagination vs Intuition

In this world, we condition our children to ignore their intuition in favor of etiquette, which is extremely unfortunate considering that a child's intuition is the purist form of communion they will ever experience.

We instinctively recognize the closeness of our children to "God", even if we are not religious. A child's empathy is awe inspiring. They can sense our feelings with uncanny accuracy. Most people typically dismiss this "sixth sense" as trivial, or perhaps even annoying, because the child cannot provide useful dialog or even articulate what it is that they are sensing.

So we send them away when they ask, "What's wrong"? Or, even worse, we lie to them, thinking they could not possible "understand".

But, it's not understanding that they lack. It is only the ability to put their intuition into words. And as they grow they eventually learn that if you can't say something then it is not important. Our culture over emphasizes the importance of words, and by doing so we condition our children to ignore the very source of their happiness. They soon become "deaf" to the same voice that called them into existence! And in place of their intuition they are trained, both formally and informally, to depend on their imagination instead.

Imagination is the perfect stand in for intuition because it can be trained to conform to social standards. It also allows us to "believe" in things that can be formed and expressed in social terms such as words and other symbolisms (i.e. idols).

But these beliefs that are based on human symbols can never provide the insight and guidance that is absolutely necessary for the heathy functioning of not just the individual but the entire planet. Without some kind of central source of communication to give us purpose and guidance, our "images of god" (i.e. imagined purposes) will inevitably result in turmoil and confusion.

That all being said, here are some ways that I have found that have helped me to recognize the voice of intuition (as opposed that of my imagination).

Intuition always demands genuine self sacrifice. Imagination demands that others sacrifice (or change).

Intuition never expects to be rewarded. Imagination is driven by reward (i.e. "heaven", "a better life", "peace", etc...).

Intuition is the strongest sense of all, so strong in fact that we can never "not hear" it, we can only ignore it. Imagination is barely "audible" by comparison, so if we only think we can hear intuition then that is a sure sign that we can't "hear" at all – we are only imagining things.
Intuition speaks from the experience of the entire universe. Imagination can only speak from individual experience.
Intuition is the basis of religious beliefs. Imagination sustains religion with stand-in beliefs.
Intuition can never be conveyed via human language. Imagination depends on human language (and imagery) to give it form.
Intuition appears contradictory and nonsensical to the unintuitive mind. Imagination strives to be rational, and even though it usually has different sides (e.g. "Pro-life" v. "Pro-choice", "conservative" v. "liberal", etc...), the side you happen to be on will always seem "to make perfect sense" to you.
Intuition never shies away from suffering. Imagination promises to end suffering while it causes more.
Intuition does not comprehend fear. Imagination defines fear and thrives on it.
Intuition will inform our imagination, if we let it. Without intuition, our imagination is uninformed (i.e. ignorant).
Intuition sees beauty in all things. Imagination see beauty in only those things that conform to it.
Intuition cannot lie. Imagination cannot tell the truth.
Intuition remembers for you. Imagination expects you to remember yourself.
Intuition never forgets anything. Imagination depends on you to forget so it can deceive you.
Intuition ties us to the Universe. Imagination separates us from everything.
That's all for now (I could go on like this forever, but this short illustration should help).
Of course "intuition" is only a word that I am using here to represent something that ultimately defies representation (in fact, any representation at all can only detract from it). So please do not be dissuaded if the word intuition means something else to you. Just keep in mind that there must be something making life happen, it is just silly to think life happens all by itself.
Also, imagination is not a "bad" thing either. In fact, it is also used by "intuition" to serve a purpose. So even as imagination deprives us of direct knowledge of, and communication with, our intuition it is still very much fulfilling the purpose it was made for (but definitely not its only purpose).
So again I say, relax, and just listen. You will hear your intuition when it needs you to hear.
There is never any rush with intuition, and imagination, of course, is always in a hurry. :)
Okay, one more:
Intuition asks us to change ourself and tells us how. Imagination wants us to change the world, but doesn't tell us how.

Dreams

Thursday, October 7, 2010

Dream World

I may have blogged about this idea once before, I don't remember. But the dream I just woke from illustrates the phenomenon too clearly to pass up a chance to document it.
The idea is that the mind somehow has the ability to create and animate distinct complex and individually motivated characters that can act and think for themselves. The following methinks clearly illustrates this:
I dreamed I was at an academic social function. Rather than a greeting line at the entrance there was a gauntlet of distinguished college officials that had to be passed through like a "farewell line". I had to leave early for some reason and after moving through the farewell line

nodding to and shaking hands with the men and women who I did and didn't know, the last professor in the line, who recognized me as one of his better students, asked me if I liked to watch movies as I shook his hand to say good-bye.
I replied that I did like movies, and he then indicated that he had some movies that I might be interested in. My mind at the time was on the reason that I was leaving early (my father, who was also at the function, asked me to come with him because he had something important to show me – I never found out what it was in the dream). So the professor's offer was a mere distraction that I countered politely by telling him I would be interested and I would stop by his office after classes started. Then I moved away from him and toward the exit where my father was waiting outside. As I moved away, by way of further expressing my interest in the professor's movies, I commented, "I hope they have lots of action in them".
Here's where it becomes clear that the professor was acting and thinking completely independently from me (or rather, the "me" I seemed to be in the dream). He said, "Well, actually, they are more of the information sort of movies".
I considered this, and realized that the professor had currently assumed that I would be interested in such "movies" (I love documentaries). So I said, "Great! I'll e-mail you!" To which he replied, "Good, just remember that you only have until midnight".
I at first did not understand what he meant. I thought he was making a personal offer to share some "movies" that he thought I'd find interesting. Then I realized that when he said "midnight", he was referring to the school's registration deadline, which meant that the "information" movies he was referring to must be part of a new course he was offering that semester, and he was pitching me the class!
He obviously did not know that I was no longer a student (in the dream I somehow still realized that I had abandoned college for my "rampage against society" and would be locked up the rest of my life, even though I was not locked up in the dream – a dream think thing).
This dream interaction demonstrates completely independent and complex, even manipulative, thinking on the part of the professor. He behaved and spoke in ways that indicate an ulterior motive; hence independent will and consciousness!
This raises some important questions. If my mind (presuming that dreams are exclusively the product of an isolated brain) has the ability to represent complex thinking and independent motives in my dreams, then why couldn't that ability be exploited unconsciously while I am awake. And in fact, through mental focusing exercises (i.e. meditation) I have determined that my unconscious mind is in fact made up an entire community of these independently thinking, and independently conscious entities, even while I am fully awake! Though I typically do not become directly aware of them unless I am asleep (or drifting off to, or on from, sleep).
So my brain not only can and does think on its own regardless of my conscious consent, but it must do so in order to function (for a less philosophical and more scientific discussion of this phenomenon read the book Society of Mind by Marvin Minsky). And if this is true (and I absolutely believe that it is) then the whole idea of independent free will needs to be reconsidered.
I am made up of independent entities that somehow function together to form "me". And since that is demonstratably true, then why might not the so-called individuals of human society really be the independent entities that make up the unconscious mind of Gaia (the World)?
This would explain a lot, and gives us a new way of thinking about ourselves as not so independent after all! For example, wouldn't we, as parts of a larger mind, necessarily reflect and ultimately conform to the purposes and experiences of the greater mind? Was the last century nothing more than literally a Gaiaian nightmare? If so, then how can we wake her (Gaia) up? Or will she "wake up" on her own? Or is she already awake?
These are the kinds of questions that I think about all the time. So now you know.

P.S.: I should address one major criticism of my "mind of Society" idea. Someone might think that there is a huge difference between how the " entities" in our mind interact (biologically) and how people interact in human society (physically). And in fact there is a "huge difference", but primarily in scale alone, but not methodology. Let me explain:
We know that ultimately our brain is made up of billions of individual cells called neurons. Neurons ultimately communicate with each other not by direct contact, but by chemical signals (neurotransmitters) that are sent and received from one neuron to the next across tiny but distinct spaces that separate the neurons (synaptic gaps).
And we know that the ability of our neurons to communicate with each other is highly dependent upon the chemical environment of the brain, which directly effects the chemical signaling process.
So our mind, ultimately, is in fact made up of billions of individual neuronic "entities" that somehow form conscious thought (but I would argue, not consciousness itself) and function (i.e. by having sensual experiences) by merely communicating with each other via chemical signals that also depend on the environment in which they are sent.
This is exactly, sans scale, how people communicate as well! The only difference is that the synaptic gaps and environment is extended out into the World.
For example, the neurons in my brain right this moment are interacting indirectly with the neurons of your brain. The added step of having the chemical messages translated to physical signals (in this case light, which is what your neurons are responding to as you read), is no more than an extension of the chemical signaling process in our brains.
So if our neurons can form a "mind" for us through indirect communication within our brain, then why shouldn't our brains be able to somehow form an even greater mind via the extended indirect communication throughout the world? There is no reason why not presently known to science. And if such a Gaia-Mind does exist, we could never interact with her directly... or could we? Or, even, are we already and just don't realize it? Who are "we" anyway? Are "we" Gaia? Why not? No, I mean really think about it; why not?

Reflections

Thursday, October 7, 2010

Wordless Lessons

If you close your mind to ideas and experiences that you think are bad for you then you are making yourself deaf to the voice of experience.
This does not mean you should stick a knife in your hand so you can "hear" a lesson. But it does mean that if you ignore or condemn the man who puts a knife in his hand (or someone's back for that matter) then you will not "hear" the lesson that this experience was meant to convey. The lesson you miss is not meant for words. If it were, then no stabbing would have been necessary, you could just be told. So no one can simply tell you what the lesson is that you will miss. You must learn for yourself. And the lesson will be repeated over and over until you do. So if you have to stick a knife in your hand in order to understand, then maybe you should.

Reflections

Friday, October 8, 2010

The Blind One

When I say that capital punishment is a crime, I am not saying so because I believe that killing someone for any particular reason is a crime.
Perhaps the word “crime” is not the correct word for what I am attempting to express since it is a word that is normally used to denote behavior that is arbitrarily defined by society as deviant and subject to censure. But I use the word only to make the point that the behavior society condemns is essentially no different then the behavior they themselves indulge by condemning the so-called criminal.
What I'm trying to say is that most “criminal behavior” is the result of individualistically motivated dehumanization of other people, and in fact that would be my definition of crime, if it were up to me.
The key terms in this definition of crime are “individualistic” and “dehumanization”.
By individualistic I mean selfish. So an arbitrarily large group of people can behave just as individualistically as an individual. I use the word individualistic to indicate the true cause of selfishness; a view of the self as essentially independent.
I also avoid the word “selfish” because it is too weak to express the truly “criminal” dimension of its definition. In our society, “selfish” does not necessarily mean “criminal”, though in my view, selfishness, or individualistically motivated behavior as I say, should be the very definition of crime.
The second critical term in my definition of crime denotes the specific mechanism used by a “criminal” to detach themselves from the person they intend to victimize. The term “dehumanize” puts the emphasis in the definition on the act of separating oneself from another person, rather than the behavior that such separation allows. It does not matter whether we “murder” or “execute” the other person; the real crime is the separation from that person that occurs in our subconscious (i.e. “heart”).
Dehumanization can be mistaken as a “spiritual” crime because of the internal (subconscious) rather than external crime scene, or “location of the crime”. But as I define it, it is not spiritual at all. It is a very real crime that any honest trial could easily expose (unlike conventional behaviorally defined crimes that are almost impossible to prove without an actual confession, which is a dirty little secret that the “Criminal Justice System” would prefer you didn't know). It is relatively easy to conceal your behavior, but almost impossible to conceal your feelings, which when perceived by an honest person (such as a child, or enlightened adult) are as transparent as glass and a direct indication of one's motives (i.e. internal state).
Of course, the problem then with my definition of crime is that unless we live in an enlightened world it can not be practically applied as a form of social control. But the beauty of my definition is that in an enlightened world it would apply itself, and social order would be maintained with no formal effort!
You may say, “Dream on!” and that I will. But my point is only this: The current “Criminal Justice System” is counter productive. It not only fights crime with crime (disguised as “law”), but it in fact generates more “crime”, even as it defines it! It must do this in order to justify its own existence! But it very ingeniously conceals this fact with a system of doublespeak and diversion (Orwell's book “1984” has been dismissed too soon! Also, the movie “A Scanner Darkly” beautifully illustrates exactly what I am saying here, not to mention uncountable other books, plays, and movies throughout history. So it's nothing new, just very well concealed – perhaps too well.)
There is just one more point that I would like to illustrate here. Since, by my definition of crime, crimes occur in the “heart”, it is still possible to kill. But killing would no longer be defined by silly laws as “murder” in one case and “execution” in another (i.e. “lawless” and “lawful”). Instead we would only kill as an act of compassion, and/or necessity (which ends up being the same thing in an enlightened world). It is because of this that I do not challenge my own death sentences. I am not an enlightened person, therefor I do not have the ability to consciously perceive another person's motives. So it is not possible for me to “judge”, even by my own definition of “crime”,

whether or not I should or should not die. And this further illustrates also why I have struggled as much as possible to not be a part of the decision process (i.e. "Criminal Justice" proceedings). In the past I have tried to prevent others from becoming involved in that process as well by asking to represent myself, and my recent decision to ask for a court appointed attorney reflects my deeper commitment to the beliefs outlined above; I have realized that trying to protect someone from judging me is a backhanded form of judgment on my own part. I was assuming I knew better than they did. I no longer make that assumption. For all I know, this is an enlightened world, and I am the blind one!

Reflections

Sunday, October 10, 2010

Dogs In Glass Doghouses

In our world (the U.S.) it is expected that a person's life consist of mostly gradual changes over time. When a person experiences a drastic change in a short time (such as the sudden loss of a loved one, a job, or home) then we recognize this as highly stressful and in some cases traumatizing.

But what we fail to recognize, perhaps because it is so far "off the map" of our cultural experience, is what happens when a person's entire world is yanked out from under their feet. Not just the loss of a loved one, or a job, or home, but the loss of all loved ones, friends, family, and all prospects of any jobs, and of ever having a home ever again. Not even a severe accident can cause this kind of loss, because even if you are paralyzed from the neck down, you still have family, friends, and community support. You can still "rebuild", and therefor there is still hope.

But what happens when even hope is taken away? What is a person supposed to do when all of their options, even the most extreme options, can promise no light at the end of the tunnel? There is one circumstance where this is the case in our society, and it is an all too common and completely ignored tragedy, called "Criminal Conviction".

I know, I know; criminals bring it upon themselves, so they "deserve what they get". But does anyone every really deserve to have all hope taken from them?

You might think that there is always hope. But if that is what you think then you do not yet understand even what hope is.

Hope is something that only exists when it is "seen". A person who sees no hope, has no hope. Just because others see hope for that person does not mean the person has hope. That is why so many "criminals" end up trapped in their hopeless worlds, because other people can "see" a way out for them, but they themselves can see no way out.

If a man does not realize that he is responsible for his own demise, then how can be responsible? He can't. It is like the dog I saw recently on A.F.V., who did not realize that the glass had been removed from a storm door, so there was nothing to stop him from going outside by walking straight through the empty door frame.

The dog would wait for someone to "open the door" before he would pass through, even after watching another person walk through the unopened door. This is very funny to us, but completely humorless to the dog.

Now suppose the dog's owner did not realize that the dog could not go through the empty storm door frame, so he leaves the regular door open expecting the dog, that is house trained, to go out on its own when it needs to relieve itself.

Of course the dog ends up urinating in the house. So the owner thinks the dog needs a "lesson", and he punishes the dog expecting the problem to be solved that way. But the dog is only confused by the punishment, and still does not realize that it can go outside anytime it wants.

And the owner soon discovers not just urine, but BM as well. He becomes irate and banishes the dog outdoors indefinitely. The owner begins to see the dog as a burden on the household and no longer a member of the family. The dog soon develops very real antisocial behaviors from the lack of human attention and is eventually put to sleep.
All of this happened because the dog could not see an option that the owner (authority) could plainly see. And there you have criminal behavior in a nutshell.
So, using this analogy, how can we open the "storm door" for criminals? Education is one way. I once did a college research paper on the effects of education in prison on recidivism (re-offense rates). Every study I found, even those unfavorable to prison education, showed a strong direct relationship between the amount of education a prisoner receives in prison and the chances that he will stay out of prison once he is released. These studies show that the relationship holds even when the prisoners are compelled to educate themselves (sort of like pushing the dog through the storm door to show him there is no glass in it). The theory is that an education helps the "criminal" overcome his blindness to his options. An educated criminal begins to realize that just because he painfully banged his no on the "glass" a few times (for example, losing a good job because of unfair workplace practices), that doesn't mean the "glass" is always there. He learns what "glass" is (i.e. workplace politics, ethics, etc...) and learns to function in a word with "glass" in it.
Of course, it will be a long time methinks before the dog owner of this world (i.e. the authorities) learn how to properly trained the dogs of this world (criminals). In fact, in the last 30 years, education programs in prison have been reduced to practically nothing. It's almost as though someone figured out a great way to make a lot of money playing "dog catcher". And the trauma that these poor ignorant "dogs" suffer is real, and profound. We punish them unjustly for their ignorance, and eventually banish them to the yard, or put them to sleep. Euthanasia ends up being our only act of kindness.

Reflections

Monday, October 11, 2010

All They'll Need Is Love

I have said that when the world awakens to itself people will become conscious of themselves only in the context of the One World consciousness, and will no longer be conscious of themselves as individuals. But that sounds like I am saying that we will lose our individual identities, and become some sort of automatons, which is not what I think at all!
In fact, we will become much more aware of ourselves as individuals, and much much more alive as human beings. All I mean by saying that we will not be conscious of ourselves is that all of our conscious energy will be spent on the One World, not on ourselves, and this will give us an overwhelming sense of purpose and being.
It might help to think of it as being deeply in love with everyone you meet, and with everything that happens. Even in the present world when we are in love with someone or something, our lives are greatly enhanced by a sense of purpose and being that is centered on the person or thing we love. Well, in an enlightened world, that sense of being in love becomes profound and omnidirectional.
So just as being in love today causes our sense of purpose to increase while our sense of importance and self consciousness decrease, so it will be when the world awakens and every living person will be connected through their love to the planet, and even to the universe, all at once.
You might envision such a world as being occupied by starry eyed hippies who sit around all day smiling blissfully but accomplishing nothing. But I believe that in such a world the human

race will accomplish more in one year than we have in the last hundred years! And that's being conservative about it!
There is so much negative energy in the world today that it's surprising to me that we can accomplish anything at all. What little we have achieved this last century will be taught to infants in the coming years in much the same way they learn to speak today. Any ten-year-old will be able to explain the relative nature of space and time, and they won't need a bigger brain than we already have to do it. All they'll need is love.

Reflections

Tuesday, October 12, 2010

Power and Control: A Consequence

When it happens, we ask ourselves how is it possible for a human being to so callously rape and murder a child? For lack of any comprehensible answer we become convinced that it simply is not possible for a human to do such a thing. It requires the heartless mind and soul of an inhuman monster.
It must be a monster. How else could a person not respond to the gut wrenching emotions that such an act solicits in anyone with any human feelings at all? And if such feelings are not present, then the person is simply not human, and therefor easy for us to make suffer for their crime against humanity. We can punish them without compunction or remorse, because the do not feel as we feel. They are inhuman and deserve whatever happens to them.
And such has been the rational behind every act of violence and cruelty propagated by humans against other humans since the beginning. The “victim” is always perceived as somewhat less than human, or rather, less “real” (capable of emotion) than the person inflicting the harm. The rapist sees the woman (or child) as incapable of comprehending his needs (i.e. emotions) and therefor deserving of their fate. The soldier sees his enemy as misinformed, and therefor less able to understand the true reality, and hence less able to comprehend real emotions. And society in general, ostracizes the criminal as we once did lepers, and for the exact same reason (it was once commonly believed that lepers brought the disease upon themselves with sin or foolishness, they deserved to suffer also).
It's called dehumanization, and without it there would be no violence in the world. The victim is a thing, a “monster” or “slut” or “piece of trash” that deserves what they get. Even as we condemn the rapist for being a heartless monster we are being heartless ourselves, focusing on our own emotions and needs (i.e. “for justice”) rather than stepping back and seeing the crime for what it is; a very “human” act after all!
We often forget that rape is not about sex. The sex is no more than a weak man's convenience, while the real goal, of course, is power and control (never mind for a moment that ultimately there is no such thing and that all effort to attain power and control is delusional, a delusion that our present culture indorses and promotes, much to its own demise). And if we consider the real goal of rape to be power and control then it is only obvious that all acts of violence and cruelty, whether “legalized” or not, are a form of rape. We might fool ourselves into thinking that we have a “right to justice” and that criminals “deserve what they get”, but the victims (the criminals themselves) aren't so easy to fool. They, typically fully realize that their “punishment” has nothing to do with “justice” or even “law and order”. They know as well as any rape victim knows it's not about sex.
You might be wondering, what does raping a helpless little child have to do with power? But it's not about power over the victim directly. It's about power over what the victim represents in the mind of the rapist. We know that a woman rape victim is often only an effigy for the women in

the rapists life who have rejected him, or perhaps even a mother who abused him. But how could a child represent such a threat to a pedophile rapist?
In the case of crimes against children, the child becomes an effigy, perhaps for a lost childhood, or maybe even for society in general. Children clearly represent everything that is precious and innocent to society. So when someone attacks a child (either sexually, as is common in the United States, or by other forms of violence, such as the rash of knife attacks on children this year in China) we should recognize that the child is usually not even the real victim. And when we respond with appall and disgust, we are giving the attacker exactly what he wants, evidence of his power and control, and support for his delusion.
The criminal himself becomes an effigy for society, as were the lepers, or even witches – all these were once symbols of societies anxieties and served as effigies as such.) The courts frequently even proclaim that the punishment inflicted is intended to "send a message" to other would be criminals. So clearly the criminal is being used to appease societies delusion of power and control over natural elements that it refuses to accept that it will never be able to control.
If this sounds familiar it should; we once punished witches for causing crop failures, and Jews for causing economic failures, and fags for causing AIDS. So it should be no real surprise that we yet identify an arbitrarily defined group of people (criminals are defined by laws that define crime – in our country sex with children is a crime, and only because of our influence has child sex, and prostitution, become crimes in other countries where child sex very rarely even occurred – until it was criminalized, thus making it a convenient weapon for weak men to wield against society), and then punish that group for causing us to suffer. Isn't that exactly what criminologists accuse criminals of doing; blaming others for their own behavior?
So how long until this pattern of very human behavior is recognized and stopped? I can answer that question with the question: How long until we stop believing in the illusion of power and control.
It could be awhile. :(

Confessions

Thursday, October 14, 2010

Murder Isn't A Solution

While I was still in prison for "raping" a 14 year old boy (when I was 16), two significant events occurred that caused me – or rather, allowed me – to decide that if I was ever to get any "justice" in this world I would have to take it for myself.
Both of these events were directly related to society's attack on sex offenders.
The first significant event, that I later used as a convenient and convincing excuse to dehumanize children so I could use them in my schemes, was the receipt of my minimum sentence (which determines the actual amount of time spent in prison until I was eligible for parole). It was set to five times over the normal range for my crime (I got 186 months, the range was 30 to 40 months, 40 being the theoretical "high end" for a first offense like mine).
My sentence was so exceptional that I nearly went into emotional shock, literally, when I was told. I lost all peripheral vision for about an hour and had memory blackouts while I tried to grasp this inconceivable reality. It took me several days to recover, and even then I thought it must be a terrible mistake. It had to be a mistake, since that was the only way I could survive the emotional impact.
Over time of course I got over the "denial stage" and began the process of developing more long term coping mechanisms. Of course, I got no counseling or professional advice, I was expected to "suck it up". It was all a part of my "punishment" (oh ya, and "rehabilitation"). So the coping mechanisms I came up with were mostly supplied by the only source I had, other

inmates, who had all learned numerous and apparently effective ways of dealing with their own "unfair sentences".

I began fantasizing a lot about what I would do when I got out. Of course, since I was only 16 when I was arrested, and still living at home and going to high school, I had no way of imagining how unrealistic and even crazy my fantasies were. But they helped me survive, and that was all that mattered.

There were two main reasons why I got such an exceptional sentence, and I was oblivious at the time to both of them.

One reason was politics. Unbeknownst to me, a small boy was attacked by a mental hospital patient who severed the boy's penis. The mother of the boy became politically active, using her son's tragedy to promote her own agenda of tougher sex crime laws (e.g. longer sentences for sex offenders). Since my victim was also a young boy (never mind that so was I) my case was "politically sensitive". If I had received anything less than an exceptionally exceptional sentence certain people in the community may have been aroused against the Parole Board which was under a lot of political pressure already from new sentencing guideline laws that were to go into effect soon.

The other reason I received such a long sentence was because of a scathing report from the "Sexual Psychopath" Treatment Program. I did not finish the program after the therapist tried to pressure my mother for sex by threatening my status in the program (this was all documented, but the Parole Board believed the therapist, not me or my mother).

The second event during my incarceration that further supported my decision to "get even" with society, was the public murder, by hanging, of one Westley Alan Dodd. Dodd had also victimized small boys sexually, so that made him akin to me. He murdered three boys and was caught trying to kidnap another boy at a movie theater.

It wasn't as though I sympathized with Dodd so much because of his sexual preferences, as much as it was his repentance after he was caught. Dodd expressed repeatedly that he could not control his fantasies and that he preferred to die rather than grow old in prison. He tried to tell people how things could have been different for him and especially for the boys he killed, "if only people would listen", instead of being so quick to judge and condemn a man like him; which was a man like me.

I understood Dodd completely. Even while I was still in prison I tried to get help, but no one would listen. It was all about rules and regs. I was not just a number, but a "bad number" that was to be dealt with systematically. Of the only two people who ever did listen to me, one was ignored by the Parole Board (Dr. Sally Sloat, a prison psychologist who told the Parole Board, in person, that I needed treatment and was an excellent candidate for treatment outside of prison – all the Board heard was "needs treatment" and they actually added more time to my sentence!).

The other was my "Man" (Lover), another inmate who also happened to have a B.A. Degree in psychology. He wasn't just ignored, he was harassed by the guards and ultimately serving more time in prison because of trying to help me (which he knew would happen when he made the choice to help).

So I understood Dodd perfectly, and when they hung him at the Washington State Penitentiary in Walla Walla, while I was there (1993), to "send a message" to other would-be child killers, like me! But the only message I heard was not the one that the people sending the message intended.

The message I heard was, "Murder is a good solution for a bad person". Except to me the "bad person" was the society that condemned me, that condemned Dodd, my "brother", and unwittingly condemned themselves to my wrath and vengeance.

I literally swore to myself on the day Dodd was murdered that I would avenge him. Of course by that time I had already decided to avenge myself, so my oath for Dodd was really a commitment

to "attack society" more than once, and I am presently sitting here in a California jail cell as a direct result of that commitment.
A prudent reader will note that I am not claiming that these "significant events" that occurred while I was in prison are "reasons" for why I ended up raping and murdering children when I got out. They are not reasons; they are a part of what I did, not excuse or reason for it. The two girls I murdered in Seattle were a part of the exceptionally long sentence I served in prison for "raping" a young man. And the boy that I murdered here in California was (is) a part of Dodd's "execution".
There are no reasons and excuses for any of it. But there can be understanding, if we stop focusing on cause and effect, which only solicits blame and excuses, and instead embrace our own part in the madness. That's exactly what I did when I picked that little girl up in Montana and carried her home to Idaho. I realized that I was a part of the very insanity that I condemned! I was not the cause, but I was a part. I saw that murder was not a solution after all, it was only another part of the problem.
So I stopped murdering. I also stopped judging, condemning, and blaming (i.e. "reasoning") and started understanding for the first time in my life.

Reflections

Thursday, October 14, 2010

Illusions Of Invention

When I am seeking understanding these days I focus on simply being open and honest with myself. The understanding comes in its own time, sometimes almost right away, other times not at all. But one thing I don't do is try to find the "reason" for something, then mistake whatever "reason" I came up with for understanding.
In our world, a world presently dominated by the religion of reason (a.k.a. "science") we are taught falsely that reasons and understanding are the same thing. If we know the reason for something then we think we understand it. And if we can't find a reason, then we think that understanding eludes us.
Amazingly, we can even have a true and deep understanding while thinking that we don't understand at all, simply because we cannot put our understanding into the terms of reason (i.e. words). This, in fact, is the very source of all human conflict and suffering. We defer to reason, and trust it instead of our true understanding which very often can not be verbally expressed or even grasped with images in our mind.
Reasoning and language are not by themselves the problem. It is only when we put our faith in symbols and reasons that we get into trouble. By themselves they are wonderful tools for expressing complex ideas and otherwise sharing our experiences (as I am doing now). But no words, nor any other symbolic system that is the product of human reason (e.g. religion, philosophy, or art) will ever truly express the real beauty of genuine understanding. Nor will these languages of reason ever be able to express or represent the understanding we need to grow out of our delusional state. As long as we put our faith in science and technology, or religion, or music, or art, or philosophy, then these same will imprison us. Only true understanding, which is direct and unsymbolized by men (yet symbolized by the universe itself perfectly and beautifully!) can set us free from the illusions of invention.

Chronicles

Friday, October 15, 2010

How A Spider Listens

When I find spiders in my cell lately I have been catching them in a Styrofoam cup that has a clear plastic lid. When I find flies, or other insects, I put them in the same cup. The spiders are kept happy, I think. The other bugs, not so much. I like to watch the spiders spin their webs, catch their food, and feed. The largest one gets most of the prizes, and she has even molted once already, much to my surprise! But she is still only about one centimeter toe-to-toe. I wonder how big she will get. The smallest are less than a millimeter toe-to-toe; barely even specks of dust. But they are just a bold as the largest. I saw one of the smallest actually pounce a fly that was the size of a house by comparison! All the spiders in my little cup (five to date) seem to be the same species. I have often said that all living creatures are potential teachers. From my spiders I have learned a lesson that I have been seeking for years. I did not understand why the Eastern teachers of peace and wisdom put so much emphasis on correct posture and form in their practice. The big spider in my cup taught me why. As I was watching her preparing and mending her web, apparently in anticipation of the particularly large fly that was in the cup at the time but not yet caught in the web, I was fascinated by her every move. But most interesting of all was when she finally moved back to the center of the web. As I carefully watched, she assumed the "listening position". She grabbed several strands of the web and put slight tension on them. I could see her do this by the way the web moved as she settled down to wait. Then, once she had the right tension on the lines and the right position of her body and legs (with her legs symmetrically arranged, probably so she could balance the slight tension on her body from the web) she did a very humanlike thing: she wiggled her behind as if settling in to a comfortable position. Then she did not move at all. She would remain completely still for as long as it takes for the "understanding to come" (i.e. the fly to become trapped in her web). I suddenly saw clearly that she was "meditating"! Many things I had read in Buddhist books suddenly made more sense to me. The need for proper posture in order to balance the slight tension we keep on the web of our experience. I already understood that meditation was a form of listening, and now I understood the relation that correct posture and form have to the act of listening. Of course, I cannot truly express the understanding I have "caught in my web", using these words in this blog. But anyone who has experienced the way nature teaches us might at least smile at the lesson I have learned. I could ask no more.

Reflections

Friday, October 15, 2010

On The Act Of Listening

To truly be able to listen we must cease all other activities of the mind. We must open ourselves up to the speaker; whether that be another person, a piece of art, or the universe itself (i.e. common experience).

To "open ourselves up" means to the offer no resistance to the ideas and impressions that are being offered to you by the speaker. That is, to not consciously attach meaning or significance to the impressions being conveyed. We should allow our unconscious mind to manage all the necessary associations for us.

We must not seek the reasons or motives behind the words we wish to hear. Doing so will contaminate their meaning with our own delusions. Instead, we should keep a clear mind. We must accept everything that is being said as though it were we ourselves speaking.

After having thus listened, we may reflect on what we have heard at our leisure. In this way understanding is given its voice.

Reflections

Friday, October 15, 2010

Looking For Reasons

If you read this blog looking for the reasons why I did the things I did, then you will no doubt find them. But they will be your reasons, not mine.

Confessions

Sunday, October 17, 2010

What Happened In Prison - Part I: "The Punk"

After I was "voted out" of the Western State Hospital Sexual Psychopath Treatment Program, my 20 year prison sentence suspension was revoked. At the very tender age of 19 I was sent to prison.

While I was still in the county jail I learned the hard way that I needed to invent a story for why I was sentenced to prison. Rape was not a very popular crime, especially if it involved a child. The weak minded inmates (typical bullies) of course needed to make themselves feel better than someone, and society already made the rapists and child molesters easy scapegoats. So I made up a story about a "burglary that went bad" and became a first degree assault. Because of my age, the length of my sentence (a rapist typically only served 3 to 5 years on a first offense in those days), and the convincing details of my story, no one ever questioned it, or asked to see paperwork.

I was classified for population at the Washington Corrections Center (WCC) in Shelton. When I arrived I still did not know how much time I would be spending in prison. The judge only set the maximum term (20 years). But the parole board set the minimum term, which would determine your length of stay until you were eligible for parole.

Because this was my first offense as an adult, I expected to get 5 years at the most. That would make me eligible for parole after about one year in prison since I would get credit for time served in jail and at the state hospital. All I had to do was hold my breath; the nightmare would be over quickly.

Or so I thought.

It turned out that the political environment concerning "sex offenders" was heating up. A small boy had been sexually mutilated by an x-mental-patient. The boy's mother was determined to get "justice" by punishing all child molesters severely, especially "homosexual" child molesters. I guess that meant me.

The parole board also had a letter that the therapist from the treatment program had written to the judge. I had no idea at the time that they could do that, so I made no effort to defend myself or contradict the numerous lies that the therapist had written about me. The therapist was one, Gary "Mike" Shepherd, and he had attempted to use his position of control over my treatment to coerce my mother into having sex with him. He was the reason I quit the program and decided to take my chances in prison. The incident with my mother was fully reported to the treatment program officials. Shepherd denied everything, of course, and accused me (in cohorts with my mother) of being manipulative and rebellious against the treatment program.

When the parole board took Shepherd's letter and the political circumstances into consideration, they came up with a minimum term of fifteen and a half years! That was five times over the expected range (of 3 years) and it meant that I would have to serve at least eight more years before even being eligible for parole!

Needless to say, I was shocked, severely! I lost part of my vision (literally tunnel vision) for some time after receiving the news. How could I possibly survive that long in prison? The worst I had expected was one more year! I was barely keeping my head above water as it was! And now...

A man in the cell next to me in the county jail had told me that because of my looks and my "attitude" (naive and immature to say the least) that I would be raped, and probably even killed, in prison. He claimed to speak from experience, and he predicted that I would "not last a year". After getting 186 months from the parole board his prophecy haunted me.

I did get raped, of course, many times. And once I was attacked by a whole gang of black men (six at one time) who scared me so bad that I screamed with a loud high pitched shrill voice, exactly like the "punk" I was, "No! Please no! Help! No! Please stop!" the entire time. They didn't actually rape me. They just beat me to the floor, and then, of course, one of them "came to my rescue". All he wanted in exchange was a small favor; a sexual favor. And then another, and another... each time threatening to "unleash" his friends if he didn't get what he wanted.

I went to the guards and told them I wanted to be moved to "protective custody" because I was being "pressured for sex". The guards told me that unless I gave them a name they would not move me. I was too scared of the men who were raping me to give up their names. They told me if I ever did that they would kill me, even in protective custody. The "prophecy" from jail seemed to be coming true, so I kept my mouth shut.

I started taking classes to get my high school diploma. I was safe in the school building, where the inmates who were raping me never set foot. I learned to like school, a lot. I became an almost straight - "A" student. Before leaving Shelton I had finished two years of high school and got my diploma.

(Incidentally: They don't teach high school in Washington state prisons any more. The best you can get is a G.E.D., so I was lucky.)

I spent my time in the living unit playing "Dungeons and Dragons" with other "kids" who were being "punked out" (pressured for sex) too. There was a little protection by staying in a group, but not much. Once several men came into my cell while "Junior" was visiting with me. I watched helplessly as they wrestled him down, pulled down his pants and put several of my personal art pencils into his rectum. They were laughing and joking the whole time. After they left, Junior curled up in a corner next to the locker in my cell and wouldn't talk to anyone. I wanted to help him so badly, but I didn't know how. (I find myself holding back tears even now as I remember this) I felt so desperately and painfully powerless.

When they put double-bunks in all the cells at Shelton I ended up moving in with Junior. It was convenient for the men who were pressuring us to have us both in one cell.

I tried everything I could think of to get out of being raped. I even asked my "classification counselor" if I could be transferred to the new sex offender treatment program at the Twin Rivers Corrections Center (TRCC) in Monroe. He told me that I had too much time left on my sentence to be eligible for the program. It was only for people who were close to getting out of prison.

I also studied religion, and hung out with the Christian inmates for awhile, until one of them raped me. I took correspondence Bible study courses, and became very familiar with the "religion" bookshelf in the prison library. I was looking for answers, but wasn't finding any. I finally said a prayer to God that went something like this:

"God, I don't know if you are real or not. But I can't find any evidence at all that you exist. I have prayed and prayed for help, but so far the only help I have ever gotten has come from myself. So I'm going to go my own way for now. I pray that if this is a mistake that you will bring me back. Amen."

That was the last time I prayed or even acknowledged God for many years. "My own way" was to educate myself, and to start sticking up for myself. Which I did. I can still remember the first real sense of power I got from seeing the look of surprise on inmate Guzman's face when I picked up a mop wringer to use as a weapon when he started picking a fight with me on the tier. Guzman had once beat me up just to steal my Timex watch that was a gift from my grandmother she gave one just like it to my brother too, one of the very few sentimental items I owned. I made him beat me up in order to take the watch but I didn't fight back. This time I was clearly going to fight back and Guzman backed down immediately. I learned a new lesson that day about bullies. They really are cowards.
My victory did not last long though, before those six black men put me "back in my place". But I wasn't ready to give up so easy.
After two years of being beat-up and raped I figured a way out. I gave the guards the name of a black inmate who I knew would not try to kill me. But neither had he ever assaulted me. So after they took him to the "hole" and me to PC (protective custody), I sent a letter to the prison disciplinary officials (who were going to punish the black inmate for pressuring me based on my statement alone) and I told them that I had lied in order to get put in PC.
It worked. The black inmate got released from the "hole", and after six months in PC (segregation), I got transferred to McNeil Island Corrections Center (MICC). At McNeil nobody knew me. And, I was older and better able to defend myself against other inmates. The rapes stopped, and a new chapter in my nightmare began.
(To be continued...)

Reflections

Monday, October 18, 2010

An Alternative To Free Will

"Free Will", by definition, demands that we able to choose independently of all influences. It does not mean we must choose independently, only that we have the ability to do so. But if we can choose independently of influence, then what determines our choice? If you say, "our character", or "our nature", then what determines those? If you say, "our choices", then you have made the age old logical error of circular reference, the same kind of logical error that kept people thinking that the world was flat for so long despite overwhelming evidence that it couldn't possibly be flat. It seemed flat, so arguments were invented (many of them circular) to explain away the evidence.
Of course, ultimately the evidence won out and now we take gravity for granted. And, we don't even bat an eye at the idea of men standing upside down some 8.000 miles below us. Someday too, we will not question the concept of dependent choice. "Free will" will seem as silly as the idea of a flat earth. But before that day comes we are going to have to collectively let go of certain absolutes that keep us from grasping beyond what our minds can directly perceive. Just as we let go of the concepts of "absolute up" and "absolute down", we will need to learn that there is no "absolute right" or "absolute wrong". Once we accept this then the idea of dependent choice will seem obvious.
And, if you think that our "character", which ultimately determines our choices, is itself determined by nature, or "God", or "the Universe", then you have already admitted that we have no free will.
Because if our choices are determined by our character, and our character is determined by something other than ourselves, then our choices are not free, they are determined by whoever (or whatever) determined our character. And that is what "dependent choice" is all about.

Dependent choice does not imply pre-destiny. In fact, the concept of dependent choice has nothing to say about our "destiny" at all. Whether or not our choices are predetermined becomes a mute question when the idea of dependent choice is fully explored and understood. It is like asking, "what holds the earth up?", after gravity is understood. The question itself no longer makes any sense, since gravity allows for a whole new way of looking at "up" and "down".
And so, dependent choice provides a whole new way of looking at "right" and "wrong". Suddenly, anyone claiming to be "the most right" about their view of the universe is exposed as a fraud. They will appear as foolish to us as a man who climbs a mountain in order to be "the closest to heaven". Most religions of the world will become empty shells of impossible "righteousness". Ironically, most religions of the world were based on the teachings of men who seemed to understand that there is no absolute rights or wrongs. When you re-read the teachings of Jesus, for example, in the light of dependent choice, suddenly what he is saying makes real sense, and no longer requires faith in imagined ideas, like absolute rightness (a.k.a. "righteousness") and absolute wrongness (a.k.a. "evil"). The "miracles" that Christ performed are seen as very good metaphors for concepts that dependent choice supports.
Just for example, Jesus healed many "lepers". Leprosy is a "skin disease" that eats the external flesh of the body while leaving the internal organs intact. Because of the way lepers were outcast and blamed for their own disease, leprosy is an excellent metaphor for how "sin" (i.e. deception) will eat away at the external "skin" of a person's "character" while leaving the internal "organs" of a person's "character" intact. Such a person's behavior (external skin) becomes more and more hideous as the disease progresses, and society soon casts them out (e.g. sends them to prison) and blames them for their sickness (behavior).
But dependent choice tells us that these "lepers" do have a disease, and, just as Jesus tried to teach us, it can be cured. Not miraculously in the "magical" sense of miracles that religion has imagined. But, in the very real "miraculous" sense of the mysterious force of "divine (unconditional) love". Just as gravity (a miraculous and mysterious force itself) allows men to orbit the earth, seeming to set them free from the very gravity that holds them there, so divine love will some day set men free from "leprosy" (i.e. deception based behavior). Some day we truly will perform "miracles" even greater than those performed by Christ (as Christ himself promised we would). But, they will not be "magic" or "supernatural". They will be achieved by mere understanding.
Faith in understanding is divine love. It is what Jesus and St. Paul really means by "righteousness". Fear and ignorance is the cause of all suffering (i.e. deception based experience). It is what Jesus and St. Paul really meant by "evil".

Reflections

Tuesday, October 19, 2010

Unconditional Love

Unconditional love is not what you think it is. If you have any ideas at all about what love is, then it is not unconditional love that you are imagining.
Unconditional love cannot be imagined. It can only be directly experienced. Once it is experienced then all other "sensual" experiences become much less important, but more intense at the same time.
Unconditional love doesn't mean ignoring your resentment toward someone. It means giving into your resentment while at the same time repenting your ignorance. In other words, it means embracing the pain we inflict upon ourselves. Not in the self-flagellation, but in the humbleness of self-effacing honesty.

Unconditional love seldom (if ever) results in one's feeling any sense of personal pleasure. The only “pleasure” a person gets from this kind of love is the pleasure that comes through our empathy for those we care about. This “real pleasure”, (a.k.a. “Joy”, a.k.a. “Bliss”) emanates from the inside out, not outside in. And, it causes all our personal external pleasure senses to tingle with the simplest experience. Drinking a glass of water can be more intoxicating than the most potent wine, for a person who truly loves.

Unconditional love does not condone ignorance. But, neither does it feed ignorance the fear that it craves. We do not “turn the other cheek” if we are afraid of being struck again. We only offer an ignorant person such an opportunity to strike us when we are not afraid, and when we truly love the person about to cause us pain. Only then will it have the power to heal.

Unconditional love does not comprehend fear. Some say that if you are not afraid then you can not know courage. But such courage is a misleading human invention that caters to false pride. I'm not saying one should not be “courageous” and face their fears. We absolutely should! But, do not then take pride in your courage, for all fear is the result of your ignorance and nothing else. And, only by facing our fears can we learn this; there is nothing to be afraid of. (Or, as I believe Roosevelt once said, “The only thing we have to fear, is fear itself!”)

So, unconditional love is not something I, or anyone, can tell you about. But I, and almost anyone else, can tell you what it is not about. Just about anything you think it is, is what it is not! But, it does exist. And, it only takes faith in its existence in order to experience it. Once it has been experienced it is simply no longer possible to confuse “imagined love” with “real (unconditional) love” ever again.

“The Tao (way of love) that can be taught is not the eternal (unconditional) Tao.” - Lao-zi

Reflections

Tuesday, October 19, 2010

Dependent Choices

The debate of free will verses predestiny is as old as civilization itself. But the debate is a distraction from the truth of the matter all together. “Free will” is a silly human invention that has no correlating concepts in the natural universe. And “predestiny” is likewise a mute argument in the light of a little simple introspection that anyone can do. But the debate persists for the same reason that all debates persist; because both sides contain truths, and both sides contain deception. Only because there are any “sides” at all does the solution remain a mystery. The solution I am referring to in this case is one I like to call “dependent choices”. It completely ignores the concepts of “free will” and “predestiny” and instead simply observes the obvious without trying to turn it into something “divine”.

The dividing question in the aforementioned debate is, “Do we have the ability to make our own choices, or are our choices predetermined?” If you consider this question without prejudice then it can seem rather silly.

First of all, the terms are not even clearly defined, and because of this most actual debates on the issues digress quickly into pointless arguments over what “choice” means, or what “freedom” is. If both sides ever did actually manage to rephrase the debated question in terms that both sides agreed to then there would be nothing to debate! The arguments are all semantics and definitions, not conceptual at all.

For example, what exactly is choice? If we agree that it is a machine-like function that any computer can demonstrate, then the predestiners win. But if it is an indeterminable “spiritual” event, then the advocates of free will have the best argument. But what if we define “choice” as, ‘the finite result of infinite causes?” I'm only suggesting one possible definition that the antagonists in this case might agree on. You can plainly see that if they were to agree to some

such definition, then the question could almost answer itself. So lets consider that question again, and see how silly it becomes using the definition for “choice” that I suggest above.
“Do we have the ability to control the infinite causes that result in a finite choice?”
It should be clear that this question has no answer. Or, if it did have an answer, it would be both yes and no. We can only control a finite number of causes, not infinite. So it's a silly question after all, as is the original version of this heavily debated paradox, when it is so carefully considered.
The question we might actually be trying to ask could be, “How can we make better choices?”
So let's apply my definition for “choice” to this question and see what comes out:
“How can we improve the finite result of infinite choices?”
Ah! Now there's a worthy question that we might actually be able to answer. But, I'll leave the answer to that question up to the “experts”, if they ever stop arguing over semantics. Besides, I've already found my own personal answer to that question about five years ago. :)
The only remaining point I'd like to make for now is my own definition of “dependent choice”. Like I've already said, it sidesteps the silly ideas and comes straight to the point: “Every choice we make is the result of infinite causes and has infinite results” (note, I am no longer using my earlier definition of “choice” here, but I am proposing a completely new definition and concept). With this definition I have stated only the obvious. And yet, it gives us a different way at looking at the “choices” we make that I think can spur whole new realizations, and perhaps even an authentic “paradigm shift” in social consciousness. Or maybe I'm just dreaming. Who knows.

Reflections

Thursday, October 21, 2010

If You Believe Me...

If someone wants to tell me what is wrong with the way I think, then I will eagerly listen to them with an open mind, and even expect to learn something. But if someone wants to tell me what is right about their own way of thinking, then I see no reason to waste my time listening to them, as I would expect to learn nothing.
And if someone wanted to tell me what is right about my way of thinking, then, if I was bored, I might listen to them merely to humor myself. Yet, if someone wanted to tell me what was wrong with their own way of thinking, then I would drop whatever I was doing, and listen to them carefully. Not so that I could learn something, but so that we all might.

If you believe me,
And you receive me,
We will be together this day.

Reflections

Friday, October 22, 2010

Dependent Parent Support

Why is it that our society demands that parents support their children, while the children are young and dependent, but we don't demand that children support their parents, when their parents are old and dependent?

Reflections

Friday, October 22, 2010

Unleashing Intuition

Modern science induces us to mistake reason for understanding. Reasoning is a mechanical process that allows us to manipulate and share understanding. But, it is useless without the understanding for it to manipulate. Even a computer can manipulate understanding. But, a computer cannot itself understand anything.

We reason with our thoughts. But our thoughts are not what allow us to understand. In fact, the process of thinking does more to inhibit understanding than to facilitate it. Thinking is a regulator, not a conductor. It restricts our understanding in order that we can do work with it. But thinking alone does not allow us to understand anything.

Monks experience their most profound understanding by turning off their thoughts (the computer-brain). Without the restriction of our thoughts to inhibit our understanding it becomes possible to experience "pure understanding". That is, perhaps, to understand understanding itself. This is sometimes called enlightenment. But it is really no more than intuition unleashed!

"And the light shines in the darkness, and the darkness did not comprehend it." (John 1:5, NKJV)

Reflections

Saturday, October 23, 2010

Your Brain On Reason

"We are led to conclude that the human being, at this stage of evolution, is a biological robot (biot) automatically responding to genetic template and childhood imprinting." - Timothy Leary in Info-Psychology (1987)

The human mind is a machine. Albeit a very complex machine that, when combined with the human body, is capable of amazing feats. If you doubt the machine nature of the mind then you probably have just not yet learned how easy your thoughts are to manipulate.

The brain is biological, yes; not mechanical or electronic. But biology is as much a system of cause and effect as any of the other machine types. So to deny the machine nature of our brain is to deny the very principle of cause and effect.

Our brain is the epitome of reason. Its primary purpose is not to determine us, but to serve us. Its function is to give us the ability to manipulate our experience. We call it "reasoning", but that is a misleading term. It implies that the mind has the ability to understand. But it does not. The mind can only process finite information. Understanding requires consciousness, and consciousness requires the comprehension of infinity. So when we "reason" we are not understanding at all. We are merely manipulating our understanding to suit ourselves.

This is why there are so many different "understandings" in the world. Because people mistake reason for understanding. We worship cause and effect as though it were a god. Or, at least some "law" of the universe set down by a god. But cause and effect is an invention of reason. And reason is the latest in a long line of false gods. We have turned to such gods for thousands of years (at least) in our delusional attempts to control forces in the world that we can not understand.

As our understanding changes, so the nature of our gods change. Any student of modern religion knows this to be true, but only a few realize the religious nature of the modern state. Our government is a religion of the false god of reason. The Christian Bible even warns us of the dire consequences of such false belief systems. So does the Koran, Torah, Buddhist sutras, and many other writings from those who genuinely understand. Unfortunately these writings have been left to the interpretation of those who still bow to reason. But fortunately the writings themselves have been preserved. So, they might yet serve their intended purpose to "guide and instruct", but not, "speak for God". Any real god must be able to speak for itself, or it is only the product of someone's imagination, and reason.

Confessions

Sunday, October 24, 2010

The Predator Awakens

As readers of my original Fifthnail blog (link, top-right) may know, while I was living in North Dakota I took up skiing for the first time. The slopes were no resort, more like just a few hills. But they did have lifts, and Thursdays were "student night", so I could use my NDSU I.D. To get rentals and lifts until midnight for only $25. It was the perfect chance for me to learn something I had always wanted to learn.

Of course there are always a lot of kids around the ski slopes, especially little slopes like these. But I wasn't interested in the children, I was there to practice skiing, and even if I happened to get a lift with a cute kid, I would be courteous, but otherwise ignore them. Like I said, my mind was on skiing, and I was enjoying myself responsibly for once.

I spent hours at a time on the slopes without a break, even in below zero weather (I'd learned how to dress warm living in Fargo). But, at some point I had to stop to use the bathroom.

On one such occasion I found myself in the small "boys room" alone, relieving myself in a urinal with my mind on what run I would choose next, or some such thing, when I heard the door to the bathroom open behind me and someone come in. As I finished relieving myself I instinctively noted that whoever came in did not move into the bathroom to take care of business, so I glanced out of curiosity over my shoulder to see if anyone was actually even there.

I saw a young boy, about nine or ten years old standing by the door, dressed as though he'd just come off the slopes for a quick pee, like me. Several children had just exited the bathroom a moment before after I had politely waited for them to finish their business before pulling out my own hose to take care of mine. So seeing the kid in the bathroom alone was no real shocker, or turn on. I figured immediately that he must be waiting for me to finish – since it was such a small bathroom with only two urinals side-by-side – the same way I had waited for the kids before me to finish, just being polite.

But then I saw him flinch with hesitation. It was the most subtle movement that I caught out of the corner of my eye just as I was looking away from him. The boy had made a move that an animal makes when it is suddenly afraid and uncertain of its predicament. Something inside of me became suddenly awake, and aroused at the same time.

Of course I did not move on the boy, he was very safe where he was. In fact – and I know many will scoff at this, but it is absolutely true – I would have risked my life to protect that boy from harm if any had been threatened. At least in that context I would have; the chalet was not a safe "hunting ground", not by far.

But the predator had definitely been stirred and awakened, and I took due notice. It wasn't the boy's appearance, age, or circumstances that aroused me, it was his fear, and his fear alone. The boy's fear had awaken a very dangerous predatory instinct.

I turned again and shrugged, nodded, and smiled to the boy, to assure him that I was finished, and that he was safe. As I washed my hands, I metaphorically scratched the predator inside of me behind the ears and thought to it: not yet my friend; not yet... go back to sleep.

P.S. We all have "sleeping predators" inside of us. Predators are born of fear, and live by it. To teach our children to "be afraid of strangers" (e.g. "stranger danger") is to prepare them to be a victim. Children who are not afraid of strangers are not nearly as appealing to child predators. That does not mean they are immune to attack, only that they are much less likely to be targeted. And, if they are attacked, they are much more likely to escape unharmed. As a "child predator" myself I speak from direct experience, not psychological theory. Several times children that I targeted as prey escaped using natural instincts that were unhampered by fear. (Once a 7-year-old boy who I had alone in the woods, a firm grip on his arm, and a sharp knife in his face, got away by screaming and fighting. He was lucky I did not use the knife, or was he? Perhaps he instinctively knew that I wouldn't. Who knows, but he got away unscathed.) I also know of other child predators who have said the same thing (Westley Allan Dodd, for one), though most child predators are oblivious to their own predatory nature, so they do not even realize that it is fear that drives their lust. The same can be said for most other predators as well.

Reflections

Sunday, October 24, 2010

Constant Scrutiny

I don't claim to understand what the ancients (wise men) understood. At least, not all of it. But, some of it is very plain to me, and even the part that I do think I understand is subject to my constant scrutiny.

Reflections

Sunday, October 24, 2010

Creations of Belief

It is only when we think that we have attained some ultimate understanding (or belief) that our ability to understand ceases (dies). True understanding is a living, breathing, changing thing all unto itself. It has its own purpose, and intelligence. It lives through us. We cannot create it or own it. It creates us!

Reflections

Sunday, October 24, 2010

The Question of Faith

"Faith" does not mean not questioning what you believe. That is how fantasies end up becoming religious doctrine.
Faith means trusting that there are answers to all your questions, even when you don't know what the answers are yet. But, it does not mean that you should not ask the questions!

Only someone who is lying to you (consciously or unconsciously) would want you to not question what they tell you (e.g. government, religions, corporations). An honest entity loves to be questioned, even challenged. It is a chance for them to be known, and to learn.

Reflections

Sunday, October 24, 2010

The Sacrifice of Understanding

Our ability to understand is the very gift of life, not our ability to “think”. Thought is something else entirely. Understanding is love. It is the offspring of infinity, and the Living Truth. We routinely sacrifice our understanding to the false god of reason every time we put our faith in human rationality. We even sacrifice our children's understanding by teaching them to trust reason over intuition.
But understanding allows this sacrifice, because if it did not then we could never come to realize that understanding is eternal, and freely given (never earned).

Reflections

Monday, October 25, 2010

Being a “Man”

There are those who believe that the “definition of a man” is someone (a male) who keeps his suffering to himself (i.e. “doesn't cry like a girl”). In my book, such “men” are weak and cowardly. It takes strength and courage to own up to and express who you are in your heart (emotionally). Attempting to hide what you feel is akin to hiding from who you are. The definition of a coward, is someone who lets fear determine their behavior. Someone who hides from what they are afraid of is a coward.
I am still such a coward. I have yet to summon the courage to express, and thus let go of, my deepest fears. It is not something I can do with words alone. I think words can help build courage though. But in order to truly face myself, I must do so in front of others.
I question whether the System wants this to happen. I suspect not, but I could be mistaken. It is the only way I will ever “heal”. It would be a miracle if it ever happens.
In the mean time, I am stuck with just being human.

Reflections

Monday, October 25, 2010

The Temple of Life

When we hide from our feelings (i.e. pain) we are only fooling ourselves. Our feelings cannot be hidden from those who can see the Truth. We can only hide from those who are also hiding. We cannot hide from the ones who walk in the light; the “Beautiful Ones”.
They see us for who we truly are, scared little children, weak and dominated by our fears. So they do not condemn us. But, they do allow us to condemn ourselves. This is so they will know when we are ready to be “re-born” and they can come to our side. When we stop judging

ourselves and our world, then we are no longer afraid. Only then do we become more than human, and join the Beautiful Ones in the Temple of Life, where death has no authority.

Reflections

Monday, October 25, 2010

The Beautiful Ones

They do not confine themselves to the flesh (at least, not usually). They live in a world of pure conscious energy. They are born twice, but only die once. Their enemy is fear and ignorance; their nature, love and understanding. Their enemy is overcome, and their nature is forever. To them, life is truly just a dream, and their waking reality is all of eternity. To us they are, angels, gods, and saints. To them we are children. They are the Beautiful Ones, and they love to help us learn and grow.

"The Beautiful Ones always smash the picture, always, every time." - Prince

Reflections

Monday, October 25, 2010

The Word of God is Spoken, Not Written

All scripture may very well be "inspired by God", but only life itself is spoken by Him. So, where do you think we should turn when we seek the Truth and Meaning of our existence? With what "words" should we seek to understand? God's spoken word? Of, man's "inspired" ones?

"In the beginning was the Word, and the Word was with God, and the Word was God." (John 1:1, NKJV)

...

"All things were made through Him (the Word), and without Him nothing was made that was made." (1:3)

Reflections

Monday, October 25, 2010

Are We There Yet?

What if the reason it is so important for us to overcome fear in this world is because heaven is a terrifying place? If we could control our fear then heaven would be as wonderful as promised, but if not, then it would be hell!
Maybe we are in heaven right now!

Reflections

Monday, October 25, 2010

The Christian Dilemma

If you are not willing to admit that everything you believe is wrong, then how will you ever know if you are wrong? All the faith in the world wont help you if you don't believe in the right thing. In fact, if you are wrong then your so-called “faith” becomes the instrument of your demise, because it prevents you from realizing you are wrong.
There is an answer to this dilemma, and the Bible even tells you what it is. But the Bible can't help you until you hear the Word of God directly for yourself.

“You search the Scriptures, for in then you think you have eternal life; and these are they that testify of Me. But you are not willing to come to Me that you may have life.” (John 5:39-40, NKJV)

Reflections

Tuesday, October 26, 2010

The Fine Art of Non-imposition

For the most part, I still believe pretty much the same things I believed before the “revelation” in the Montana wilderness that caused me to turn myself in. The one main difference is – and this is a big difference – that I no longer believe that I have the “right” to impose what I believe onto other people.
Every critical decision, and most lesser ones, that I have made, since the revaluation, has been in accord with this simple realization. Including my decisions to bring Shasta home, allow myself to be arrested, cooperate with the authorities (prosecution and defense lawyers), to not speak to media (and write a blog instead, so the truth as I see it would be freely available instead of packaged and sold), and to not resist, attempt to influence, or appeal, societies decisions in my regard.
I spent the whole first part of my life believing the lie that I needed to change people to my way of thinking in order to make the world (any world) a better place. After the “revelation” I saw that this was as far from true as night is from day (which is an analogy with deliberate innuendoes concerning the fact that night and day can only be properly observed by someone standing on the surface of a revolving world). The world can only change, and is changing, according to the will and intentions of infinity. There is nothing I can do as a limited being that will ever cause the world to change any differently.
But, I also came to realize that my limited self has an infinite counterpart that is very much capable of changing the world. And, as I have just stated a moment ago, already is! I do not need to make a conscious effort to improve the world. All I need do is have faith that it is already being improved. I will then do whatever needs to be done without thought or effort. Joseph Campbell calls this, “following your bliss”. The hippies called it, “believing in Him”. I have called it, “listening to your intuition”, but it can also be simply stated as, “letting go (and letting God)”. Whatever you call it, it is a delicate balancing act that can be (and fortunately is) maintained only by ridding oneself of worldly fear, which is not easy to do, until you have done it, then it is the easiest thing in the world. “An easy yoke to bear”, as the most famous man in all of history is purported to have once said.

Reflections

Wednesday, October 27, 2010

A World of Real Miracles

Life is eternal and there is no escape. We try to escape by lying to ourselves, but in the end (usually our end) the truth prevails, and life goes on without us.
Didn't I just say that life was eternal? How then, you may ask, does "life goes on without us?" Simple, we are not eternal, but the life that gives us consciousness (and the ability to understand our experiences) is eternal. We are finite and limited beings that life created and occupies according to its own intentions. Life's intentions accommodate all of eternity. Our limited intentions are pure fantasy by comparison. Life is forever; we are not.
But, we can live forever with life, and through life; as life lives through us. We can share the eternal nature and consciousness of life. All we have to do is stop lying to ourselves, telling ourselves that we create life (that is, believing ridiculously that somehow our consciousness is a product of our brain). We pretend to be gods, with god-like "free will" and even eternal existence. This fantasy prevents us from realizing and sharing the true eternal nature, and continuity of being, that only the life inside of us can offer. Life, consciousness, does not belong to us, and we certainly did not create it with our puny little monkey brains! And even though life does not need us, it loves us. Even the most despicable person is a treasure beyond the value of the universe itself, as far as life is concerned. I know, because I am one of those "most despicable" people, and yet I witness life's love for me every day! The first time I witnessed it (or, more correctly, the first time I had the courage enough to acknowledge it as my creator) was on the mountain with Shasta. Shasta's innocence was like a healing salve that freed me from the iron like grip of the mask (lies) I wore. I truly wish people could see the miracle in this alone, then perhaps they would stop believing in their fantasy miracles, and start living in a world of real miracles.

"Imagine there's no heaven.
It's easy if you try.
No hell below us,
Above us only sky."

Reflections

Thursday, October 28, 2010

A Definition For Murder

I have written profusely about the destructive and anti-productive properties of fear, often even referring to it as the source of all "evil". But like all other aspects of our experiences in life, fear has a purpose. So I should stress, that like all "evil" things, it is important to learn how to master and control fear, not eliminate it. Fear needs you to "be afraid, be very afraid", in order to control your thoughts and behavior.
Our goal should be to feel fear without being afraid. Roosevelt would have been more precise (though less dramatic) if he had said, "The only thing we have to fear is being afraid." All he was really saying, of course, was, "Let's not be cowards!" Isn't the definition of a coward, someone who is afraid of fear, and thus allows it to determine what they do, and, perhaps even more significantly, what they think.
When we let fear control our thoughts then we end up rationalizing our cowardly acts. The murderer thinks, "He deserves to die because..." It doesn't matter what excuse he invents, or

even whether it is invented spuriously in the mind of a cowardly killer, or formally in the courts of a fearful society. All that matters is that the excuse justifies our submission to fear, so that fear can stay in control.
But what is a coward if not a child? Perhaps being afraid is the only way we can protect ourselves while we are still too immature to respond rationally (and without rationalization) to the threats we perceive. So maybe we should not be so quick to judge and condemn a coward, because doing so is itself a cowardly act. Instead, maybe we should see the coward for the child they are, whether that child be a 35 year old man, or a 200 year old social system. (Notice how only the young and immature social systems in the world still have criminal death penalties. The European Union will not even accept a country that still executes its criminals.)
If "being rational" means acting on reason, and "rationalizing" means inventing excuses, then how can we tell the difference? Actually, there is a simple test that the militaries of the world have used for thousands of years. They call it, "clear and present danger". If you kill for any reason less than this, then you are only rationalizing a cowardly act. And, that makes you a murderer. But, don't worry. You'll grow up someday. I did.

Reflections

Thursday, October 28, 2010

"Justice Delayed Is Justice Denied"

I have suggested that we use "clear and present danger" as a measure of the validity for the reasons we use to commit violence (i.e. to kill). But I realize of course that there are no simple rules for determining when we should or shouldn't kill.
For example; I have also asserted at times that perhaps it would have been best if someone had simply put a bullet in my head at that Denny's restaurant in Coeur d'Alene five years ago (where I was found in the company of a little girl I had kidnapped after murdering her family) instead of putting me under arrest.
You may think that society must determine my guilt before it can justify killing me. But that is exactly the kind of irrational fear based thinking that makes real justice (justified action) impossible.
Despite what our fear motivated system wants you to believe, it is simply not possible to determine rationally what should be done about a dangerous (or tragic) situation out of the immediate context of the situation itself! As soon as you change the context of the situation, you also change the appropriate rational response. And attempting to re-create the circumstances in court in order to determine a rational response is impossible. It can only result in the fabrication of rationalizations (i.e. excuses) for delayed actions.
In other words, by arresting a suspect in order to delay justified action (i.e. justice), we completely destroy any chance of genuinely justified actions (true justice). It does not matter how meticulously preserved the crime scene is at the time of the crime, or how carefully the evidence is weighed in court. No matter how hard you try, you simply cannot just suspend the crime so you can decide what to do about it later. This is a fundamental flaw with the entire justice system. And the system itself is acutely aware of this flaw, so it expends tremendous resources just trying to cover it up, and even more effort futilely trying to fix it. Better and better crime scene preservation and evidence analysis only results in more money being spent while justice is delayed and perverted further and further.
Attempting to invoke any kind of social justice by delaying action is clearly never going to be accomplished. The outcome can only be less and less justice the further we move the rationalizing process away from the circumstances being rationalized. It is a sand trap with only one solution: don't step in it!

They say “justice delayed is justice denied”. I wonder if they realize how true that is. As for taking justice into our own hands, perhaps there is no place else where it belongs!

Reflections

Thursday, October 28, 2010

Crapshoot Justice

You come home after a hard day at work and discover your front door kicked in and several valuable items (T.V., stereo, laptop, etc...) are gone. You feel violated and even terrified by what has happened. What should you do?

In our crap shoot justice system, you are expected to call the police, so the burglars might be caught, and justice served. There are many theories that support this course of action, such as; that catching the criminals (and locking them up) will stop them from being able to commit more crimes. We also rationalize that the punishment will somehow discourage other would-be criminals from violating the law once they learn about the potential consequences. Then of course there is always the retribution itself, which makes us feel better.

But in truth, none of these theories hold water. The criminals eventually get out of jail, or prison, and typically end up committing more crimes than they would have if they had never been caught (this bears out statistically). Other “would-be” criminals are actually encouraged by the thrill and danger that the possibility of getting caught provides. Tougher punishments have historically resulted in more, not less crime (with few, but highly touted, exceptions). And the retribution is of course just another word for vengeance, and we all know where that leads.

So what can we do? We can't just ignore the crime and let the violator run free, can we? Or, can we? What if we did?

Most burglaries are committed by immature people (under the age of 25). That means that if we leave them alone there is a good chance that they will “grow up” and become responsible member of society all by themselves. You never hear about all the criminals who don't get caught and end up becoming very law conscious citizens over time (usually a few years). You may think that's ludicrous, but once again, statistics bear me out.

Consider that, in areas of the world with practically no crime, such as rural China, there is also practically no law enforcement. Sociologists have known for a long time that the hands-down best deterrent to crime is a close knit community. Even in America, the best crime prevention/reduction programs are the ones that emphasize community integration, and reintegration of the criminals back into the community. These programs are proven to work, and the cost-benefit analysis is astonishing as well. But the “justice system” itself is the primary opposition to these programs, both in the polls and on the streets! (For example, by pushing for longer sentences that only increase the length of time a criminal is kept separated from society while increasing the chance he will commit more crimes when released.) That is, of course, because the justice system needs crime to survive, and there are no official mechanisms to check it's appetite for criminals. It is a “beast” that only appears to control crime as it consumes criminals, then blames the fowl smelling excreta that oozes out its other end on the criminals that it feeds on. I know, because I was once excreted from the system's ass. So when I hear a cop or some other “official” refer to me as a “piece of shit”, I just smile and say, “exactly”.

Reflections

Saturday, October 30, 2010

"Lights out for predators on Halloween"

Sometimes the depth of the ignorance of people in American society still amazes me, even after being so amazed so often in the past.
In the news today was the bold headline. "Lights out for predators on Halloween", that was accompanied by an article boasting of "Operation Boo", carried out by the California Department of Corrections and Rehabilitation (uh, isn't "Correction" and "Rehabilitation" supposed to be the same thing? I guess some genius state official figured that two lies were better than one, even if they are just different words for the same lie!) Apparently, all registered sex offenders who are on parole are forbidden to participate in Halloween. They must remain at home, with lights off, and are not even allowed to answer their door.
Talk about alienating sex offenders (which in most cases is exactly why they became sex offenders in the first place). This is a perfect example of how "the System" works against proven effective rehabilitation efforts (such as community reintegration) by imposing "media friendly" programs that do absolutely nothing to reduce criminal activity. Of course what "Operation Boo" does accomplish is that it gives "visibility" to a government agency's supposed efforts to "protect our children". But, the only thing they are protecting of course is their jobs, and perhaps their delusion of heroic purpose.
I would be willing to bet dollars for dirt that if anyone did an effectiveness survey for "Operation Boo" (though not surprisingly there is considerable resistance by the System to all such surveys), they would find not only any significant reduction in sex crimes committed by the targeted sex offenders (parolees), but over the course of the few weeks that follow "Operation Boo", they would discover a distinct increase in the number of sex offender parolee parole violations and re-offenses.
Of course, no one will ever do such a study, and I suppose that makes my prediction a safe one to make. Which makes a point not so much about the potential results of such a study as much as the point that so many operations are carried out by government agencies while the only ones reporting on the supposed effectiveness of the operations are the agencies themselves. And, they invariably use extremely slanted, controlled, and unscientific data to make their programs appear effective. Not even the press steps in (like it claims to do) to provide any "public oversight", because then they would be cut off from getting so many lucrative headlines handed to them on a silver platter, like "Lights out for predators". How juicy is that?

Dreams

Tuesday, November 2, 2010

A Dream Not Forgotten

In a dream that I had when I was 21 years old in the cell-blocks at McNeil Island Corrections Center (M.I.C.C.), I dreamed that I was a massive twelve foot tall barely humanoid creature. I was stooped over in a hospital room, and there was an anonymous man, of normal stature, laying in the bed in front of me. I somehow knew that in order to prove that I could be a "demon" I had to eat the man. So I picked him up as easily as picking up a child, and began biting his leg. I was repulsed, so I started laughing and snarling as I chewed on the man's leg in order to stave off my repulsion. Then suddenly two tremendous black shadowy arms wrapped around me from behind and pulled me backwards and down. I fell through the floor of the hospital room and quickly found myself being pulled helplessly down into the blackest blackness. As I fell backwards, the powerful arms constricted my chest and arms, so I could not move or breath! I felt a sense of fear at that moment like nothing I had ever experienced before, or since. It was sheer unrestrained terror, that no worldly experience could ever replicate. Then I somehow knew that I was dreaming, and desperately willed myself to wake up. I woke with a violent start and gasping for air. I was back at M.I.C.C., in the top-front bunk (nearest the bars) of an eight-man prison cell, on "Dog-tier", one story up. It was morning and the other inmates in the cell were also just waking up and in various stages of dress as they got ready for mainline (breakfast). After catching my breath and taking several deep breaths to calm down, I climbed down off the bunk and sat down on the locker next to the bars. The man who slept below me was a friend, and he was there sitting on his bunk. I began to tell him about my dream. But some of the other inmates in the cell overheard, and one of them began raging on me about dreaming that I was a demon. I got angry and told him to shut up. Encouraged by his own friends, he began taunting me even more, "What'cha gonna do, eat me!" I jumped up and attacked him in the middle of the cell. I was so angry that I quickly brought him to the ground, with me on top, and began forcefully slamming his head into the concrete floor. He stopped resisting after the first blow to his head on the floor. The inmate was dead, but I had my hands around his neck and kept using that hold to lift and slam, lift and slam his head into the floor, until his face started to distort. Then I watched in amazement as his face transformed into that of a hideous demon, and he started laughing at me as I banged his head even more and more furiously into the floor and strangled him at the same time. I screamed (and these are the exact words that I remember clearly to this day), "No! No! I don't want to hate! I want to love Jesus, but he won't let me!" Then I woke up again, this time for real. I was in the same bunk, but the lights were off and a guard was just then walking past the bars at the front of the cell with a flashlight doing a security check. Everyone else was still asleep. It was the middle of the night. My heart was racing, and I sat up to think about what had just happened. Could that really have been just a dream? Or was it some sort of message; a warning? I didn't know, but I decided not to take it too seriously, though it was a dream that I never forgot.

Reflections

Tuesday, November 2, 2010

Consciousness Arising

Consciousness and probability are inextricably intertwined, I have observed in the past that consciousness is the product (or "offspring") of infinite probability. This is a very difficult realization for even me to grasp, and I am certain that the words I am using to express it fall miserably short of being even an inspiration for most. But, alas, it is my task to at least try.
In another post, I have expounded on what I referred to as evidence of a "probability limit". But now, I realize that what I was contemplating was really just consciousness at work. The purpose of consciousness is inexpressible, and hence, so is its "work". But we can observe consciousness as it is expressed in the universe around us, and more intimately within ourselves. We can even experience pure consciousness directly by various means (from drugs, to meditation, and many other ways). But we will never be able to express that experience in terms of the limited experiences we have through our senses. So what I am about to state will be meaningless, unless you are one who enjoys intimate contact with consciousness directly. Then perhaps you will be able to make some sense of this, since it comes straight from my own direct experience of consciousness. And, while how we express true experience may differ (as all the different religious attest) the experience itself is always the same. It is only how we relate it to our limited experiences that differs.
First, I should be specific about what I mean by "infinite probability". In order for there to be any probability at all then there must be some event that can happen in at least two different ways. This is simple probability. The simplest event of all is whether something exists, or does not

exist. I call this the prime event. A variation of the prime event is what I call the time event. The time event is really the same thing as the prime event, only how we view, or describe, it changes. Instead of something either existing or not, we say that it is either moving forward or backward in time. This "view" is better for understanding pure (infinite) probability, because it allows us to think in terms of something we already experience, time. But, keep in mind that this "time event" view is actually less "true" than the "prime event" view, yet neither view is absolutely true (though the "prime event" is perhaps the purist definition of "God", or "infinite intelligence" that I have ever proposed, by itself it is also the most meaningless!)
With the time event, we say that something exists when it moves forward in time, and does not exist when it moves backwards in time. So, with this view, it is clearly possible for something to go from a state of existence, to a state of non-existence, and back again. So then, our simple probability is defined by the two possible directions in time.
As strange as this sounds, there is a corresponding event that has been observed numerous times by particle physicists. When a positron (i.e. anti-electron) collides with an electron both particles cease to exist in a burst of energy. Positrons are also known to be mathematically identical to an electron moving backwards in time. (I'm not making this up, see my earlier post "Time Travel is Real" posted August 16, for a further explanation and references). One theory is that the positron and electron are really the same particle seen changing direction in time, and appearing to us to cease existing in the process. But, I do not need particle physics to support my ideas here, because I am speaking from my own direct experience of consciousness, not external observations (the later being quite primitive in contrast).
So, now that we have defined a probability event, we can begin speaking in terms of probability. In the simplest terms we say that the probability that something is moving forward or backward in time (i.e. does or does not exist) is finite. That means that even if we cannot calculate what the probability is, we know at least that there is some value for the probability by virtue of the fact that only one or the other state can be true in any given infinitesimality (yes folks, that is a real word, even though it may not appear in your dictionary. It means an infinitely small instant, or for the purpose of this discussion; a timeless instant). Either the something is moving forward or backward in time (and does or does not exist).
Now here is the reason we use the time event instead of the prime event for our visualization: if an entity (i.e. "something") does exist, and hence is moving forward in time, then given any length of time (a non- infinitesimality) said entity can in fact either exist or not exist in an infinite set of infinitesimalities. In other words, there can in effect be an infinite number of time events! And since each time event is said to have a finite probability, then an infinite set of finite probabilities is, of course, the definition of infinite probability.
Now, what does all this have to do with consciousness? Well, hopefully, if I had laid my words right, I have set up an interesting test for an age old dilemma. We have only to ask, what exactly determines the probability of a time (or prime) event? Or, to completely rephrase the question, what ultimately determines the choices we make? This is the same exact question, only now you can see the direct relationship it has to consciousness!
The answer is consciousness, of course. What else could it be? If it were pure chance then there would be only chaos and profound lawlessness in the multiverse (since we're talking infinite infinities, "multiverse" is a better term for "universe", since the former refers to all possible universes, not just ours). As I have already expounded on in my previous blog post on the probability limit, pure randomness cannot account for the obvious law and order that makes up our universe. There must be consciously directed probability, which is what I previously referred to as the probability limit.
And so, infinite probability (a.k.a. "God the Father") gives rise to the very consciousness (a.k.a. "God the Son") that shapes and determines the space/time experience we call reality (a.k.a. "The Spirit of God"). And if you carry through with this revelation correctly, then you will discover that is meshes perfectly with not just the true teachings of the Bible, but also with the basis of

every other world religion. Everyone of the Fifth nail blogs serves this revelation. Every word that has ever been written is about this revelation. Though many words have been written to conceal the truth, all words are written about the truth. When you can see the meaning in this, then you will never be deceived by words again. Consciousness, which is the "Word of God", cannot lie.

Reflections

Sunday, November 7, 2010

One is Enough

I happen to know that there is at least one person who reads every word of this blog with an open mind, and an open heart. And that one is more than enough to justify the effort. Thank you, silly girl!

Reflections

Monday, November 8, 2010

Worse Than Rape

Anyone who claims that child rape is universally the most evil and despised crime in the world has obviously not been around the world very much, nor even studied history. In fact, it has been only very recently in history that any society has been able to generally value children at all. Even the great United States not very long ago legally condoned the commercial and systematic abuse of children in ways that would make most modern child rapes seen kind by comparison.

And I'm not defending child rape as no doubt some idiot would claim if I did not specifically say so (and will probably claim anyway just because it makes them feel righteous to denounce a child rapist). Child rape is clearly wrong, but there are far far worse evils in this world. And, you don't need to look to history to find them; just check your back pocket. Any U.S. Currency you find there is evidence of your own guilt in causing millions of children to suffer from hunger, sickness, homelessness, exploitation, and worst of all, hopelessness! I won't bother explaining why this is true, because if you don't already know then you really shouldn't be reading this blog. You should be learning about world economics, and about how easy (and common) it is for strong countries to just take whatever they want (resources) from weaker countries. Talk about rape! Right now the U.S. Has it's economic hard-on so far up the Middle East's ass that they can't even take an economical shit unless we let them. And their very real flesh and blood children are the ones feeling it the most. (Please don't tell me you thought 9-11 was about religious fanaticism! You'd be fanatic too if you had to watch your children starve, and go without medicine and shelter, just so some stronger country could have its pleasures.)

Like I said, check your wallet next time before you cry out ignorantly about child rape being so "evil". You might just discover that you are the one with a hard-on for vulnerable children!

Dreams

Tuesday, November 9, 2010

Sweet Sweet Innocence

I dreamed yesterday that I was visiting a planet where the people lived on an island under constant threat from attack by intelligent creatures that lived beneath the surface of the oceans. Except for their tiny island, their entire world was covered with clear blue water. The sky was permanently overcast by tremendous amounts of moisture from the great ocean, but this protected the islanders from a sun much closer and harsher than our own here on Earth. While I was there an attack came and the alarm was raised for everyone to defend the island. I moved outside and down to the beach where everyone was running around in a panic. Orders were being yelled and ignored. Then I saw groups of islanders opening fire at other groups of islanders, who returned fire to defend themselves. Soon a full scale battle broke out, but there was no attackers! At least, none from the sea. The islanders were fighting each other in the ever escalating confusion and chaos. I began walking along a seawall, where I saw several large horse-like creatures that had been brutally slain in the fighting. Their large mutilated bodies seemed to emphasize the insanity of the "battle". Then I came to the end of the seawall and turned inland. Just off the shore, and behind the battle lines, I saw where new horse-like creatures were being brought in to replace other ones killed. They seemed unconscious when they arrived, and they were secured with straps inside the crates, lying flat on their sides. I approached one of the crates that had a smaller, pony-sized, creature. As I watched the pony was unstrapped and revived (woke up). It quickly got to its feet and I saw that it was very much like a child's fantasy pony, with a blue coat and colorful mane, complete with wings that seemed to attach themselves to the animal rather than being a part of it. I suddenly felt very much as though I was in a child's dream, like no dream I had ever been in. And as if to emphasize my own alien presence, I then noticed a little girl, about six-years-old, who I knew to be a princess, and the recipient of the flying pony (and perhaps also the "dreamer"). I watched as the pony took to the air and flew majestically out over the sea past and through the many rainbows that made up the sky. It was so beautiful and so innocent at the same time that I began to cry happily. I followed the little princess, who followed the pony, as it flew back toward the castle where I had been before the fighting had started. But now there was no more fighting, it seemed almost everyone was dead or no longer able to fight. I was still crying when we arrived at the castle gates, and as I watched the little girl go inside I couldn't help but notice what a sexy little ass she had, even as I cried over the beauty of her innocence. Then I woke up. I'll let you interpret this dream however you wish. But let me say this; for me, it was a great lesson!

Reflections

Tuesday, November 9, 2010

Shame On Me

It is satisfying to know that I will be murdered by consensus of the people of the most powerful nation in human history. Shame on me for feeling that way, and shame on you for wanting me dead. It makes me feel like some sort of martyr. :)

Dreams

Tuesday, November 9, 2010

Art Conscious Dream

I dreamed today that I had returned to college for an art class. I arrived early for class and found the instructor, a middle aged black woman, at the front of the classroom contemplating a painting that she had painted and was presenting for that days lecture. The painting was an abstract watercolor self portrait, black on white canvas, about 3x4 feet tall. It stood on a pedestal at the front of the room facing toward the seats. The instructor stood near a lecture podium as she mused over her work of art from a few feet in front of it. I approached without speaking so as to politely not disturb her. I stopped near the front of the room and also began contemplating her portrait. She then began speaking to me as if we were already in the middle of a conversation about the painting. She said, “Notice how some parts are well defined, such as my arms and my hair, while other parts are intentionally obscure, such as my legs and torso.” I noticed what she was talking about in the painting. The “well defined arms” she spoke of were black rectangular shapes that seemed to extend either out of or into the painting, depending on how you looked at it. The “hair” which clearly defined the position of the subjects head, was a sharply defined black arch near the top of the painting. The “legs”, and other parts of the painting were extremely vague by comparison. After a pause, long enough to allow me to take all this in, she said, “The parts that are well defined express the focus of my consciousness as I worked on the painting. The parts that are blurred are areas that my mind was trying to avoid being aware of. For example, see how blurred and misshapen the legs are? That is because my legs were causing me pain at the time.” I saw exactly what she meant, and I could almost tell her exactly how her legs felt just by looking at the painting. Then I suddenly “opened up” to the painting and I started “seeing” reflections of my own consciousness in it. I said to the instructor, “Yes I see what you mean. The blurred undefined areas seem to change, according to my own mood, while the clearly defined strokes keep me anchored to the subject.” I caught her nod of approval out of the corner of my eye. Then other students started to arrive for the class. (The dream continued, but was less interesting after that)

Reflections

Wednesday, November 10, 2010

Thank Goodness For Ignorant People!

I blog a lot about fear and ignorance, but only because I have been, and yet remain, one of the greatest cowardly ignoramuses that I know. My only claim to accomplishment is that at least I realize that that is what I am. And I'm not ashamed of it either! But, nor am I proud; why would I be? Realizing that I am a deceived person keeps the blinders of pride off my eyes, and helps me see the world around me much more clearly. It helps me to not be so quick to judge, and hence destroy any chance I might have to learn and experience new things!
So, while I observe the ignorance of other people often, I do not condemn it, nor would I even wish they were not a part of my world. For so wishing would be to wish for my own demise, and that would be silly. The man who spits in my face is as much my brother as any other.

Reflections

Wednesday, November 10, 2010

Gnosticism

Everyone knows that an agnostic is someone who does not believe in God. But, actually that's not quite right. Agnosticism is really just the belief that it is not possible to know whether or not

God exists. So, it is even reasonable for a Christian to be agnostic. Such a person would say, "I can't know that God exists; that's what I have faith for!"

But few people know what a gnostic is (no "a"). Gnosticism actually dates back to before Christ. But the first Christians, or at least some of them, considered themselves Gnostics.

Gnosticism is not a religion. It is merely a way of thinking about religion and life and anything for that matter. A gnostic views all knowledge as coming from a single source. This does not contradict the Christian view that all things are created by the One God. It is just a different way of viewing the same thing. But, perhaps an important difference.

The gnostic Christians were actively suppressed very early after the birth of Christianity. Many of their doctrines were seen to contradict the teachings of Christ, which is rather strange since a true gnostic would never subscribe to any one doctrine. So accusing them of contradicting Christian doctrine would be like accusing someone of not liking vegetables just because they like meat.

But to the early Christian church, anyone who did not believe exactly what they believed were considered heretics. (This is proven over and over throughout Christian history and accounts for so many "denominations" and divisions of the Christian religion today.) To this day, the very hallmark of Christianity, is the insistence that you either believe what we believe, or you are wrong. In other words, Christian's by their nature (the nature of Christianity) believe they are "right", and everyone else is "wrong", even when only a very few of them think they are "right" (i.e. Christian cults).

But the gnostic Christians were not like that. They believed that all knowledge (and hence, all beliefs) led ultimately to the source of Knowledge, that being of course, God. So there were as many different paths to knowing God as there are different things to know. But they emphasized being able to know the difference between true knowledge (or just "knowledge") and false knowledge (or, more correctly, "deception").

To a gnostic, deception is "the devil", in the same sense that knowledge is "God". Deception is the source of all "evil" and "suffering" in the world. The "devil" is not a magical creature that lives beneath the earth (or in some other reality, as Christians believe today) but he is a very real and present phenomenon of intellectual action that we must resist not in fantasy, but in reality. Learning to recognize and resist the "devil" is the obligation of every servant of God. And we do so by seeking true knowledge, which allows us to discern deception. The only weapon against deception is truth. But truth can only be properly wielded against deception (evil) by those who have the necessary qualities of a "true believer".

Those qualities are outlined in the Bible (and numerous other books for that matter), so I won't go into them here. But I should point out that merely pretending to have these qualities does not qualify you to do battle with evil. The qualities I speak of can only be granted by God himself, no man can obtain them according to his own desire or will (which the Bible also clearly says in many places and many ways in order to be clear on this point). And hence, no man can come to know the source of all knowledge unless they have indeed been chosen by God.

The popular Christian belief that we have so-called "free will" (or the oxymoronic "limited free will") and that life is some sort of test to see who deserves to live forever, is a spiritually childish notion to a true gnostic.

Even though gnosticism was suppressed and literally outlawed by the church, it has quietly survived all these years. To a gnostic this is no surprise. They know that the truth (i.e. source of knowledge, a.k.a. "God") is the living and conscious force behind all of nature. So gnosticism cannot be destroy like some belief system or religion. Even if all men were destroyed, and a completely new intelligent species involved, there would still be Gnostics, even in the new species.

But, of course, gnosticism is just a word. You don't need to know the word to be a gnostic. I call myself a gnostic only very hesitantly after studying the history of gnosticism and learning that its principles are precisely my own. I did not adopt gnosticism, it adopted me.

P.S. It is difficult, if not impossible, to ever completely, or even correctly, define gnosticism in terms of human language. Like I have said, it is not a religion, not even "pure religion", it is only a way of seeing things that allows one to "see" the religious paths, but it is not a "path" itself. It is like Ti-chi, in the sense that Ti-chi too, when correctly practiced, is a "way of seeing". You could say that gnosticism is a kind of intellectual Ti-chi. Except, unlike Ti-chi, gnosticism can not be taught person-to-person. It can only be learned God-to-person.

Reflections

Saturday, November 13, 2010

Fabrications Don't Help

I sincerely hope that when people read the parts of this blog that talk about my past life's experiences and present experiences, including dreams, that they don't try to analyze the information in order to support, or even form, some "theory" about what made me a "psycho-sex killer" (or whatever). I gave up trying to figure that out when I picked Shasta up and brought her home, and I know more about me than anyone else will even begin to know. (Which is why I openly deride all the psych-doctors who attempt to "evaluate" anyone.)
I have said that I am writing this blog in hopes that people might understand; not my experiences , but themselves. I write about my honest experiences because I'm sure that at some point what I write will contradict any "theory" about me out there. I predict this based on the simple belief that all such "theories" are mere fabrications that ultimately explain nothing except how the mind works in the person who fabricated the "theory". So by exposing the fabrication I hope to expose the fabricator to themselves! Only then will they even begin to understand me! (The best psych-doctors are the ones who see me in themselves, or vice versa. But, even they fail catastrophically as soon as they pretend to document, or otherwise articulate, their understanding.)

Confessions

Sunday, November 14, 2010

Prison Rape

Before I ever arrived at the Washington Corrections Center in Shelton, Washington (W.C.C. state prison) I had been told by just about everyone I spoke to that I would be "targeted for sex" by other inmates, and probably beat-up, or maybe even killed, just because of the way I looked. I was only 19 years old, six feet tall and 138 pounds soaking wet. I had no body hair to speak of, and no facial hair at all. According to my psych-evals, I was also very immature and effeminate (though I had no idea at the time what being "effeminate" meant). They say the three things that will get you killed in prison are sex, drugs and gambling. But the one thing that will get you killed or hurt the fastest is fear. Fear draws predators like death draws flies. With my age, my looks, and my fear, I was a walking rape just waiting to happen. The first men to rape me were two "sexual psychopaths" who were from the same sex offender program at Western State Hospital that I had been expelled from in order to be sent to prison. I don't remember their names (they were not in the same "treatment group" that I was in at the program), so I'll just call them Big John and Kevin. Big John was a huge youngster (but still several years older than me). In fact, he was the "biggest white guy" in the whole prison. But he was also soft spoken and easy going.

He was the one who first came to my cell and told me that because we were both “from the program”, we should be friends. He asked me if I wanted to get high, and invited me to come down to his cell with Kevin, at the very end of the tier, away from the guard station, to smoke a pinner (a small marijuana joint, common in prison). I knew enough at least to avoid a set up like this, but Big John and Kevin were x-program members, so I thought I could trust them. Yes, I was that naïve. Big John was a pedophile. So, he resorted to trying to manipulate me with conversation in order to get me to do what he and Kevin wanted, after he got me into his cell with the door closed. He promised me that no one else would find out and that it would be “mutual”. But, I said I wasn't interested and tried to leave. That prompted Kevin to grab me from behind. He was a little shorter than me, but heavier and much stronger. Kevin was a stone-cold rapist, and seemed to enjoy the prospect of violence. He forced me down onto the end of the bunk, then told Big John to grab my hands (since I was trying to fight him) so he could pull down my pants. But, Big John still preferred manipulation over physical force, so he told me, “We're gonna do it one way or the other. You may as well just go along so we won't hurt you” (which, incidentally is the same logic that police proffer when subduing a “suspect”). I agreed, and stopped resisting. I let Kevin pull down my pants while I was still bent over the end of the bunk. He penetrated me from behind while Big John put his erect penis in my mouth as he laid on the bunk and told me how to pleasure him. This was the very first time I had ever had anal sex (top or bottom), and it was also the first time anyone ever told me how to “suck dick”. (All my previous experiences with oral sex had never consisted of more than placing the penis in the mouth while masturbating, including the oral “rape” that I was in prison for.) After Kevin ejaculated inside of me, they switched places. And, with more threats of violence, Kevin persuaded me to pleasure him orally too, even after he had just had anal sex with me. The entire experience was revolting, but I was too frightened to not do what I was told. Luckily there was only a little pain (other times that I was raped in prison were much more painful during the act of penetration, I learned the hard way why “bending over” is always a good idea when you are getting anally raped). There was nothing “mutual” about any of it, at least not until a few days later (after other inmates had found out that I was “easy”, and started pressuring me with threats of violence to have “one-way” sex with them). Big John told me to come down to his cell again, so we could talk. I went, expecting to be raped again, but this time he was alone (not that he couldn't have raped me all by himself if he wanted to), and instead of demanding sex from me, he offered himself to me! He told me not to tell anyone, not even Kevin. He gave me oral sex until I was half erect, then he laid back on his bunk and put his legs in the air and told me to “put it in!” Well, the sight of his giant hairy ass was more than my poor little fellow could bear. I lost what little stiffness I had, and told him I wasn't really interested in the “mutual” thing anyway. He was kind enough to let me go, with a few further, admonishments to not tell anyone, of course. But I did tell, my friend and fellow “punk”, Junior. And Junior told a black man who was pressuring him for information about me. And the black man told his friends, who told their friends, until, of course someone finally told Big John, “what Duncan was saying”. By this time I was living on a different tier, from a futile attempt to get away from being “pressured for sex”. But Big John came onto my tier and a huge crowd followed him to my cell to witness the confrontation that it seemed everyone but me knew was about to happen. He came into my cell and pretty much accused me of lying about him, then punched me in the face. There was no way I could even hurt this guy if he gave me ten free shots, so I fell to the ground, and confessed profusely that I had lied about him. He pretended to be satisfied, and left. The show was over. I should actually credit him for not doing much worse. By all “rights” he should have put me in the hospital (and at the same time I thought he was going to). But his true nature was not violent, he only did the bare minimum of what he had to do to protect his “reputation”. He let me off easy, and I learned to keep my mouth even more “shut” than before. Now I knew that I couldn't tell the guards, or even other inmates, about what was happening to me. I never felt more scared and alone in all my life. By not at least trying to fight back against Big John, I unwittingly "announced" to the whole tier that I was "fair game". Anyone who wanted to have sex with me from then on didn't even have to threaten me themselves. All they had to do was threaten to tell Big John that I was "talking about him" again, and they could make me do anything they wanted. Especially since before Big John left my cell, after punching me in the face, he threatened to do "a lot worse" if he ever heard of me talking about him again. And all the "vultures", "wolves" and "big cats", were no doubt salivating at his words (these are the different kinds of prison sex predators, each with their own tactics and tastes). Once again, I was the last one to realize what was going to happen next. The wolves ganged up (six of them attacking me at once), the big cats pounded in turn, and the vultures moved in for the left overs. If I hadn't been transferred when I was, I probably would have been killed; if not by someone jealous "daddy's" shank, then for sure by the even more gruesome, Mr HIV (which was in it's heyday at the time). I eventually began getting aroused while I was being used for sex. At first it confused me, I wasn't trying to be aroused at all. I remember the first time it happened, as I lay on my stomach on a black man's bunk with my pants down around my ankles, and the man himself laying on top of me kissing the back of my neck while he had anal sex with me. I felt myself getting an erection, and thought it was just more evidence that something was "wrong" with me. I got transferred to another prison soon after that, and had learned how to "act tough" (i.e. not show fear) so I didn't draw so much unwanted attention, and the rapes stopped. But then the fantasies of getting used began. It gave me a way to take control back from the men who had taken so much control away from me. At least, in my mind, at first. But eventually I started "letting" men use me for sex, but only if they treated me with respect. And hence, I became a prison queen. But that's a different story.

Chronicles

Sunday, November 14, 2010

Going Bald

I went to "rec" today in order to shave my beard off and cut my hair. For "rec" (short for what the jail calls recreation), I am allowed to go up on the roof of the jail to a domed cage about half the size of a basketball court. There is a basketball, and hoop, and even a handball (much more than most other jails have). I'm allowed one and a half hours, by myself of course, twice a week. But I usually only go once every other month or so, to cut my hair and shave my beard off; like today. The cordless electric trimmers that they let inmates use (only during "rec") have been an ongoing issue. Because of the constant use they get, they usually only last a few months before the battery stops taking a charge. I've seen at least four different models of cordless trimmers since I've been here, and they seem to get cheaper and cheaper (and stop working sooner) each time they are replaced. There haven't been any trimmers at all available for the last month or so. But I was told they finally got some new ones about a week ago, and I was past due to get my beard wacked off, so today I went to "rec" accordingly. But the "new" trimmers were the cheapest I've ever seen. They would not hold a charge for more than a minute or two at a time. And I had already started to cut my hair when the charge ran out on the first trimmer. They had two, so I exchanged them and tried to continue cutting my hair when the second went dead too. So I shot some hoops while I waited for them to charge some, then tried again. By the end of my hour and a half of "rec", I had wacked off most of my overgrown hair, but now I had an uneven mess of stubble all over my head and face. Fortunately I had anticipated a problem like this and had a backup plan. They don't let inmates have real razors to shave with (they issue one inch wide "toy" razors that are so dull that they literally rip the hair instead of cutting it, no lie! They're called "no shank razors", but about the only thing they are good for is making shanks. And, they are so easy to tear apart to get the blade out that they should be called "easy shank razors". Somebody's making a lot of money by just calling them "no shank razors" for nothing, a very typical "industrial complex" rip off) but I ordered some "Magic Shave" (depilatory cream) from the jail commissary, and after "rec" I went to the shower and smeared almost a whole tube of the stuff all over my head and face! And, behold, 15 minutes later I was as bold as Kojak (but twice as handsome) :) (This is the first time I've ever shaved my head in my life, and I get no thrill from it, so it will probably be the last time too.)

Dreams

Monday, November 15, 2010

Waking Up From Murder

I just awoke from a nap. I was dreaming that I was visiting my step family, who in real life have said that I "deserve to die". Actually, in the dream, the family I was visiting was a bizarre hodgepodge of past friends, step family and even a reality TV family (kind of a cross between "19 kids and counting" and "little people, big world"). I was sitting in the dining room where two of my real life step-nephews seemed to be doing homework for school. By way of making polite conversation I asked them what grade they were in. The one sitting closest to me, Nick, who in real life, as in the dream, is a very independent young man, told me, "eight". I said, "Do you mean, eighth grade?" He said contemptuously, "No. We don't have 'grades'. We have 'levels'. We're not like other schools." I asked, "What do you mean?" And he said, "We believe in the death penalty." As I started to inquire further I woke up. But even as I lay awake in my jail cell, more questions for my nephew poured through my mind. 'Do you think some people deserve to die?' 'What do you mean by "deserve to die?"' As I lay there, I realized that a person's position on the death penalty is a good divider between basic types of belief systems. And this dream seemed to indicate so by apparently defining an entire school system based on the belief in the death penalty. If you believe in the death penalty, then you essentially believe that some people "deserve to die" (or conversely, "do not deserve to live"). And you can't believe that unless you also believe that there are (and should be) some standards that people must live up to in order to "deserve to live". You also, by implication, believe that those standards are determinable. And, more importantly, that it is possible to weigh an individual against said determined standards. In short, if you believe in the death penalty, then you believe that humans have the ability to determine (by judgment) the moral worth of other humans. And this belief will determine not only your position on the death penalty, but also your position on many other issues as well, such as whether or not war can be justified on moral grounds (i.e. "in the name of God"). Even a person who calls themselves atheist, is bowing to a false god, if they believe such a thing. I won't go into all the reasons it is impossible for us to morally judge each other, numerous other books have already been written about that (especially the Bible!). But I just wanted to observe what believing in the death penalty really means. I believed I had the ability to judge society once too. And I believed that my ability to judge was superior to those whom I judged. And I carried out my judgments, until a little girl showed me that my ability to judge was pure delusion. That was when I "woke up" in real life!

Reflections

Thursday, November 18, 2010

Fear No Evil

If I were afraid of death I would not have been able to bring that little girl home and turn myself over to the present authorities. In fact, you could say that it was the fear of death that I overcame which allowed me to do what I wanted to do in my heart all along (stop killing). It amazes me that people do not understand that threatening someone with death only alienates them and makes them that much more likely to try to hurt someone. But I suppose I should not be too amazed, since I also once rationalized my own fantasies of how people would react to my threats, by thinking that they would regret what they did to me. Of course, now I realize that no one regrets my having been sent to prison as a kid for 15 years, to be raped and perverted by the System. And, even those who realize that what happened to me was wrong don't seem to realize that they were the ones who did it to me (or, more precisely, the attitudes and beliefs that allowed me to be crucified as a child). I too once could not see my ignorance. And now that I have had my false beliefs illuminated for what they are, I do not suddenly believe that I know the truth. Instead, I realize that I know nothing! How could I possibly trust my own knowledge ever again after learning that my most basic lifelong beliefs were all lies! I can't. But, at least I'm not afraid of death any more. Nor am I afraid of being deceived, because I realize now that as long as I do not believe that what I think is true, then I cannot be deceived. I suspect this is what Jesus meant by "believe in me". He was simply trying to tell us to believe what is in our heart, not our mind. If you believe that Jesus was a Man/God that lived 2000 years ago, then you believe what you have been told by other men. These things exist only in your mind. But if you believe that it does not matter whether a man called Jesus of Nazareth ever walked the earth at all, but that His "teachings" are still important and useful for guidance and instruction, then perhaps you will be saved yet.

Reflections

Thursday, November 18, 2010

Freedom of Sexual Expression

I just read that it is important for gays (generally speaking) to believe they have no choice about being "gay". Supposedly, they need to believe they have no choice in order to attenuate their shame.

Wow. I should have known this already, considering my predominantly gay sexual adventures. But I did not realize this (in the general sense). I knew that some gays felt that way, but not most of them. I always assumed that most gays understood that being "gay" was a choice. To me, it has always been important that my sexual exploits were the product of my own volition. If who I enjoy having sex with is not my choice, then what choices do I have at all?

There is no more intimate form of communication between two people than sexual expression. If I cannot choose what I "say" sexually, then I have no choice in anything I say. Because of its extremely intimate and personal nature, sex, to me, is the most meaningful form of speech. Without freedom of sexual expression there is no freedom of speech.

Perhaps this is why men who seek power over other men throughout history, i.e. religions and governments, have always suppressed sexual expression. It is only obvious that if men cannot express themselves satisfactorily they will readily turn to other men to do so for them, which is what we call social intercourse. If so, then it becomes obvious how social concepts such as "justice" and "freedom" and "security" can be so emotionally charged, because they are proxies for pent up sexual energy!

Wow! So governments and religions derive their power by suppressing and then redirecting the emotional energy of our libidos! How weird is that? No wonder we are constantly fighting and killing each other. If all this is true, then in a better world, sexual expression (and so-called "preference") will be completely untethered. I suspect the only "law" in such a world would be the One Law that Jesus speaks of in the Bible, "Love thy neighbor as thyself" (which is the same thing as loving God when it is understood correctly), then the thought that "God condemned homosexual behavior" will be seen as ludicrous by everyone, because everyone will be "gay" (i.e. willing to do whatever feels good without compunction).

Confessions

Thursday, November 18, 2010

The Mark Of A Convict

I used to boast, when I was in prison, that my first infraction was for assaulting a guard. I didn't even have to lie. I'd just say, "I hit a guard in the head with a garbage can lid." Technically that was the truth, and recently when the Federal prosecutor brought that infraction report into court as evidence of my "past violent behavior in prison", I didn't challenge it. But, here's what really happened. I was working in the kitchen "garbage room" with another inmate. Our job was to take the garbage from the room to the back loading dock, and empty it into the garbage truck when it arrived. The cooks had changed the oil in the friers the day before. So there were about a half dozen boxes of empty Crisco cans. Each can was the same size as a regular can of Crisco oil and each one also came with its own plastic lid for resealing the can if it is only partially used. Each box held about 24 cans and consequently, about 24 plastic lids, which the cooks threw into the boxes loose with the cans after emptying them. So my co-worker and I were throwing the lids at each other like frisbees. They were harder to catch than to throw, so the object was to try to catch the lids the other guy threw with one hand, while throwing lids back with the other, all as fast as we could; scoring short-lived bragging points for "good catches". The kitchen guard, c/o Tobin, was a laid back older man who I thought was "friendly", as far as my very limited experience with guards went at the time. So when he walked into the garbage room and told us to get back to work, I jokingly threw one of the lids at him and shouted, "Tobin! Catch this!" (Those were the exact words that Tobin himself wrote in the infraction report). I expected him to turn when I called his name, but he was saying something to my co-worker, and turned about a second too late, just in time for the five-inch plastic lid to hit him on the forehead above his left eye, by surprise. I laughed and said, "Opps... you were supposed to catch it, sorry!" The other inmate and Tobin suddenly weren't smiling. I didn't understand it at the time, but I had just violated a subtle, but serious prison taboo; inmates don't familiarize themselves with the guards, no matter how friendly they are. Of course, Tobin was not injured in the least. But, a line had been crossed and he had to make sure that I understood I was never to cross it again. He wrote me up for "Assault on a guard", one of the most serious infractions possible. I couldn't believe he wrote me up at all, much less for such a serious infraction. I thought he was such a nice guy. But, I had a lot to learn and this was to be only my first of many "lessons", over the years, that came in the form of unexpected infractions. I learned that there is an invisible but well defined social stratum line between guards and inmates; guards above, inmates below. I learned that while conventional etiquette crossed that line freely enough, familiar things such as trust, genuine concern, and any kind of intimacy, were strictly barred from crossing between the two strata. I learned that no matter how friendly a guard was, they could never be my friend. I eventually learned to hate the "System", and that was an important part of my prison education that helped keep me alive. Other inmates can "feel" this hatred in each other, and it's not easy to fake. It is the mark of a convict, and the basis for a code that I learned and lived by in order to survive, and "stay out of trouble". Of course, it is also the basis for what prison officials call, "criminal mentality", and what psychologists call, "anti-social personality disorder". Inmates are trained to hate the System, by the System. And nobody seems to care; not even when that hate gets escalated by the same "Criminal Justice" System into a murderous rage.

Reflections

Friday, November 19, 2010

The "Serial Killer" Fence

Attempting to classify the traits of a "serial killer" (or any criminal for that matter), in order to determine what causes them to become killers, is as stupid as trying to figure out why some snow flakes land on the edge of a fence by studying the characteristics of the snow that has landed there.

Yes, the snow there has certain properties that are distinctly different from snow that has landed in the yard. The snow on the fence is more loosely packed, but harder (colder) at the same time. But those characteristics are not what put the snow on the fence. They were developed only after the snow had landed on the fence, from the additional exposure to the cold and wind. Actually, the snow flakes that land on the fence may be a bit larger, or perhaps more damp, on average, than other flakes, allowing them to stick better and not getting blown off again by the wind. But knowing these characteristics still won't help you keep snow off the fence. There will always be variations in the size and dampness of snow flakes, after all, "no two are ever alike", remember?

And so it is with studying "serial killers" (or other "social flakes"). They might be "harder" and "colder" than the average "flake", but that has little to do with why they kill. Killing causes a person to become that way. And sure, statistically, they may have more often been bed-wetters, or fire-bugs, or abuse victims, before they ended up on the "serial killer" fence, but that information is completely useless. More than 99% of the people who wet their bed, start fires, or were abused as children, never become "serial killers".

In one of the books, that I was studying for my case ("Using Murder: The Social Construction of Serial Homicide" by: Philip Jenkins), the author points out that the famous FBI Behavior Sciences Unit (B.S.U.) is as helpful to police as the Psychic Friends Network. The information they provide is generalized and useless. Any specific details that they do come up with are as often wrong as right.

The only reason for the B.S.U.'s popularity is due to movies such as, "Silence of the Lambs" and "Red Dragon". But while the profiling techniques in those movies were authentic enough, the characters being profiled were fictitiously "shaped" in order to let the FBI profilers be the heroes in the end. There was nothing authentic at all about the overall pathology of the killers in these movies. While the "Cannibal" and "Dragon" may have been based on real people, their psychology in the movies was a hodgepodge of unlikely combinations of various mental illnesses.

And yet after these movies came out the FBI Behavior Sciences Unit in Quantico, VA, received overwhelming public support, despite the fact that in the real world this Unit was floundering from a series of serious profiling errors, and no significant successes. The only thing positive most police investigators can say about the BSU information they get in a case, is that it helps them "think outside the box". They say the same thing about consulting with psychics.

So, if we want to keep snow off the fence, then we'd be much better off taking a closer look at the fence itself! For example, how do we define a "serial killer", and how does that definition help to actually put people on the "serial killer" fence?

The whole concept of "serial killer" is new, but there have been people who fit the definition all throughout history (see Jenkins's book, "Using Murder" for a really good analysis of this). So tearing down the "serial killer" fence wont stop "killer flakes" from falling out of the sky, but it would, perhaps, at least get people to start looking up!

P.S.: Incidentally, for what it's worth the FBI's profile report on my crimes (that was written after my arrest and "confession") said that my case was anomalous. Almost none of the "elements" of my crimes matched up with their general profiles for other "sex killers". I keep trying to tell them that my crimes weren't about sex, or even violence. (Believe it or not, I loath violence, and have only ever resorted to it after much deliberation. "Violence when there are alternatives is immoral. Violence when there are no other alternatives is survival." I had alternatives to my own violent behavior in the past, but even after the most careful and meticulous deliberation I never saw what my alternatives were. At least not until a certain eight-year-old little girl named Shasta helped to open my eyes!)

Reflections

Friday, November 19, 2010

What I Am

In the original Fifthnail blog I was as honest as I could be without exposing myself as a child rapist/murderer. So at times I even made carefully worded denials of any interest in children at all. These denials, of course, were deliberate lies. But in this "Fifthnail Exposed" blog, I no longer need to hide my sickness or perversion. I am what I am, and attempting to deny the truth at this point would be a futile attempt at vanity, not to mention self defeating.

The "revelation" that caused me to bring eight-year-old Shasta home and surrender myself to the police, did not "cure" me. I still have fantasies of raping children, and even masturbate as often as I feel like it with little or no compunction.

Several times after I was arrested in 2005, I tried to suppress my deviant fantasies and would go weeks at a time, "fasting" from all "pleasurable thoughts". These fasts would often include going without food at the same time. I continued these fasts, off and on, for about two years after I was arrested, thinking that I had to be able to "control my desires" in order to be "pure" and "completely honest".

And during these fasts, I often told my attorney's about my attempts and failures, at self control, thinking that being as truthful as I could with them would help me to become more honest. I even "confessed" to the FBI, at one point, with this same goal in mind (which I explicitly explained to them as the reason for my talking to them against my attorney's advice. I said, "God told me to be honest with you".)

But, as it turned out, it was easier to starve myself for weeks at a time (the longest I ever went was about two weeks with no food) than to get control of the violent fantasies that kept coming into my mind. They seemed to have a life and will of their own, to survive!

I started noticing that the fantasies would react to specific external circumstances. When guards, or other inmates, projected insults at me, I could be doing something completely innocuous, such as reading a book, or writing a letter, and even though I tried to ignore the insults, the fantasies of deviant sex would come seemingly all on their own.

So I started "experimenting" with different reactions and techniques. For example, I discovered that if I allowed myself to react to the insults, by shouting back for example, that the fantasies were much less likely to come, or if they did come they were much less persistent. I also noticed that even if the insults were not directed at me, for example, when I overheard inmates or guards talking derisively about some other "sex offender", the fantasies would still react as if somehow to "defend" me from harm. I remember explicitly reporting this realization to my attorneys at the time. I told them, "It's as if some unconscious part of my mind is trying to protect me!" I was realizing that my fantasies were the product of completely unconscious processes that were attempting to attenuate the pain of reality, even though consciously they often caused even more pain! (For the first several days after my arrest in 2005, I was in a kind of emotional shock that kept any fantasies, and barely any thoughts at all, from coming into my conscious mind. I thought that perhaps I had been "freed" from them at last! But on about the fifth or sixth day I had calmed down and recovered enough that this unwanted "defense mechanism" decided to kick in, and I started having fantasies about having sex with Shasta and her brother, Dylan, at the mountain campsite. When the fantasies came and demanded my attention the way they do, I curled up on the cold concrete floor of the jail cell, and cried. The pain came from knowing I was not "free" after all.)

On the way bringing Shasta home in the Jeep, I had promised her that I would never have "bad thoughts" (i.e. fantasies) about her again, not even after I was arrested (she knew I was going to turn myself in). I truly believed I could and would keep that promise, because at the time I was able to relate to her in a completely non-sexual way. In other words, I was not having any sexual desires for her at all, much less fantasies. Not since before my arrest in 1980 had I been able to relate to a child with no sexual thoughts. So, I thought I had been "miraculously cured" on the mountain when I decided to bring her home. It was a "cure" I had been praying for, for a very long time. But, I was wrong.

I am still the same "sick" and "twisted" pervert that I have been all my life. Yes, I admit, even as a kid I was a "sicko". But as a kid that "sickness" was only the result of a severe lack of healthy sexual information and experience. I could have easily been "cured" with just a little time all by itself (as recent studies show happens frequently – i.e. under confidential agreements, many responsible adults who have never been arrested, or accused of sexual crimes, have admitted that as youths they engaged in sexual behavior that could have gotten them arrested, often even feloniously. And I have personally known several such men, who are now very law abiding and respected members of society – one man, for example, who molested both me and my brother when we were 12 and 10 years old respectively, while he was 17, is now a Captain in the Navy. And he didn't just "touch our privates" out of curiosity. He did things to my brother and I with a bicycle pump in our butts that was perverted even by my present standards! Now he has a wife and kids of his own, and a very respected career.)

Eventually I realized that I was running around in circles trying to "control my fantasies". I noticed that I was starting to fall into the same behavior cycles that I experienced when I was in prison years ago trying to "cure" myself.

So, I stopped trying to suppress my fantasies several years ago. I rationalize that there is no danger of me acting out my fantasies ever again, so why not "let them go" and try to learn by watching what they do. It's kind of like living with primitive anthropoids in order to better understand them. In the past I tried to control them with external pressure. Now I'm just trying to understand them from within instead.

I've been learning a lot, and have even reflected on some of those lessons (in mostly non-sexual contexts) right here in this blog. Perhaps, if I live long enough, someday I will learn something that might help other people, or even society in general. But, I realize that's a thin hope. I'm just content to know that I don't have to struggle anymore. No matter what happens, for the rest of my life, I will be what I am. And that's okay.

Confessions

Tuesday, November 23, 2010

What Happened In Prison - Part II: The Convict

McNeil Island Corrections Center (MICC) was a “real prison”, compared to the Washington Corrections Center (WCC) that I had been transferred from in 1984. The main cellblocks were five tiers high, with the traditional bars on the front of all the cells. Most of the cells were 15' deep and 20' wide and housed eight men on four sets of bunks, two bunks against opposite walls, and a single toilet and sink against the wet wall at the back of the cell. By this time my hatred for the System had finally begun to take root, and this gave me a little bit of status with the other inmates who called themselves “convicts”. I'd learned to hide my fear behind cold expressions and not let myself be bullied by the more aggressive inmates. Luckily, nobody at MICC knew about how I got raped and “punked out” at WCC in Shelton. I was also finally able to grow a little bit of hair on my face and it seems that went a long way to help deter all but the most hard-core predators. So after a few half-hearted attempts to pressure me by a few of the seasoned predators, I was pretty much left alone. And then something interesting happened. I started to attract the attention of a different kind of inmate. These were older more experienced convicts who I guess saw something in my youth and determination to stand up for myself that must have reminded them of themselves when they were younger. Several of these older convicts took me under their wings, which they wouldn't have done if they had not seen me standing up against the pressure. (They were “older” to me but still young themselves, not more than 30 years or so). None of them ever made any sexual advanced toward me, and having their friendship pretty much squelched all the remaining interest I got from would-be attackers. But, more importantly, they taught me how to not just survive, but to thrive in prison. Instead of just waiting for the “System” to assign me a job (like I did at Shelton), they encouraged me to go after a job I wanted. So, after I was assigned to the dish-tank in the kitchen, I went straight to the head-cook and told him I worked as a “cook-five” at Madigan Army Medical Center. And that I wanted to cook instead of wash dishes. (The “cook-five” job was part of the “Youth Summer Employment Program” that I was part of for four months while at the Dyslin's Boy's Ranch, so I did actually know something about institutional cooking). The cook asked me a few questions about safe food handling and how to operate and clean he steam kettles and grills. After I answered his questions he hired me on the spot. That was another “lucky break” for me, because the inmate cooks were all part of the older more experienced convicts in the kitchen who formed a privileged clique that even the guards gave some respect to (mostly since these older convicts kept things running smoothly, which made the guard's job easier). And the cooks ate well, very well! At MICC there was a butcher's shop attached to the kitchen. And the inmate butchers were part of the cook's clique. So we had steak and eggs for breakfast (not all the time, but often enough), and fed on juicy pork chops while everyone else ate “Mexican surprise”. And, of course, we were also “in” with the bakers, so doughnuts and cake were status quo. Actually, I'm exaggerating here a little, but only just a little. We weren't supposed to eat anything except what was on the menu, so we had to be discrete. But I'm not exaggerating at all to tell you that when we walked out of the kitchen with a half dozen “Dagwoods” (deluxe sandwiches) wrapped in plastic and tied around our waist for our buddies back in the cell blocks, the kitchen guards never shook us down. They knew not to. In the mean time, I had also signed up on the school floor for the Vocational Electronics Program. I had always been fascinated by TV's since I was a kid. Not just the TV programs, but I wanted to know how TV's actually worked. The waiting list for the electronics program was over a year long, but one of my older convict friends suggested that I go out to the electronics shop and talk to the instructor. So I did. Fred Schuneman had built the electronics program himself, almost from scratch. And inmates who signed up for the program usually only did so with little real interest. So when I showed up in his office begging to be moved up the list because I had “always wanted to learn electronics”, he didn't hesitate. I got into the program right away, and did well. I especially liked the hand's on labs, and the self-paced format, which allowed me to zip through the material quickly. Before long, other students started to come to me for help, and I became a sort of unofficial teacher's aide.

So, I was now working in the kitchen and going to school at the same time, which kept me pretty busy. In my spare time, on the weekends, I liked to play volleyball on the yard, and spend time in the library reading books about computers and psychology that I could barely understand. I read about computers for the same reason I was taking electronics lessons. I had seen an Apple IIe computer once, and even though I wasn't even allowed to touch it at the time, I just knew I had to find out how it worked. So I began reading books in the library on computers, and even computer programming, long before the first time I actually touched a computer. I read books on psychology and self-help, because I always wanted to understand my "sexual deviancy" problem. I thought that if I understood how my brain worked then I should be able to "fix it" myself. I definitely wasn't getting any help from the "Correctional System", and I had decided that "God" wasn't going to do anything for me either. So, my only hope for getting well was to educate myself as much as I could. I took what few psychology and self-help classes were offered by the school, but mostly I familiarized myself with the "psychology and self-help" bookshelf in the library at MICC, as I had once familiarized myself with the "religion and philosophy" bookshelf while I was at WCC. Education was my only hope of ever returning to a "normal" life on the streets, so I took it seriously and read everything I could get my hands on that I thought might help me understand what was "wrong" with me.

Back in the kitchen the institution was starting to cut back on the food budget by reducing how much food inmates could have. One morning as I was frying eggs on the serving line (inmates could have their eggs cooked to order in those days), a guard came and told me to only serve two eggs per inmate. I ignored him and just kept giving the inmates who came through the line as many eggs as they wanted (usually four, sometimes six). After awhile the guard came up and told me again to serve only two eggs per inmate. I said, "Okay". But when the next inmate asked for four eggs, I gave him four eggs, even while the guard was still standing there. The guard left in a huff. Then, another inmate cook who saw the guard leave in a hurry and heading back toward the cook-supervisor's office, came up to me and asked, "What was that all about?" I told him that the guard had told me to serve only two eggs and I refused to do it. The other inmate cook left, also toward the supervisor's office. A little while later I saw the guard and other inmate cook return to their usual positions on the serving line, which surprised me since I had expected to get pulled from the line and given an infraction for "refusing to obey an order", or worse. But I finished serving that morning with no further incidents. As it turned out, the other inmate cook also realized that I would probably be infracted and pulled off the line, if not fired. So he went to the supervisor and while the guard was still complaining about my refusal to obey, the other inmate said that if I were pulled from the line none of the other convicts would take my place, and if I were infracted the entire morning crew would quit. So that explained why I didn't get in trouble. Nowadays inmates could never pull a stunt like that. They'd lock down the whole prison first. But back then, the convicts had a lot more power than today. Because I was programming so well, with a full time job and school, and staying out of trouble, I ended up getting moved to "preferred housing". At first I went to "Two-house", which was an older cellblock that was only three tiers high and all single man cells. While in Two-house, I began very discretely giving sex pleasure to one two other convicts (I only remember one specifically, but there may have been two). I would come to the TV room during late-night wearing only a long bathrobe, which was commonly done, but I'd only have on a pair of sport-jocky underpants beneath the robe (or sometimes nothing at all), and a pair of thick wool socks that acted like slippers, and made it appear as though I had on more clothes beneath the robe. Then, after I was alone in the TV room, I'd take off my robe and masturbate to fantasies of letting other inmates have sex with me. I usually did this all by myself, but after a while, at least one other inmate noticed that I spent a lot of time in the TV room at night alone, so he started hanging out later than usual to see what would happen, and sure enough, I started letting him watch me masturbate and I even let him touch me while I was naked. But we never had intercourse, not even oral, and I never let him do more than just touch me with his hands while I masturbated. I got off on the power and control I seemed to have over him. We ended up becoming good friends (since we would converse a lot while all this was going on), and he never tried to go any further than I was willing to let him. He respected me, and that was a new experience for me when it came to sex. I should also note that while masturbating by myself in the TV room at nights seems bizarre, it made sense to me because by doing so I could cut off my fantasies of child rape. Masturbating in the TV room was a way for me to get excited without fantasizing about children. The risk of getting caught provided a kind of adrenaline kick, while the environment itself, a place where inmates normally congregated, provided tactile support for my fantasies while at the same time interfering with any kind of fantasies about children. It was like therapy for me, in more ways than one, not to mention, great exercise, since I often got very physical as I acted out my fantasies (e.g. dancing erotically in front of the room while I fantasized a room full of cheering inmates eager to have sex with me). I should also point out that in all my years in prison I never once got into trouble for my sexual behavior. Unlike other queens and homosexuals, who typically had more infractions for having sex than they could count, I never got caught or infracted once. There were a couple of times I came close to getting caught, but I never actually got caught. Nor did I ever contract a single sexually transmitted disease, not even crabs or herpes. I like to think this was because I was always very careful. But, I would not be being completely honest if I did not admit that I had at least some help from lady luck. Though I never needed a lot of luck, mostly because I was never as sexually active with other inmates as I was with myself. I often fantasized about having sex with ten inmates at a time, but I rarely ever had sex with even one (not counting the times I was raped at WCC). Even after I came out on my own as a queen (openly gay) I was almost completely monogamous, almost, but now I'm getting ahead of myself.

When a position came open in the electronics shop for a toolroom clerk, I quit my job in the kitchen and went to work for Fred Schuneman. The pay was the same (19.5 cents per hour, or about 23 dollars per month), and there were far fewer fringe benefits, and somewhat less prestige. The other workers in the electronics shop were mostly regular “inmates”, as opposed to “convicts”, but I didn't mind. The important thing to me was that I could be closer to computers. There were two Apple IIe computers in the shop, and every once and a while I would actually get to use one (usually by volunteering to do some tedious typing or other work). Then one magical day Fred came into the toolroom where I was working and asked me if I wanted a computer to work with. The shop had ended up with a spare Apple IIe from the school that was in the shop for repairs, but it had already been replaced at the school by the time it was fixed. So now the computer was just taking up room in the shop. Fred decided it may as well take up room in the tool room where I could use it. This was the first computer that I had essentially unrestricted access to, and I was more than ready for it. I had been studying not just programming languages, but also computer architecture, digital electronics, and just about anything else I could that had to do with computers. And now I could for the first time start applying what I had been learning. In the first month with the Apple computer I wrote a machine-code program that could beat anyone at a game called Mastermind (a colored peg sequence guessing game). I had assembled the program by hand, without the aid of another program called an assembler. I used the technical specs for the 6502e processor chip, and punched in hexadecimal numbers as the instructions instead of higher level command words. In other words, I did it the old fashioned (and very hard) way and I learned. Then I built a light-pen from spare electronic parts around the shop, including the machine-code “driver” for the pen, which plugged into an empty chip socket on the mother board of the Apple IIe. And soon after that (I had saved my pennies from work and bought a real compiler program called “Merlin”, so now I could start writing more advanced programs). I wrote a graphical compression algorithm that allowed my programs to create animated graphics with the very limited memory of computers in those days (my Apple had only 128 Kilobytes of RAM!). This was years before I ever heard of “gifs” (the popular little animated graphics all over the Internet today), which pretty much do the same thing my program did back then. When the vocational welding instructor saw me demonstrating my animation program he asked if I could use it to create a quiz program for his welding class that would have animated graphics along with each question. I said I could, and I did. I called the program “Quiz Wiz” (and years later I wrote a much more sophisticated Web-based version of Quiz Wiz for another vocational program at Monroe, Washington, that, last I heard, is still in use today.) I even once wrote a firmware hack (a program that takes over for the software that comes built into the computer hardware) that I called “Err-go!” and submitted it for publication to a popular magazine for Apple II computers called “Nibble”. My article was rejected, but I still think it was a great hack (it let Applesolf BASIC programmers write programs that could jump to labeled subroutines instead of just numbered routines, a feature that is standard today). In other words, yes, I had proven myself to be a genuine wiz kid. And, I took on all of the haughty airs that go along with such status. Well, I wasn't that haughty, but haughty enough to demand people to “leave me alone!” while I was working on the computer. I eventually got moved out of the tool room and took over the shops main computer, which was a suped-up Apple II e (with 512 k memory and 40 Mb external hard drive! Woo-hoo!). I became, officially, one of the shop techs (doing actual electronic repair work), but I spent most of my time on the computer.

An important aspect of my obsession with computers is that it provided me with a strong distraction from my sexual exploits. By the time I was turning myself into a computer wiz I had been moved to a housing unit called Summit House. It was the ultimate in “preferred” housing units. I could, and would, sit up in the laundry room at Summit House half the night, writing programs and studying, using the large tables, that were meant for folding clothes on, as my study desk, with books and papers spread out all over. I did not have time for fantasies, or dancing naked in the TV room. Computers seemed to be my salvation. Well, maybe not my “salvation”, but they had a definite impact on my fantasies. I recall that while I was studying computers, I still masturbated frequently. But my fantasies had become almost exclusively adult oriented. I never did “like” fantasizing about children. It was “pleasurable” to do so, but it always made me feel bad. So being able to fantasize about sex with other men was much preferable, and with my new social status as a “wiz kid” I found that I had a place in the adult world after all. For the first time I started feeling like I was an adult, not just a kid anymore. I was 24 years old.

I graduated with honors and special recognition with an AS degree in Electronics Service. At the graduation ceremony I was approached by a woman from Institutional Industries who congratulated me on my honors then offered me a job programming IBM computers in the industries offices. The job would pay five times what I was earning in the Electronics Shop, (over a dollar an hour) and was by far one of the best paying jobs in prison. But, I politely declined her offer, citing loyalty to the Electronics program. I felt I should “give back” what the program had given me.

Suddenly my world got turned upside down, again. Only this time in a good way! The Parole Board had been ordered by the courts to bring the minimum terms of all inmates in their charge, “within range of the SRA” (Sentencing Reform Act – a new set of laws that was supposed to provide predetermined sentences for all crimes and get rid of the Parole Board). Well, as I've mentioned before, my sentence was more than three times over the SRA range, so the Parole Board had to reduce my time. When they did so, they set a new sentence that was still over the SRA range for my crime, but it was under what I had already served! So what I expected to be a routine review hearing turned into a parole hearing! They asked me if I had any parole plans. I said, no. They asked what I would do if I were parole. I said, I didn't know. I simply wasn't prepared. They asked if I was willing to get sex offender treatment on the streets, and I said, of course. And then, right then and there, completely out of the blue, they found me parolable! It was over! I was going home! I'm emotional even now as I write this and remember how happy I was. My mother was still living in Tacoma at the same house I had been arrested at as a 16-year-old boy. I could go live with her, get a job, help her pay the mortgage (she was close to loosing the house because of not being able to keep the payments up). And everything would be okay again! I was going home, at long long last! But, that's not what happened, not even close. It was another seven years before I actually got out on parole, and by then my mother had long lost the house, and I had long lost any hope of ever returning to a "normal" life. By the time I finally did get paroled I had only one purpose in life, revenge! It was the only thing I felt that I had to live for after what "they" did to me over the course of the next seven years. They destroyed every last hope I had and threw all my efforts to heal myself right back in my face. But, that's another chapter, that I call "The Transition".

Reflections

Friday, November 26, 2010

What It's Like

It's like trying to walk on a 14-inch wide steal I-beam, a thousand feet up in the air at the top of a sky scraper under construction. Some people can do it easily, they say it's no different than walking on the ground, you just need to be a bit careful about where you walk is all. The trick, they say, is to not look down. Some people can't do it at all! If you put them on such a beam, and all they had to do was crawl ten feet to safety, they wouldn't be able to do it. They'd cling to the beam with both arms and legs, eyes tightly closed and beg hysterically for someone to get them down.

Still others, like me, can at least manage to crawl, but never stand without support, much less walk. And the irony is that this "beam" that I can't walk is only ten inches to a few feet off the ground for most people. But it's a thousand feet to me, which most people don't seem to understand. They call me a coward and a sicko because I can't walk what to them is as easy as a walk in the park. But, a park that has children in it to me is as much a tightrope in my mind as a crack house is to a crack addict. And strangely enough I've smoked crack, but I've never had any problem putting the pipe down. I always used drugs and alcohol intermittently, and never when I could not afford to. Those were "beams" I could walk blindfolded (I'd go months and even years without getting high at all, even when I could afford to. I once gave a crack addicted friend of mine my last "rock", then asked him politely to go smoke it by himself and not to call me anymore. To him, crack was that 14-inch beam a thousand feet in the air, and I knew that if he ever fell he could end up hurting me too. So, I respectfully ended my association with him, though I still considered him a friend. The only time I ever saw him again was once, to give him a Christmas card that featured a picture of my cat, that he had reluctantly let me have when it was a kitten and could not take care of it himself. I gave him the card so he would know I still considered him a friend, and so he could see how the cat had grown. I never saw him again after that, nor did I smoke any more crack until shortly before my arrest in 2005, about two years later).

We all have 14-inch beams that we can't walk in our lives. Most people are lucky enough to never find themselves confronted with having to navigate their exposed beams. But others must face their beams every day. If you put a crack addict in jail where he can't get high, he's fine. But for me, my "beam" is literally attached to my body and "not looking down" is a lot harder to do than it sounds!

Reflections

Friday, November 26, 2010

It's All In My Head!

Trying to control my fantasies about sex is like trying to walk across a 14-inch steal I-beam a thousand feet in the air. Knowing that the sense of vertigo that causes you to fall is all in your head doesn't help. Telling yourself over and over that, "you can do this!" doesn't help either, at least not for long. A safety harness might help a little, if only the people manning the ropes weren't so eager to just let you fall (i.e. parole/probation officials) so they don't have to help hold you up anymore. But even with a safety harness the apprehension and dizziness don't just go away.
There is a solution though, and one that could help a lot of people: simply stop building sky scrapers! In practical terms, stop making sex such a lofty thing by placing intellectual structures beneath it that simply don't belong there (such as "love" and "commitment" and "taboos"). Let sex be what it is in nature, an animal drive without baggage. Then maybe people like me wouldn't be dropping out of the sky so much.

Reflections

Saturday, November 27, 2010

Help Me!

How does it make me feel to admit that I still masturbate to fantasies of raping small children? It makes me feel like crap. It makes me feel like I am a failure at self control. It reminds me that I am not better than human. And it forces me to rely on my belief that I am no less than human as well. It causes me to feel inferior to even those I have judged in the past as ignorant and cowardly. It compels me to face my own ignorance and craven nature. And it gets me to think about my "sickness" in a context I might otherwise not have been able to appreciate, an "exposed" context.
It also appeals to the depraved part of me. The shame that I experience awakens the part of me that needs shame in order to feel justified. I do not indorse this part of myself, I only acknowledge it in order to better understand it myself; to bring it "into the light" of social consciousness. But it is craven and pathetic, and derives great pleasure from being exposed, from even exposing itself, like a person exposing their sexual parts to another unsuspecting person for the pleasure of it. (Which is why I only "expose" myself in this blog, which has ample warnings attached to it to prevent anyone from being "victimized". Unless, of course, they want to be "victimized", but in that case it would be their "sickness" not mine at play).
Of course, I do not "expose" myself for the pleasure of it. I am extremely careful not to give that part of myself that much control over my words and behavior. I've learned what a heinous mistake that can be, in the past. But the part that wants to understand; the part that takes no pleasure in my shame, or any pleasure in asking others for help. But by exposing myself in this way I am asking you for help, no matter who you are. If you are a caring person at all, then I need your help to get better. I am convinced that I cannot "heal" myself. It was from trying to heal myself in the past that I became so desperately depraved (i.e. "sick").

How can you help? Simply like this: read my words, open your heart, and try to understand. You do not need to relay that understanding to me, or to anyone else. If you understand, the understanding will relay itself in ways that our conscious minds have yet to fathom.
How can you hurt? By judging me and condemning me. In this way you "feed" my sickness, the depraved part of me that wants you to be offended and "sickened" by my "exposed" private parts. If you want to hurt by shaming me, I'll certainly understand, I once needed to hurt people by shaming them too in order to feel justified. But if you have the courage to help me instead, then thanks!

Reflections

Sunday, November 28, 2010

Little Choices

By exposing myself on the web I am hoping ultimately that I might solicit some understanding that might otherwise not be possible, since this kind of exposure is so severely discouraged in our society. I am acutely aware that my sickness is a "choice", but it is not a conscious choice. If it were then I would have simply consciously chosen to not be perverted and depraved a long time ago, and a bunch of people would be still alive today. You might think that it's a simple matter of an accumulation of a lot of little conscious choices over time that has made me the way I am. And, that may very well be true, but if in the course of making those choices I never consciously knew the end result, then the choice to be what I am today was still an unconscious one. And blaming me for what I am because of choices that I made in the past that I did not comprehend the consequences of, is itself a choice that has consequences that you may not be conscious of. Just ask yourself, how did we become such a perverted and depraved society? The answer is easy: it's a simple matter of an accumulation of a lot of little conscious choices over time, like the choice to judge and condemn "sex offenders", and thus creating a whole new pathological role in our society that will continue to grow in numbers until we, as a society, overcome the ignorance and cravenness that drives us to make all those "little choices". My "sickness" is yours too!

Dreams

Monday, November 29, 2010

A Pencil In My Eye

A few months after I was arrested in Idaho in 2005, while I was still desperately trying to understand what was happening, I had this dream, which I told my attorney's about and also wrote about in a journal that I was keeping at the time. I dreamed that I had a pencil stuck in my eye, and when I tried to pull it out my brains started to come out stuck to the pencil. I was in an outdoor plaza and people were walking all around me, but they either ignored or even avoided me by walking clear around me. I cried desperately, "Please, help me! I'm hurt! Please help me! Help!" But the people continued to ignore me, some just looked right at me but kept walking. They could see me, but why wouldn't they help me? When I woke up from this dream I found I had been crying in my sleep, and I quickly realized that it was not just a dream. It was an apt metaphor for my "sickness" in real life, and the way people just stared at me, but no one would help. Also, in real life, like in the dream, I am effectively blinded in one eye, which prevents me from being able to perceive depth. But in real life the "eye" is my "heart", or, the part of my subconscious mind that allows me to “see” (ie. Love, understand, etc.) the world I live in and the other people in it. To me, the world is a flat, two-dimensional reality. Of course I know about depth, and the three-dimensional nature of the world, just as a man with one eye knows the world is three-dimensional. But, like a man with one eye, I simply can't see the same way other people see. I know the depth is there, but I can't “see” it (which could explain why I once proclaimed in another dream, “I want to love Jesus but He won't let me!”). This dream perfectly depicts the nightmare that has been my life. The “pencil” is still there today, and it still hurts like hell all the time. It often gets bumped causing flare-ups of pain that I will never be able to prevent as long as the “pencil” remains in my eye. But Shasta, the little girl I couldn't kill, helped me “see”, by letting me look through her eyes. And what I saw changed the way I see things forever. I saw a whole new dimension to reality that I once knew, but had long since forgotten! I knew that without Shasta I would be “blind” again. But the glimpse she gave me was all I needed. She restored my hope in love. I suspect there are a lot of one-eyed people in the world, but not for much longer. We only need each other to “see.”

Dreams

Saturday, December 4, 2010

Desert Decisions Dream

I dreamed last night that I was driving down the street toward the house I lived in as a kid at Ft. Lewis, Washington, on “Davis Hill” (an NCO housing area), but the street unexpectedly continued past where my house should have been (and for some reason the road was made of bricks, or cobblestone, instead of pavement). So I stopped at some sort of government information center to ask for directions. I told the person inside the info-center that I was looking for the house where I lived as a child at “8513 Lawndale” (which was where I lived after Ft. Lewis, in what is now Lakewood, WA. I don't remember the actual street name for Davis Hill). The official said he recognized the address and that it was nearby. He pulled out some maps to show me and began marking streets with a marker. I remember looking at the maps and seeing what they looked like. But, nothing I saw was familiar to me. The man marking the map ended up tracing far more streets than it should have taken me to find my old house. Then he gave me the map along with this curious instruction: “Follow the lines, especially in the desert, that's where the new decisions need to be made.” (The “decisions” were new roads on the map)

Dreams

Saturday, December 4, 2010

Coincidental Dream?

I frequently have dreams that mysteriously seem to correspond to things I see in the media the following day. Last night I dreamed that I was in a police evidence room where several shelves contained opened boxes of strawberry shortcakes that the employees would eat, even though they weren't supposed to. In today's newspaper, the “Dennis the Menace” cartoon showed Dennis' mom serving him a slice of strawberry shortcake. Coincidence? Well, even though this kind of “coincidence” seems to occur to me often, I still tend to dismiss it as just that, a coincidence. But today the coincidence was just a little stronger that usual; the shortcake in the Dennis comic showed the strawberries sandwiched between two cakes, exactly like in my dream! Strange? Well, consider this: when I normally think of strawberry shortcake I always expect the strawberries to be on TOP of the cake. In fact, I cannot remember ever seeing shortcake with the strawberries in the middle, until today, in my dream, and in the Dennis comic. Still coincidence?

P.S. In the same paper was a "Pardon My Planet" comic that seemed to coincidentally correspond to my recent "Pencil in my Eye" blog post about a world full of one eyed people with no depth perception: In the cartoon a woman says to her boyfriend, "Sure, Gandhi said, 'An eye for an eye makes the whole world blind.' I think instead that the loss of depth perception would make it really hard to shoot each other anymore." I never knew Gandhi ever made such a statement, but I agree with him, not her (she was just being silly, but the coincidence is unmistakable – Carl Jung calls this "synchronicity".)

Reflections

Sunday, December 5, 2010

Gnostic Breath

The gnostic appreciates knowledge in much the same way that an artist appreciates beauty. The appreciation cannot be taught, but it can be learned by anyone interested enough to enjoy the benefits. And as an artist portrays beauty through his medium as an expression of his own experience, so the gnostic might express his own experience of knowledge through words. But, words are not the only means that a gnostic will use to express his experience. A true gnostic expresses his experience of knowledge with every breath, and every action he takes. He cannot help but do so.

Reflections

Sunday, December 12, 2010

Fantasies of Nature and Nurture

When I fantasize, I often let my fantasies "run free". "Run free" is the only term I can think of to describe what actually happens. My fantasies seem to take on a life all their own that frequently leaves me pondering their intentions, which regularly seem to contradict my own.

I don't think letting them run free is irresponsible in and of itself, so long as they are confined to my own experience and not imposed upon others (i.e. acted out). In fact, I often think that I learn things from my fantasies, about myself, and about sexual instinct in general.

For example, when I was living as a female in prison, I was taken by surprise once by a fantasy that imagined I could become pregnant. This seemed as unsexy as anything to my mind (I had no psychological association that I was aware of that connected "getting pregnant" to the sexual pleasure of letting a man make love to me anally), and yet when the fantasy came to mind (while I was being made love to by a caring man) my arousal level unexpectedly skyrocketed! Suddenly I wanted to passionately whisper to the man who was inside my body, "Yes! Yes! Give me your babies!"

Was this mere perversion? Or, was it some sort of instinctual response to sex that lives inside all of us, not just "Jennies" (genetic females). Well, judging by the unexpected intensity that the mere idea of being made pregnant by a man I cared deeply for (and hence, wanted to "keep" him in my life) caused me to feel, I'd say it was something that came from nature, not nurture at all.

There are many other things I have learned about myself mostly, but also about being human in general, by letting my fantasies "run free", and just paying close attention to what they do.

Reflections

Sunday, December 12, 2010

Unconscious Realms of Consciousness

If you are conscious, then even when you "empty your mind", your mind is infinitely far from being empty! The empty mind is merely the un-focusing of attention. Or, put another way, it is consciousness focused on itself. In this state you have the ability to explore consciousness.
By "explore" I mean that you can effectively move about within the world of the "unconscious", which is in fact an infinite world (as anyone who has ever achieved this level of consciousness well knows!), but that does not mean that it is without structure or laws.
In fact, the laws of the unconscious mind are the only true laws in nature! The first and most important law, for example, is "Do not be ignorant!" (Of course that is only one way to state the law in limited human terms. Another way to say this same thing is, "Love God!" And/or, "Love thy neighbor as thyself!" Which all mean the same thing.) Because this is an absolute law, it cannot be broken, but it is possible to exist in a self imposed state of ignorance (and fear, which is, to "hate God") but this is purely illusory and has no basis in the conscious or unconscious universe.
I should explain what I mean by "no basis" just to be clear: Ignorance (and fear, which is inextricably intertwined with ignorance) is no more than a substanceless shadow. It can only be perceived at all in the same way we perceive shadows, not by what is there, but by what is NOT there! So, in the same sense that shadows don't exist, so ignorance (and fear, and hate, and "evil") has no "basis in consciousness". That does not mean it is unreal, or cannot cause real harm. Just as a shadow can weaken or even kill a plant (by depriving it of sunlight), so ignorance can weaken and even "kill" (destroy) a human "soul"! But also realize that as long as a plant is not kept in the shadow all the time, most can survive and even thrive on very little sunlight. And so it is in the realms of consciousness.
"Light" in the realms of consciousness is "Love" and "Understanding" (which are the same thing). The "physical" world only exists by virtue of mutual ignorance that causes "fixed illusions", that we all share. Modern science has been studying the edges of this illusion since the beginning of the last century. Quantum physics has clearly established the link between consciousness and the "physical world" for some time now (though few scientists will even admit to themselves what the data from their experiments shows; that we don't even exist! Or, to put it another way, we only exist as "conscious energy" or "thoughts".
So, a person with a truly "empty mind" is one who has lifted the veil, and sees consciousness for what it is; the source of everything we call "the universe" or "reality". In such a state of understanding (i.e. Love) this person can move about to any point in space and time of the physical world, but not just space and time, to any point in consciousness itself! That is why such a person cannot easily relate their freedom of movement (a.k.a. freedom of choice, though "movement" in a much better term, it still does not fully express the actuality) into human terms. This is what it means to "know the will of God". It is to know your own true will! (If you think you already know your own will, then think again! Who decided when you would be conceived? You did! And when you truly realize this – by "visiting" that point in consciousness! - then you will understand what I mean!).
So the next time you meditate – and if you don't meditate then why are you wasting your time by reading this! - try to realize the freedom you have, by letting go of your physical mind (your

thoughts and perceptions) and “moving” into the unconscious realms of consciousness, and “see” what you find!

P.S. By “meditation” I do not necessarily mean anything as formal as Zazen (but anyone who practices Zazen regularly will easily follow what I am saying – though they'd probably disagree on a few technicalities). All I mean, is simply the practice of “emptying the mind”, or just “quieting the mind”. Most people meditate without even realizing it when they engage in some kind of “relaxing” activity, such as running, or working on a stamp collection, or such. As long as you suspend your thoughts long enough to become aware of consciousness itself, sometimes perceived as “existence” - so if you do something that makes you “feel real” then you are probably meditating.

Reflections

Tuesday, December 14, 2010

Random Choices Make Us God

I read in a book on the science of chaos once, about a popular novelty random-motion desk sculpture that has three steel balls attached to stiff wires that are driven to rotate chaotically around each other by a magnet in the base of the sculpture. The book explained that a little simple math (relatively speaking) indicates that the motion of the steel balls can be completely altered in as few as 20 cycles, by the gravitational pull of a building five blocks away.
That means, if it were possible to create two machines that were identical all the way down to the quantum level, and set them in motion with the exact same force, even inside a vacuum, the mere fact that they occupied different positions in space, even if only a few inches, would cause them to lose synchronization within 20 or so cycles and start rotating in completely independent chaotic patterns with no discernable relationship to each other's movement.
Within 40 to 100 cycles, the gravitational pull of a building sized object on Jupiter would have the same effect. And within, say, 1.000 to 10.000 cycles, such an object orbiting the nearest star (about three light-years away) would also cause our matched machines to “forget” their common origin (assuming of course that nothing else in the universe changed during those 1000 or so cycles).
With a little extrapolation it becomes clear that our machines could not remain in synch for more than a few years if nothing else changed in the entire universe, except the existence of a single molecule in a galaxy far-far away!
If that single molecule, billions of light-years from here, has the ability to alter the course of motion in our random-motion machine here on Earth (and every molecule in the universe has this ability to influence what happens), then it also has the ability to change the entire course of history on this planet, in much less than a few years!
What's my point? Is this just a novel but meaningless mental exercise? I think not. In fact, everything I think is also effected by that distant molecule. And that brings me to my point.
If any molecule in the universe can change what “random” thought I may be having two or three years from now, then how can we say that I have volition of thought (much less “free will”)?
Of course the first, and most obvious, response to that question is that, “the motion of the machine may change, but the machine itself does not change. It still behaves according to its own nature”.
But what determines the “nature” of the machine? Wasn't it “designed” by mere thought? So, this response to my question fails when you consider that the machine's very existence, and its “nature”, are determined by all those distant (and near) molecules in the first place. My question stands; where is our free will?

Actually, there is a solution to this puzzle, but not one that most people can accept (at least not yet). The answer, assuming we do in fact have “free will” (which we must, or all is lost!), and the only answer, is that we, in determining what we do and think, also determine the existence and state (location and motion in space and time) of EVERY SINGLE MOLECULE IN THE ENTIRE UNIVERSE FROM THE BEGINNING AND TO THE END OF TIME! There is no other solution. Hence, we are God, or we are nothing!

Reflections

Tuesday, December 14, 2010

Baal's Hypocrisy

If it is no excuse for a man to abuse children because he was abused, or to rape because he was raped, then why is it okay for society to kill him because he killed?

Reflections

Thursday, December 16, 2010

Who I Am

My mantra: The greatest enemy of knowledge is the presumption of knowledge.

My motto: The only thing I know for sure, is that I know nothing for sure; except, I am.

My greatest hope: To know who I am.

My greatest fear: To know who I am.

My greatest accomplishment: Embracing my greatest failure.

My greatest failure: Not knowing who I am.

My current theological bent: Gnosticism (True and direct knowledge of ”God”, and/or the source of our existence, is attainable through honest introspection, and is reflected in all external experiences)

My former theological bent: Agnosticism (Experience is all there is, and the source of experience, a.k.a. “God”, is unknowable)

My current practice: Self sacrifice without self debasement.

My former practice: Self debasement without self sacrifice.

My current occupation: Seeker, student, fool (in that order)

My former occupation: Fool, student, seeker (in that order)

My greatest personal asset: An open heart.

My greatest personal handicap: A broken heart.

My favorite animal: Domesticated cats.

My least favorite animal: Domesticated humans.

My current life goal: To remember who I am.

My former life goal: I forgot.

Reflections

Saturday, December 18, 2010

Crime Isn't The Problem

Crime is a symptom, not a problem. This would be an obvious truth if it weren't for the tens of millions of people who have invested their lives in the "blood letting" of society. Like the so-called healers of old, they have a vested interested in keeping people ignorant of the truth and an even stronger reason for lying to themselves. If the truth were generally known, that all their efforts are all for show, and any effects they have are purely incidental, then they would be exposed for the charlatans they are. And even worse, for exacerbating the problem while pretending to cure the symptom!

The problem is age old, but that does not mean it cannot be solved. The solution is as old as the problem itself, and every great book of truth has expounded on the solution, from the Holy Bible to the Buddhist sutras, for thousands of years.

I myself have been writing about it non-stop since I stopped killing and turned myself in. This blog is centered around it. And life itself proclaims it loudly, for those prepared to hear.

The problem is fear, the solution is faith.

The problem is isolation from the source of our existence (which begets fear), and the solution is returning to the source (which requires faith alone).

You don't need to believe in God, or Buddha, or even science to realize this truth. You have only to be honest, with yourself. The more honest you are, the more self evident this truth will be, and the less fear you will have, and the less suffering you will bring into the world.

But being honest with yourself is the hardest thing you will ever do. If it is not hard for you to be honest, then you are either still deceived – and bringing suffering into the world, even if you yourself do not realize it – or, you are an enlightened being, at one with the source of all things. Which is to say, that becoming honest is the hardest thing you will ever do, but being honest is the easiest! Or, as I've written before, the "easy yoke to bear", is the hardest one to don.

Any observer can note that our present social system, especially the so-called "Justice System", does everything it can to support and promote the illusion of isolation from the source of our being. It fosters and advocates an "Us-Them" mentality that denies the oneness and unity of all things.

It is easier to pretend we are better than someone else, and blame "them" for our problems (our suffering) than to take responsibility for our own actions – which is the only real "authority" anyone has! When a man robs or assaults another man, the present social system literally demands that the "victim" report the "crime" and cooperate with the "authorities" in the "pursuit of justice". But no one ever expects the "victim" to take responsibility for the "crime", perhaps by admitting that he should not have been flaunting his gold jewelry in front of young drug addicts

(and what was he doing with gold jewelry in the first place, while there are starving people in the world he could have given a job to instead of buying "shiny metal" status symbols to wear?).
It was easier for me to accuse the police of being self-righteous cowards that ignorantly drove me to commit my crimes, than for me to admit that I need the police (as human beings) and that I myself was responsible for their self-righteous attitudes by acting so cowardly myself by attacking children in order to hurt "Them".
That is until I saw through the eyes of my last intended victim that she was me, and they were too! I saw this truth as plainly as I saw her. Even now it is hard for me to fathom how I had been so blind! But, the reason for my blindness is just as plain at the same time; Fear.
I was terrified because I believed the system's lies; that I was alone in the world, and would die alone, and forever. But when I finally saw the Truth – the same Truth that all the ancients talk about, and that modern science even confirms – that I was not alone, and that I would never die! Then I no longer had a reason to hurt "them", because I knew that they were me! And crime, for me at least, lost it's meaning.

"The intellectual who no longer feels attached to anything is not satisfied with opinions merely; he wants certainty, he wants a system."
"...Whether it wants to or not, the (System) consolidates and establishes injustice. It helps men to forget their ills instead of curing them." - Raymond Aron, French political philosopher

'We would rather be ruined than changed; We would rather die in our dread; Than climb the cross of the moment; And let our illusions die." - W. H. Auden (1907-1973) American poet

'There is no such thing as the State, And no one exists alone; Hunger allows no choice, To the citizen or the police; We must love one another or die." - W. H. Auden

Reflections

Sunday, December 19, 2010

There Are No Cruel People

I don't believe in cruelty. I believe there are people who do cruel things, but not because they are cruel, only because they are confused.
I believe that cruelty is a human invention, not a human trait. Even though we observe what appears to be cruelty in very young children, if we look more carefully we will see that the behavior they exhibit is really no more than raw survival impulses that have not yet been honed by social instinct. To punish them for being "cruel" is how cruelty itself is instilled.
The parent who punishes such behavior is the one who is really being cruel. A more responsible and loving parent, who has faith in their own child's development, will see the behavior for the aberration it is. And rather than responding out of fear that there is something "wrong" or even "evil" with their child, they will instinctively either ignore the behavior (which is usually, but not always, the best thing to do the first time or two that it is displayed), or they will take some "corrective" action other than punishment, such as distracting the child from the negative "cruel" behavior, by giving them a hug for some other positive "kind" behavior, helping to hone the child's rough edges rather than agitating them with punishment, which only teaches the child to avoid the parent (i.e. authority) not the behavior. Punishment often even makes the "cruel" behavior seem appropriate to the child. After all, the punishment itself is no more than a demonstration of the "cruel" behavior it is supposed to avert!
And when you extend this understanding of how children are taught to be cruel by fearful parents to the way a fearful society teaches its citizens to be cruel with a "punishment" based

justice system – a system that demonstrates cruel behavior and calls it “justice” - then we might start to understand how we bring crime upon ourselves.

“All Penal Laws court Transgression & therefore are cruelty & murder...” - William Blake (1757-1827), English poet

“Cruelty is a tyrant, that is always attended with Fear.” - Thomas Fuller (1654-1734), English cleric

“I was trying to punish society... I wanted justice for what happened to me (in prison)...” - Joseph E. Duncan III (b. 1963), American “Serial Killer” statement to the court (September 2008)

Reflections

Sunday, December 19, 2010

True Religion

Only when we fail to recognize the intelligence that created us do we feel unloved by the universe. If we think of our existence as the result of random events, then how can we feel loved at all? The love we seek from other people under such circumstances is empty and superficial because they too are only mortals whose love can and will be taken away someday.
So this failure to recognize the intelligence behind our creation is a critical failure. It keeps us trapped in a perpetual state of fear. And even worse is our attempts to substitute direct knowledge of that intelligence with the rationalized constructs of our own mind. We create false images of the intelligence that created us, and then invest tremendous amounts of time and energy into substantiating our false beliefs. This is the phenomena we call religion.
If there were a true religion, then it would not need to be promoted, defended, or even defined. It would exist regardless of human endeavors. I believe such a religion does exist, only I hesitate to apply the word “religion”, or even the term “true religion”, because then it would become too easily confused with all the other false religions that use the same term (all of them do, by implication at least).
If I could, I would define religion as the open acknowledgement of divine intelligence. By this definition then all religions are accommodated, both the one true religion (as yet undefined) and the many false ones. All religions openly acknowledge higher intelligence, though they typically go on to embellish their image of that intelligence with all sorts of human attributes and qualities. A true religion would, of course, not use such embellishments, either directly or by implication. So maybe we'd be better off to refer to it as “pure religion” rather than “true”. This at least would acknowledge the fact that all false religions have a true element at their heart. This also allows us to recognize the validity and value of false or “embellished” beliefs.
This concept is not very unlike the core principles of Catholicism. They seem to believe (as I understand) that all the rituals and symbols that comprise the external church are really only humanized versions of a much purer and truer inner church that is the charge of all Christians (Catholics) to cherish and to protect. But I believe even Catholicism fails in its mission to preserve the “true faith”, as evidenced by all the atrocities it has committed. No true religion would ever feel so compelled to establish itself in the world of men.
True religion is not only already established in our world, it is the very foundation of it! A worshiper of such a religion would know this and without fear wait patiently for his church to arise. Not only that, but he would know, by virtue of every breath he takes, that he is loved and cherished by the entire universe as well. Such a man would not seek out human love and companionship. He would not have to, for he would be loved by all seekers of the truth, who

would see him in its light. Yet, at the same time, he would be despised by those whose faces are yet turned away from the truth, for to them the truth is an ugly and sinister thing, and so anyone bathed in its light will appear ugly and sinister to them. Such was the fate of Jesus and it is why even he predicted a similar fate for all followers of the true religion.

Reflections

Tuesday, December 21, 2010

What Education Is

Education is a word that is used to refer to the process of discovering the depth of our ignorance.

"...certainty is the enemy of true knowledge. Knowledge is a process, a journey toward, not an arrival. People who believe they possess certainty are capable of any atrocity, ranging from the concentration camps of the Nazis to the cross burnings of the KKK. Because they are certain they are right, these people feel they can justify any act of subhuman cruelty. Throughout history, it has been the doubters, the assailers of accepted truth, who have moved the species forward. A corollary to this thought is that the only thing you can truly learn in life is the depth of your own ignorance."

Al Goldstein, Publisher
Screw Magazine
New York

Dreams

Wednesday, December 22, 2010

Multiple Me's Dream

This morning I had a rather unusual dream. I dreamed that I was in a larger than usual two-man prison cell alone. I decided in the dream to masturbate to a fantasy of being used by other inmates (something I used to fantasize about often when I was in prison years ago). So I pulled down my pants and laid down on a bunk in the cell on my stomach, and began my fantasy (which usually began with me seducing the other inmates by letting them see me naked). Then suddenly I heard a guard coming. So I jumped up and pulled up my pants... or at least one of me did. When I looked back at the bunk, I was still laying there! Only now I was completely naked, waiting to be used. The guard came into the cell as I was whispering desperately to my other naked self to "get up!". But the guard, a female, walked in and saw both of us, me standing fully clothed and me laying on the bunk naked, at the same time. But she could not see who the naked man on the bunk was because he had long hair (which in the dream I thought how strange it was that my hair had grown so quickly – because in real life right now my hair is only crew-cut length), so she clearly thought we were having sex, a prison rule violation. But I told her it was "Just me" on the bunk as I slapped the other me on the ass to get him to look up so she could see his face. Once she saw that it was in fact just me, I pointed out to her that there were no rules against masturbating (except I was not using words, and the true meaning of what I "said" to her was more like, "having sex with myself", though it also meant "masturbating" at the same time). She agreed, and then left, apparently satisfied that no rules were being violated. I only remember one other time that I dreamed of multiple "me's". And in that one other dream there were four me's! Two me's, one a young man, and the other a young boy, were playing on a lake dock together, and in the water, while an older, middle age me-me (the one who was having the dream) watched them from a near-by hill, while a much wiser and disembodied-me "stood" behind me-me. I asked (again without using words) the disembodied-me what I could do to "help the boy" (referring to the boy-me on the dock), and the disembodied-me replied, "He needs to know he is forgiven/loved" (again not with words, so "forgiven/loved" is the closest I can come to what was actually said. Actually, an even more correct term would be, "unconditionally forgiven/loved", but of course in the dream all of this was expressed with just one word that seemed to be "forgiven"). Both of these multiple-me's dreams seem to have important messages from me to me. Is that weird or what?

Reflections

Thursday, December 23, 2010

Learning to Drive

I do not follow where my mind leads. I instead let it wonder on its own, always watching it carefully, like a loving parent watches an immature child.
I know that my mind will never have true wisdom. So unlike a child it will never become independent of me. Perhaps my mistake in the past was to burden my mind with moral responsibilities that it was never meant to manage.
My mind is a remarkable machine, but no more (or less) of a machine than my body. My mind and body are essentially the same thing; a living organism. But I am the life in my body and in my mind.
In my dreams my physical form is frequently represented as a car that I am driving but can never quite completely control. I can actually gauge my mastery over my form (mind/body) by simply contemplating my ability to drive in my dreams. So far I'm not doing very well, but I am making progress at least.
It is possible to gauge my mastery of form when I am wide awake, but more difficult because I must watch not what just my mind does, but also what my body does and most significantly, the consequences that occur in my life. To ignore the consequences of my actions would be synonymous to driving a car without looking out the windows (which I frequently find myself doing in my dreams).
My thoughts are like a steering wheel. So, if I don't look where I am going then it does not matter which way I turn my thoughts. This is why, in my efforts to learn how to "drive", I am presently concentrating on what is going on around the "car", and watching closely what effect my thoughts (and actions) have.
Slowly, but surely, I am learning to drive.

Reflections

Thursday, December 23, 2010

My Children!

When I say that my fantasies have a will, motive and even consciousness of their own, I do not mean to imply that I have no power over them. In a sense, I realize that I am the "parent" of my fantasies (and thoughts and actions for that matter). So by attributing will and consciousness to my fantasies I am not attempting to shirk responsibility for them. I am only recognizing them for what they are: My children!

Reflections

Monday, December 27, 2010

Life vs. Death

What is life in prison without the possibility of parole? That is a very subjective question. To some, it is a life worth living, restricted, but a life nonetheless. To others it is not life at all, it is no more than a living nightmare of deprivation, worse than death.
I belong to this later group. I say, “Give me liberty, or give me death!”. And I mean it. But I don't mean, as the original author of that statement, that I would rather fight to the death than be enslaved for life. I simply mean that I would rather be murdered by sanction of the state than live out my natural years in a modern penal institution.
And, it's not because of the restrictions that such a life would entail. It is not because of the lost so-called privileges of a free citizen. It's not because I wouldn't be able to have, or do, certain things. I could (and for many years have) live easily without such “freedoms”. But what I find it difficult and even excruciatingly painful to live without is intimate contact with someone I care deeply about.
It does not need to be a lover, just a brother, a sister, or mom, or dad, or even a good friend. And by intimate contact I don't mean sex, or even physical contact at all. I just mean regular interaction, such that that person shapes my thoughts (and behavior) every day. Such contact would free me from my “sickness” (this is a part of what I began to realize just before I surrendered to the present authorities of this world), and it would give me a chance at self-actualization.
Without someone to love, and to love me, in my life, I have no chance of ever coming to know my purpose. Without that chance, that hope, I would rather die. Not because I give up on life, but so I can move on with it! Maybe in my “next life”, in this world or some other, I will be able to appreciate what I gave up so much to learn in this world; that without love, there is nothing. Without forgiveness, there is only insanity.

PS: I realize, of course, that a “self-actualized” person would be able to love everyone. But, I also realize that we need someone to love to help us become self-actualized.

2011

Reflections

Saturday, January 1, 2011

The End Is Near

Relatively soon people will begin to realize that there is no space or time.

There is only consciousness.

We will also come to understand that consciousness is the inevitable product of infinite probabilities.

Science will fall, harder than any religion has ever fallen, taking with it all modern social systems (as well as what is left of religion).

Out of the chaos, Consciousness will arise, as the One True Religion, if you can call it a religion at all.

And all suffering in this world will abruptly end, and the new world, that we have been building unconsciously for millions of years, will manifest in the "physical" realm of space and time.

Reflections

Sunday, January 2, 2011

On My Honor

A man who protects his honor is a fool. If his honor needs to be protected, then it is not honor, it is vanity, or worse, pride.
Honor is the knowledge that you are worthy of existence. There is nothing that you can do as an individual separated from the universe to deserve honor. Honor is deserved by virtue of your existence alone.
This should not seem surprising, after all, it is no different than what Jesus tried to teach.

Reflections

Sunday, January 2, 2011

Infinite Responsibility

I am responsible for what I have done to harm others, but not as an individual. To presume that I, as an individual, somehow am capable of making even the most common decision is an error. Every choice I make, from when to brush my teeth to whether or not to kill, is made as a consequence of literally infinite factors which are impossible for me as an individual to weigh. So, does this realization (or "claim" as some would have it) somehow release me from, or lesson my responsibility? Absolutely not! It increases my responsibility infinitely! And it forces me to stop focusing on myself as an individual, and consider myself in the true light of my being. It compels me to come to know the eternal source of my volition, since it is clearly the only possible way for me to take responsibility for my actions, past and present.
Only by not striving to know my true infinite self (which means learning to love unconditionally or forgive absolutely) do I shun my responsibility and bring more suffering into this world whether I realize it as an individual or not.

Reflections

Sunday, January 2, 2011

Individuality Is Nowhere

When I speak of the perils of individuality (and there are many) I do not mean to imply that we

should not be individuals. In fact, if my assertions are understood correctly, then it should be clear that only by viewing ourselves as one undivided being is it possible for us to be truly individual at all!
What I'm saying is that we become more individual only by denying the illusion of separation from the universe. If we see ourselves as separated from the universe, then no matter what color we dye our hair, or how unique the clothes we wear are, or even how strangely we behave, we are pathetically no different than every other deluded person out there. Only by becoming conscious of our true being do we become truly unique, and only then do our individual characteristics (such as hair color and behavior) have any meaning at all.

Reflections

Tuesday, January 4, 2011

Nothing Is Random

In order for there to be free will there must be meaningfulness. A choice is not a choice unless the constituents of that choice are given weight with meaning. Without meaning, a “choice” is only random. Random choice is not free choice. Fortunately, careful contemplation has revealed that purely random choices are impossible (this is supported by numerous scientific studies). If random choice is not possible, then only meaningful (free) choice remains. So, life as we know it does in fact have meaning.

What we perceive as random events are really events for which we are not conscious of their meaning (or purpose). Hence, when we witness a violent crime we commonly label it “random”. Or when we experience some natural catastrophe we think it too is random. But randomness is a meaningless word in and of itself. Everything has meaning, this is a self evident truth of being. We can find peace by embracing this truth. We can also find meaning.

Reflections

Wednesday, January 5, 2011

Honestly Ashamed

As much as I try to deny it, I am chasmically ashamed of what I have done and for what I am. I have denied this shame in the past because I recognize it as a primary source of my negative self destructive behavior. My attempts to deny my shame have not been motivated by a desire to make myself look better, or even feel better. But, I thought that if I deny my shame then perhaps I would not be ashamed, and my tendency toward anti-social behavior would be at least somewhat alleviated. Now I realize that my shame is not something that will go away just by denying it. Perhaps it will never go away.
I have also attempted to turn my shame into humility, with what I thought was some success. I was certainly humbled. But now I suspect that ultimately while humility embraces shame, it does not replace it. I must learn to live with my shame written on my face at all times, or I am not being an honest person. Perhaps that is all humility really is; being honestly ashamed.

Reflections

Wednesday, January 5, 2011

The Mask of Shame

Pride is no more than a mask that shame wears in order to hide from the self. It is a fig leaf that we wear to hide our shame from God. To see this, we have only to consider the pride that is so commonly taken in the clothes we wear. We clothe ourselves primarily to cover our nakedness (the quintessential symbol of shame). By turning the clothes we wear into a symbol of pride, pride is revealed as no more than a mask that shame wears.

Reflections

Wednesday, January 5, 2011

Bad Actor

The best actors are able to convince themselves that they aren't acting while they are on stage. This is true especially for the stage of life.
For some reason I have never been able to convince myself that I am not just acting out a role given to me to play. I suppose that's why I am such a bad actor.

Reflections

Friday, January 7, 2011

The Ultimate Servant

A true understanding of eternal life must not devalue life in the present. “Heaven” cannot be a place in space and time. Which means that it is not some place you go after you die (or otherwise leave this world). Heaven must exist in the here and now. Otherwise it is meaningless and even contrary to the Ultimate (Divine) Truth. Why this is so should be self evident under honest introspection.

A true understanding of eternal life will only enhance life in the present. It will cause our current existence to take on profound meaning and purpose. When we understand and believe our infinite nature then all struggle against death ceases. Death becomes our obedient servant, and safe to ignore; no longer a tyrannical master demanding our constant attention.

Reflections

Friday, January 7, 2011

According To The Laws Of Physics

According to the known laws of physics, if life is eternal then it must also be infinite. That means that in order for life to stretch forward into infinity, it must by definition also stretch backward into infinity. This is the meaning of the saying, “If it has a beginning, then it has an end”.

Also according to the laws of physics, if life is infinite in time then it must also be infinite in space. Einstein proved over a hundred years ago that time and space are one and the same thing. And since then, that proof has become a foundation of all modern physics. So in order for one person to have eternal life, all life must be eternal and all life must be one and the same life.

This is the meaning of the saying, “There can be only one (eternal being)”.

And alas, according to the laws of physics, if all life is eternal, then every finite experience we have in life is locked into infinity. That means it is predetermined and undetermined at the same time. In physics they call this a state of superposition. It is the meaning of the saying, “If it has an end, then it already has”.

Reflections

Friday, January 7, 2011

The Rise and Fall of Death

The modern scientific view, that natural death caused by aging is a disease, is perhaps the most fatal error science has ever made. In the day that we perfect a “cure” for aging death itself will rise up as the supreme ruler of this world. In that day humans, who previously only anticipated death with trepidation, will universally fear death more than the loss of their soul. In that day death will become the ultimate source of fear, and by said virtue, the ultimate despot over the entire world (or at least the parts that have “the cure”).
Fortunately, every prophecy of this event – and there are many such prophecies – also predicts that death's reign will be very short and disastrous. But we don't need prophecies to tell us this future. It is written plainly throughout our history.

Reflections

Thursday, January 13, 2011

The Ultimate Uncertainty Principle

The ultimate uncertainty principle says: It is not possible to know you are right and to be right at the same time.

This is perhaps the most profound realization I have had yet. It has the power to change the world, if it could ever be understood and embraced. But by its own assertion, it cannot be understood by direct observation.
Like Heisenberg's uncertainty principle, which says that observable quantities like position and momentum cannot be precisely known at the same time, this ultimate principle pins down the enigma of the dual nature of all energy and matter, including consciousness itself.
If consciousness is a form of energy, then Einstein proved over a hundred years ago that it is interchangeable with matter (by his most famous equation: e=mc^2). So why should we be surprised to find in quantum mechanic experiments that consciousness seems to effect matter? In fact, consciousness, as quantum theory predicts, exists in both wave and particle form at the same time. We routinely observe this dual nature of consciousness all the time. We call it the conscious and unconscious mind.
The conscious mind (our individual consciousness) is the manifested “particle” state of conscious energy. The unconscious mind is the probability “wave” form of conscious energy. So every thought we have is manifested consciousness and the “silence” between thoughts is infinite conscious potential (the probability wave).
In order for something to be right, it must be the truth and it must be real (truth and real being pretty much the same thing). If something is true and real then it is also right. But a thought,

which is a manifestation of infinite probability, is not real. It exists finitely, at a point in time. So nothing we can ever think will have the quality of infinity. Therefor, neither can it be real, as only something infinite can be said to be real at all (this should be self evident when carefully contemplated). Only infinite consciousness is real. So only a person who exists in a state of infinite consciousness can be right! Any thought such a person has of being right will immediately expel them from the state of infinite consciousness into a state of finite consciousness. This is the same thing that happens when a quantum of energy is observed. It becomes finite, as numerous scientific experiments confirm. (It is the "Quantum Enigma")

Reflections

Thursday, January 13, 2011

Blade of Truth

This blog is written in such a manner that anyone who knows what they are looking for will find it here, then hopefully quickly go away. But those who do not know, well, perhaps they will find what they are looking for too, but it won't be in this blog; it will be inside themselves.

The truth can never be written. But when it is written about, it can have many edges that can cut many ways. My hope in writing this blog about the truth, is to dull some of the more dangerous edges, while leaving the most important edge safely buried, but sharp as ever.

In the hands of an ignorant person – like a scalpel in the hands of a child – my words can do considerable damage. Not to me, but to others, especially the ignorant person wielding these words so foolishly.

But in the heart of an honest person, these same words can cut away calloused deception in the darkest (unconscious) recesses of the mind, exposing profound truths that may not always appear very beautiful at first. I cannot say what those truths will be, or even how they will appear. But I can tell you much about what the calloused deception looks like.

And that's what this blog is all about.

Chronicles

Saturday, January 15, 2011

Circle Jerk

Yesterday (Friday) I had a "status hearing" before Judge Downing here in Riverside County (Indio, California). The trial for the case here is tentatively set for some time in March. But the defense attorneys cannot possibly be ready to go by then. So I must either consent to another time waiver (which allows the trial to be delayed again), or dismiss counsel and go to trial pro se (representing myself again). The problem is that I desperately need some basic dental work (fillings) to keep my teeth from needing to be pulled. Because I have been in short term confinement facilities (Jails) for the last five and a half years (since my arrest), and jails only provide "emergency" dental care (basically they only do extractions) and nothing else, I can't even get a general exam to find out what is wrong with my teeth. And my teeth hurt. At least three probably need small fillings, if not a root canal filling. I have always taken care of my teeth.

I brush daily (though the only toothbrush I can have in jail frays badly after only two or three uses) and would floss too, but the jail doesn't allow dental floss (it's supposed to be a "security risk", but if I want strong nylon string to make a weapon with all I have to do is pull it out of my mattress, which of course, other inmates do all the time, destroying the expensive mattresses in the process). So I still have all my teeth and have never needed anything more than a few fillings, as I do now. The only way I can get the dental work I need is to get this pointless California case over with so I can go back to Federal prison and have my teeth cleaned, examined and repaired. If I waive time and let the trial be pushed back again (the defense attorneys are asking for "at least 12 months") then I will not only end up loosing some of my teeth, but I will also have to sit here for up to two months in pain while I wait for an "emergency" appointment to have the teeth pulled. So, I told the defense attorneys that I will not waive time for the trial unless they can guarantee I will have my teeth taken care of. Actually, I asked them about getting my teeth taken care of several months ago (as soon as they took over the case after I stopped representing myself last year). I even told them explicitly that my dental work was my number one concern. But after several months they basically told me that there was nothing they could do. So I told them I had no choice but to get the trial over with in March so I could go back to Federal prison and have my teeth taken care of. Ultimately, what happens here in California is purely for show and will have no bearing on whether I live or die. If the Feds find me not competent on appeal, then any California death sentence will be rendered moot. And if the Feds find me competent, then they will kill me long before California even gets their hands out of their pants (and don't think too much about what they are doing with their hands in there). So there is no reason why I should sit here in jail and let my teeth rot in my mouth while they enjoy a good long circle jerk with me in the middle of the circle. (I actually wouldn't mind them jerkin' off over me so much if my teeth didn't hurt. It's not that I enjoy the attention of anything, it's just that I understand the "need"... believe me, I understand!) So now the defense lawyers are attempting to solicit funds (defense funds) to pay for a private dentist plus transportation and security to have my teeth worked on. But it appears to me as if they are placating (the requisition they showed me as evidence of their efforts was severely ill prepared and underestimated) and trying to get me to waive time without a guarantee. They don't seem to realize how painful a sore tooth can be! They seem to think that I should just buck-up and sweat it out. And I might have considered doing that, IF the trial were anything more than a big pants pocket circle jerk. So, I did not waive time yesterday at the hearing. The court rescheduled another progress hearing for February 22nd. If I don't waive time then the trial will have to go in March, and I will have to represent myself again (since the lawyers cannot be ready by then). That's okay, I just hope my teeth will hold out until March!

Reflections

Saturday, January 15, 2011

The Power of One

When two or more people bond to each other, a synergistic consciousness arises that has the power to take over and direct the lives of the individuals who comprise the bonded unit. We normally take this for granted and seldom realize the extent that this higher consciousness dictates our lives when we are a member of such a unit. Instead we continue to perceive our thoughts and actions as our own. But if we question the source of our motivations, and if we question them honestly, such as through deep contemplative meditation, we soon find that strikingly few if any of our thoughts originate in our own mind. They are the result of our extremely complex unconscious experiences, which are determined by the groups or units that we are bonded to, such as family, community, world, and ultimately the universe. This process of unification occurs on all levels of nature and consciousness. Quarks bond to form mesons, mesons (electrons, protons, etc...) bond to form atoms, atoms bond to make molecules, molecules form compounds, compounds (proteins, amino acids, etc...) become cells, cells bond to make organisms, and organisms bond to create us. But it doesn't stop there. We bond together as families, and families form communities, which make districts, states and nations. Nations bond (ultimately) to form hemispheres... which comprise the world. Actually, all bonded units are polarized into what you might call hemispheres. Male-Female, The Left and Right, and The East and West. Of course, it is what the Chinese have long called yin and yang. All bonded entities have yin and yang.

All bonded entities have yin and yang.

The synergy of bonding is so common that the language of every culture, even the most primitive, revolves around it. Our most important and meaningful words reflect it. When we speak of love, we speak of this bonding force that any poet knows has a life and will all its own. All religions attempt to appease it by honoring it. Whether we call it love, or God, or life force, it is all the same. I call it consciousness, but only because that word best expresses my own experience with it. (I actually call it many things: "The Living Truth" was my favorite for a while after the first time I directly experienced it.) But it does not matter what we call it. It only matters that we recognize it, and acknowledge its divine sovereignty.

Reflections

Friday, January 21, 2011

The Cause of Understanding

The only thing I have to be ashamed of is shame itself. There is no shame in being an ignorant fool, it is only shameful to deny that you are one. To be such a fool is the very definition of being human. To deny our foolishness is the cause of shame. To embrace it is the cause of understanding.

Saturday, January 22, 2011

What I Deserve

There is no corresponding element in nature for the intellectual concept of just deserts. Obviously then, no one really deserves to live or to die. And yet nearly all of the pain and suffering inflicted by people against other people is done in the guise of what someone else deserves.

The rapist believes either his victim deserves to be raped or he deserves the pleasure of raping her. The soldier believes the enemy deserves to be killed. And the jurist believes that the murderer deserves to die.

You might think that some people clearly deserve to die, such as a man like myself, who has raped and murdered children. But if I deserve to die, then so do you.

“No man is an island”. And no man exists or behaves independent of social influence.

To say that I deserve to die is to ignore the very reasons that I raped and killed in the first place. To ignore these reasons is to ultimately condone what I did, in the sense that you are allowing it to happen all over again!

Blaming me, and then killing me (a.k.a. Scapegoating) accomplishes nothing. Oh sure, it temporarily relieves the anguish that is primarily caused by fear. That is, it pretends to remove the problem, while at the same time making the real problem get worse, usually much worse.

The problem in my case was that I was rejected and punished by society for perfectly natural behavior that resulted from confusion as a child over the very mixed signals I got over my sexual feelings. The problem was exacerbated by societies own irrational anxieties over juvenile sexual interests. I acted out of my confusion with no intentional malice. And for the one hour of sexual imposition that I forced on another boy I was sent to prison for 20 years, where I was convinced by means of psychological torture that I was a “sexual psychopath”, and repeatedly raped and physically abused by other inmates. And when I finally got out of prison I found no hope of social redemption, or acceptance.

The boy I raped became a man who is to this day convinced that I got what I deserved because of what I did to him. He thinks being forced once to swallow another boy's semen has “scared him for life”. He seems to have no idea of what it's like to be the confused boy who made him swallow the semen. Even then, when I was but 16 years old, I would have traded my misery for his in a heartbeat. He at least has sympathy and compassion for his one confusing experience. All I got was a lifetime of much much worse pain and confusion, with no sympathy at all.

And so is it really any surprise that after I started to realize that I wasn't a “sexual psychopath” at all, that I had (and have) a real heart that was sorely wounded, and yet I was systematically forced to play the role of the “monster”, a role I despised... is it then any wonder that I wanted justice?

I quickly realized, as all convicts do, that if I wanted any justice at all I would have to take it for myself. And so I did; indeed, so I did.

And now I only laugh, morbidly, when I think about how society thinks I “deserve to die”. If anyone could ever deserve to die then I am certainly one. But, so was Jesus. After all, his crimes (open blaspheme) in that day and age were considered far worse then child rape or even murder. A man who killed a common child in those days would have been sued for the value of the lost child, not even criminally charged (unless he could not pay the restitution, and that would have been a completely separate offense). But a man who blasphemed was the lowest of the low! It was an attack on what society at the time considered most sacred and innocent of all. Why else do you think they spit on him and demanded that he be crucified? In their eyes Jesus got exactly what he deserved. Only Pontius Pilate saw the insanity of it because it wasn't his image of god that was blasphemed.

So I laugh, yet I cry at the same time when I think of all the children yet to be raped and murdered because they live in a society that does not yet know how to take responsibility for what its citizens do. And I cry even more for all the children in our society who grow up to be men like me, still confused by their own behavior and even their own thoughts because the world they live in offers them no help, no understanding, and no sympathy at all. Society attacks such men with the same hatred and vehemence that it once attacked Jesus with. And, for the same fundamental reasons; blaspheme of sacred social images of the holy and innocent.

(No, I'm not suggesting child rape should be condoned. All I'm saying is that children would not get raped if we learned to take responsibility for when it happens instead of blaming the rapist and "putting him away" or "punishing" him. After I was arrested as a 16 year old boy, I wanted "help" more than anything in the world. I knew there was something "wrong" with me, but I didn't know what. Almost all so-called "sex offenders" feel exactly the same way, at least they do the first time they get in trouble, but after that they quickly learn that there is no help, so they almost always eventually resolve to just "be what they are" and keep on hurting themselves and other people. All of which is completely unnecessary, if instead of blaming them and punishing them we simply asked them, "What's wrong?". Then listen to what they tell us, and sincerely try to help!)

The only solution is really so simple that I frequently cry when I think about how so many people (especially children) suffer so unnecessarily. The solution to crime is love (understanding), anything else is just more crime.

Reflections

Sunday, January 23, 2011

Honesty is a Contradiction

To say one thing and do another is hypocrisy. But, to say one thing and then say another is honesty. The nature of truth is such that it can never be fully expressed with words. So, if your words do not contradict themselves then you are probably not being honest. In fact, a sure sign of a dishonest person is extreme verbal consistency, usually accompanied by hypocritical deeds.

"Consistency is a paste jewel that only cheap men cherish" - William Allen White

Reflections

Sunday, January 23, 2011

There Are No Facts

Modern science is only just beginning to realize what mystics have known all along; that the truth is a potentiality, not a fact.

Reflections

Tuesday, January 25, 2011

An Ode To The Killer

I know the reason why
I know the reason for your hate
And I know the reason for your pain

I know the reason for my love
And I know the reason we're not the same

God's Love
God's Love is the reason
And God's Love will bring you down.

I wrote the above in a small black journal in 1997, the day after Anthony Martinez was raped and murdered. (The police have this book in evidence and actually presented this page of it as evidence in the Federal trial to kill me, though they never referred to it in their arguments, so the reason that they presented it remains unclear)

This poem came to me while I was driving away from Indio, California (where I am presently jailed). I had to stop to write it down. It seemed important. It ended up being prophetic in a way I could never have imagined at the time I wrote it. It was indeed God's Love, as expressed through the innocence of a little girl, that caused me to stop killing and turn myself in.

Reflections

Tuesday, January 25, 2011

The Reason Why

To ask why I did what I did is to ask why I was born. No matter what answer you give or get, no answer will ever be all there is to it.

If you truly want to understand, do not ask "Why?". But instead ask, "Who?".

Asking "Why?" changes nothing, and only allows the pain to continue. But, asking "Who?" will change everything, and turns the pain into understanding, so we can grow, and so we can heal.

The answer is who I am, not why.

You are who I am.

And that, is why.

Reflections

Tuesday, January 25, 2011

Cold Compassion

Compassion is not a feeling or an emotion. To feel sorry for someone, or to feel sympathy is not compassion. I felt sorry for every person I killed. I thought that meant I was a compassionate person. I was wrong.

Compassion is the will to act out of understanding. Feeling sorry for someone often actually prevents us from being compassionate. Compassion understands emotional anguish, but it does not cater to it. True compassion is as emotionally cold as a natural predator. In fact, a true predator is driven by compassion, not lust, or wrath, or any other emotion. No rapist is ever really a true predator.

But, cold compassion is not unloving or inhuman. True compassion rises above feeble human feelings and raises us into the realm of eternal life. In truth, real compassion can only come from the eternal sense of reality, which is a world that surrounds us in space and time though we are unaware of it until our self deception (and illusion of space and time) wanes.

The emotions that we commonly call compassion (such as sympathy) lead us to do more harm than good when we turn to them for a sense of purpose. In and of themselves, these feelings are benign, and clearly even necessary. Like hunger, sympathy serves an important role toward our physical well-being. But also like hunger, sympathy can become a dangerous addiction that compels us to overfeed our egos the way hunger, when not checked, compels us to overfeed our bodies.

If you doubt what I am saying here, then you effectively doubt the wisdom and compassion of the Universe (i.e. “God”), which sadly, most people do; even professing Christians, Muslims and Jews. Consider the child that is born only to suffer a few years of poverty, disease and starvation, then dies for lack of just a few dollars worth of food and medicine. Now, consider this child living over a thousand years ago, so the lack of food and medicine is “natural”, and not any man's fault.

Is the Universe without compassion? If you say yes, then you do not yet understand what compassion is, and nor can you realize the true meaning of salvation. Salvation is the realization of true compassion.

Reflections

Wednesday, January 26, 2011

Why I Don't Kill Myself

I suspect that when this body dies that the psychological sickness that has haunted my life will die with it. But at the same time I fear that the CAUSE of the sickness will persist in one form or another after my death. And that is why getting at the cause of my sickness is so important to me.

If I thought the cause would somehow die with this body then I would destroy it myself without hesitation. I have no reason to doubt this kind of resolve, since my history bears my tendency to put principle before my own life. The thoughts I think may be subject to the disease I suffer and therefore are not to be trusted. But, what I do, and have done in the past, is subject only to my true nature, and therefore can be trusted to illustrate the truth. So I am as sure as I can be that the cause of my sickness is not in my body, or my mind. For if it were then I would have killed myself long ago.

Reflections

Thursday, February 3, 2011

We Need A New Religion

Articulating our understanding of consciousness will ultimately require a new religion. Science cannot do it, and the older religions hardly even try because they too are clearly inept.
Our most advanced methodology for deriving an understanding of the nature of our world is constricted to external experience. In fact, early on science was apt to conclude that external experience was the only thing that could be considered real. Extreme sects of this belief system, such as Behavioralism, even became widely accepted. Such views are in decline today (though remarkably still clung to by many) because of the overwhelming number of experiments (i.e. experiences) that contradict the very existence of any external reality at all.
Science is currently struggling, as all religions do when experience begins to contradict the basis of their methodology, to find a new definition for God (a.k.a. Theory of Everything) that will conform to its way of thinking. But the inevitable is already clear: Science has failed in its mission to explain the ultimate nature of the world, and there is evidently no chance of it ever succeeding.
We need not just a new science, but a whole new way of approaching the truth. We need a new religion The holy scientific method has been exposed as another false, or at least limited religion at last. Now we can move on, forward to a better religion, or perhaps backward to a purer religion. Whatever we do, we must abandon science, for it has not only failed to provide the ultimate answers that we crave, but in so failing it has brought us to the brink of self annihilation. We instinctively know that if we cannot grasp the true nature of our reality then we will never be able to claim our relationship to it (i.e. inherit heaven). We must know our ultimate Father before we can ever truly know ourselves.
So the search goes on, and I will humbly make this one small suggestion to those who would join the ultimate quest: Look within. And the new religion must needs do the same.

Chronicles

Wednesday, February 23, 2011

My Teeth Hurt And Other News

Yesterday my attorneys "made an offer" to the state to allow me to plead guilty if the death penalty is dropped. It would be smart for the state (actually, the county) to accept this offer since a trial in this case would pointlessly cause a lot of unnecessary anguish for the family of the boy who was kidnapped and murdered, as well as for the community in general. Ultimately, whether or not I am killed by the state (Federal or local) will be decided in Federal court. California can do little to nothing to effect what the Federal system decides. So forcing the families and community to go through an ugly trial would be pointless and maybe even cruel. As far as I'm concerned, it doesn't matter whether it goes to trial or not, except that I'd really rather not be a witness to such futile anguish. That, and my feegin' teeth hurt! So I hope the "deal" is accepted so I can get back to the Federal prison in Terre Haute, Indiana, so I can get my teeth taken care of! Because I have been in one county jail (i.e. "short term confinement facilities") after another I have been unable to get basic routine dental care. So, now, after almost six years of no floss and shoddy toothbrushes to try to keep my teeth clean my teeth have had enough and are starting to rot in my mouth uncared for. I imagine that just a hundred years ago I would have no place to complain. Back then most people didn't understand the relationship between oral hygiene and dental health. But this is a supposedly informed world these days, and I would hope that I'm not the only one who realizes that no general dental care means painful tooth problems and loss. So far I've managed to keep all of my teeth in my head where they belong (sans third molars, which I paid to have removed while I was living in Fargo, for hygienic convenience). I've never needed any dental work more complicated than a single-surface filling, or filling repair. I have no caps, bridges, root canals, or anything. I never even had to wear braces. But now, after over five years of forced neglect, I need at least one root canal, and probably several more fillings. So, I'm complaining, yes. Because like the trial here in California, there is no reason that I should have to suffer. (Unless you take a sick view of "justice" by thinking that I deserve to suffer severe tooth aches because of what I did to those children and their families. But in that case why shouldn't I just be drawn and quartered? If you think I should, then I wouldn't blame you. I'd just welcome you to the club!) If the offer is not accepted then I will stick to my plan of trying to get the trial over with as quickly and painlessly as possible. Even if that means firing my attorneys and representing myself again (which is definitely what it would mean). I'd have to fire my attorneys in order to not delay the trial any further simply because there is no way they can be ready for trial in less than at least another year (probably more time than that given the complexity of the case and the multi-jurisdictional issues involved). And if they are not ready then the judge can waive my so-called "right to a speedy trial" over my objections, in order to give my own attorneys time to prepare. And, since the only way I can get my teeth taken care of is to get back into Federal custody (i.e. "long term confinement facilities" which provides basic dental care) I would have no choice but to fire my attorneys, if the plea offer is not accepted, so I can get the trial over with and then sent back to Terre Haute. I don't like being so drastic, but I don't like being in severe physical pain even less. Let's hope the case is settled quickly to avoid a rotten mess of a trial!

Reflections

Saturday, February 26, 2011

Demanding freedom

I am physically confined in a concrete cell eight feet by ten feet, and yet I am just as "free" as anyone else.

I'm not just telling myself that I am free in order to escape my imprisonment through denial. In fact, I don't believe I am "free" at all. And that's my point; nobody is!

Can you walk on the sun, or even the moon for that matter? Of course not. And neither can I. So we are not free.

But wait, this is no mere word play with exaggeration. This is a serious restriction on our freedom! We do not recognize the seriousness of it because we just accept it. But we don't have to accept it at all!

We were meant to be truly free! And if we don't demand our freedom from the universe then we make ourselves slaves to it.

Demand to be free! And don't stop until you are.

Reflections

Wednesday, March 2, 2011

Natural Compassion

I have written in this blog that compassion is not an emotion. This may be a confusing misuse of words on my part. Compassion is not an emotion, but it requires us to be able to feel emotion. You could say that compassion is the ability to listen to our emotions, but it is not in itself an emotion.

To have true compassion it is necessary to be able to let our emotions guide our behavior and thoughts without interference from our ego. When the ego gets in the way we end up letting our thoughts rule our emotions instead of the other way around. This always results in suffering of one form or another, either pain or pleasure. Regardless of the result, our egos can never be compassionate, though it frequently tries to convince us we are being compassionate when we have thoughts that invoke feelings of sympathy for another person. By raising your consciousness you become aware of these thoughts and begin to be able to distinguish between the false emotions they generate (false compassion) and the genuine emotions that come directly and unhindered (innocently) from your heart ("heart" is just a convenient term for the complex inner-workings of your unconscious mind). Only by learning to listen to these emotions do you begin to naturally have compassion.

Reflections

Thursday, March 3, 2011

The Most Important Thing You Will Ever Know, Period.

Since I am about to convey you the absolute most important thing that you will ever know in your lifetime, I suggest that you take the time now to find a comfortable place to sit in a quiet location to give yourself plenty of time to reflect on what you are about to learn. I'll wait...

Now, before I tell you this most important thing of all, I should warn you that once it has been conveyed to you everything else in your life that you thought was important will of course be drastically affected. Thus, I further suggest that you take a moment to reflect on the things that are important to you and then decide if you really want to let them become less important by hearing what it is that I have to tell you. Do this now...

Also, having the most important knowledge in the entire universe just suddenly dumped into your mind can cause severe shock, or worse, even physical damage to your brain, if you are not prepared to contain the information. So you should make sure you are mentally braced for the impact and willing to accept all risks as well. I'll wait while you do this also...

Okay, there is just one more thing that you need to do before learning this life altering information. This is necessary for my own peace of mind, so that if anything bad happens as a result of my letting you in on the ultimate truth then at least there will have been some contingency. Please at this time make sure that your last will and testament is up to date...

Alright, I'm sorry about all the delays. But you realize of course that this is no ordinary piece of information that I am about to relay to you. So a little preparation is certainly warranted. And now, at last, I can tell you. But first, I must give you one final chance to make sure you are ready, or to change your mind. Please only continue when you are ready...

Are you ready? Are you sure? Okay, here is the most important thing you will ever know: You are...

(Due to unspecified technical limitations to human faculties of reason, this blog post has been interrupted and suspended. We apologize for any inconvenience this may cause to your higher brain functions. In the event of complete psychological collapse, call your mother (or some other loved one). Thank you for your patience and understanding.)

Reflections

Wednesday, March 9, 2011

Judge Not...

We can, and do, only judge ourselves. It is not possible, under any circumstance, to judge another person. We can pretend to judge someone else all we want, and others can even pretend along with us. But, regardless of what we convince ourselves, in the final analysis, it will be only ourselves we have judged.

To realize this truth is to realize the futility of jurisprudence and the source of true justice at the same time.

Chronicles

Saturday, March 12, 2011

Baby Huey

Baby Huey is who I think of every time I see this one particular baby-faced and overweight deputy. But unlike the comic duck, this deputy is filled with prejudice and hatred, especially toward me. I'm not sure why, since I have never so much as even acknowledge his existence beyond what is expected of me to exist peaceably in this jail. And even less than that actually, in his case, since he seems offended if I speak to him even in courtesy. So I don't speak to him at all. No sense upsetting the baby duck.

It is difficult for me to love and understand a person like “Huey”, because his level of ignorance seems astounding to me. But I am usually quick to remind myself that if I can't love and understand someone like him then I will never truly love and understand myself. And, loving and understanding myself is tantamount to loving “God”, which I believe is the most important task of all.

So, instead of suppressing my negative feelings toward him (and people like him), I realize that these feelings are only a symptom of a more basic flaw in my character. And, I let the feelings run their course, but under close observation. I am trying to understand my emotions, by seeking the source of their steam. I can only do that by paying close and objective attention to them, sometimes even interrogating them to try to expose their hidden causes buried in the dark unconscious realms of my psyche. I frequently succeed, and have learned immeasurable volumes about myself and my relationship to “God”, this way. But I still feel like I want to hurt people like “deputy Huey”. I am clearly still missing something important and have more to learn.

So, I keep my head up, eyes, ears, heart and mind open, and hands inside the car. I'll figure it out eventually! :)

Reflections

Monday, March 14, 2011

What The *BLEEP* Do I Know?

I am careful to frequently assert my ignorance throughout this blog. But that doesn't necessarily mean that I'm just talking out of my ass like so many people do.

Everything I write is what I believe to be the honest truth, usually with careful consideration of the possibility that I may be unconsciously blowing smoke. I am always acutely aware that I have been frequently and gravely mistaken in the past about what I honestly believed to be true.

So my ignorance disclaimer is a way for me to protect my pride, I suppose. It allows me to speak freely and honestly without trapping myself in my own ignorance. If I learn tomorrow that I was mistaken about something I wrote today, or last week, or even ten years ago, I can just point to my disclaimer and unabashedly correct myself.

It gives me the freedom to grow and to learn to be even more honest. And it gives you the best assurance you can get that I'm not just bull*BLEEP*ing you! :)

As I have said before, if a person is not contradicting themselves then they are not learning and growing. And, if they are not learning and growing then they cannot possibly be being honest.

The most honest and wisest men in history have always contradicted themselves, frequently even in the same sentence. And the most dishonest and manipulative men have always stuck doggedly to their guns, defending their "truths" even to their dying breaths.

(It is interesting then that in our culture we quickly condemn the person who contradicts himself, even if it is only to correct a mistake, while at the same time we revere and reward the person who never changes their mind and hence never learns anything. We even teach our children to "not tell lies", but what we are really teaching them is to not contradict themselves, and hence to not be honest by admitting their mistakes. Is it any wonder then that there is so much strife and dishonesty in this world when we so unwittingly worship deception?)

Chronicles

Tuesday, March 15, 2011

L.W.O.P.?

I must admit that I am a bit befuddled by the people of Riverside county's decision to not sentence me to death and give me L.W.O.P. (Life Without the possibility of Parole) instead. Of course this was not a decision made by any one person, or even by any select group. It was a decision ultimately made by the people of Riverside, and that's what has me perplexed. The District Attorney by himself could not have decided to not seek the death penalty without committing political and social suicide. I get the impression that the new D.A., who just took office a couple of months ago, seems to realize the importance of maintaining the "integrity" of his office. He would not undermine the power (a.k.a. authority) of his position by making decisions that were insensitive to the so-called "will of the people". (And to his credit, I also don't think he would make the common political mistake of pandering to that "will" either.) So if the D.A. Is being as responsible as he seems to be, then how is it that I'm not being sacrificed on the alter of social justice? The popular media in this county has been following my case doggedly ever since my arrival here two years ago, and yet no one has raised a voice at all (at least not that I have seen in my limited perusals of the local paper) to demand that "justice be served" in my case. Why? Perhaps I'll never know. People still seem eager to execute other less notorious offenders. And my offense is not just high-profile, it is also extremely offensive, to say the least. (In case you don't know, I am in Riverside County Jail for charges of kidnapping a ten year old boy out of his own backyard where he was playing with several other children. I then drove him to a secluded desert ravine, raped him, then murdered him and left his bound and nude body to be found decomposed and ravaged by scavengers several weeks later. And if that wasn't bad enough, I got away with it, and there were no suspects in the case until I told them I did it after I was arrested in Idaho for a completely different – and even more violently shocking – case, eight years later!) So why spare me? Of course, there are the so-called "practical" reasons. For example, the county is in a fiscal crisis (what county isn't these days), and a death penalty case typically costs millions for the initial trial alone. But, that could never be used as an excuse to not prosecute such a high-profile and extremely heinous case as mine. So, what about the fact that I am already sentenced to three death sentences (for the Idaho case) in Federal court? That would make any death sentence in California seem superfluous, and indeed it would be insanely superfluous if I had continued to not appeal the Federal sentences. In that case I would have been executed by the United States long before California even got its hands out of its pockets. But, as you may know, I have decided to allow the Federal defense attorneys to proceed with their appeal. Yet still, the Federal appeal will be decided years before California even appoints an appeal attorney for me. And if my Federal appeal is denied, then again I will be executed before California even starts the appeal process. But, if the appeal in the Federal case is somehow miraculously won, and the Feds don't execute me after all, then, and only then, the California death sentence would act like a kind of (albeit very expensive) backup execution. Wouldn't that be "justice" (I'm just going by my own impression here of what most people think "justice" is, of course I would never call any kind of killing "justice"... "necessary" maybe, but not "justice"). Wouldn't that be enough to justify the expense of sentencing me to death here in the Golden state? I guess not, because nobody raised a stink when they heard the D.A.'s office was considering a plea agreement in my case that would "take death off the table". Maybe the people of Riverside are just tired of hearing about this case. The "shock" value has worn off a long time ago, and now all that's left is disgust, and even that has turned sour over the years. So there's no " entertainment" value left in the story for the media to sell... But wait, maybe this plea agreement will actually end up giving the story new life! People could be shocked and disgusted all over again at the new D.A.'s audacity for accepting such a deal. The media would love that they could spin it a dozen different ways and get a good few weeks of good "entertainment" out of it. We'll just have to wait and see on that one. Who knows? Obviously there are any number of reasons for why the people of Riverside county in California has spared me a death sentence trial. But the reason I like the most, and the one I personally prefer to believe (lacking any evidence against it, of course) is that the people have somehow, perhaps on the level of the collective unconscious, realized that killing, at least in this case, is wrong in a way that could potentially expose the "wrongness" of the death penalty in every case. I stopped killing and turned myself in and have taken full responsibility for my actions since. While these facts are relatively under reported (nobody likes to hear about a "monster" who doesn't act like a monster should act) they are out there, and even the most oblivious person must realize the significance of the fact that I didn't "get caught", I surrendered. So maybe people are starting to wake up a little bit to a larger reality, where monsters no longer live in the shadows, or beneath beds. Maybe people sense, if not realize, that the death penalty is a crime too. Maybe...

Chronicles

Wednesday, March 16, 2011

Checking Out Of The Hotel California (News Update)

The Riverside (California) D.A. accepted the plea offer that will give me "Life Without The Possibility Of Parole", twice, in exchange for my guilty plea and admission to all special circumstances (aggravators). As I understand the reasoning behind the DA's decision, they figure the Federal death sentences will be carried out long before any California sentence; so why bother? It also gets the case out of everyone's hair (since I can't appeal the California case now). The plea has already been entered and accepted by the court (yesterday, March 15) and the actual sentencing is scheduled for April 5th (three weeks away). Shortly after my sentence (presumably within a day or two) I will be flown back to Terre Haute, Indiana (Federal prison). I am still waiting for a decision in the Federal appeal. If they accept my belated consent (i.e. notice) of appeal then the Federal appeal process begins from scratch (even though it has been two and a half years since I was sentenced in Federal court). I'm not sure what will happen if they do not accept the appeal. Probably the appeal attorneys will just file another appeal to the US Supreme Court. I don't know how long that takes though. Probably a year, or two, I would imagine. Either way, I'll be back in Terre Haute on Death Row for a while, and will continue this blog from there.

Reflections

Sunday, March 20, 2011

Death Is Not A Failure

When we fail to see beyond death, then death appears to us as a failure. But death is no more than another transformation of being essentially no different than the transformation that already occurs from one moment to the next.

Who you were before you read the above paragraph is dead. And, who you are now as you read these words is a new creature. Yes, you have much in common with your former self, and yet for all the characteristics that you share with that other manifestation of yourself you can never ever be that person again. Your minute-old self is as dead as your now-self will be a thousand years from now.

So, you died. But is this then failure? Of course not. It is only transformation. And when the transformation from one moment to the next becomes so drastic that we no longer are able to psychologically make the connection between the two selves, such as when the body dies, that does not mean that the connection is lost either.

Who we are, the "I am" at the core of our being, is what connects all life, and all things together. When we realize this we become immune to the illusion of death. When we can see the stream of consciousness that runs continuously through all life, then death becomes a respected servant, and no longer a source of fear or apprehension.

This is what it means to put death beneath our feet. We see that death is a necessary part of eternal life, not our enemy at all. To defeat death is not to destroy it, it is only to see it for what it is; a necessary part of our journey through eternity; another transformation, nothing more. And certainly not a failure.

In fact, death, like defeat, will only make what dies stronger. This is why killing a killer makes no sense. It only makes the killer – that is, the reason the killer became a killer – stronger. No person exists without a cause. And killing a person without understanding their cause only strengthens it. To understand the cause is to gain power over it. And the only way to understanding is to seek its reflection inside of ourselves. Killing the killer is like smashing the mirror because you do not like what you see there. It is the failure to recognize yourself, the only real failure that can ever happen.

Reflections

Saturday, March 26, 2011

Go away!

If you are reading this blog with the intention of coming to some conclusion about Joseph Duncan, then let me make it real easy for you: He is a sick, perverted, child-rapist/murderer, coward, selfish, petty, small minded, ignorant, queer, weakling who doesn't deserve to live.

There, that should make you happy.

Now, GO AWAY! Your wasting your time here.

But, if you are reading this blog in order to understand yourself (i.e. the world you live in, which is the same thing), then please don't let my insanity deter you and read on...

Reflections

Saturday, April 2, 2011

The Weakness of Anger

If you think that getting angry makes you stronger, it is only because you are weak to begin with. Anger is a sign of weakness and fear, nothing more. The only strength that comes from it is superficial and desperate. The only purpose anger serves is to help a mentally weak person to overcome obstacles that any strong healthy person can surmount in stride.

There are no obstacles in life that a mentally strong and healthy person cannot overcome; not even death.

Reflections

Sunday, April 3, 2011

What Poe Didn't Know: An Answer To A Dream Within A Dream

I took your kiss upon the brow!
And, in not parting from the Now
Thus much let me avow -
You were not wrong, to deem
That your days have been a dream;
But, if hope has flown away
It alights upon another day,
And if in your vision you have none
Is it thereby forever gone?
All that we see or seem
Is yet, a dream within a dream.

You stood amid the roar
Of your own tormented shore,
And held within your hand
Those grains of golden sand -
"How few!" we heard you weep
With seas of sand beneath your feet,
And yet you weep – and yet you weep!
My God! why do you vainly grasp
What must defy our mortal clasp?
My God! why do you seek to save
The very sand that fills your grave?
If all that we see or seem
Is but a dream within a dream,
Perhaps the answer you should seek
Is who we are, when not asleep!

Inspired by: A Dream Within A Dream, by: Edgar Allan Poe

Reflections

Friday, April 8, 2011

I am a Cowardly Ignoramus

To be clear, when I say that I am the most cowardly ignoramus that I know, I do not mean so disparagingly. I am simply making an objective observation. I am not consciously or intentionally a coward (i.e. ruled by fear), nor am I deliberately ignorant. But when I observe my own behaviors and thoughts I find evidence of both of these attributes. And though I may suspect others of behaving similarly, I can only have direct knowledge of my own cravenness, never anyone else's. Thus, I say I am the most craven person I know, because I am truly the only craven person I know.

I have also said that my greatest accomplishment has been being able to embrace my greatest failure. By this I do not mean that I condone my own cowardly ignorance, but neither do I condemn it. Instead I metaphorically say to it, “You are welcome inside my home (mind, heart, etc...), as long as you do not mind me keeping the lights on!”.

What I mean, is that every idea, emotion, thought, and experience that I have is subject to the constant “light” of consciousness. In other words, I tell my own mind, “I'm watching you!”. And then I do watch, as consciously as I can.

And what I see is an ugly mess (in places). But rather than quickly turning off the lights again, like most people do, I accept what I see, and set about the arduous task of putting things in order and cleaning up the messes, instead of merely denying my own sloven past.

I will probably not finish “cleaning house” before I am released (i.e. murdered by the government). But, my goal is not so much to have a “clean house” as it is to learn how to clean. Sometimes I even “make messes” just so I can clean them up again, and learn how to do it better.

So when I point out evidence of psychological messes in other people's lives, I only do so out of the understanding that comes from having cleaned (or at least found) those same messes in my own “house”. I do not mean to condemn or judge anyone. I'm not saying, “You should not be that way”. Instead, I am only trying to say, “You should be aware of the way you are!”

And when someone else says to me, “You are a coward!” I like to ask, “Could you please be more specific?” (that I might learn something new about myself!)

Reflections

Monday, April 11, 2011

Screams Nobody Heard

I took the two children into the mountainous wilderness of Western Montana. I had killed an entire family, a man, woman and teenage boy, just so I could kidnap these two, a boy and a girl, aged nine and eight, to rape and molest at my leisure.

I stood naked at the edge of a cliff overlooking a dirt road that twisted and turned along the contours of a narrow valley. It was the only way to get to the clearing where I stood, staking my claim.

The children were behind me in the Jeep. They too were naked, watching and fearing my every move as I exposed myself to the forest, to the sky, and to them.

I dared anyone to see me, as I contemplated my situation. In a moment I would rape the children, but I felt compelled to do something else first; some necessary part of the script that would make my revenge more legitimate.

The instructions came, just as they always did, right when they were needed. There was something I had to say, but what?

Suddenly I knew.

I screamed at the top of my lungs, my voice straining, booming across the valley, forming words, and challenging anyone to hear.

I screamed, “Where are you now? You fucking pigs!” Not a question, but a demand; and a challenge.

And I screamed, “How'ya gonna stop me from havin' my way with these children now, fucking coppers?!”

And I screamed, “What happened to all your power and authority, pigman?!”

Then, breathing heavily, I waited for an answer. But none came. Nobody heard my screams. Nobody would rescue the children. That was exactly the point that I needed to make. It was a symbolic formality that in my mind would justify what I was about to do to the children.

I turned around and walked back to the Jeep. I looked at the naked children, my prize. I saw the questioning terror in their eyes, and I imagined I could smell the smoldering fear in their hearts. For a moment I wanted to cry, but I laughed instead. I laugh so as not to cry.
I then pronounced their sentence.

“I'm gonna rape you”, I said, “and nobody's gonna save you, and nobody's gonna hear if you scream.”

Then I raped them.

And nobody tried to save them.

And nobody heard them scream.

Confessions

Saturday, April 16, 2011

The Last Time I Ever Fell In Love

I turned 21 years old in prison protective custody where I sat for six months in a ten-by-six cell while the classification people decided what to do with me. It was a two-man cell, so I could play cards, and even have sex with my cellmate (if you can call being forced against my will to lick his smelly-ass balls while he sucked my dick and masturbated himself, having sex. Some people call it rape, but by then I could hardly tell the difference.) I also managed to study a high school US History book and then write several essays that were counted as class credits; the last few credits I needed to get my high school diploma. So I finished high school in protective custody too. Besides having forced sex and finishing high school I also fell in love... uh, with a real girl, not my cellmate. Her name was Anne Campbell, and she was my younger brother's 19-year-old x-girlfriend, and mother of his son. She wrote to me and sent me a picture of herself holding her baby boy, C.J., my nephew. My brother left her after getting her pregnant. I don't know why, but I suspect he accused her of getting pregnant in order to snare him. Whatever the reason, he abandoned her with the baby and shortly there after she started writing to me. Maybe she thought if she couldn't have one brother she would settle for the other; I don't know. But, she hinted that I would make a good father for C.J., and she made me feel not just wanted, but needed. I desperately wanted to make up for my brother's abandonment and my own criminal past. I imagined – fantasized really – that the parole board would realize how much she needed me and release me so I could take care of her and her child. In effect, I fell desperately in love with her. My desire to take care of her burned genuinely in my heart. I so desperately felt that my desire to help Anne was so strong that all my "deviant" desires would just go away, IF I could just be her husband. Indeed, I didn't fantasize at all about rape or sex with children while I was in love with Anne. She was my cure, my purpose, my love! I needed her, and I felt she needed me. I thought we would "save" each other, if only they just let me go, so we cold get married. Of course that never happened. I proposed to her in a letter, but she respectfully declined, and then gradually stopped answering my letters. I, of course, was heart broken, again (the first time my heart broke was when my first real girlfriend, Sharon Winget, was forbidden to me to contact by the sexual psychopath treatment program. They said I couldn't write her or call her because she was one of my "victims" because I had sex with her while she was under-age. Never mind that it was consensual, and that she was less than two years younger than me, and that we were both in the same grade together in high school, and that we wanted to get married after high school... the SP program rules were clear and inflexible...she was a juvenile, and I was declared an adult by the court at the age of 17, so that made her my "victim"... this was necessary for my "treatment"). The hardest part about being in prison is so tough that nobody even talks about it; it is the pain of being separated from the people you love, especially when they need your help and you can do nothing. About a year and a half after my proposal to Anne, my nephew, C.J., was repeatedly abused by an army GI that Anne moved in with to help take care of the baby. C.J. Was permanently brain damaged from the abuse. He would never be able to develop mentally beyond the age of two as a result. The man who caused this brain damage by hitting the small boy only served a few months in jail for the abuse, and was then released on probation. If the same man had simply ejaculated in the boy's mouth he would have been sent to prison for 20 years and forced to register as a "sex offender" for life. But instead, to this day, C.J. Must still wear diapers, crawls on hands and knees to get around and can only speak a few simple words. His favorite words are, "I love you". He is 28 years old.

Reflections

Saturday, April 23, 2011

A Few Of My Beliefs

I believe that the core essence of my being is pure consciousness.

I believe that all consciousness is one infinite thing that exists in all places and all times at once.

I believe that my finite conscious experience, this present life, is no more than a page, or maybe just a name, in the eternal "book of life".

I do not believe that this present life (my finite conscious experience) is eternal in any sense, nor would I want it to be, not even if I were a respected and wealthy king.

I believe death is a cherished friend of eternal life.

I believe that what I do today is more important than what I do tomorrow and more important than what I did yesterday. And, tomorrow I will believe the same.

I believe that each moment that I am alive (in the finite sense that any momentary experience has) extends forwards and backwards into infinity at the same time. No moment is ever truly finite, or otherwise separated from infinity.

Reflections

Saturday, May 7, 2011

The Yellow Brick Road

A person who focuses their attention on the only thing in our experience that it is possible for us to know to be real soon begins to realize that all experience is a manifestation of that one thing.

What is the one thing? It is that we exist. Or as Descartes has exclaimed, "Cogito ergo sum". I think, therefore I am. Descartes called this the first principle of pure philosophy. It is the starting point of the path to truth. The beginning of the Yellow Brick Road. But we must first kill the Wicked Witch of the East (our ego?) and claim her Ruby Slippers (consciousness?) as our own before we can begin that journey.

And of course, we all know where we will end up; right back where we started; Home!

Reflections

Friday, May 20, 2011

A Place For Me In The World

If I were to be miraculously exonerated of all crimes and set free to do my own will once more, I would like to go to Africa, as an AIDS worker. I realize that this will never happen. We are still a long way off from anything resembling constructive justice (our current system being almost exclusively destructive in nature). But some day, men like me will have a positive and constructive place in this world. I'm just saying that I think mine would be in a part of the world were ignorance is rampant and feral. I'm certain that my deviant sexual tendencies would naturally atrophy in such a place. I would feel valued and significant. And I would be kept busy working my ass off, so I'd never have time to day dream (i.e. fantasize). Any time that I did get would be too precious to squander on mere sexual fantasies. I'd use it to either meditate or contemplate ways to help the people I worked with.

Methinks I'd be happy there.

Reflections

Sunday, May 29, 2011

God's Advantage

God gave Himself all the advantage He would ever need when He invented Time.

Reflections

Saturday, June 4, 2011

To Know Me Is To Love Me!

If you can put what you believe into words then you do not yet know what you believe.

I say that I believe in One Consciousness (i.e. “One God”). But to say this is not a true expression of my belief. My belief transcends words. That is why I often seem to directly contradict myself. I can say just as honestly that there are an infinite number of gods (or conscious beings). Though these statements seem to contradict each other they are both true, but only in their own sense of expression. The ultimate truth about the unity or duplicity of consciousness is inexpressible. But – and this is important – it is knowable! (Gnostic)

In fact, it is directly known by all conscious beings. It is what I might call true belief, if that term wasn't as wore out as it is. To me, true belief is what everyone believes, but only a few realize. All religions are based on true belief, but no religion manages to convey it. It is impossible to convey, at least not with any human words.

To know God is to know yourself; and to know yourself is to know (and understand) me!

Reflections

Friday, June 10, 2011

Philosophical Vanity

Any philosophy, theology, or ideology that presumes humans to be more significant than other living creatures is biased and useless.

If we cannot see ourselves as a part of the continuous spectrum of life then we only deprive ourselves of any significance at all.

So, if we have souls, then so must germs. If we have eternal life, then so must an insect. And if it is possible at all to know the source of our being, then it must be possible for all beings to equally know that source!

That does not mean that our individual relationships with (i.e. understanding of) our source must be the same. It only means that our ability to have a relationship with (or and understanding of) our source must be derived from the same principles. It is a mistake to take any intellectual understanding of our existence as divine or empirical at all. True understanding must have such a nature as to exist independently of all thought or intellect.

Reflections

Friday, June 17, 2011

Materialism vs. Science

It has come to my attention that I have been mistaking materialism for science. But now I realize that I have been giving science a bad rap.

Materialism is a metaphysical ideology that even most scientists confuse with science itself. To claim that something metaphysical is unscientific is to imply that materialism is not a metaphysical viewpoint. My own confusion, often referring to science as a neo-religion, has been the result of my mistaking materialism for science.

Materialism exhibits all of the dogmatic and irrational faith-based belief systems that has defined religion from the beginning (note, shamanism and Buddhism are not religions by themselves, but are turned into religions by those who like most scientists today, turn the experiences expressed by the shamans and Buddhas into dogmatic belief systems).

The book, Science and the Near-Death Experience, by Chris Carter (see Fifthnail book list), has an excellent chapter that addresses just this confusion (chapter 16, p. 235). It opened my eyes, but note, that does not mean that my views have changed, only the words and terms I use to express those views have changed.

Reflections

Friday, June 24, 2011

My Eternal Life

I do not pretend to know what my experience will be after the body of Joseph E. Duncan III dies. I only know that my experiences will never end.

I do not know this because of anything I have read or have ever been told. And I do not know this because it comforts me to believe it. It does not comfort me; it humbles me and would terrify me if I let it.

But I have faith in the Universe that determines every experience I will ever have. I believe that all experience is ultimately purposeful. And I believe THAT because it DOES comfort me.

In other words, I don't KNOW my experience (i.e. my life) is purposeful, I only BELIEVE it is because to believe anything else causes me to suffer. And I don't BELIEVE I will live forever, I KNOW I will from having direct knowledge of The Eternal Being.

Reflections

Friday, July 1, 2011

Christian Love

Shortly after my arrest in 2005, a Christian minister from a local parish came to visit me. I told him the following story in order to illustrate my understanding of divine love. The minister was so impressed by the story that he worked it into his next Sunday sermon. It was not well received.

Imagine that you walk into your young son's bedroom and find a naked man standing over your child's bed covered in blood. You look down and to your horror see the nude and sexually mutilated body of your child laying in a large pool of blood on the mattress. Your son is clearly dead.

When you look back at the man you see that he is holding a knife, also covered with blood, that he obviously used to murder your child. He waves the knife at you menacingly and warns you with wild eyes and a sinister smile to stay away.

Instead of attacking the man, or running away, you speak calmly and with steady assurance, and tell the man, even as your heart wrenches and tears pour down your face, that you forgive him, and that you understand why he has done this terrible thing.

Your tears and pain are for the loss of your son and equally for the terrible state of pain and confusion and desperation that you sense in the man who has killed your son. You beg the man to let you help him, and he is so stunned that he just stands still while you pick up one of your child's shirts from the floor and use it to wipe your own son's blood off of the murderer's body.

Gradually the murderer realizes you are no threat to him and he lets you lead him into the bathroom, where you run water and provide him with what he needs to get the rest of the blood off.

After he gets dressed, you take him into your kitchen and prepare some food to his order for him to eat. When he finishes, you tell him again that he is forgiven, and more importantly, that you love and understand him. You try to make him understand that you can feel his pain and confusion.

Eventually the man leaves, and you call the police to report the murder. The police don't believe your story about the man who killed your son, especially when you tell them with tears in your eyes that you forgave him and let him walk away. They arrest you and soon you are charged, convicted, and sentenced to die for the crime. But, of course, your only "crime" is unconditional love.

Actually this is an embellished version of the story I told the minister back in 2005. But the points it illustrates are the same. This is how God loves us, and it is how His Son commanded that we love each other.

The minister I told this story to later told me that several of his parishioners withdrew from his church's congregation when they learned the source of this story and that he was visiting me in jail.

The minister himself stopped coming to visit me when I refused to "accept the Lord Jesus Christ as my personal Lord and Savior". I told him that such "verbal circumcision" would only dishonor the genuine nature of forgiveness and love that I had already experienced. No words could, or should, ever express the divine presence that overcame me on that mountain. It was an ultra-personal experience that no words will ever adequately express.

I have not heard from that minister in over four years. I have come to suspect that he thinks the devil was attempting to influence him through me, merely because I raised doubts in his mind about his own beliefs; another sad case of blinded faith ingoramatitis.

God commands us to love and understand each other. No man is a devil deserving to be hated, though all men hear the devil's voice (deception). You can believe the lies, blindly, or open your eyes and see the Truth for yourself. God's command to love unconditionally is no more than a command to open your eyes, and to wake up!

And this command is spoken plainly and directly in our "hearts". You should not need to "believe the Bible" in order to realize God's command. You should also realize that it is a command, not a suggestion. God is not telling us that we should try to love as he loves. He is commanding that we do so.

God would not issue such a command if it were not within the power of every living soul to comply. There will be no excuses on judgment day.

Dreams

Thursday, July 7, 2011

Samurai Me

I suspect, but so far only suspect, that my present incarnation was designed to teach me humility. And given the obvious intensity of the lesson, if indeed it is a lesson, perhaps there was a nearly insurmountable amount of vanity and pride in some other life that I am compelled to account for.

I once had a very vivid dream that I was a samurai provincial lord waiting on the side of a hill for first light over a small village. In the dream I understood that it was necessary to kill everyone in the village, men, women, and children, as a way to control the prosperity of my province. I did not feel bad about what I had to do, it was just "necessary", that was all. In fact, even though I knew my samurai warriors would attack the village very soon – it was predawn and they were to move in and start killing the people as they slept at dawn – I was preoccupied with thoughts of a teenage boy lover.

The dream was so real and detailed, and contained numerous elements that intrigued me enough that I decided to read what I could find about samurai.

I discovered several things in the dream that were historically plausible that I was not consciously aware of when I had the dream.

For example it was not unusual or even unsavory for a samurai to have a boy lover. If anyone had enough nerve to say anything derogatory about a samurai's sexual exploits they would likely be killed, or end up having to kill the samurai that they derided as a matter of honor if they themselves were also a samurai (if they were a subordinate samurai then they would be required to kill themselves).

Also, the killing of an entire village as a form of "management" was very common. I would never have imagined this to be true before my dream. But even before I confirmed it in a history book I knew the dream was right. It just made sense somehow.

At one point in this same dream I encountered a completely incongruous character; a man lounging in a reclining lawn chair wearing a Hawaiian shirt and Bermuda shorts sipping on a margarita, who seemed to be watching me as if he were enjoying a show.

In character with the samurai I believed myself to be, I drew my sword and raised it over my head in a challenging manner and charged down the hill toward what to my mind was an invader. But to my consternation the strange man, though clearly unarmored and at my mercy, showed no fear at all!

Precisely because he showed no fear, and ONLY because he showed no fear, I stopped my attack. I believe there was some baffling exchange of words, but I no longer remember the nature of the exchange. But the interesting point here is that I behaved exactly as I only learned later that a samurai might behave in such a situation. The strangers lack of fear and obvious poise caused me to assume he had more power than me. This is very much a samurai kind of rational, or so I read later, after the dream.

I also read that samurai tended to be very conscientious in regard to their role and purpose in this world. It would not be unusual at all for a samurai to earnestly question the purpose of his own existence. While of course the samurai were never supposed to question their role or their loyalties as samurai, they often did dedicate their lives toward higher purpose.

So, it would not be unfathomable to suspect that if I were once a samurai lord in some other life that perhaps even then I knew that I needed an entire lifetime (at least one, maybe more) of abject humility in order to counteract the extreme imbalance and disconnectedness that one lifetime of a severely proud and vane samurai lord would likely have wrought.

Or maybe I'm just subconsciously trying to make myself feel better about all the terrible things I have to be ashamed of in this life. Who knows? Anything is possible!

Reflections

Friday, July 15, 2011

Dancing With Desire

How do we dance with desire? Oh, but how we have forgotten. Our children will help us remember. They dance so well, without thought, or inhibition. They dance too, without shame or sin.

This is the dance; to be free to move, to speak, to show how we feel. This is the dance, consciousness arisen. To know only the truth, and fear only one false move. This is the dance, unforgotten .

To dance with desire is to dance in God's arms; safe, loved protected, desired. It is also to dance in our neighbor's front yard, unbidden; insane to a world that is insane to you.

It is what want wants. It is what need gets. It is what desire is. To dance with desire is to live, knowing only that you are alive, and will be forever.

Reflections

Saturday, July 23, 2011

The Coldest Blooded Killer Of All

Have you ever been a bully? Think honestly about this, because the truth in this matter can be very enlightening.

When I was a kid, more often than not I was the victim of bullying, in school, in my neighborhood and even in my own family. But on one or two occasions I clearly remember becoming the bully. And I remember the reason I did so in every case: peer pressure.

I once turned on my own best friend, simply because for a rare moment I felt accepted by a group of other boys for doing so. I actually tried to apologize to him later, but he just shrugged it off and said it was okay, he "understood", which made me feel even worse.

But I didn't understand. It was the first time I ever really succumbed to peer pressure. As a younger child, for some reason, peer pressure did not seem to be a part of my world.

Once, around age six, I was playing with a group of other boys around my age in a playground sandbox. Suddenly several of the other kids started yelling, “Oh no! Here comes that stupid German kid!” (we lived on an Army base in Germany, and sometimes German families would come visit the American families on base). All the other kids scattered; except me. I just continued playing with my toy jeep in the sandbox as I watched the unfamiliar boy approach. He came straight up to me since I was the only child who didn't run away from him and began a jovial though mostly one-sided conversation with me in German.

So what happened between the age of six and fifteen, when with a group of other boy scouts on a camping trip I started calling my best friend names along with the other scouts because he was the only kid who couldn't run fast enough to jump up onto the supply truck for a free ride back to the campsite? Mob mentality; a.k.a. peer pressure, that's what happened. It is the coldest blooded killer of all.

Reflections

Friday, July 29, 2011

Desire, My Friend

For some reason a lot of people seem to think that desire is an obstacle to absolute truth. But I doubt if that is what Christ, or even the Buddha meant when they indicated that we must overcome, or control, desire in order to come closer to God (the ultimate truth).

Desire itself is obviously a completely natural and even critically necessary part of nature. Without desire we would not feed, procreate, or even breath. So how do we “overcome” something that is such a fundamental part of our existence?

Obviously we cannot get rid of desire. Somehow we must make our peace with it. The same can be said about death as well. The Bible tells us that when The Christ returns He will put death “beneath His feet”. It does not say that death will be destroyed, or otherwise illuminated at all. Instead, it clearly indicates that death will be a servant (that's what “beneath His feet” means).

So perhaps desire is meant to be our servant as well. Maybe the idea is to be able to control and direct our desires, not to simply illuminate them.

William Blake wrote, “Those who restrain desire, do so because theirs is weak enough to be restrained;...”

I think Blake is right. Strong desire cannot be restrained by any human effort. Most people realize this to be true, but then they say that with “God's help” we can overcome any desire. But, if that were true then why is the innermost sanctum of every church plagued with uncontrolled desire of usually the most base sort? Even St. Paul wrote of God's refusal to assist him in overcoming his own “affliction” (with desire), and he wrote extensively about his own struggles with it (though most “Christians” prefer to ignore, or even worse, “interpret”, what Paul wrote in order to support their own beliefs, of course).

So, if we cannot restrain desire, what are we expected to do with it when it interferes with our communion with the Ultimate Truth? Well, if there were an answer to that question that could be simply put into words then there probably would never have been a “fall from grace” in the first place. Yet, while I can't speak for everyone, I can express my own thoughts on the one approach to this dilemma that seems most honest to me.

I think we should become friends with our desires! Rather than pushing them away, which only forces them to become more devious and manipulative, we should embrace them, “talk” to them, and more importantly, “listen” to them. As we get to know them we will find (at least I have) that they are a lot like people, and not “bad” people at all!

Of course, in order to befriend our desires we must learn to communicate with them. I find that the best way to do this is to start by “listening” carefully. In practical terms that means paying conscious attention to them. I “listen” most intently to my own desires while I am meditating.

Of course, I also “listen” carefully while I am engaging them. I think most people “tune out” when they are “giving in” to their desires. This is a mistake. It promotes detachment and alienation from an important part of yourself, namely your desires.

I have come to realize that my desires are so much like individual people, with egos and the whole nine yards, that if I treat them with love and respect they in turn tend to treat me the same way. Likewise, I have found that by ignoring them and berating them disrespectfully I only end up incurring the same treatment from them.

My desires seem to behave in complete disregard for my feelings and interests if I don't treat them with the same love and respect that I would give my own children. And in many surprising ways, they are exactly like my own children! Sri Aurobindo seems to understand this as well. He writes that our thoughts (and desires), “... are forms, and have an individual life, independent of their author”. In his book, Powers Within, Aurobindo discusses this concept at great length and expounds on the importance of recognizing our thoughts as our own children that we send out into the world to find their way, and whom eventually “return home” to you.

If we try to control our desires with threats and intimidation, then, like children, they end up rebelling against us and even intentionally acting in spite of us. But if we listen to them, and try honestly to understand and love them as an extension of ourselves, then maybe they will even confide in us what their own desires are! To achieve this level of communication takes time and patience. But once you have gained their trust, then they will share their own motivations with you; motivations that they normally keep to themselves (“unconscious” to you) out of fear that you might turn this knowledge against them. It is in effect like knowing the name of a demon. It gives you power over it, but it does not let you destroy it. How you use that power will ultimately determine your eternal fate.

So, I believe that the only true path to lasting and meaningful control over your desires is to develop a mutually loving and respectful relationship with them. Get to know them, and let them get to know you. Like any parent-child relationship, it is important that you yourself set a good example. You can only do this of course, by coming to know and understand your own purpose (i.e. primary motivation) in life. If you do not already know this, then I'd suggest you find out. It is YOUR True Name, the one that will or will not be found "written in the book of life" at the "end of days". If you ever expect your children to respect and obey you, and tell you their "names", then you will have to tell them yours.

If we think of God as "Love", then perhaps it is only with his help after all that we will ever win the obedience from our desires that can only come with love and respect. In this case God is perhaps teaching us by example (as I believe He always does). He never asks us to do what He Himself isn't willing and able to do; not even be a human being with human desires!

If your desires are completely out of control (as mine clearly were when I raped and murdered children), then you cannot expect to earn their love and respect overnight; or even at all, especially if they are relatively "grown" and mature desires. But, with enough patience and time, you can come to know your desires well enough to at least befriend them. And if, like me, your relationship with your desires is severely strained with a painful past, then perhaps a friendship is the best you can hope for. In that case you will have little hope of ever winning their devotion and obedience, but at least you can be friendly (non-abusive) with each other, and talk, share secrets (which otherwise would remain "unconscious" to you), and perhaps even dance arm-in-arm once in a while, as good friends should.

Reflections

Friday, August 5, 2011

What Exactly Is Karma?

I have read many things about Karma, but nowhere have I ever read about how to realize what Karma is without being told.

If you can't realize something without being told, then that thing is either false, or not significant to the truth. This is why I try to emphasize discovering the truths that I write about for yourself and never just take my – or anyone else's – word for it. The truths you discover may or may not correspond with what I write, but it does not matter if they do or not. The only thing that matters is that you can feel and experience the truth, so that it is real to you. It does not have to be real for me or anyone else; only for you.

Karma is real to me, but not in the same way that it is often expressed by other people. My experience of Karma is a real and direct experience, not something I have read somewhere.

Karma, as I experience it, transcends time. It is instantaneous and eternal at the same time. Not only do I receive back all the energy, both yin and yang, that I put into the universe, but I receive it back at the exact moment that I express it, and I receive it back for all of eternity also.

We can be (and are) forgiven for anything we do, but we can never escape the consequences! Karma forces us to live with the consequence of out actions for all of eternity, past and future. I suffer today for crimes that I will not commit until a hundred years from now. And I reap the joy of compassion that I expressed two thousand years ago at the same time.

This is the Karma I know through my direct experience. But even as such it is not a static belief unsubject to change. My experience of Karma could be different tomorrow, and I will let it be different if it wants to. Who am I to determine what Karma should be? I will let it be what it wants to be without judging it, but always heeding what it has to teach me.

Reflections

Friday, August 12, 2011

Beyond Evolution

Natural selection is not something that only effects genetic material. It is dynamically intertwined with reality itself. Even the very thoughts we think are the result of a process that selects which ideas come into our conscious awareness according to the successfulness of the idea in competition with other ideas. A completely conscious person can actually become aware of this process and even consciously modify the selection criteria. Partially conscious people also modify the selection criteria of their awareness all the time, but they do it unconsciously.

This process – conscious or unconscious – is the basis of intelligence itself. What we perceive as intelligence in ourselves is the result of a process that extends out into our world, and even into the universe. Our brains are no more than organic transceivers for this intelligence. The more we open ourselves to it, the more "intelligent" we seem.

It is not possible to have any thoughts independent of your experience. Even basic instinctive urges are motivated by experiences that are stored in your genetic material, much as complex psychological reactions are the response to experiences stored in the synapses of your brain.

Yes, this implies that we are no more than automatons, or at least our bodies are. Yet, the intelligence that our bodies (and minds) respond to is WHO we really are. Enlightenment is the event of identification with the intelligence, and source of our physical form and all experience. Delusionment is the event of mistaken identification with the experience itself.

Both enlightenment and delusionment are necessary for any experience to occur at all. They are the fundamental events of reality. To have one, you must have the other. It is the constant transition from one to the other that comprises what we call experience.

Reflections

Friday, August 19, 2011

You Tell Me

I just realized that to think in terms of our "relationship" to other people, or to the universe, or even to "God", is a tremendous mistake.

A relationship implies a connection between two or more entities over some distance. The form of connection itself is not important. It can be either physical or simply metaphorical. The important aspect of a relationship is the distance between the entities being related to each other, not the form of connection.

The reason the distance is so important is because without it there is no need for a relationship! Without distance no "connection" of any sort is required. In fact, without distance, no "connection" is even possible. Because without distance there is only one entity, not two.

So, before we can have a relationship we must establish a distance and hence separation from the entity that we wish to have a relationship with. And that's the problem; distance and separation are scientifically – not to mention metaphysically – known to not exist!

Scientist call it "nonlocality". It was first theorized in the 1960's by John Bell and later proven in numerous lab experiments based on Bell's theorem. And it's not what Bell's theorem proves that makes it so astounding; it's what it disproves! Bell's theorem, and the consequent rigorous scientific experiments, disproves the concept of "locality", or "separation between physical objects".

In other words, distance between objects is scientifically proven to be impossible. This is the "quantum enigma", that baffled Einstein until he died (Bell's theorem was intended to directly address Einstein's assertion that quantum theory was "incomplete" because it could not account for the locality of objects in space, i.e. distance and separation).

So, there you have it. It is impossible for us to have a "relationship" with anything or anyone, because we are not separated!

This is obviously what "mystics" have been saying all along.

The Bible does not say that Jesus is our "connection" to God. It says over and over that He is God, and He is Us! He is "in us" and we are "in Him" at the same time; not separate at all!

The Buddha taught that it is impossible to become enlightened; we can only BE enlightened. Becoming something implies a distance (in time) that must be bridged (connected). But, "being" recognizes that no such distance exists.

So what are we waiting for? What's keeping us from believing what we already know to be true?

What are we afraid of?

You tell me!

Reflections

Friday, August 26, 2011

Projective Identification Of Discompassion

To imagine that it is possible for a person to live without compassion ("human monsters") is a vice of ignorance.

We often convince ourselves of this possibility when we ourselves observe discompassion in our own thoughts and behavior.

Rather than take responsibility for this perceived failing in ourselves, we unconsciously shift it out into the world upon some convenient entity that seems insensitive to our experience.

And in order to prevent ourselves from realizing the connection between what we project and our own internal fallacy, we exaggerate the fault in the externalized form to the very extreme of its manifestation. We imagine that the target of our projected discompassion is a completely heartless human being with no sympathy at all (and therefore, ironically, deserving of our own lack of sympathy and compassion).

Because of this, some psychologists (and philosophers) say that we “become the monsters that we imagine”. But, the truth is that the only reason we imagine the monster in the first place is because it was already living inside us.

The “monsters” we perceive in the world are invariably products of our own discompassion, and the “evil” that they do is no more than a manifestation of our attempt to deny responsibility for the ugliness inside of ourselves.

So is “society” to blame for the monsters it imagines? Not at all! No one is to blame. The so-called monsters themselves are no less, and no more, to blame than anyone else; they do the same counter-projecting back onto society (or other people who project onto them).

No one can be “blamed” for not taking responsibility. In fact, blaming someone, even yourself, is just another way to not take responsibility. This is why I don't “blame” society for wanting to kill me (at least, not since I surrendered almost six years ago). If I blame them, or even myself, then I accomplish nothing. So instead I focus on what I can do to be responsible for what has happened, without blaming anyone.

If society wants to blame me, and project their discompassion onto me, to hide from their own responsibility, that's okay, for them. But not for me.

Reflections

Friday, September 2, 2011

Unemotional Love

Real love is not an emotion. A friend of mine once told me that real love is a choice. I thought I understood at the time, but I didn't. I thought he meant it was a choice to feel love for someone. But now I realize that real love is a choice to make someone else your top priority in life. Even if doing so causes you to feel unloved and forgotten, or any other emotional pain. Real love does not seek emotional pleasure, but finds happiness in suffering. As long as that suffering is for another person.

This can be confusing if it is not understood beyond words. For example, some people confuse masochistic suffering as real love. But in that case they are also confusing emotional pleasure with true happiness. True happiness, like true love, is not an emotion. It is simply a form of knowledge without confusion and doubt. It is knowing your purpose, and your ability to fulfill that purpose. Not a vague or imagined purpose. But a real and clear purpose that makes you smile when you think about it, even if you are in deep pain.

Another common mistake people make is thinking that love must be reciprocated. True love is rarely reciprocated, at least not in the present world. This is because real love is so rare in this world. The odds of two people being able to genuinely love each other actually meeting is very small. And even when such people do meet, they tend to unconsciously repel each other. Unless they come in close intimate contact. In that case they will lock into each other and become one. But this is extremely rare in the present world, and when it does happen it usually goes unnoticed by all but the two (or even rarer, three) who have become one.

I believe our destiny as a world is for everyone to become locked into each other to form one global "body-mind". And I'm not the only one who believes this. I believe it because of what I have experienced within myself as reflected in the world. In other words, because of my direct experience, not because of something someone told me, or something I read. I always emphasize, it is not something that can be understood with words. It must be experienced. And so must real love, and real happiness.

Real love is when someone else's happiness is imperative to your own. And enlightenment is when everyone else's happiness is imperative to your own. And we make others the happiest by honestly being who we are.

Reflections

Friday, September 9, 2011

Demonstrations Of True Love

I have written a lot about the nature of love, faith, hope, fear, ignorance and many other things, but nothing I have ever written has ever been meant to imply that things should be any different than what they already are.

I have written about our destiny as a world, and about the lessons we have yet to learn before true peace can be known. But that does not mean that things are not already as they should be. In order for us to learn and grow we must make mistakes, even hurt each other and ourselves. So, when I say we must love unconditionally, I do not mean that we are wrong, bad or evil, if we do not love so. The truth is that we do love each other unconditionally already, but only a few of us yet realize it (and even I can not yet say honestly that I am one who realizes).

To say we must love unconditionally is really only saying that we already do. But it takes true faith (which is no more than the complete dominance over fear) in order to realize it. Once we do realize our love for each other then it becomes no longer necessary to demonstrate that love; it becomes pointless to continue pretending to not love each other, which is how we so often attempt to unconsciously demonstrate our love. We pretend to hurt each other for the same reason a child pretends to cut open another child while playing doctor, or even to shoot and kill their best friend while playing at war. It is a game (how can anyone deny that it is a game after honestly observing the silly rules, a.k.a. laws and reasons, that we play these games according to) that we play as an immature species, in order to learn for ourselves the ways of the much greater Universe that we must some day inherit.

So everything is exactly as it should be, but never as it will always be. Life is change, change means death and rebirth. Life is eternal after all.

Reflections

Friday, September 16, 2011

God Is A No-Brainer

As soon as you start to think about whether or not God exist, or even about what God expects from us if He does exist, then you have already completely missed the point.

God is a no-brainer. If you don't have a relationship with Him that does not depend on what you think, then you have not yet realized what your relationship to Him is.

Most people who call themselves agnostic are actually closer to God than most people who call themselves Christian. This should be obvious to anyone who has stopped thinking about God and started knowing Him.

Most agnostics believe in the self as the only arbitrator of their existence. Because of this, without realizing it, they have identified their connection, and hence their real relationship to God.

Just because they don't call it God, or Jesus, or Buddha, or Krishna, or anything at all, does not change what "It" is. Only a person who is caught up in the delusions of the mind would let words inform their relationship to the Universe, God, Self, whatever.

The fly knows as well as I, that God is, and cannot lie.

My brain thinks it knows God too, yet still asks, "Why?" instead of "Who?"

Reflections

Friday, September 23, 2011

Survival Without Struggle

The principle behind all martial arts is survival without struggle. This principle flows naturally from the knowledge that it is not possible to fail.

This is not the same as saying, "Failure is not an option", which only invites struggle. Instead, a martial artist says, "Regardless of the outcome, I will not fail." If I am defeated, then I will become stronger. And if I am victorious, then I will humbly look for a stronger opponent.

There is no anxiety or apprehension. There is no struggle in the conflict; only an exchange of power and a transformation of being.

This is the way of the peaceful warrior. It is the way of the shaman, the Christ, and the Buddha. It is the only way that makes any sense at all.

Reflections

Friday, September 30, 2011

What Is An NDE?

After I inadvertently revived the nine year old boy (Dylan), that I had hung by the neck until he stopped breathing and let loose his bowels (which commonly occurs when lower brain function is lost), the first words he spoke were, “I thought I was in heaven...”

I immediately asked him what he meant. He told me, “I saw a light... I thought it was heaven.” I questioned him more about his obvious near-death experience (NDE) later on, and he told me that the last thing he remembered about being hanged was me pushing his head down so he couldn't breath. The next thing he remembered was floating in a pitch black space, and then he saw a light in the distance that started getting bigger (closer?). He “felt” that the light was heaven. Then the next thing he remembered was that his neck was suddenly really sore and he was laying on his back on the floor (of the cabin) and I was yelling questions at him.

After I saw that he was conscious (moaning and in pain) I started demanding that he tell me his name and how old he was. I did this to see if his higher brain functions were working (I was aware that he could have been brain damaged from lack of oxygen to the brain).

When we spoke later I told Dylan that the light may or may not have been significant. I explained to him that there were different theories about what he experienced, but it was a commonly reported experience from people who nearly die.

After telling him what little I knew about current NDE theories (from heaven to hypoxia), I asked him if he still thought it was heaven that he saw. He shrugged and said he didn't know. I also asked him if he could choose between “there” (the light) and “here” (being alive) which he would choose. With only a slight hesitation he said he'd rather be alive.

Because of Dylan's NDE I decided recently to read up on the latest information about them. Not much has changed since I last read about such things. Everyone seems to think they know what NDEs are, but I'm not convinced by any of them. I don't really have my own theory, but I don't think anyone else has a good theory either.

I don't believe that the OBEs (out of body experiences) that typically go along with NDEs are any more (or less) real than dreams. But I also think that our dreams are perhaps the best clue we have as to the nature and possible significance of the NDE.

In fact, I'm convinced that dreams hold the key to the nature of the universe itself. If we ever come to understand what a dream is then we will also then understand reality itself, not to mention NDEs.

After all “(everything) we see or seem is but a dream within a dream.” And that's what I believe (thank you Poe).

Reflections

Tuesday, October 4, 2011

Dylan Was A Bully

I've been reading hundreds of pages of newspaper articles about the “child molester/killer Joseph E. Duncan III” going back to May of 2005. Since my arrest I have generally been unable to follow the press and/or just not interested. So I didn't know, for example, about Michael

Anthony Mullen, the man who murdered two men who were registered as sex offenders in Bellingham, Washington. According to the article, which I just read today for the first time Mr. Mullen wanted to "send a message to sex offenders" because of what he read in the papers about the "Joseph Duncan murder-sex abuse case". I actually applaud Mr. Mullenfor for at least acting on what he believed. Even though what he believed was a bunch of lies fed to him by our industrious "free press", at least he had the courage to take some action and hence direct responsibility for what he perceived as "wrong" with the world. He apparently later decided that spending pretty much the rest of his life in prison labeled a "murderer" was a bit more responsibility than he bargained for, so he murdered one more person; himself. I don't mean to call him a coward for killing himself. In a way, that took courage too. I just wish this present world were not such that people like Mr. Mullen are taught to think in terms of victims and offenders. You are either one or the other according to popular sentiment. But in the real world it is almost impossible to be one or the other, as I think the demise of Mr. Mullen clearly shows. Mr. Mullen lamented the brutal death of Dylan Groene (who I personally murdered in the name of my own deluded sense of justice), calling Dylan "a hero" even though Mr. Mullen never met the boy. Mullen did not see himself as a "bad guy" at all, writing, according to the article, "I care too much if anything. I've always hated bullies, and pedophiles are the worst kind". I wonder what Mr. Mullen would have thought if he met any one of the numerous smaller and weaker boys at Dylan's school that Dylan used to get in trouble for beating up, "just because they're dweebos!" so Dylan himself told me. I don't mean to dishonor Dylan's memory and he certainly did not deserve what I did to him. But, the truth is, Dylan was a classic playground "bully" and everyone who knew him knew it. That's a fact that you'll never see in the papers and it's a fact that might have kept Mr. Mullen from becoming the very the very thing he hated, a bully, if it had been reported. If we want to have a truly free press, then we must allow the press to report the truth. But we don't. Instead we want to judge everything that is reported, just as these words here will be judged instead of heard, even though I am stating simple truths with no other motive than to expose the lies. And we do not honor Dylan, who was a real child and human being, not some fictitious "angel" who always smiled and never hurt anyone. We cannot honor his memory with a lie, so I am honoring him here, as no-one else dares, with the Truth; Dylan was a playground bully. What does that change?

Chronicles

Sunday, October 9, 2011

Ride Free

On the way back from the jail shower this morning February 3, 2011, one of the deputies who was escorting me mentioned a biker video and his wish that he could just ride free like the bikers in the video. I piped up and said, "But oh, you can!"

He replied, "Yah, but how would I put gas in the bike?" and I stupidly retorted, "You'd figure out a way, legally, to do it. People would feel for you and help you out."

I wish we could have carried on the conversation, but before we could get much further we were back at my cell and the deputy removed the handcuffs and then went about his duties.

I've been here in Riverside county jail for over two years now, and I have never had a single conversation with any of the jail staff. The most I have ever spoken with them is in little snatches, like this morning, and even then only rarely. Usually when I am being escorted I keep quiet, which I suspect the deputies prefer since any conversation at all with me could potentially land them in a witness box, a fate that they generally rue.

But, if I could have continued our conversation this morning I would have liked to explain to that deputy (who seems to be a genuinely nice person) that he wouldn't need to depend on handouts for gas either (which even I would not abide). With just a little planning he could arrange to work for his fuel as needed (which wouldn't be much if the bike were in good condition), or even live off investments.

I would have enjoyed discussing the possibilities because it is something that I have often thought about. In my thoughts (and I mentioned this also to the deputy just before our conversation was cut off, but did not have a chance to explain), if I had just jumped on a bike and took off after the first time I got out of prison then I would never have felt the need to "get even" (i.e. rape and murder) with society.

Why? Because I would have been FREE! The entire time I was on parole I never felt free and frequently expressed this sentiment to anyone who would listen, especially the parole officers. I thought I would feel free after I got off of parole, but the sex offender laws would never allow that either.

I was confined to being a "sex offender" for the rest of my life and this confinement amounted to numerous and often painful restrictions on my existence. It determined were I could live, work, even play. I couldn't even engage in normal adult social activities without feeling the chains of my confinement chaffing against my psyche. The sex offender laws made me a pariah; state sanctioned discrimination in the most insidious form ever, driving sex offenders to re-offend by undermining their social support structures. Study after study prove that a good social support structure is essential to keeping an x-offender out of trouble. So why do we keep passing laws that make it practically impossible for a person to be socially accepted?

Because we love sex crimes in the news that's why. The popular media cashes in on this perverse love all the time, so there's no point in denying it. I never had a chance to not reoffend, it was just a matter of time.

But, if I had ridden off on a bike I could have escaped the prison of pariahism (hey, I know that's not a real word, but just go along with me here) by remaining anonymous and slipped the sex offender chains completely. So my frustration would not have festered in stagnant confines of social laws and I would not have ever felt the need to lash out in desperation at the perceived source of my misery.

There are actually many "sex offenders" who have made this kind of escape from social bounds, which the authorities are only too happy to constantly remind us. It implies that the reason sex crimes aren't going away in spite of all the intense new laws, is because of all the "unregistered sex offenders" out there. But what they don't tell you is that as a group, "unregistered sex offenders" are practically invisible (i.e. off the criminal justice radar). That's because very few of them reoffend. The overwhelming majority of them who do get arrested do so for not registering, not for committing some new crime. And every single one of them site the same reason for not registering: so they can socialize without fear, not so they can commit new crimes.

I don't suppose I'll ever get a chance to say all this to any of the deputies here in jail, though the information (in the right mind) could go a long way toward helping someone understand why I did what I did, and much more importantly, suggest ways to keep it from happening again (hint:

killing me to "send a message" is not only barbaric, it only makes the problem worse!)

Someday society will understand, and maybe then we'll all ride free!

Reflections

Friday, October 14, 2011

The Ugly Truth

The truth, no matter how ugly it seems to us, is the very Heart of the Universe, in the same way that a child, no matter how ugly it seems to others, is the heart of its own mother – even if that truth, or that child, is as "ugly" as me.

Reflections

Friday, October 21, 2011

System Of Abuse

If the checks and balances that are in place to protect us from abuse of authority are not secure enough to protect us from an x-convict who is given authority, then they are not secure enough to protect us at all.

By restricting positions of authority to those without a record of irresponsible behavior we only foster an illusion of non-abuse, while at the same time establishing a system ripe for abuse by those who are more adept at getting away with it, if not more prone to do it.

The officials in the position of authority are the ones most deceived by this illusion, since it promotes their self image of being a "good guy", even as they routinely engage in abuses that would make most criminals look like kind hearted idiots.

For all its worth, the system itself spends almost all of its energy defending the illusion of protecting society. A significant portion of this effort goes directly and indirectly into propagating the very threats it then pretends to protect us against.

The saddest part of this insanity is that it is well documented and has been expounded upon by numerous people since the system was born thousands of years ago.

But, the system itself is a master of deception, which means it can evade the truth better than any master illusionist. Even its ability to deceive so many and keep people generally blinded to any attempt (such as this blog) to expose the truth, has been written about in incredible detail. But its defenses are seemingly impenetrable.

Seemingly.

Reflections

Monday, October 31, 2011

Murdering God

It may be better for a man to commit murder and admit he was wrong than for a man to do nothing and believe he is right. The one murders the flesh and learns the truth, while the other preserves the flesh, but murders God.

How do you murder God? Easy, just ask the pharisees. (Hint: The Romans killed Jesus, but the pharisees were the ones who murdered him. Murder is a choice, not an act; though it often results in violent acts)

Reflections

Saturday, November 5, 2011

God Is Who I Am (And Who You Are)

Presume there is One God.

If God knows everything I know, then God is who I am, and then some (albeit, an infinite "some"). Think about this.

Let me say it another way.

I am the sum of my experiences. To be sure, by "experiences" I mean to include all internal as well as "external" experience (though I quote "external" because technically all experiences are strictly internal and only seem "external" to us). So all my thoughts, feelings, memories, moods and other characteristics are all, "my experiences". Even "who I am" as a person is included in this definition of experiences.

So if God knows everything I know, then God knows all of my experiences, including the experience of "who I am". In order for God to know "who I am", God must experience "who I am". And the only way to experience that is to also experience my limitations!

This is important. God cannot know me, unless God experiences "who I am" in the exact same way that I experience "who I am", with all limitations!

Is that even possible? Well, according to the Bible, yes! What do you think the whole concept of Jesus is about? Over and over Jesus tells us, "I am just a man, not to be worshiped. And yet I am the infinite God, whom you must obey." Jesus was "God made flesh", which means "limited god". Christians admit that Jesus was "limited and unlimited at the same time". But they conveniently forget the significance and the importance of the limited aspects of Jesus. (Though the book of Hebrews spends considerable effort attempting to emphasize the importance of the Christ's limitations, without which he could not be a mediator between God and man.)

Now think about it some more.

Wasn't Jesus really just trying to tell us that God knows us, and even while knowing us God still loves us? Wasn't the profundity of the message of Christ that we are known, and loved? Jesus was only trying to tell us that our "salvation" depends on our realization that we are accepted ("forgiven") by God "the Father" who knows us "through the son", which means "in the limited sense of our being!"

The message of Christ is not some supernatural divine new law or decree sent by God. It is simply an affirmation of our relationship to God "the Father". A new understanding of the ancient and eternal reality!

You shouldn't need religion to realize this!

Reflections

Thursday, November 10, 2011

Round One

After admitting in this blog that I still like to masturbate to deviant fantasies, I've decided that I should re-affirm my "reasons" (i.e. ignorant rationalizations) for doing so. And the most honest way to do that is to speak from direct experience. And, since it has been some time (2 years, at least) since I actually attempted to suppress my fantasies, then the only way for me to speak from direct experience is to suppress my fantasies now, otherwise I would just be relaying what I remember from the last time I did so, and memory is never a reliable witness.

So a couple of days ago I decided to actively suppress my fantasies, and this is what I have realized so far:

As usual, my mind has come up with some seemingly fresh and appealing reasons for NOT giving in to my fantasies. These reasons, as usual, relate mostly to my current interests and experience. I'm reading some books on ESP that talk about OBEs (Out of Body Experiences) and NDEs (near-death experiences). This subject interests me because of the vivid lucid dreams I frequently have, as well as other experiences in my life that seem to indicate that there is much more to life than meets the senses (hence, "extra-sensory"). So my mind has come up with reasons to not indulge deviant fantasies based on these experiences.

For example, what if ESP is real, and my thoughts (and fantasies) are projected into the collective unconsciousness of the world? Then I could be causing real harm without even realizing it!

Actually, I have thought of this before, but it seems fresh to me because of the books I am reading about ESP, that have changed my view somewhat on the topic of paranormal science. (I used to think it was a bunch of hocus-pocus, but after reading "The Conscious Universe" by Dean Radin, I am convinced that there is real scientific evidence for ESP, that has been systematically suppressed by the establishment.)

But, as has happened thousands of times in the past, a stark truth has stepped into my consciousness, a truth that I have never been able to deny (though I have often tried). The truth is this: I cannot trust what I think! I am still just learning to trust my actual experience again, after being so long out of contact with it because of what I thought. My delusions have distorted my experiences for so long, for awhile I was having a really hard time distinguish the two (i.e. separating my experiences from my delusions). So any thought I have that suggests a course of action (i.e. behavior) is extremely suspect. Especially if that thought is detached from experience, as any such thoughts of ESP usually are (sort of).

Of course, I could rationalize that my experiences seem to support ESP, but unless I have some kind of direct unequivocal support (books and dreams are not enough) then I cannot give credence to the idea. This does not mean that I reject ESP, or the possibility that my fantasies could be doing real harm to the world still. It just means that I cannot base my decisions on such ideas, since they are, as yet, unconfirmed. To me, the rational that it is better to believe in God, because if He is real then you “win everything”, and if He is not real then you “lose nothing”, is a lie. If you believe in God and He is not real, then you lose any chance you might have had at discovering what IS real! And that IS everything! This rational applies to all questionable truths, not just whether or not God is real.

And now my mind counters; but how will you know if ESP is real or not, if you don't TRUST it? Ah, now there is the classic zealot's parry! And a tempting feint to boot! But, an experienced “swordsman” knows better than to attack such logic. It is a clever circular reference that turns the energy of any attack back onto the attacker. No rational argument can overcome this “faith defense”. But it can be undermined, by simply observing that the same could be said for any belief!

And my mind is familiar with this backhanded attack as well, so it says, ah yes, but should you not at least explore the possibility? Otherwise you would never learn anything at all!

And there my mind has a valid point, touché! My only counter is to concede the bout, or, make a desperate thrust for the heart; at what point, I ask my mind, should I stop “exploring” one possibility and turn my attention to some other?

My mind easily answers this question; when you have run out of new territory to explore.

Ah ha! My own feint worked! My mind has dropped it's guard and left me an opening at the end of the match for a counter-point: All of this, I say, IS old territory!

I have had such bouts with my own mind so many times that the only real challenge is to come up with moves that I haven't thought of before. And this I do as well, for both sides.

All this of course is an illustration of only a single round of an ongoing battle that I invariably get into when I try to suppress my fantasies. In fact, the ultimate reason that I stopped trying to suppress them is primarily to simply avoid this battle, and enjoy a little peace. If some harm is really being done by my fantasies, then it must come to the surface of my consciousness sooner or later. I can't force it to the surface by “believing in it” or I risk creating another delusion. I only believe in what I can experience directly and so far that is only one thing... me! Or, more succinctly; who I am (which if you read this blog at all you will know is not in any selfish sense at all – I believe that all things are caused by me, even you! So I believe in you too, or, at least I would if we ever met, that is, if you ever became a part of my direct experience).

And so, the battle rages on, in this case for your benefit, not mine. I still prefer the peace that comes from not resisting or trying to control my fantasies at all, but instead just observing them (in a safe environment) and letting them teach me what they may.

Reflections

Thursday, November 17, 2011

Just Blame Me

For most of my adult life I have believed that all of my problems were other people's fault and that anything good that ever happened to me was the result of my own hard work and determination. Of course I had a lot of strong evidence to support this belief system, not to mention being raised in a culture that clings to fault finding and hero worship as if nothing else matters. Without our villains to blame and our heroes to idolize most of us would feel lost in a pointless existence.

Reflections

Friday, November 25, 2011

How Much Longer Must We Kill?

The question anyone who supports the death penalty should ask is, will our culture always support the death penalty?

If they answer yes, then their ignorance is irrepressible. But, if they answer no, then they should ask themselves, how many more victims of the death penalty should we tolerate before we start making reparations?

(If the Confederate States had asked this question about slavery then perhaps America's most shameful war could have been averted.)

"I hold that man is in the right who is most closely in league with the future." - Eisenhower, quoting Ibsen in his '56 acceptance speech

Reflections

Friday, December 2, 2011

The Mind Hunter Farse

I started to read "The Mind Hunter" (a book about an FBI profiler who claims to be able to understand the mental processes of serial killers) and couldn't get past the first few chapters before I decided there was no point reading any more since it was more fictional than the five o'clock news (which is almost pure fiction).

The whole idea that serial killers somehow think differently than "normal" people is as full of hype as the idea that there is such thing as a "normal" person. If you handed an FBI profiler a letter written by a catholic nun and told him it was written by someone who kills children he would point out several things about the letter that "indicate" the writer is a psychopath (this has been done in numerous studies with even more dramatic and alarming results than this simple example with nuns even hints at).

But people love to think that they are "good" and the only way they can do that is by separating themselves from people who are "bad". And it does not matter if the thing that separates them is as superficial as skin color, or as arbitrary as sexual preference. The goal is always the same; to make ourselves feel superior to someone else.

Even though this concept has been studied and documented for hundreds of years, society in general remains as ignorant as Nazi Germany to the damage they are doing to real human beings, not to mention their own children.

When, oh when will we stop sacrificing our children to Baal?

Reflections

Monday, December 12, 2011

A Delusion?

Dr. Richard Wacksman is a secret government agent. He was recruited the same way all field operatives are recruited by the S.G. (a.k.a. "M.O.M."). They caught him engaged in extremely illicit activity and used the threat of prosecution and exposure to force him to work for them. MOM routinely recruits professionals in this manner and they have tens of thousands on their payroll.

Rich was assigned to be my "handler" after I absconded from Washington State in 1997. His orders were to make contact and befriend me, nothing more. Later he received orders to entice me to come to North Dakota, where I could be better controlled (my handlers in Seattle let me slip out of their collar) since MOM's primary base of operations are dispersed throughout the badlands in Western North Dakota (under the cover of nuclear missile silo security).

I was being trained as a "mad dog". Mad dogs are used by MOM to keep the American social mass under control during tense social maneuvering procedures. I was "set loose" (subconsciously ordered to attack a subrural American family) as a diversion (thought I don't know what from specifically). My "training" began while I was at McNeil Island Corrections Center. I was recruited and trained subconsciously to be a mad dog, then "leashed" and placed in the community ready for action. But I slipped my leash and killed three children without "orders". I was not exposed for the murders because I was too expensive and still servicible.

Dreams

Sunday, December 18, 2011

All That We See Or Seem...

Sometimes my dreams over the course of two or more nights seem connected in ways that defy common imagination. It is the kind of connection that only some sort of factually existing alternate reality could have. I hope the following accounts of two separate dreams that I had last night and the night before will express my meaning.

First of all, for the last two nights (3-4/3-5-2011) I have been having (or perhaps just remembering) more dreams than usual. But, that is not unusual. I sometimes go a few nights with almost no dreams, and others, like the last couple, I seem to dream constantly while I am asleep. Often even I seem to start dreaming as soon as I close my eyes.

So, the dreams that follow are picked from a hodgepodge of dreams, though these two specifically occurred on separate nights and in the midst of other seemingly unrelated (and unconnected) dreams.

The first dream in and of itself was a bit unusual. In this dream I was at a well attended outdoor induction ceremony for some sort of Harry Potter like magic college. I was in fact one of the inductees, and found myself wearing scholarly (or wizardly?) black robes suitable to the occasion.

The dream seemed to begin just as I was called forward from a group of other inductees, some of whom I knew to be my friends, and was compelled to take an oath of class by the traditional means of repeating short statements that were meted out to me by the headmaster.

I remember having trouble hearing the oath I was expected to repeat, and at one point I was certain that I flubbed my lines. The headmaster paused at that very point, and the entire student body fell silently still. I was not sure if this was because my oath was complete, or if my mistake had been a drastic faux pas.

At any rate, the headmaster announced my acceptance into the school and a huge cheer went up from the entire student body as well as the group of other inductees who all started dancing around in celebration.

I too started dancing and waving my arms at everyone causing my robes to ceremoniously fly all over. I even leaped into the air at one point and actually few for about twenty feet and a good ten feet off the ground with my robes fanned out around me like a giant black bird. I did this to demonstrate my own worthiness to be a member of this college, though it was apparently the extent of my ability to fly at the time.

I “flew” back to my position in the group of other inductees and rejoined some of my friends in that group. I remember excitedly explaining to them that at my graduation I would be able to soar around in the sky flying for real!

Then the ceremony continued, and another boy's (we seemed to be teenagers) name was announced and called forward to be inducted. He was also a friend, or at least someone that me and my friends knew, though he was not in our immediate group. In addition to the black robes that all of us were wearing, this next boy also had a cowl drawn up over his head and as he walked forward he turned about so everyone could see – and appreciate! - the truly sinister appearance of his face buried deep in the cowl. My friends and I commented to each other on how ghastly he was. We were impressed as only teen boys could be impressed by such a thing.

Well, the dream continued for just long enough for one or two boys (whom I didn't know this time) to be similarly inducted, each followed by rampageous cheers and a brief ceremony as the boys demonstrated in one way or another their prowess, usually by climbing a tall heavy curtain that hung from the wall of a nearby building and cutting off a piece of fringe from the top. This fringe cutting was some sort of tradition that I myself felt bad about not having engaged in.

So, that was the first dream, though there were a few other details that I'll just skip. What made this dream a bit unusual was how out of character I was in the dream. The person I was in the dream was clearly very outgoing and sociable, revealing in the attention of not just his friends, but an entire student body! In real life such attention would have made me very nervous. I am usually uncomfortable with the direct attention of more than just a few people at a time, especially if I am expected to win their acceptance as in this dream. And yet, in the dream I felt only the excited anxiety of a popular and accepted teenage boy in his element. It was not "me" at all, not even close.

The second dream, the one I had just last night, was far less extravagant in detail, but nonetheless interesting for the reasons I have already asserted above; the uncanny connectedness to the first dream.

In the second dream I seemed to be some sort of student of a very old university campus. I was apparently walking between classes. I was by myself, and as I just said, there were few details that I was aware of. It was like a vague "snapshot" memory of some mundane and ordinary day in the life of a college student.

There was no conscious connection between this "campus" and the previous dream. I did not think it was a magic school, but it could have been. I did not realize I was dreaming at all. In fact, it seemed my mind, in the dream, was blank. I wasn't thinking or feeling anything in particular at all. I was just moving (walking I presume) toward a building where I knew my next class would be.

That was all. Actually, the dream continued, but I cannot remember anything except a vague memory of being inside the building, which was some sort of very old church.

Again, I emphasize that this dream was vague and in no way seemed connected to the dream from the previous night. But, at some point later in the dream I remember looking at a brochure that had an idealistic photo of the same building I had entered earlier in the dream. I remember looking at the photo and realizing that this was the brochure that my parents must have used to select the school. The picture made the building seem much grander than it was in actuality.

That was pretty much all for the second dream. Now, here is the strange connection: according to the brochure, the building in the second dream was a monastic temple, but distinctly not Christian! That would mean that I was attending classes at some clearly mystical (i.e. magical) school!

Could it be that this was the same school that I remembered (i.e. dreamed) being inducted into the night before? If so, then why did I not appear to realize this connection while I was having the second dream?

Actually, and this is the uncanniness of it, the only reason I would have realized the connection is if the connection was subjective! In other words, if the connection were not "real" (i.e. objectively existing in some other "reality"), then it would have been necessary for the connection to be established subjectively in order to provide continuity.

But, if the connection were objective, and actually existed in some "real" sense, then there would be no reason for me to realize that connection within the experience (i.e. the dream) itself. You would not expect to "realize" the connection between any two random events of your life unless you were actually relaying those events in some narrative (i.e. subjective) form.

The fact – unfortunately a fact that only I can confirm to myself – that the dreams seem objectively and not subjectively connected at the same time is what I find so astonishing! Could this be evidence that dreams can at least represent some kind of objective experience?

Or, perhaps an even more intriguing question might be; is there any such thing as objective reality at all?

If dreams can represent objective experience – which is not to say that they always do, just that they can – then why couldn't our everyday "reality" just be a dream?

Of course I am admittedly biased on this point, believing as I do that dreams and so-called reality are intimately connected. But, like the proponent of any unproven theory, I get understandably excited every time I encounter some apparent evidence supporting my belief, as these two dreams seem to do. (The real challenge, of course, is to keep my mind open to the possibility that I am mistaken; maybe dreams have nothing to do with reality. But, so far I have found no convincing evidence or argument to support such an antithesis.)

Alas, I find myself once more compelled to quote the great dreamer, Edgar Allan Poe:

"All that we see or seem Is but a dream within a dream."

Sunday, December 25, 2011

The Gradual Soul

Nothing in nature is ever completely unique. Everything exists on a spectrum, so that any difference at all is only gradual. It is not possible for anything to exist outside of some gradual spectrum as a unique entity in and of itself with any significantly discrete characteristic. Everything has a direct predecessor and descendant of like kind. And, everything evolves, or changes over time.

This is the most basic teaching of Buddhism called transiency. It is an ancient concept, and it cannot be rationally denied. And yet it is so often ignored and even contradicted for foolish reasons.

For example, people frequently claim that the individual "soul" is uniquely human. This is an error of the gravest sort. It pretends to provide a "spiritual" means for us to experience the oneness of the universe, or to "commune with God". But, instead all it does is instill a deep sense of separation from the spectrum of consciousness that is the source of our being and our "soul". It teaches us that we are separate to begin with, and therefore we must find a way back.

But we are not separate to begin with. The appearance of separation from the universe, from each other, and from "God", is only an illusion. We are perpetually joined to everything through a spectrum of consciousness.

It does not matter how you define the soul. If it exists at all, by any definition, then it exists on a gradual spectrum. And, if humans have a soul then in some form so do all other animals, reptiles, and even insects and germs.

If what you believe cannot account for this graduation of the soul, then it accounts for nothing, and you should demand something better to believe... evolve.

Reflections

Saturday, December 31, 2011

The Perfect Poem

Life is a Poem
Written by God
With only one Word
And no revisions

156

Volume Two

2012-2013

2012

Reflections

Sunday, January 8, 2012

Descartes' Principles

The First Principle

Everyone has heard René Descartes most famous axiom, "I think therefore I am". But, few people realize the full context and profound importance of this truth.

Here is a translation of the greater context of what Descartes actually wrote:

"I observed that, whilst I thus wished to think that all was false, it was absolutely necessary that I, who thus thought, should be somewhat; and as I observed that this truth, I think, therefore I am, was so certain of such evidence, that no ground of doubt, however extravagant, could be alleged by the skeptics capable of shaking it, I conclude that I might, without scruple, accept it as the first principle of the philosophy of which I was in search."

First of all, it is important to realize that the basis of Descartes famous assertion, as is clearly indicated above, is that, "all was false", which is to say that nothing we experience can be considered anything more than an illusion. Forget that modern science (i.e. quantum physics) bears this out; it is self evident to any careful thinker. As Descartes himself puts it elsewhere:

"What is there then that can be considered true? Perhaps this only, that nothing is certain."

And I myself have often stated, "The only thing I know for sure is that I know nothing for sure; except I am."

The "except I am" is my own expression of Descartes famous aforementioned axiom. Of course he actually wrote in Latin, "cogito ergo sum". But, contemporary historians note that the correct form is, "cogito cogitationes, ergo sum", or "cogito me cogitare, ergo sum". Using these forms, then a better translation that more correctly reflects what Descartes was trying to say is, "I am aware, therefore I am". Or, more precisely, "I am cognizant, therefore I am".

The importance of this "first principle" is that there is nothing else we can be certain of, except that we exist! But Descartes did not just stop there. He went on to ask, what can be derived from this most basic truth? And while that is presently about the extent of my knowledge of Descartes, I myself can derive a second, third, and even fourth principle from his well established first.

The Second Principle

The first principle is, " I am cognizant, therefore I must exist". From this it is possible to derive other important information about our existence.

For example, if I exist – as the first principle claims – then I must also be eternal. The basis for this second principle is as unshakeable as the first. Since clearly anything with a beginning (and hence an end) cannot be said to exist at all. "If it has a beginning, then it has an end; and if it has an end, then it already has." Anything that is not eternal is only an illusion in time (and space), and therefore does not exist. So, if I exist, then I am eternal. This is what I call the second principle.

So, I do not need to be cognizant of my eternal nature in order to know that I am eternal. It is as self evident as the first principle.

The Third Principle

The first principle says, I exist; and the second, I am eternal. So a third principle now becomes apparent, and is really only an extension of the second principle.

If I am eternal (in time) then I must also be infinite (in space) since space and time are essentially the same thing (which mystics have been saying long before Einstein came along and proved it mathematically).

Since I am infinite, the I know there is nothing that is not me! This is critically important, because it informs us that everything we experience is as much a part of who we are as anything else we experience. I am you, and you are me. To realize this in your heart is to be enlightened. To realize it in your mind is just another illusion.

The Fourth Principle

The fourth principle flows naturally from the first three: I exist, I am eternal, and I am infinite, therefore there is nothing that I am not.

I am who I am, I am the creator of all that I experience. I do not need to be aware of my divine nature, or my infinite power. The fact, whether I realize it or not, is that I am God.

Realizing this truth is incredibly humbling. In fact, if you think you are God, but you are not humbled by the thought, then you simply do not yet realize the truth of it.

From this truth wisdom flows. As God, we can plainly see the folly of judging others, and realize how by doing so we are literally judging ourselves. We learn the value, and power of forgiveness, not as a rule, but a divine law that can never be broken. We see that all struggle is futile and pointless. Peace becomes our nature, since to struggle makes no sense to someone who truly realizes they can never die.

Reflections

Sunday, February 5, 2012

Wagering On God

Pascal wrote, "You must wager...Which will you choose?... Let us weigh the gain and loss in calling "heads " that God is. Let us weigh the two cases: if you win, you win all; if you lose, you lose nothing. Wager then unhesitantly that He is."

I have heard this argument before. The fact that anyone would actually resort to such logic in their attempt to answer the single most important question of their eternal life is appalling to me. It is a good example of how our foolish reliance on reasoning prevents us from ever experiencing that which is directly in front of us. I can hardly imagine that God, however defined, would acknowledge such a superficial attempt of belief. The wager itself is a cop out, one that if taken, win or lose, will cause you to lose everything.

Knowing God should be no more of an exercise in reason than knowing your own mother, in fact, even less so. To question the existence of God is to question your own existence. There is no reasoning more complex than, "Cogito, ergo sum", necessary to reach the required solution. If there is no God, then there is nothing. God is that that is; nothing more and nothing less. To wager on His existence is to wager on your own existence. It is a fools bet.

Reflections

Sunday, February 12, 2012

No Easy Solution

I have often lamented the insanity and injustice of persecuting sex offenders. It is a form of madness that invariably leads to more sexually abusive behavior in our society while pretending to prevent it. But I have never offered any ideas of how to fix it.

The omission has been deliberate. I believe that once the insanity is clear then the sane thing to do will also become clear. But the "sane" thing to do is never something any human laws will ever be able to fully emulate. The only sane thing to do is to love and an accept an offender, then trust love to solve our dilemmas for us. It is a solution as old as time itself.

So the "sane" thing to do when someone rapes a child might be to simply kill the rapist immediately, out of mercy (since no one would commit such an act of violence unless they are badly wounded psychologically and in great "spiritual pain"). Or it might be to simply ignore the rapist and help the child. It all depends on what love tells us to do, not logic.

Logic is cold and incapable of compassion and understanding. So as wonderful as it is for solving scientific problems, it will never be able to solve our moral ones. (In fact, attempting to apply logic to moral questions is the very crux of the insanity of our so-called justice system. This is also why psychology, sociology and even anthropology should not be considered sciences at all. They are pseudo-religions and will never be anything more.)

Reflections

Wednesday, February 15, 2012

Black History

In the US, February is Black History Month. But, black history is my history too.

Reflections

Thursday, February 16, 2012

Enemy Mine

The only way to truly understand the enemy is to become the enemy. If you are unable or unwilling to do so then you must resign yourself to perpetual conflict.

Reflections

Saturday, February 18, 2012

Son of the One

I have often believed in the past that I could stop masturbating and fantasizing anytime I wanted. I used to think that the only reason I continued to be sexually deviant was in order to "get even" with the System. In my mind, I would use the shocking nature of my behavior to lash out at those who would be shocked by it; my enemy, the complacent citizens that comprise the body and mind of the System.

I needed to believe those things in order to convince myself that I was in control of my life. I needed to blame society for all my problems in order to have any sense of control at all over my life. If I were to blame myself for my problems – and I did not know how I was to blame – which I did not, then the sense of loss of control would be overwhelming. So I had no choice but to either blame society, and retain an illusion of control over my life, or blame myself, and surrender all control.

Ultimately I learned that I didn't have to blame anyone. I also learned that I never was in control, and never will be! I witnessed directly the incredible intelligence that directs my life. I believe now in the ultimate benevolence of that intelligence, since I saw how all the pain and sorrow in my life have been the result of... loving guidance. The blows that caused me such anguish were delivered by the will of the ultimate craftsman as my life was shaped into a work of art that no human artist will ever mimic; a living, loving, faithful, adoring, Son of the One!

Confessions

Sunday, March 4, 2012

What Happened In Prison – Part III: The Transition

It has been several months since my last "What Happened In Prison"-posting. I have been working on this, "Part III: The Transition", during that time, having thrown away at least three nearly complete attempts and starting over from scratch each time. This has been the most difficult time in my life. It was the period between 1987 and 1990, when the circumstances of my incarceration finally forced me to accept that I would never go home again, and in my mind: **never go free**.

My chains had become psychological, and they were forged as surely as carbon steel to be completely invulnerable to any attempt on my part to break them. And it was against these invisible bonds that I began to rebel, and hence unwittingly define my identity and role in society; that of a social outcast, a pariah, and a "dangerous monster". It was a painful time of transition for me, filled with the raw (newly formed) emotions of betrayal, and the beginning of my desire for revenge against "the machine".

Revenge was the only salve available to me that could ease my pain. In this preamble I wish to achieve two things: First to explain why this posting has been so long in coming. And, second, to establish the proper mood (solemn) and perhaps add a little deserved gravity to the events that follow. You are about to read (or not) about the actual birth of a real life "monster" from the very womb of social ignorance. Or, to put it a bit less delicately, what follows is a description of the Beast itself, taking a shit.)

"Ignorance is the womb of monsters." - Henry W. Beecher

In 1987, seven years after my arrest and incarceration for forcing another boy – two years younger than me – to take off his clothes and put my dick in his mouth (rape) I got an unexpected break in the fifteen-and-a-half-year-sentence imposed by the Parole Board. The Parole Board was ordered to adjust the sentences they set, and to bring them within the sentencing range set by the Sentencing Reform Act (SRA) in Washington state. The SRA would have set my range at five to seven years, maximum (under no circumstances was I supposed to serve more than seven years, according to the SRA).

I had already served over seven years under the "old guidelines", so the Parole Board (now called the ISRB, or, Indeterminate Sentencing Review Board) was forced to reduce my time and find me parolable. All I needed was an approved parole plan and I could go home, three years sooner than expected! Or, so I was led to believe. It would end up being more than another seven years before I managed to "fight my way out" of prison with the help of litigation filed on my behalf by an attorney. But that comes later in this story.

At the time when I was found parolable, in 1987, I still believed that someday I would be able to go home and the nightmare that began because of what I did when I was a confused 16-year-old boy would then come to an end. Yes, I was still that naive.

So, I submitted parole plans to live with my mother in the same house where I was arrested in the front yard seven years earlier. My plan was to get a job, working with computer and/or electronics repair work – skills I had learned in prison – and to pay my mother rent. This would have allowed my mom to keep the house which she was otherwise losing because of unpaid mortgage, assuming the plans were approved. My counselor, Mr. Dennis Wheeler (a name I came to remember because of the subversive role he played in bringing about the addition of many more years to my already extraordinary sentence) assured me that these were good parole plans. He also assured me that all the subsequent plans I submitted through him were all good as well, while he simultaneously and covertly recommended to the Parole Board that all my plans be *denied* - which I didn't learn about until years later when a lawyer disclosed to me Mr. Wheeler's "unofficial" reports to the Parole Board that I had no way of knowing about. In these reports Mr. Wheeler recommended even that my parole plans to the Interaction Transition House ("I.T. House") *also* be denied. His recommendations were not based on disciplinary problems or even because of lack of structure in the parole plans. The I.T. House plans were considered the best parole plans a person could have at that time.

It took up to two years to be accepted by the program and I had to participate in the weekly I.T. House meetings inside the prison to win their acceptance. But Mr. Wheeler was "concerned" about my "unstable sexual behavior", which is prison-admin-speak for "flamboyant homosexuality". Even though I never got in trouble in prison for having sex. Most "out" prison homosexuals have more "504's" - sex infractions – than they can count. I never got one, not even after over 17 years in prison population, most of the time being "out" as a homosexual a.k.a. "queen". Yes, I had sex in prison. But not lasciviously. Most of the time I only had sex regularly with just one person, "my man". I maintained and adamantly respected a monogamous relationship for almost the entire time I was out of the closet in prison. I was "Big Al's girl", and everyone knew it.

Apparently, Mr. Wheeler and later the I.S.R.B. decided that flamboyant homosexuals were dangerous to society. Even though the prison psychologist, who in her official report to the I.S.B.R., wrote that because of my efforts to confront my sexual identity, I was a "much smaller risk to re-offend" than I was before. The psychologist's name was Dr. Sally Sloat, a name I remember because of her persistent efforts to convince the I.S.B.R. that I was not "sexually unstable", but actually a better candidate for parole than I had ever been.

When the I.S.R.B. first found me parolable in 1987, my first concern was to make sure that I would not re-offend. So, on my own initiative, I began meeting with Dr. Sloat regularly in order to discuss my treatment options on parole, and my current attempts at self-treatment. The prison had previously turned down all my request for treatment because I had "too much time left". So, seeing Dr. Sloat was my only option, which I took voluntarily, and under my own initiative. When I told Dr. Sloat about how my fantasies of letting men use me as a woman seemed to make my fantasies about children go away, she revealed to me that all of my "psych-tests" (e.g. MMPI) indicated that I had "strong feminine characteristics". She encouraged me to "explore my sexual identity", as a way of understanding and controlling my deviant sexual fantasies about children. So, with the help and support of Dr. Sloat, and "my man", who Dr. Sloat knew about, I came out of the closet, specifically as a transsexual, which translates as "queen" in prison.

My man, Big Al, was an intelligent, well-educated (with a BA in psychology that he earned in prison) and highly respected convict throughout the state prison system at the time. He was also the prison imam (Muslim leader) and devoutly dedicated to his beliefs. The entire time I lived with Big Al, he always performed his daily prayers and observed all of the other Muslim religious conventions, except one: *he fucked the hell out of me almost every night that he could, and I loved it!* As for how a devout Muslim, an imam no less, could possibly reconcile such a serious offense against Muslim practice as homosexuality, all I can say is that Big Al was not homosexual at all. To him, I was just a "female trapped in a male body", but I also had a very female-ish body and he never treated me as anything but a female. When other Muslims confronted him about his relationship with me (which he never tried to hide) he would tell them: "It's between me and Allah". In other words, none of their business. And he backed this up with several sutras straight from the Qur'an.

Big Al took a huge risk to his reputation as a Muslim in order to represent me (be "my man") in prison. But he did it because he supported Dr. Sloat's idea that I needed to establish my sexual identity if I wanted to have any hope of escaping my deviant sexual past. He knew all about my crime and about how I was bothered so much by persistent sexual desires for children. In fact, he was the one who initially suggested I go see Dr. Sloat, and told me I could trust her. He did not pretend to be qualified to give me the help I needed. But when Dr. Sloat suggested that coming out of the closet would help me get over my pedophilia tendencies, Big Al cared enough to support my efforts, even though he knew well that he was risking more than just his reputation; a lot more! Because of his open relationship with me, Big Al lost his preferred housing status at McNeil Island. He also ended up losing his custody security level (from medium to closed), which caused him to be transferred back to the state penitentiary on the other side of the state (away from his family). And he is still in prison to this day, having been found parolable himself more than six years ago, but yet to be released on parole, perhaps again because of his relationship to me. But, the thing that impressed me the most, personally, was when he risked his life in order to protect me.

In a move clearly intended to separate me from "my man" and thereby putting me in danger from other inmates, prison officials placed me in a unit where Federal inmates were being housed (on a contract with the BOP). Even though Big Al could receive none of the conventional benefits of representing me any more (namely, sex) because of our separation, he nonetheless let it be known that I was his girl, and if anyone messed with me they would answer to him. He did this after I had made a mess out of trying to solicit the biggest, baddest, and handsomest Federal inmate in my new unit to be "my man", and represent me. His name was Kato (or at least that was what he liked to be called), a tall and muscular half-Asian, half-black man who lived in Korea as a youth and studied Kung Fu since childhood. He was an enforcer for the Asian mafia in America (not necessary the U.S.), or at least that's what he and his "crew" claimed. Whatever he was, he was clearly a dangerous man. He practiced his Kung Fu Katas (fighting exercises) every day, but was forbidden by the institution to teach other inmates. He talked all the time about Kung Fu, and about his time in the Special Forces, and about all the special training he received. He was especially proud of a form of Kung Fu called "Praying Mantis" that he claimed to have learned while he was AWOL in Cambodia, from traveling priests who took him in to exchange styles (he taught them several of the styles he learned as a kid in exchange for being taught the Praying Mantis style). He claimed that he also taught Kung Fu in America, and he himself had learned from various masters, though he always insisted that he was not a master because of his lack of spiritual reverence, not because of his lack of skill. I believed all of it.

So, I considered having Kato as my "man" a step up from Big Al; at least that's what I thought at first. But Kato was (surprise, surprise) only interested in using me for sex (and letting his "crew" use me). It didn't take me long to figure that out and as soon as Kato made a clear breach of contract (by not defending my honor as he should have), I bravely dumped him. I say "bravely" because getting dumped by a prison queen is a hundred times worse than getting dumped by a real woman, and Kato totally did not expect me to do it. When I told him to his face that I no longer considered him as my "man", I saw that same demon flash behind his eyes that I came to know so well behind my own not much later. He would have killed me right there, if he could have gotten away with it. But instead, he ordered his "crew" to teach me a lesson on his behalf. I found out later that he was under "orders" from his mafia bosses to stay out of trouble, which is why he did not just "bitch slap" me right then and there. And that was when Big Al stepped back into the picture. But when Kato found out that "some state inmate" was speaking up for me he sent his "crew" after Big Al instead. But, what he didn't realize (and neither did I at the time) was that Big Al had a "crew", too - a much bigger "crew"! So, Kato and Big Al ended up negotiating peace terms (that amounted to an apology to me, but without reparations, from Kato for allowing his "crew" to disrespect me) down in a back room of the prison laundry (Kato's turf). I was genuinely afraid for Big Al, and warned him not to negotiate on Kato's turf. But Big Al assured me that Kato only thought it was his turf. Well, things worked out, or at least Kato and his "crew" never messed with me after that (and neither did anyone else).

For a while at least I was probably the most chaste "queen" in prison population in the whole country! Big Al and I could only see each other on the prison big yard, where we met almost every day, and spent hours, just talking, as we sat on "our throne" (a bench seat that overlooked the yard) that other inmates left open for us. He agreed to be my "man" only if I agreed to give him say about who I had sex with, and I could only have sex with people he knew well enough to know for sure that they did not have AIDS, which was almost nobody. I only had sex with one other person on one or two occasions during this time, but I won't say who, though Big Al, of course, knew.

The harassment from the prison officials kept up. As part of my transition from convict to prison queen I had quit my job in the electronics shop in order to take a job in Institutional Industries, so I could work with Big Al. He was a data entry clerk and I became a programmer in the same office. But no sooner than it took for me to establish my ability to run circles around the other so-called programmers (I single-handedly cleared out the six month backlog of dBase report requests in less than a month), I was "fired" by the institution. Not because of anything I did – the industries staff loved me since they could now request complex reports that they could never get before. But, I was fired because I "knew more about computers than the institution's go-to-guy" which made me, supposedly, a "threat to security". Of course, the real reason, again, was a thinly veiled attempt by prison officials to separate me and Big Al. Even though we weren't in the same living unit any more, our reputation as a couple (i.e. lovers) was growing stronger all the time. And that, for some reason, bothered the hell out of the prison officials. Also, around this time (1989), I was scheduled for another parole hearing.

My counselor (no longer Mr. Wheeler) assured me that it was a necessary routine hearing to reconfirm my paroleability status after having all my parole plans denied over the last two years. So, I was completely unprepared to defend myself when the board members started asking questions about my "risk to re-offend", questions they had never asked before, not even when they found me paroleable two years earlier. Dr. Sloat was at the hearing (she insisted on being there, even though my counselor tried to discourage her from appearing – apparently, she understood the real purpose of the hearing, even though I did not). But, even though she adamantly backed up her report, saying that I was a much less risk to re-offend than before, the ISRB revoked my paroleability and added the first of several more extension years to my sentence!

I would say that this was the proverbial "straw that broke the camel's back", but it was more like a ton of bricks when a straw might actually have been enough! After all my efforts over the years to straighten out my life were thwarted, by one broken promise after another by the "system" to "help me get better", and after I was betrayed by the sex offender therapist who tried to use his authority to coerce my mother into having sex with him, and after this same therapist wrote an almost completely fabricated report to the court (in order to protect himself from backlash) that caused me to get such an extreme sentence for such a juvenile crime, and after I was then repeatedly raped and assaulted by other inmates (until I learned how to protect myself) while prison officials denied my requests for protective custody, and after I did everything I could to "heal myself", even going to the prison psychologist as a last resort, and after my mother lost her house because my parole plans to help support her were denied, and long after the rest of my family had pretty much given up on trying to support me; after all that, the ISRB dropped this ton of bricks on me out of the blue.

I couldn't "go home" after all. I snapped. To say the least, I snapped. And the stress of trying to identify myself as a woman in a male institution didn't help. I had very little information about what it meant to be a transsexual and the only support I got was from my "man" and from Dr. Sloat. Many of my "friends" stopped talking to me. And most of my new "friends" only wanted one thing (need I say what?). There were times when I was so nervous about trying to appear effeminate in the prison population that it felt like there was a physical force surging through me that made me so stiff I was afraid I'd fall over. I never felt that kind of stress ever before, or ever since. Not even at my death penalty trials or hearings; not even close.

It was around this time that I also started having my first "paranoid delusions". But my rational mind, and self-education in psychology, kept me from letting the delusions take control. No matter how convincing the delusions seemed – *and they were very convincing* – I was always able to reason them away. Or, at least out of my conscious mind. Who knows what havoc they might have wrought unconsciously.

When I mentioned these delusions to Dr. Sloat, she recommended that I see the prison psychiatrist. Which I did, and he prescribed some kind of psychoactive drug. But I didn't like how the pills made me feel (like my brain was being mildly electrocuted), so I stopped taking them and rarely spoke of my delusions with anyone after that. They didn't seem to interfere with my ability to function, or at least so I thought. Even when I did talk about them I always played them down by calling them "paranoid thoughts", even though I realized they were much more than just "thoughts"; they were a part of my reality (or, a significant aspect of my overall experience at least). So, when the ISRB yanked my paroleability and added several more years to my sentence because of my attempts to understand who I was - and hence, why I was in prison (i.e. why I raped a 14-year-old boy), so that I wouldn't reoffend - yes, I snapped. I cried. I screamed. And I mourned. But, I kept it all inside.

Showing such emotions in prison was a sign of weakness, even for a queen. But Big Al saw my feelings, though at that point I stopped seeing Dr. Sloat and was never honest with a prison psych-doctor ever again. My "man" watched helplessly as all the hurt, and frustration, and betrayal, congealed at last into a dense ball of rage that I buried beneath thoughts of revenge and vindication so that I wouldn't have to feel the pain. It was the only way to make the pain go away, other than religion I suppose. But as much as I respected Big Al's faith in Allah, and as much as I myself had even come to acknowledge a conscious force much greater than myself in the universe - to me, religion was just another "delusion" that I ignored or rationalized away just like all the others. The consolation of revenge became the only source of relief I had.

When I was 17 years old sitting in Pierce county jail awaiting to be tried as an adult for raping that other boy, I wanted to die so bad that I cried for days, almost non-stop. But in lieu of picking up a razor or rigging a noose, I made a pact with myself instead. I always remembered this pact very clearly, because it let me live with what I had done. In the pact I swore to myself that no matter what happened (as a result of the charges against me) over the next several years and that no matter how much I changed as a person, or who I became, that I would never, NEVER, under any circumstance or for any reason, cause such harm to my family again. You see, I wanted to die not because of my shame, or even because of what I faced. I wanted to die because of how I hurt my family, my father, mother, sisters and my brother. For the first time in my life I realized how important my family was to me. So I swore that I would die (kill myself) before I ever did anything to hurt them again. But, when the ISRB revoked my paroleability in 1989, I realized that it was a pact that was impossible to keep. The system would not only never allow me to heal, but my mistake as a 16-year-old kid would be used to keep hurting my family for as long as I lived. And I couldn't kill myself either, because that would hurt my family even worse. So, I changed my original pact to say that I would never hurt my family directly. In other words, nieces and nephews and even "friends of the family" were all "off limits" to my "sickness". And I have always honored this version of my pact even at times when it would have been extremely easy not to. But, after 1989, when I realized that my best efforts to fix my life were a vain dream, and that I would never be allowed to stop paying for the mistake I made, I also made a new pact that the modifications to my original pact now allowed, even *demanded* in a way: I would make society pay, even if that meant I had to die in order to do so.

The purpose of my life changed at that point from repairing the damage I had caused my family (which I finally saw as impossible), to causing as much damage (pain and suffering) to society (which I blamed for not letting me heal) as possible. So now, instead of educating myself to work towards "getting better", I would from now on educate myself to work toward "getting even". In the past, my reason for living – my "pact" for life – was to heal myself and my family. My whole life centered around this effort. Even when things seemed impossibly difficult, I kept going for this hope, this goal.

In 1989, all that changed. My life now centered around a new goal, and a new "pact". From now on I would not only stop trying to "heal" but I would strive to become the "sickest sicko" alive, so I could hurt society with the very "sickness" that it would not let me escape. And, just so the reader understands: I did <u>not</u> blame the ISRB or people like Mr. Wheeler. They were just ignorant servants of "the Beast". And I did <u>not</u> blame the men who raped me at Shelton Corrections Center. They were just victims themselves, even if they didn't think so. I didn't even blame Mike Shepherd, the therapist who sexually assaulted my mother, and lied about me in his "official" report in order to protect himself. No, I blamed the entity that gave rise to all these ignorant people. I blamed the "system", which is the name I gave to the faceless masses usually called "society". I blamed no one person, or group of persons, more than I blamed society itself. I didn't even blame the "secret government" that my mind convinced me (to this day) was behind all criminal behavior and sexual perversion in society. Even if it wasn't a delusion (I still can't honestly say if it is or not), it still could not be held accountable for all of my pain and suffering, because it was "super-secret" after all. But, in my mind at least, society had to held accountable. The "system" could be hurt, if not damaged. I could at least make it cry, to feel some of the pain that it caused me and others like me. If I was never to be allowed to heal, then neither would I let "the Beast" live in peace.

With as much vehemence and emotion that I put into my first pact, I now (in 1989) swore that no matter what happened, no matter how long it took, no matter how my life changed, for better or for worse, and no matter who I became, I would make society pay. And, the only way this pact was able to ease my pain, is if I knew I would keep it. And I knew I would. And I did. <u>Not</u> because I wanted to, but because <u>I had to</u>.

(Anyone watching the videos I made even the infamous "cabin video" with the Groene children in Montana can see that I did not "want to" do what I was doing. *I had to* do it – or, at least that's what I believed until Shasta broke the "evil spell" that this "pact" had become for me).

I told Big Al: "Someday, they'll make the mistake of letting me out". He tried to warn me that it was my mistake to think that way. But I didn't listen, and it was something we never spoke about again. He named that part of me "Joe", and "Joe" and Big Al didn't like each other at all. So, when Big Al and I were together, "Joe" stayed in the dungeon I made for him in my mind. Big Al also named my feminine personality. He called her "Jazzi". He said that, sometimes, when she "took over", my whole face changed like a completely different person. A very beautiful person in his opinion also. As best as I can fathom, using the radar of hindsight, "Joe" was "Jazzi's" protector before I'd met Big Al. But "Joe" protected "Jazzi" mostly by keeping her hidden, which Dr. Sloat and Big Al convinced me was not healthy. But, after 1989, "Joe" was the one who went into hiding, and in a strange reversal of roles. "Jazzi" became "Joe's" protector. These were not "split personalities" in the clinical sense (since they were each fully aware of each other), but they were also as distinctly different from each other as any "split personality" could be. I could go on for pages about all the ways "Joe" and "Jazzi" were different. But, to keep it short: they were complete opposites in every way you can imagine. But, one thing "Joe" and "Jazzi" had in common was that they were both emotionally based creatures. Because of this, they both shared the common weakness of all emotionally based people: they were both "intellectually challenged". And that's where "Jet" came in.

Yes, Big Al identified "Jet" also, but I gave "Jet" the name I grew up with because "Jet" was the central personality that held "Joe" and "Jazzi" together. "Jet" provided the intellect and rational basis for all of "Joe" and "Jazzi's" behavior. "Jet" was also the mediator for the other personalities. He realized the importance of "Joe" and "Jazzi" because they gave his life (my life) meaning and motivation. "Jet" needed "Joe" and "Jazzi" as much as they needed him. But "Jet" was all brain and no heart. He could always think clearly, even in the most dramatic situations (such as during a murder, or even a life threatening situation). In such circumstances, "Jet" could easily push "Joe" and "Jazzi" aside and "take care of business" with no emotional "interference" from them.

You might say that "Jet" was the "psychopath", but I think it is misleading to assume he existed independent of emotion. Yes, "Jet" seemed to act and think completely without emotion, but without "Joe" and "Jazzi" (my emotional selves), "Jet" would have never had any reason or motivation to act at all. This is why I say there is no such thing as "a true psychopath" (a.k.a. "an emotionless person") like is so commonly depicted in the movies. Even the most depraved and "monstrous" people are ultimately driven by their emotions. In fact, it is only the intensity of their emotions that enables them to behave so extremely, <u>not</u> *the lack of* feelings at all.

Though, like me, like all of us to one degree or another, they have split off from their emotional selves. The only thing that makes me unique, perhaps, is that because of my intense efforts to understand my own mind (and problems), and with the help of intelligent and knowledgeable friends like Big Al and Dr. Sloat, I became aware of this "split" from my emotional selves, and thus "Joe", "Jazzi" and "Jet" were "born" into my conscious mind, rather than unconsciously like in most "normal" people. I think that if so-called "psychopaths" do share one trait in common that distinguishes them from "normal" people, then it would be a very high level of self-awareness, which allows them to act without emotion when necessary. But, if that were true, then there are an awful lot more "psychopaths" running around than we'll ever know!

So, regardless of all the philosophical ramifications, in 1989, "Jazzi" stepped into the limelight, and "Joe" retreated to his dungeon. I would no longer concern myself with "getting better" because now I accepted that I would never have a "normal" life. There was never any such a thing. Instead, my primary focus became "survival" and, to me, because I needed "Joe" to survive, and "Joe" needed to be "fed" in order to live, "survival" meant "revenge", because that was all "Joe" cared about: hurting those who hurt me. But, "survival" also meant "love", thanks to one special lady named "Jazzi". So I kept both "alive" inside of me. Alive, but completely separate, which became my bane and my "sickness". (I have been struggling since my arrest and "revelation" in 2005 to unite "Joe", "Jazzi" and "Jet" into one person by essentially "dismantling" the "walls" between them. It is a difficult and often very painful process because it forces me to learn how to live with the pain that the walls were built specifically to "protect" me from. But I've learned that, in the end, the walls come down anyway, ready or not. My goal in life presently is to be as "ready" as possible when they *do* come the rest of the way down!)

As I already mentioned, Big Al eventually got an infraction for "threatening a staff member" and, although this is considered a serious infraction, it is one that an inmate can never defend himself against because all the staff member has to say is that they "felt threatened" and <u>that</u>

defines the "offense". I've know inmates to get this infraction for just glaring at a staff member and, of course, going straight to "the hole" as a result.

In Big Al's case, he told a guard to leave him alone (i. e. stop harassing him), "or else". And that was enough to get him taken to disciplinary segregation ("the hole"), and to lose his "security points" so that he got sent to the maximum security penitentiary in Walla Walla, Washington (the other side of the state). And so the prison officials finally had their way. Big Al and I were as "separated" as any two inmates could be in the Washington state "corrections" system. We were in completely separate prisons with different security levels on opposite sides of the state. We couldn't be any more "separated" than that, or so they seemed to think. But I had different ideas.

As soon as I learned that Big Al had been set up and taken down, I came up with a simple plan to join him. I went to the prison "hobby shop" and, in front of "everyone", I climbed up a wall and across an I-beam to a small second story window in the back of the hobby shop that led into the administrative offices for Institutional Industries (were Big Al and I both once worked). It was after hours, though (in the evening), so the offices were empty and "locked up". Rumor has it that I broke into the offices in order to avenge Big Al by planting a virus "bomb" on the computers there. Actually, all I did was take off all my clothes and run around the offices naked while masturbating to fantasies of being "trained" by a bunch of inmates (this was "Jazzi" after all). I was simply enjoying the rare privacy that I had while alone in the offices.

Of course, the real reason I broke into the offices was because I knew I would be "ratted out" (by one of the inmates who saw me climb through the window), and that the resulting infraction would be serious enough to get me sent to Walla Walla, to be with Big Al. And it worked perfectly. Later that same night (after I had "had my fun" in the offices, I climbed back out through the same window and returned to my cell), the "goon squad" (a team of guards) showed up at my cell door and took me straight to the hole.

A few weeks later, I was on the "chain bus" for Walla Walla. And so began the next chapter of my adventures as a prison queen in one of the notoriously "toughest" prisons in the nation, Washington State Penitentiary.

Reflections

Sunday, March 11, 2012

My Ignorance Defines Me

Most people, methinks, define themselves according to what they think they know. But, when I was just 23 years old (in prison of course) I realized that more than anything else, my ignorance defines me.

What I don't know separates me from the universe in which I find myself more than what I know. And since ignorance separates, and knowledge joins, it is what I don't know that determines my limitations and my boundaries. And isn't that what a definition is? A description of limitations and boundaries.

Even when we think in terms of what we know, we are really only conversely experiencing what we don't know. I might think that I know my eyes are blue gray, but doesn't that just mean that I don't know how to say what color they really are? In other words, I don't know what color my eyes are at all, unless I am actually looking at them in the mirror. And then they are the color they appear, not the color of some words or even ideas I might hold in my mind.

It is thus my ignorance that I express when I believe myself to be expressing knowledge. And it is this ignorance that defines me.

Reflections

Sunday, March 25, 2012

One Choice

I have already said that as children of God it is given to us to play God by pretending to judge (condemn and glorify) other people and circumstances. But, behind our immaturity is a universal dynamic that ultimately determines our capacity to either play God or Be God. That dynamic is the result of a single choice that everything in the universe must make.

Yes, we do have free will, the freedom to choose. But, in the final analysis that freedom comes down to one, and only one, choice. It is a choice we all must make. We can choose to know the ultimate Truth, or to remain ignorant. To know the Truth is to be conscious of it. It is not a choice you make with reason or rational. To remain ignorant is to remain unconscious of the choice itself. To be unconscious of this choice is to be considered but a child of God, and to be condemned by your own ignorance and your own choice (i.e. your own judgment) to experiences that seem either random (chaotic) or determined by other pretend gods (human or otherwise).

The events in the life of such a child sometimes appear to the child as its own "choices" as well. But these are just pretend choices and their purpose is the same as all the other pretend experiences that the child of God has. We pretend to judge, pretend to suffer, pretend to love, and even pretend to die. But, as I have said, we have only one real Choice.

The Choice itself cannot be truly articulated in finite terms. Even though I have not yet attempted to expound on the actual Choice, I have already made several statements about it that inevitably imply things about the One Choice that are not quite right. Just for example, I stated that everything in the universe must make this One Choice. But the word "everything" does not truly express the nature of everything. It implies that there is more than one "thing" in the universe, which is not really true. But it is also not really true to say there is only One Thing (or God), though in some contexts this is closer to the Ultimate Truth.

The most correct expression is in regards to the duplicity or unity of the universe would be to say that it is both One and Many at the same time. But this too is not a true and correct picture, not to mention that it is also very confusing for most people, especially God's children (or perhaps more correctly, God's Child, since the many-one aspect of the universe applies to God's children-child as well).

So you can see then that the One Choice is also an infinity of choices at the same time. It cannot be grasped by any means of finite reason. You must make this choice in your "heart" as they say, not with your mind. But, it is possible to know what choice you have made, that is, to know the Ultimate Truth. This is why the mystics who have made the right choice always say that you will know when you do. But if there is any doubt or question in your heart at all, then you are still only pretending.

Be patient, the time will come for you to make the right choice. In the meantime have faith. It will only be pretend faith of course, until you have come to know the Ultimate Truth. But, you do not need to know the Ultimate Truth in order to have faith in it. And nor will having faith help you to know the Truth. But it will ease your suffering and make the games of childhood a little more tolerable. Especially as you get close to maturity and the games become more and more transparent and superficial to you.

There is nothing you can do consciously in order to facilitate your knowledge of the One Choice, any more than you can consciously make your hair grow (or not grow). People who tell you to "not sin", and "obey God", or even "believe in Christ", are pretenders who have yet to realize the choice they are making to pretend. But, at the same time, people who have made the right choice will, without conscious effort, do all of these things, and more.

The Bible does not tell us how to make the right choice (nor does the Bible itself even claim to do so). No book or person can tell you that. But the Bible, and many other books of truth, can tell you how you will know when you or someone else has made that choice. Such a person will not sin, will not lie, will love unconditionally, and will make forgiveness mode of justice. But, doing all of these things does not constitute making the right choice, or salvation for that matter.

P.S.: I'm still only pretending myself. But, I sense strongly that I am on the cusp of true understanding. I believe that I have already made the "Right Choice" at least once (when I brought Shasta home and turned myself in), but I was unable to sustain that choice (i.e. keep making the right choice). I also suspect that once I am able to make the Right Choice again, then I will probably not bother attempting to write about it. I will fully realize the futility of words, as I only partly realize now. In the meantime I continue to ignorantly hope (pretend hope?) that my words will at least help others get to the cusp as well. No words will ever take you further, they can at best only point you in the right direction.

Confessions

Thursday, March 29, 2012

What Happened In Prison – Part IV: The Queen

„I will remember, because a queen can never forget." - Juana of Castile, in The Last Queen, by: C.W. Gortner

By the time I arrived at WSP (Washington State Penitentiary in Walla Walla, Washington) in early 1990, I was a full-fledged and completely weaned prison queen. All my nervousness about being seen as queer had left me, and was replaced by the more normal social nervousness over meeting new people and adapting to a new environment.

As strange as it may seem, I was actually looking forward to Walla Walla, even though it was reputedly one of the most violent prisons in the country. I was fed up with all the petty games and attitudes from the wannabe prison (MICC), and hope WSP would be better. I had no concern at all for my safety because I was, after all, Big Al's girl and nobody messed with a fully represented queen in a real prison.

Right away as soon as I stepped off the chain-bus I knew things were going to be different. The guards actually treated me with politeness and respect. They even took me into a private area in order to strip search me out of view of the other inmates. And I could have sworn the guards themselves were looking at me lasciviously, though that was possibly just my own devious imagination at work.

From the intake processing area all the inmates from the chain-bus were taken to a temporary housing unit for a few days of observation before we would be classified for regular housing in the prison.

As we were being dressed out in the temporary unit (given clothes to replace the orange transport coveralls) an inmate I'd never met before covertly gave a full pack of cigarettes along with a message from Big Al that he would see me at mainline (in the chow hall).

I passed some of the cigarettes out to other inmates who I had befriended on the bus and they in turn passed them out to their friends. Suddenly I was very popular and it felt strange.

As a queen I had to get used to people I'd never met before talking to me as if they knew all about me. I was a celebrity of sorts since people talked about almost everything I did. For example, almost everyone I met had heard about how I „dumped" Kato, the kung fu expert and asian gang leader at MICC and „lived to tell about it". They also knew that I had broken into the furniture factory offices at McNeil Island and „planted a computer virus" in order to avenge Big Al.

Usually it was the things people „knew" about me that I didn't even know about myself that were the most interesting. Things like:

„Hey, Jazzi! I heard you turn tricks with the turn keys!"

Oh, I didn't know that.

„Hey, Jazz! I heard you got AIDS..."

Oh, really?

That AIDS rumor actually followed me all the way to Kootenai county jail in Idaho in 2005. The FBI asked my attorneys to get an HIV test for me because they „heard" that I was HIV positive from a former cellmate of mine. Ya, right. (That particular inmate used to sit on his bunk and masturbate while he watched me exercising in the cell. He was not my cellmate for very long – after I told Big Al what he was doing)

All this attention was a bit disconcerting for me at first, especially considering my so-called „antisocial" propensities. But I ultimately learned to relish it as much as anyone would, revelling in all the positive attention while ignoring the negative; usually.

I got almost no harassment at all from the other inmates. The worst insult I got came from a prison guard who waved a hot dog at me as I was going through the serving line in the chow hall to get my food one day.

„Do you like weaners?" He asked, apparently to get a laugh from the other inmates around because there weren't any other guards within earshot.

If an Inmate had been stupid enough to attempt to insult me like that I probably would have picked up one of the hot dogs off my own tray and thrown it at him while saying something like, „sure, but I like to share!"

Something like that might have been what flashed through my mind as I stopped and just glarred at him. The guard must have seen something in my eyes at that moment that frightened him, because I remember seeing the fear flash just for a moment on his face before he covered it up with a nervous laugh and a sudden order to, „keep moving!"

The fear on his face, even if just for a moment, told me he was a coward. So I dismissed him and the entire incident. By the time I got to my table, in the „blacks only" area of the chow hall, I had forgotten all about him. But he unfortunately didn't forget about me.

Later that night I was called out of the unit six dayroom and escorted by a group of three guards down into the counselor's office area; a secluded area after hours with all the lights turned off. I didn't understand why I was there until one of the guards turned on me suddenly and glowered in my face.

He said menacingly, „If you ever look at me like that again I'll find a way to mess you up!" (an exact quote by the way)

It took me a full second or two to realize that I was being threatened. And then another second or two to figure out who the guard was and why he was threatening me.

„Oh!" I said „You're that guard from the kitchen!" I was smiling at my own realization.

Yes, smiling. I thought the threat was funny because it was so pathetically childish. I actually chuckled, as I said, „Is that all you want?"

The guard said, „Yah, just remember what I said". Then he ordered me to return to the unit dayroom unescorted. So, I turned and started to leave.

But, as I walked away I couldn't resist a parting shot, I said over my shoulder, „You don't know who you're messing with; I'm not some duck..."

...that you can intimidate, is what I'd meant to say. But, before I could finish the guard cut me off by yelling at me – he had just gotten exactly what he wanted from me all along; a „threat". In that „authoritative command" voice, that cowards like him love, he screamed, „Lock up! Now!"

I had fallen for the same kind of trap that got Big Al shipped out of MICC. It's an easy trap to fall into, even if you know about it. Fortunately I was already in a maximum security prison so I couldn't be shipped out. But I could go to the hole, and that's exactly what happened. I returned to my cell and after a few minutes the goon-squad arrived, and cuffed me up to take me to segregation. The guard from the kitchen was with them and kept making comments that were intended to get me to „resist". But I knew better than to give him a chance to „goon" me also. (Getting „gooned" is prison slang for getting beat up by the guards. All they need is the smallest excuse in order to make the paperwork look good and then they can beat you up all they want. But they need that excuse, however small, before they can get away with it. And don't think for a moment that it's just a few „corrupt" guards that do this. It's part of how „the system" works, and just one of the hypocritical aspects that made me hate it so much. Rodney King knows what I'm talking about!)

At the disciplinary hearing the guard from the kitchen denied waving the hot dog at me and threatening me, of course. And so, more evidence of my „antisocial" behavior in prison was added to my official record.

And that was the story of the worst insult I received. But the greatest compliment came from a young inmate in the unit six shower room.

The showers were only open for a couple of hours each evening after mainline (chow). It is a single large tiled room with about 25 or 30, or so, shower heads spraying water from the walls. No stalls, of course, and a guard booth right there in the shower so there'd be no funny business. There was always a crowd in the showers.

I used to usually go with Big Al as my „escort", more for symbolism than because there was any real danger from other inmates. Sometimes I'd even go by myself, but I liked having my „man" with me.

I'd always be sure to prepare ahead of time by putting on a pair of jocky underpants in a way that allowed me to keep my „embarrassment" tucked up between my legs in the shower, with my testicles actually held up inside the abdomen.

I wore these „panties", as I called them, for the whole time that I was in the shower, and would discretely wash under them to get myself clean.

So, anyway, one day, as I was drying off and getting ready to leave the shower room, a young inmate standing next to me who was also just getting out of the shower, suddenly asked me a question completely out of the blue.

Shyly, he asked, „Do they let you take female hormones here?"

I answered in my girliest voice, „I wish!"

Then I wondered why he would ask a question like that. I didn't know him and have never spoken to him before. And I thought it was obvious, by how flat chested I was, that I'd never used female hormones. So, out of curiosity I asked him, in turn, „Why do you ask?"

Without hesitation he answered, „Because you look so much like a real woman with no clothes on". And then he quickly moved away, apparently embarrassed by his own comment.

It was obvious that he did not intend to flatter me. I could have kissed him right there in the shower, if he hadn't run away so quick. To this day I can think of no time that I was ever more proud of how my body looked.

I just realized that I forgot to tell about how I got moved into the same unit, and even the same cell, with Big Al.

At first they put me in a special unit that was still in general population but had only one-man cells. It was in that unit that I got to meet and know a legendary prison queen named Star.

There's really not much to tell about my meeting Star, except that she was past her girly prime and no longer bothered to even try to appear effeminate, though everyone still called her Star and refered to her in the feminine.

In her day Star was a legend. Not for her good looks (she was too big and muscular to ever pass for a real girl) but because of her principles – you couldn't be a more „solid" convict than Star was – and her exploits.

Once Star grabbed a guard and put a shank to his throat and paraded him around the prison demanding „justice" for some violation of her principles. (Perhaps he made the mistake of waving a hot dog at her provocatively!)

Needless to say, Star was one of those people who was never going to get out of prison. But I loved and respected her as a human being all the same. She never once ever tried to disrespect me and she taught me a lot about what it was like to be a queen in the „old days".

She befriended me more out of love and respect for Big Al than for me, I suppose. But that was because she knew that if Big Al respected me (and he did) then that meant she should too. So she did.

Well, as much as I appreciated being in the same unit with a legend (I'd heard a lot about Star long before I ever got to Walla Walla) the only unit I wanted to be in was the one Big Al was in. So, the first chance I got I requested to be moved to Six Wing.

That chance came at my first „unit team" hearing about one month after arriving at WSP. They asked me about how I intended to protect myself from other inmates and I told them that I had „a friend" who would make sure nobody messed with me.

Then they asked, „What if someone bigger than your friend comes along?"

And I looked them straight in the eye, and said, „There is no one bigger than my friend". And I meant it, though I was thinking more about Big Al's reputation than the size of his arms.

The move was not only approved, but they actually moved me directly into Big Al's cell, even though I never once told them who „my friend" was. Like I said, everyone knew I was Big Al's girl!

So, sans the first month, the entire time I was in WSP I lived with Big Al. We had a four-man cell all to ourselves for almost the entire time, with only a few brief interruptions – one of which I've already mentioned (the masturbator who thought I had AIDS).

Our cell was in the middle if a bottom tier and directly in front of a guard both. But the guard both was empty and locked up every night after lock down at nine o'clock. So, the guard both never seriously interfered with our love making at all.

And we certainly made love. Almost every night after lockdown, I would start by giving Big Al a therapeutic back rub (his huge muscles almost demanded to be massaged) that would always end up being a sensual back rub. I'd rub his back before we had sex, and he'd rub mine afterwards, if I wanted him too. But usually I'd be so wore out that all I wanted to do was climb into my own bunk and go to sleep (or masturbate alone, see below).

In case you're wondering how two people with male „equipment" can make love as a man and a woman, then let me tell you. After Big Al was good and relaxed from me rubbing his back (actually, shoulders and arms mostly) he would roll over onto his back and I'd spend some time working on his chest and arms from the front.

I'd usually be either naked with my penis out of site between my legs or wearing a sexy pair of women's panties (I had several pair that were more or less homage gifts from another inmates, who were lucky if they ever even got to see me wearing them). So Big Al would be at full attention in anticipation of what was coming by this time.

After working his front muscles for a while I'd begin massaging his legs and groin area, then bend over and begin giving him a dick massage with my tongue and lips. This was more for his pleasure than mine though. I got my pleasure soon enough.

Then after we were both so hot with anticipation that we could hardly contain ourselves, I would lay down next to him with my back to his front, „spoon" style and we'd entangle our legs together in a special way that we both agreed was „the best way", then I'd reach back and guide his manhood into my „pussy".

And he would fuck the hell out of me. But not violently, just passionately. All the time kissing on my neck, my shoulders and even my ear. I would also frequently twist my upper body around, while he was still buried deep up inside of me, so we could kiss, deep and wet, on the mouth.

We'd fuck like this for up to a half an hour, sometimes even more and then Big Al would release inside of me, usually in the midst of a deep passionate kiss, which was how I liked it. And then we'd sometimes just lay together while he went semi-soft with his dick still inside my ass, enjoying the profound intimacy of it. This was the human intimacy that the „system" had tried to rob from both of us, but which we defiantly stole back every night we could.

As for my own orgasm; I would usually wait until after I'd climbed into my own bunk then slowly stroke myself to an orgasm while I could still „feel" Big Al inside of me. This bothered Big Al because he wanted to be sure that I was being satisfied too, and he always would assure me that he didn't mind if I masturbated while we were together. But, he himself would never touch me „down there". I think it was because he wouldn't touch me there that I preferred to wait to pleasure myself alone. I wanted to be his woman, and jacking off in front of a man just didn't „feel right". So, I preferred to do it alone.

These were my happiest days in prison, easily. Big Al and I shared a special status in WSP that most staff and inmates seemed to respect. It was as though everyone knew what it was we were „stealing back" from the system and honored our courage for doing so.

It took courage because the one thing the „system" tries to destroy more than any other is the human spirit. So Big Al and I were making ourselves targets by simply daring to express our love for each other out in the open.

We were together as much as we could be, on the yard, in the gym, in the chow hall. And most people seemed to appreciate what we represented. Even the guards (usually) and especially the higher ranking guards (sgts. and lts.) who had been around in the „old days", seemed to really understand the value of what Big Al and I stood for. Which is why I was moved directly into Big Al's cell, and why, unlike at MICC, we were seldom harassed as a couple.

Big Al would go to work during the day out in the Industries administration offices (they'd hired him right away because of his experience – and connections no doubt – in Industries at MICC). So we'd always have money to keep extra food and cigarettes in our cell (I didn't quit smoking until I got out to WWCC about a year later). I even kept track of big Al's money (or „finances" if you can call an inmate account that) since I had so little „money" of my own.

I did not have to work because I have a „bad back" (I have a very slight curve in my spine, a.k.a. scoliosis, that can only be seen by measuring an x-ray. It never really bothers me, but it makes a great excuse for getting out of work in prison). So, I'd stay in the cell and read, or watch TV. Or, I'd go to the library or big yard for something to do. I also attended weekly Yoga classes and an occasional college course if I saw one that interested me on the school schedule.

It was a stress free existence and with my „man" always by the side it was as close to freedom as anyone will ever get in prison. Maybe even freer in a way than what many people have outside of prison.

But I was only inside WSP (the actual penitentiary) for a little more than a year before I'd gotten enough security points back to be transfered to a „medium security" prison again. Big Al took longer to get his security points back for some reason, but I don't remember why.

So, I got transferred by myself to WWCC, which is literally right next door to WSP, though in a completely separate compound. Big Al and I decided to accept this temporary separation because we knew it would only be for a few months.

Because WWCC was medium security instead of max, I had a few more privileges and a little more freedom (not much) than inside WSP. But, without Big Al around, I also had more time on my hands (alone time), so my deviant fantasies came back (which had all but left me while I was with Big Al, that is unless you consider transexuality to be „deviant"). I had no real interest in having sex with other inmates, since none could approach what I had with Big Al. So my fantasies turned once more to children, only this time I didn't even try to resist them. I had no reason to.

And since I couldn't just stay in my cell and masturbate all day, I ended up enrolling in school full time (at WWCC I was required to „program" in one was or another, „bad back" or not). They had much better college level course offerings from the local community college. So I started work on an AA in general studies and got straight 'A's" and on the Dean's list frequently.

The only thing interesting that happened during this alone time (without Big Al) was that I managed to catch a mouse in my cell with a homemade „humane" mouse trap, that actually worked. I had made it out of two one-pint ice cream containers, a rubber band and a paperclip. I was proud of this feat, though the mouse soon escaped to be never seen again. Apparently some mice at least can learn quicker than most humans.

Oh, I also saw a full grown tomcat attempting to mount a very young kitten just outside my cell window once. I thought that was interesting; a child molesting cat, in prison! Hmmm, go figure that one out!

Westly Allen Dodd, a man convicted for raping and murdering young boys, was hanged inside WSP while I was at WWCC. The execution was meant to send a „message" to other would be child-killers; like me. I got the message all right, loud and clear. But I don't think it was the one I was supposed to get. The execution only strengthened my resolve to get even with the

"System".

After about six months Big Al got moved out to WWCC and directly into my cell. I'd been living alone with no cellmate until Big Al came... and came... and came... (joke).

While I was still inside WSP I had taken out a free personal ad in the SGN (Seattle Gay News) and started writing and occasionally calling the men who answered my ad. That's how I met Dave.

Dave drove across the state (from Seattle) to visit me for the first time while I was at WWCC. We became fast friends.

Dave ended up hiring an attorney to „look into my case". The attorney began reviewing my prison records and basically learned what I already knew; I was being shafted by the system.

So the attorney started writing some letters to the ISRB, to basically let them know that he was representing me and that they had better start obeying their own directives (i. e. the law).

With the help of letters written to the ISRB by the attorney that my new friend, Dave, hired, I was finally found parolable again in the Summer of '93. But, this time there was a catch. I had to "map out" before my parole. That meant that there was a list of supposedly progressive steps to more freedom, and programs to prepare my for the streets, that I had to take before actually being paroled.

Needless to say, it was years yet before I get paroled. And even then it took many more letters and actual litigation (to procure an order from a judge) before the ISRB consented to my release. In the mean time I was being transported (i.e. shipped) all over the state from one institution to another, supposedly to fulfill my "map" requirements.

This "merry-go-round" ride (a tactic they use to try to keep inmates from being able to file litigation) kept me from completing the one program that would have really helped after I got out. I was on my last semester of classes needed to complete an A.A. degree in General Studies when the merry-go-round ride started. So, it didn't keep me from filing litigation (Dave's lawyer was doing that for me), but it did keep me from finishing the three-credit English class I needed to get my degree. And, it also interrupted the Spanish II class I was taking, which would have been directly transferable toward a university degree years later. With those Spanish credits I would have a B.A. in Computer Science today. But, instead I had to go for a B.S. degree instead which took more time (and money, of course). Apparently their "map" program - slash, merry-go-round - was more important.

And so began the next chapter of my prison adventure, where I managed to fight my way out at last, with the help of a friend on the outside, a lawyer, and no small deception.

Reflections

Sunday, April 1, 2012

The Crime Of Punishment

The threat of punishment has never been, nor ever will be, a significant deterrent to crime. The primary criminal deterent has always been social consciousness. And, the primary cause of crime has always been the lack of social consciousness.

The threat of punishment works to undermine social consciousness, and by doing so only ends up promoting the very behavior it purports to deter.

Social consciousness can be instilled in a person's character at any age under proper conditions, though it is most commonly instilled during childhood. In order to instill social consciousness the person's personal experiences must reflect an ability to trust social mechanisms and social structure.

The lack of social consciousness is always caused by social experiences that demonstrate a lack of benefit to the individual while at the same time demanding personal sacrifice and suffering.

The primary benefit of a healthy social system is a sense of belonging and purpose. It is the perceived absence of this benefit that leads directly to criminal behavior. This is also the very first thing that is forcefully and thoroughly stripped from a person as soon as they have any encounter with the so-called Correctional System as an offender. It should be no wonder at all that such people, even if they had a relatively intact social consciousness going into the "System", rarely have any social consciousness at all coming out of the System.

The only way to restore a person's sense of social consciousness is to restore their faith in the social system. Punishment does the exact opposite. Criminals rarely believe that they deserve to be punished. (Recently corrections officials have figured out that the offenders who genuinely believe their punishment was deserved are far less likely to re-offend. The officials don't seem to realize that this is a cause, not an indicator. The criminal behavior itself is an indicator of the more serious problem of lost social function.)

Punishing the criminal is tantamount to killing the messenger. It doesn't solve anything and usually only makes the problem worse. The only solution (and one that has been proven to work) is to develop a system that promotes, instead of destroys, social consciousness. But that would diminish the need for the government's power, and we couldn't let that happen, could we?

Reflections

Monday, April 9, 2012

Video Evidence In The Press

In a video that was displayed as evidence for the prosecution during my Federal sentencing trial over two years ago, I told Shasta that her wish for "a million-billion dollars" was impractical and asked her why she didn't wish for me to take her home instead. We were making wishes and writing them on a piece of wood that we would then burn so that the wishes would be carried to the astral plane for consideration. Shasta and Dylan both wished for money, and then Shasta wished for jewelry and Dylan wished for a fancy car. I wished for forgiveness.

After I questioned why neither of them wished to go home Shasta quickly added, "Oh, ya! And I wish to go home too!", at which point I said, "At least I wished for something I might get..."

In the video, also at the time it was made, it was clear that I was admonishing Shasta for her first wish (for money and jewelry), not the one (to go home) that she added after I prompted her. And yet when the media reported on this video, on two different local news stations and in the papers, they all reported falsely that my comment, “At least I wished for something I might get...” was directed towards Shasta's third wish, “to go home”.

The intention of this misinformation by the press was obvious. It was to make me seem as cold-blooded and cruel as they could, even though in the video I was being fatherly and kind at the time, and the children were both clearly under no duress. I'm not denying the cruelty of what I did to these children. I'm simply observing that in this particular video no cruelty was evident. Several people who watched this video said that if they didn't know the children had been kidnapped they would have thought it was a video of an ordinary family camping trip. And yet the news media chose to portray a fabricated misconstruction of the events depicted in the video.

And, what's even more interesting is that not just one media outlet chose to run this misinformation. As far as I could tell, they all did! (At least the four sources that I saw for myself – two TV news broadcasts and two newspapers, one local, and one from Spokane). And it wasn't as if all these news sources themselves had the same source. There were several reporters in the courtroom from different agencies. And yet they all reported the same misinformation about this video!

Why? The paranois me wants to scream, “conspiracy!” But the more practical me realizes that the truth is probably even scarier than that. The technical term, I have since learned, for this kind of media distortion is called, “framing”. The idea is to portray the information in “packages” that the viewers expect. How information is packaged (or framed) for viewing is a part of the consumer culture. It allows information to be distributed in a convenient form. If something doesn't “fit” inside the “frame”, such as a serial killer behaving as a compassionate person, then the extraneous information is “shaped” to fit, as it was in the case of my comment in the evidence video.

I site only one specific example of media framing in this blog post. But every story you see, in fact, ever piece of information you see in the media, is framed one way or another. This framing distorts public perception so severely that it allows serious misperceptions to be regularly propagated. Society in general takes certain “frameworks” for granted, such as “sex offenders are less human” or “terrorist are irrational fanatics”, in spite of clear evidence that indicates otherwise. These false presumptions lead to distorted decisions that end up causing a lot of people to suffer unnecessarily. They also – coincidentally I'm sure – produce a greater need for authority, in order to maintain social order.

Of course there are numerous well reputed books written on this topic (e.g. Using Murder: The Social Construction os Serial Homicide, see “Booklist” linkon the upper right of this page), so there is no need for me to expound on it here. I just wanted to shed a little light on it in the context of my own experience; which is what this blog is about. In my case alone I have seen so much distortion of information that I do not consider my “public image” to have anything to do with me at all. Joseph E. Duncan III is a media monster, not a person at all, and certainly not me! My hope is that this blog will help anyone interested in the real person behind the name to see that I am no more, and no less, than a human being. Yes, I have done extraordinarily terrible things. But, nothing I have ever done, despite how my actions have been packaged and sold by the media, has ever been outside the range of human behavior; not even close.

I'm not saying what I did is somehow acceptable; it is not. But it is human, and the more we deny this (the more we "buy" what the popular media is selling) the more we allow this kind of destructive behavior to continue, and of course, the more we need "authorities" to "protect" us (which is another false framework sold to us by the media because they profit tremendously from it).

Reflections

Sunday, April 15, 2012

What Words Will Never Know

I have suggested in this blog that at some point in your life you may realize that you are God. But I think it is important to understand that when this event occures you will probably not actually think, "Oh, I am God!"

Actually, if you think anything at all it will likely be something relatively silly, like, "Oh, the sky is really blue!" or "My gosh, I'm here!". What you actually think will not by any means express the true realization that you have, not even if you spend the rest of your life writing down what you think about it (as I seem to be doing). :(

When it happened to me the only thing I thought was something like, "I'm not afraid anymore!" (I don't really remember my actual thoughts when it happened, but I do remember that I kept repeating those words out loud). At the time I was on the side of a small mountain in the Montana wilderness with a little girl I had kidnapped and intended to kill. The actual realization I speak of came as I was standing nude in the forest with a large rock poised over my head in my hands that I was about to use to crush the skull of the naked and blindfolded little girl as she stood in front of me.

When the realization hit me – and it had a distinct emotional impact that was anything but "peaceful" - I suddenly turned and threw the rock off into the trees as I let out a primal scream of sheer terror! I had realized, without words, what I had been running from realizing for almost all my life.

I realized, as I have just said, that I am God! And, at that moment, and for many hours hence, I stopped PRETENDING to be god, and for the first time in my life I took responsibility for BEING God.

Of course this is just one way of trying (and failing) to express something that I know can never be expressed, at least not with mere words (though my life and choices I have made since that moment on the mountain have become a form of expression in themselves of what actually happened, but this form requires a lot of intuition to even "hear", much less understand). I could also say (and have) that I realized that I was directly responsible for everything that was happening (and had ever happened) to me. It doesn't sound as psychotic when I put it that way, but the meaning is the same. In fact, almost everything I have written in this blog has in one form or another been an expression of the realization I had at that single moment on the mountain.

It was not as "peaceful" as some say such a realization should be. And because of this it took me a long time to correctly articulate what it was that I had realized. Not to mention that by the time I was arrested in Cour d'Alene, Idaho, many hours later, I was already beginning to lose touch with what I had realized. I was quickly slipping back down into the muck of my own ignorance that I had somehow lifted myself out of long enough to bring the girl home and let myself get caught.

It has taken me over five years to work my way, slowly and painfully, back up out of that muck to the point where I can at least write these words, if not fully re-embrace that realization of Godhood itself.

I have also come to suspect that perhaps the reason the experience of "enlightenment" was not a peaceful one for me was because I was not ready for it. I was still not mature enough for such a powerful experience. In a sense, it was a premature birth of sorts, and I was fortunate enough to be able to crawl (almost literally) back into the safety and comfort, that the womb of deception provides, before my premature "heart" gave out from the stress of pumping harder than it was ready to.

But, as I always say, I don't know. I probably won't know until I am born once more into the light and what I now believe to be the REAL WORLD. Until then I will keep spouting from the depths of my ignorance, knowing it is not someplace I will remain forever. Someday, I will realize once more that I Am God, and I hope the next time it happens I can leave all words and thoughts peacefully behind.

P.S. When I said that I threw the rock down in terror, I meant in terror of the Truth. But when I started repeating, "I'm not afraid anymore!" I meant I was not afraid of "them" (i.e. the system).

Dreams

Monday, April 16, 2012

Tent City Paradise Dream

I just awoke from another one of my future-paradise-world dreams. The last words I remember from the dream, just before the guards here woke me up for breakfast, were, „We are here to learn about each other and to understand each other so we can live together". It was one of those lengthy and complex dreams that seemed to traverse several different dream worlds in one incongruous but continuous sequence. It seemed to begin with me living in a friend's house with his family. But, they sent me on an errand and when I went to get the family car it was gone. Even the bicycle that I used was missing. I realized that the family wanted me to leave and not come back, it seems I had over stayed my welcome. So, I left on foot and walked away through a suburban neighborhood, not sure of where I was going to. I decided to head in the general direction of where I thought downtown would be. But, that required me to head into some woods. I followed a foot path for awhile that went along the top of a steep hill covered with trees. Then I came to a large old tree that leaned out over the hill. I leaned on the tree to keep from falling down the hill, but my weight was enough to cause it to come crashing down. It almost landed on a man who appeared to be working in the woods (a ranger?), but just missed him. It then became apparent that the man was there for me. He had come from the future (or perhaps just some other world) to get me and one other person to come back to his world with him, where we were needed for some important reason. The other person was a good looking young man, but he seemed confused and not sure what was happening (as though, perhaps, he himself were having a dream in which he was only half conscious). The man from the future embraced both of us with something on his arms that caused our connection to the world we were in to weaken, so that we could then walk away from it. It was as though we could walk fast forward in time, and even though we passed by other people, they were all motionless, frozen in time if you will. We left the woods, to a paved plaza, then a large hall. I asked the traveler if I could stop to see my mother. He said it was normally against the rules, but since she was nearby I could go see her (to say good-bye?). My mother (apparently) lived in a hospital (retirement home?) but after climbing a broad and long stair-case to get to her room, she wasn't there. Some other old people told me she had moved. So I went back down the stairs to meet back up with the traveler, only now it was just him and me. The other young man was gone (perhaps already in the „future"). The next thing I remember is being inside a large steel (or perhaps iron?) ball with the traveler. The ball clanked loudly as it rolled with us inside of it, but we remained stationary. Then it stopped, unexpectedly according to the traveler. We had not yet arrived at our destination. So we both got out to see what the problem was. We were stopped in a large wheat field, and there were several intelligent harvesting machine/robots blocking our path. The traveler spoke to the machines and told them that we had priority and that they had to let us pass. But, the machines disagreed claiming that the harvest had priority (was it possible that we were the „crop" being harvested? Maybe). We had to make a run for it, though I'm not sure if we were escaping from the harvesters or just trying to get past them a to a wall at the edge of the field. As we ran, the harvesters started throwing parts of their machines at us. We made it to the wall, which had an opening that opened into a courtyard. But now there was a female with us who I knew, somehow, to be my girlfriend. I did not question her presence, as though she had been with us all along (was she the handsome young man from earlier?). The traveler had a (magic?) liquid that he used to help us escape the harvesters. But, the liquid turned him into an egotistical demi-god and he stopped trying to help me and my girlfriend and started trying to use the power the liquid gave him to impose his will upon the harvesters, perhaps unsuccessfully because I did not see him anymore after that. But, my girlfriend had some of the liquid too, and now she wanted to use it to scale a wall that kept us in the courtyard. Our only way out seemed to be up. But, I warned her it was dangerous to use the liquid if you were not ready for its power. She used it anyway. For a moment I became her. I felt the liquid taking effect inside of her/me. It arose like a blissful emotion, the erupted as a song that seemed to come down from the sky so that the entire world could hear it. It was a song of pure emotional energy taking on the form of music; a love song, divine, pure, innocent, love. It was a song that had power and those who could hear it were summoned to yet another world. I felt her/me rise up into the air, carried by the music, to that new world. Then I was just me again. My girlfriend's presence was no more, as if she had never been there. I found myself in a chamber filled with ten foot high tents, shaped like those domed changing tents you see on beaches sometimes, only bigger. There were others, all of whom I knew had been summoned here like me. We were all walking past the tents, and into a large auditorium. There were people everywhere, a crowd, all talking, asking each other questions, like, „Who are you?" „Where did you come from?" „Why are we here?" Then there were some announcements over some unseen PA system. We were told that we had each been chosen for a specific reason that made each of us unique in our ability to contribute to a new society that we would build together. The announcement mentioned gays, people with different religious backgrounds, different technical experts and even a „multiple murderer", which it seemed everyone knew meant me. But, no one reacted negatively to the fact that I had killed people. They seemed to understand that I was not a danger here in this world, and somehow my past gave me some trait or traits that made me important to this new community. When the announcements finished, I went back to the area where the tents were. This is where we would sleep, and engage in „intimate forms of communication" with each other (sex, for just one example). I found a tent that had one lavender and two yellow five inch dots over the entrance. I knew this was to be my tent and that I would be sharing it with a couple of gay men, who were already inside when I entered myself. After I entered, the tent spoke to us. It said, „We are here to learn about each other and to understand each other so we can live together”. This same message was repeated in all the other tents as well, as soon as all its respective occupants were present. That's as far as this dream went before I was awakened by the prison guards for breakfast. But, somehow I don't think it really ended, but somehow just continued without me (this me).

Reflections

Sunday, April 22, 2012

Last Laugh

I wish that you could see me
Right here before your eyes
I wish that you could be me
'Cause then you'd realize

The blackest nights that we flee
Only dream of blacker lies
Loathing we should be free
Lights in darkened skies

I wish that you could see me
In there behind your eyes
Perhaps then you could be me
And laugh at death's goodbyes

Reflections

Sunday, April 29, 2012

It Always Comes Back To Fear

Fear is the primary ingredient for hate. We cannot hate without it. The secondary ingredient is ignorance (sic) a.k.a ignorance. All other ingredients contribute to the flavor of hate, but not to its substance.

I have found through close personal introspection that every time I get angry (a clear symptom of hate), if I look behind the facade of reasons for my anger I will consistently find fear lurking in the subconscious shadows of my mind.

Reasons are the spices that flavor our hate, but they always only serve to mask the putrid flavor of raw fear and rank ignorance. Our capacity to reason has become our bane. It too easily allows us to live in a delusional world, where ravenous monsters of our own creation exacerbate the vast cesspool of reasons we need to spice up our hatred into its many palatable forms; outrage, indignation, irritation, frustration; even lust and desire.

But reasoning, as powerful as it seems for solving our problems, cannot see past its own creations to the very core of its own existence. Reason can not grasp the formless reality of the source of our being. And yet, only by recognizing this source can we overcome our fear, and our ignorance.

Yet, perhaps overcoming fear does not mean being rid of it! Maybe we need fear, and even the various forms of hatred that it substantiates, in order to live life as we know it. Which is to say that without fear and ignorance, there might not be a world for us to live in. The entire universe as we know it could merely be an illusion that must be sustained by a balance between faith and fear, knowledge and ignorance, love and hate.

By overcoming our fear we put it „beneath our feet", compelling it to serve us rather than rule us. This is the message of the Bible, the „Gospel" that saves. It is the knowledge of eternal truth that brings salvation and infinite peace.

But you cannot overcome fear with reason. Reason is fear's invention. Fear is the ultimate master of reason and so reason can never be used to overcome fear. Fear will even deceive us into believing that we can defeat it with reason. This is the fallacy of nearly all worldly religions; they seek to justify their beliefs, and to destroy fear (i. e. „evil") rather than to overcome it.

Fear knows it cannot be destroyed. Fear itself fears only being overcome, and forced to submit to the will of „God" as expressed through women and men. It also knows that it can never be overcome with reason. That is why it has established so many belief systems that seek to either „destroy evil" or otherwise overcome evil with reason.

Only faith can overcome fear. You cannot fight it, you must release it.

We use faith to control our fear, not destroy it.

Reflections

Tuesday, May 1, 2012

People Like Me

As long as society continues to demonize people like me there will continue to be people like me. I am a product of society's fear. As long as fear is allowed to dominate, people who spread fear will thrive. And, it does not matter from which side of the system they spread fear from, the result is always the same; people like me.

Reflections

Tuesday, May 1, 2012

Release Day

Ignorant fear mongers will do doubt claim that by referring to my execution as a release day I am merely denying the reality of my circumstances. But, whose reality am I denying? In my reality, which is to say, in my experience, death is no more than another step in life. By calling it a release I am denying nothing, but embracing death's true form by using a term better suited to its purpose and effect. For those who have never been to the edge of the world, a world with edges is all they know. And, for those who have never been to the edge of life, a life with death is all they know. It is only this deluded reality that I reject by calling death what it more truly is: a release, and an opportunity to move on with life!

Reflections

Sunday, May 6, 2012

The Right To Be Wrong

I have said that it was the realization that what I was doing was NOT wrong that caused me to stop killing and turn myself in. But this is not entirely true, or at least, it gives an impression that is not entirely true. So, let me contradict myself a bit, so I can make myself a little more clear. What I should have said was that I realized that what I was doing (i.e. raping and murdering children) was not wrong IN THE WAY THAT I THOUGHT IT WAS WRONG at the time. But it certainly was wrong in another way that I previously did not suspect, and I "realized" this at the same time as well. It was not wrong because it was perverse, or unnatural, or morally corrupt. I needed it to be wrong in those ways in order to justify what I was doing. Only if what I was doing was an affront to "human decency" would my actions deliver the blow they were intended to deliver to the heart of The Beast that I thought was my mortal enemy. I needed my crimes to be socially condemned in order for them to be justified. I realize that the concept that social condemnation directly attributes to anti-social behavior is a difficult one for most people to grasp. So, I won't even try to expound on it here, since others far more astute than I have already done so many times in numerous books. But, the converse realization. That what I was doing WAS wrong in another unexpected way, is much simpler to express. I realized that I had no right to impose my beliefs (or my "trip" as Timothy Leary would say) onto other people! This is such a simple and basic truth that it seems so completely obvious once you realize it. And yet it is also the easiest truth to rationalize away, as most of us do, one way or another. So, that's what I realized was "wrong" about what I was doing. But, I should note that nothing is ever "wrong" in any absolute sense. I realize now that it is only possible for me to know what is "wrong" for me, and me alone. That is why the above realization - that I must not impose my "trip" on others - is so important. Because I cannot possibly know what is "wrong" for someone else. But, that's essentially just saying the same thing; we all have the right to be wrong ourselves, but not the right (or ability) to judge wrong in others.

Reflections

Sunday, May 13, 2012

How Intelligent Are We?

What if everything we think of as human intelligence is not really intelligent at all? What if we turn out to be one of the most ignorant species on our planet? Think about it. Isn't intelligence ultimately a measure of our ability to understand our environment and then use said understanding to propagate our existence? If so, then clearly humans are pretty dumb after all. We are destroying this planet with a voraciousness rivaled in nature only by malignant cancer. How intelligent is that?

Dreams

Tuesday, May 15, 2012

Curiouser and Curiouser Dream

I dreamed last night that I was a modern American soldier stationed in a foreign country. We were there to provide social support serviced (food, shelter, and some semblance of order) to the people who were in a "region of unrest". Our squad received orders to prepare for an attack from guerilla forces near-by, but we were only armed with mock weapons. The military apparently did not expect that we would need to actually fight. Our job was to protect the locals. So, we gathered them together in a community hall where we could defend them easier. At the gathering there were benches arranged like pews in a church for people to sit on. I took a seat in the front pew. While I was seated a young boy motioned for me to hold him the way children do. So, without thinking anything about it I picked him up and set him on one leg and held him with one arm in an assuring manner. After holding the boy innocently for a few minutes I remembered that the other people around me knew I was a child sex "offender", and I became slightly self conscious about it. But I also realized that the boy needed the reassurance of being held by an adult. And since I had no sexual interest in the boy at the time I decided his need was more important than my discomfort. A few minutes later everyone in the room stood up to begin a procession line to receive a portion of food (one bite of scrambled eggs). When I stood up I set the boy on his own feet and he wondered away, apparently satiated for now. The woman next to me was tending to a three-year-old little girl. The woman asked me to watch the girl while she excused herself to the bathroom. I said I would, and let the child hold onto my pant leg while I continued to monitor the progress of the food line. The little girl did not seem frightened or uncomfortable, so I did not pay her much attention since she did not seem to need it. A moment later the little girl apparently became curious about the difference between a man and a woman, as she began touching my privates on the outside of my pants. At first I did not pay her any attention because I did not realize her attention and touches were deliberate. But then she grabbed me out right and began trying to determine what I had between my legs. At that point I gently removed her hands and calmly told her that it was not appropriate behavior, which seemed to satisfy her. What I found most interesting about this dream is that I did not feel "judged" for being a "sex offender" even though everyone in the dream knew about my past. It was this lack of feeling judged that allowed me to respond appropriately to the child, instead of trying to take advantage of her natural curiosity.

Confessions

Wednesday, May 16, 2012

Nine Lives And An Evil Monster

When I was living in Fargo I once saw a cat get hit by a careless taxi driver while I was on my way home from a movie with a lady-friend. The incident took place on a residential street, with no other traffic. The cab obviously did not try to avoid hitting the cat, and then afterwards didn't even slow down, much less stop to see if the cat was okay. My reaction was to immediately slam on my brakes, even though I was not the one who hit the cat, and I tried to jump out of my car to help so quickly that I got tangled by the seat belt, which I had forgotten to unfasten. When I finally managed to get to the cat laying in the middle of the road it was still trying to run, even though its head was completely caved in and one eye was hanging by the nerve outside its socket. Needless to say, for all its effort, the poor cat only managed to move its legs in jerky sporadic motions, as if it were trying to run in its sleep. My lady-friend, Joni, was soon approaching from the other side of the car, and when I heard her ask if the cat was okay I bid her desperately to stay away, knowing she was a cat lover too, like me. I didn't want her to see the terror of what I was seeing. I asked Joni to get an old towel out of the trunk of my car, which I then used to wrap the cat up and carry it on the side of the road. By that time the cat had stopped trying to run, but I could tell that it still labored to breath for several minutes more. I cried silently to myself as I waited with my hand on the cat's fir for it to stop breathing. I wanted to comfort it, and contemplated breaking its neck in order to end its misery. But, fortunately, the cat stopped breathing on its own before I could even figure out the logistics of doing so. I then picked up the dead cat and carried it back to my car, where I placed it, still wrapped in the old towel, into the trunk. When Joni asked me what I was doing with the cat off to the side of the road, I told her that I was just waiting for it to die. In truth, I didn't want her to see that I was crying. We ended up taking the cat to a small strip of woods next to a cemetery for people, where we buried the cat, towel and all, in a shallow grave. We made a hurried marker out of some sticks, said a prayer, then left. Joni and I both watched the classifieds for a few days, looking for any ads for a lost cat. We also drove through the neighborhood where the cat had been hit looking for any lost cat signs, but saw none. Of course, this entire time I was only pretending to be concerned about the cat and its possible owners, all the while fantasizing secretly about raping children and terrible things like that. I don't actually remember any of these fantasies, or feeling like I was faking anything, but I must have been, because I am an evil monster after all, or so they tell me.

Reflections

Sunday, May 20, 2012

There Are No Lesser Evils

If someone hates hate, then they only hate themselves. True love loves hate, but any hate that is loved becomes love, not hate. To understand this, it helps to think of hate as darkness, which is simple the absence of light, which of course is love. So hate is no more real than a shadow, and neither is "evil". We can experience a shadow with almost all of our physical senses, but when you think about it, shadows don't even exist! So, to hate hate, is like seeing a shadow, and creating an even bigger shadow in order to get rid of it! Of course you can't destroy a shadow with more shadow. Only light can destroy a shadow, but of course the light doesn't really destroy anything. It only changes the darkness into illumination! And so love changes hate into understanding, and "evil" into "good". But "good" doesn't really exist either. Good is no more than a "non-shadow", so it is common for people to mistake a bigger shadow that encompasses many smaller shadows, as something "good", or perhaps "a necessary evil". There is no such thing of course. Necessary evils only seem necessary to people who's hearts do not yet shine enough light to illuminate the darker experiences of their life (like me, for one).

Reflections

Monday, May 21, 2012

See No Evil

There is no evil in nature other than the evil we imagine as human beings. We only imagine evil because we are fearful, and we are fearful because we ignore the one truth that perpetually offers itself as our salvation from an eternal life of evil. Religions frequently form around this truth. Some religions believe they must protect it. Others think they must spread it. But, no religion understands it, because if it did understand then it would know that the one saving truth is completely independent of our experience, and does not need to be protected, or spread, or even served. It only wants to be acknowledged (i.e. loved). And, as soon as we do acknowledge it in our heart of hearts, we are freed from fear, and from all forms of imagined evil. Acknowledgement (love) of the one truth is not something we do as an act of volition. We cannot choose to "love God". God chooses who will love him, and how that love will manifest. It is an event that occurs as any other event in nature, as the result of an infinite sequence of circumstances that no human mind could ever begin to fathom. We pride ourselves on our knowledge of the Universe, but we have not yet even begun the understand. Evil is not real, not really. We invent it, and we create it. But in the end, the truth will destroy it, or rather, reveal the lie of it.

Reflections

Sunday, May 27, 2012

Playing God

Most people in our society enjoy playing god. We even teach our children how to play this game practically from the moment they are born. A person who plays god well is admired as a successful person, and the person who plays poorly is condemned and outcast from the social playing fields. What does it mean to play god? It is the simple act of pretending to judge the merits of other people and circumstances. Our entire culture is permeated with the paraphernalia of this game. Newspapers, TV, magazines, the Internet, are all primarily concerned with providing us with the superficial information that we need to play. We become addicted to this game at a very young age, so young that we typically cannot even remember a time when we did not judge every person we meet and every experience we have. To judge seems completely natural to us, and we typically feel the need to do so constantly. For most people sitting quietly for a few moments without judging something creates a strong sense of unease and anxiety. And like any sport, there are many different levels of play, from the amateurish judgment of backfence gossip, to the world impacting judgments of politicians and religious leaders. But no matter at what level we play, it is still just a game. To BE God is a completely different matter. To BE God is never a game. Each and every one of us has the ability to Be God, but very very few have the courage to do so. So we PLAY god instead. I'm playing god right now as I write these words. I am judging myself and other people's ability to play the game. It is not a conscious process for me, but at least I am conscious of it. I realize that I am playing god because I exhibit all the behavioral indicators of the game (and the addiction). First and foremost, I am engrossed in human language. The fact that I am using words is a primary indication that the game is being played. Human language has become one of the greatest facilities of the game. Not all human language is used for playing god. But generally speaking, the more a person's lips are moving (or pen) the more likely they are caught up in the game. This is especially true any time that words are used to form some sort of opinion, of course, even if that opinion is only vaguely implied (as I am doing now, by vaguely implying that I know what the hell I'm talking about!) Yet for all the pain and suffering that playing god entails, it is not “bad” or “wrong”. And while it certainly invokes “evil”, it is not evil in and of itself. Ultimately it is still only a game played by the children of God. It helps us to learn so we can grow up and someday take on the responsibility that comes along with Being God. As we mature we eventually begin to lose interest in the game, and naturally become more involved with the process of creation (which, of course, is an ongoing miracle). We do this because as we judge less we begin to understand (and hence love) more. Through understanding we acquire the ability to shape and change our world (and the universe). Pure understanding, uncontaminated with judgment, has the ability to create. But pure understanding requires complete non-judgment, a return to innocence if you will. This is also what it means to truly forgive, and be forgiven. A person who is BEING God does not need to judge. But, God lets His children judge themselves, so that they will know when they are ready to stop playing children's games and grow up, becoming One with Him. Though the game is one of judgment, we are not learning how to judge. We are learning how (and why) to not judge. We are learning how (and why) to forgive. Only by learning this lesson will our need to judge (and to play god) diminish. And, pretending that we know how to forgive (i.e. by judging first so we can then pretend to forgive) is just another way to play the game (one that seems particularly popular with the least mature children of god who frequently call themselves Christians). You will know when you have learned this lesson (how to not judge and to genuinely forgive), because you will at that moment realize that you ARE God! And it will be the most humbling realization you ever have!

Reflections

Sunday, June 3, 2012

What I Saw, That Changed My Life

I saw that all life is eternal. I saw that I existed only by my connection to this eternal life. I saw that all things exist via the same connection to eternal life. I saw that what I am is animated and given purpose only by who I am. I saw that who I am is eternal. I saw that what I am would perish, but only after it had served out its purpose to who I am. I saw that all things serve the purpose of who I am. I saw that my purpose was to learn, and to understand. I saw that learning was an act of love, and understanding is the compelling force behind the act, and faith is the medium through which the force becomes action. I saw that lying was an act of hate, and ignorance is the compelling anti-force behind every lie, and fear is the medium that the anti-force conjures in order to justify deception. I saw that a great war was being fought between love and hate, understanding and ignorance, faith and fear. I saw that good and evil are deceptions used to keep fearful people ignorant of love. I saw that I was a fearful person.

Reflections

Sunday, June 10, 2012

Addicted to Us

I am convinced that drug addiction, like sex addiction, and perhaps like all addiction, is a sociological condition, not a psychological one. Which is to say that it is induced by pathological conditions in our social system, not by individual psychosis. It is a grave mistake to place the blame for addiction on the addict. Such a person clearly is not in conscious control of their own behavior, and said lack of control can be relatively simply traced to their social experience and background. Native Americans have an extremely high susceptibility to alcoholic addiction. Some studies have pointed to genetic vulnerability, but these studies have not withstood scientific scrutiny. Currently there is no commonly accepted theory for their vulnerability to alcohol. Perhaps the solution could be found by studying the social impact on the disease. For example, what is the addiction rate of genetic Native Americans who are isolated from the Native American culture. I predict it would be much lower than other Native Americans. Maybe I'm talking out of my hat (in fact, I am), but if Native American alcoholism can be tied to sociological conditions, then what other forms of addiction could be similarly explained? The implications would clearly be staggering. So, perhaps for once we should listen to what an addict (me) says, and take a look at ourselves as a society instead of pointing fingers (which is all our so-called criminal justice system seems good at). Blaming the addict only exacerbates the problem by encouraging the self blame and the shame that is invariably associated with all addiction. This habit of blaming the addict may actually be the social construct that causes the addiction. We should at least question addiction in this social context. But, since any general solution for addiction would cause a significant collapse in a whole sector of our present economy namely, the "Correctional Complex", the more valid my suggestions may be, the less likely they would be seriously researched. And that is the result of another perhaps even related disease called capitalism. And since just mentioning that word gets my blood pumping, I'll stop now before I start exhibiting the symptoms of my own addiction to judgementality.

Reflections

Sunday, June 17, 2012

The Book of Life

Christian's don't believe in Christ; they believe in their own belief systems (b.s.) instead. The Christ is the Christian bible even tries to warn them of this error (see John 5:39-40 for example). But of course they cannot help making this mistake, because they have not "received the love of the truth", so God sends them a "strong delusion, that they should believe the lie" (see Thes 2:9-12). And I say this not because the bible says so, but because it has been made clear to me. I have learned not to trust the "wisdom of men's words", it was such "wisdom" that drove me to murder! And it is exactly this same false wisdom – wisdom born in fear and ignorance, not love – that drives men to want to murder me even now. Please read John, chapter 8, and look past the words and into the heart of Jesus, into my heart, and into your own! The gospel cannot be read in any book, except the Book of Life itself! ("...our sufficiency is from God, who also made us sufficient as ministers of the gospel, not of the letter, but of the Spirit; for the letter kills but the Spirit gives life." - 2 Cor 3:5-6, "You are a letter of Christ... written... on tablets of flesh, that is, of the heart." - 3:2-3)

Reflections

Thursday, June 21, 2012

Blame Excludes Responsibility

Blame excludes all responsibility. You can't have both at the same time and they are not the same thing despite what those who project blame for a living (i.e. witch-hunters) want you to think. Blame shuns responsibility while only pretending to actually be responsibility. One way it does this is by using oxymoronic language such as, "personal responsibility", in order to confuse things, which makes it easier to convince people that blame is the same as being responsible. But there is nothing "personal" about real responsibility. It is action taken for the benefit of everyone, not just an excuse, like blame, to do nothing while everyone suffers. Responsibility takes action to solve a problem long before blame even points its accusing finger. It might not always solve a problem on the first try, but it knows that finding fault and placing blame never accomplishes anything and usually only makes things worse. Even though blame likes to pretend it makes a problem better it never does, because it can't. The best blame can do - and one of its favorite tricks - is to confuse the issue behind a veil of emotionally charged accusations and a lot of superficial action. For example, using punishment and reward "systems" to try to compel other people to take responsibility. But compelling someone to take responsibility is like trying to force them to love you! It can't be done. It might result in a false and temporary display of convincing compliance, but the display never lasts long before it turns into rebellion and spite behind the oppressor's back, which of course only make the problem worse in the end. Responsibility must be accepted freely, and it doesn't need to be rewarded. Like love, it is its own reward. Anyone who has ever been genuinely responsible, even just once, understands this. Those who can only place blame never will.

Chronicles

Saturday, June 23, 2012

It Never Ends

I am sitting on the floor of this concrete cell with two blankets and a sheet wrapped around me to keep warm.

The vent noisily blows cold air.

It is well past lights out.

The only light comes in through the small security window in the steel door.

I am sitting in the light so I can see.

I can't sleep.

And, I can't wake up.

I am thinking about God, the universe, reality...

The guard shines a flashlight through the window, sees me sitting on the floor writing, and is gone to the next cell in less than a half second.

I want to have a lucid dream so I can talk to someone.

I want to know who, what, when, where, and why I am.

I want to be free, from life.

I want to cry, but I can't.

I don't know why.

I want to die, but I can't.

I don't know why.

It never ends.

It never ends.

It never ends.

The pain never ends.

The beauty... never ends.

Reflections

Saturday, June 23, 2012

Sex Offender Society

The Sex Offender Society (SOS) is an organization of registered sex offenders. It does not matter if you have or have not ever committed a sex crime. You can register as a sex offender at our website, or in person at one of our pride parade boths. Free SOS T-shirts will be given away this year to all new registrants at the Seattle, San Francisco and Minneapolis parade booths. The T-shirts read: "REGISTERED SEX OFFENDER, keep women and children away! (men preferred)" SOS is light-hearted. But provides real support and information for all registered sex offenders (criminal or not), not just gays. Our organization is founded in the future, and is based on the simple belief that all people are sex offenders, and all sex offenders are people. Note: SOS does not advocate or condone sex crime, or any sexual behavior that compromises another person's freedom to choose their own sexual behavior. If you would like more information about SOS, then you'll have to use your imagination; because no such organization exists... yet. PS: If the SOS website existed (sexos.com, pronounced "sey-ohs-dot-com") it could have the following information and features: A comprehensive history of sex offender registration laws; including history of criminal registration (i.e. Nazi Germany) and current legal challenges. History of sex crime. History of persecution. Detailed listing and analysis of registration laws, cross-referenced by state. Sex offender registration lists, and searches, by state and national. SOS registration list, which includes offense type (not necessarily criminal) and optional descriptions, as well as other information that the "offender" determines should be made public (not the police). Periodic newsletters (e-mail subscriptions) to introduce new website features, legal challenge updates, and "Sex Offender of the Month" feature, as well as other features, such as "Tips and Tricks" (on how to legally avoid parole and police traps) and maybe a feature on "Legal Sex Offenses" (such as types of gay sex). Ideally the site wouls allow the SOS registered members to vote on new features (such as chat rooms, e-mail alerts, photo options, etc.) and also encourage member contributions (i.e. articles, stories, pictures, tips, etc...) The site would basically attempt to provide much needed community support for "sex offenders" in general, while being careful not to promote sex crime.

Chronicles

Sunday, June 24, 2012

Musical Cells

This morning I got to play the musical cells game. But it wasn't very fun because nobody got stuck without a cell and had to go home. :(

It seems that every 21 days inmates here in the SHU (Special Housing Unit, a.k.a. the hole) get moved to a random different cell (for "security" reasons, of course). The cell I just got moved to is a lot dirtier than the one I was in before, but other than that it's actually a lot better. This cell has a new mattress that's a lot softer than the old one (well, okay, it's really only a little softer, but it feels a lot softer after so much tossing and turning every ten minutes on the old one because it actually starts to hurt to lay in one position too long - especially because of how boney I am), and the new mattress even has a built in pillow which isn't the greatest, but it's certainly better than no pillow at all, which is what I had before.

The old cell was also just on the other side of the regular population inmate basketball court. It seems the backboard was attached to the wall just outside the cell, so I'd hear loud banging all day and in the evenings, and sometimes even late at night after lights out when the guards get bored and decide to shoot some hoops (and mess with my head perhaps, since they all knew I was in that cell).

I also got a cell with a stool this time, so I can actual have someplace to sit and eat, or write, as I'm doing now. And, I can see a little bit out the window to where the paint has thinned out some. So all in all, today is a good day.

Dreams

Monday, June 25, 2012

No Way Out

I have been reading a book on lucid dreaming and hoping to improve my abilities as an oneironaut (pronounced oh-NIGH-ro-knot, and meaning „explorer of dreams”). But I haven't had much luck lately. All hopes of lucidity aside, I did have an interesting dream last night, or rather this morning, after breakfast when I went back to sleep (which the book says is the best time for lucid dreams). In fact, I think maybe this could be one of the most intriguing dreams that I've ever had. I'm going to need some time to think about it, that's for sure. It could end up being a real game changer for me.

The dream I'm talking about was actually kind of sandwiched between two other seemingly unrelated dreams that I don't remember for some reason. But, the significant part all seemed to happen in this sequence:

I was in a plain rectangular room with just one door. The room seemed to be a private waiting room of some sort. There was a young boy in the room with me, but I don't remember why he was there or what he was doing. I was waiting for my attorneys to finish confering with each other about my case in another room just down the hall from this one.

There were two young women standing in the doorway who I knew to be investigators working for the attorneys in the other room (though in real life I have many investigators and attorneys who have worked on my cases all of whom I call my friends, these dream counterparts did not correlate with any of them specifically). The women were obviously keeping an eye on me while acting all friendly and pretending to just be keeping me company. I easily saw through their facade and was irritated by it. When I tried to leave the room they made excuses for why I should stay. I started to feel like a prisoner.

Finally I became overly impatient and pushed my way past the two women into the hallway outside the door, ignoring their pretentiously concerned protests. I walked down the hall to the left and passed another room where I saw the five or six attorneys sitting of a conference table. They didn't seem to notice as I walked by with the two investigators on me heels.

The hall opened onto the promenade of a large indoor shopping mall (indoor malls have been a recurring theme in my dreams for the past several years now). I walked quickly into a mall restaurant, past the dinning customers, and directly to the kitchen. I was hoping that the women following me wouldn't come into the kitchen out of propriety. But, they stayed right behind me the whole time.

I wanted to loose my tail without making a scene (by trying to run away from them for example). So, true to my real-life character, I stopped to think about the problem and find a solution. I laid down on a metal kitchen table with my face toward the women so I could see them. They were once again posting sentry, this time at the entrance to the kitchen. I watched them for several minutes and noticed a three or four second gap in their vigil when they traded places at the door. The next time they turned their backs while trading positions.

I was ready. I got up quickly and dashed for the rear door of the kitchen. It lead to a hall in the restaurant that gave access to the customer restrooms. I was out of the women's sight, but not for long. I needed to hide fast before they found me again.

I darted into the men's restroom, then quickly climbed over the rear stall wall. Rather than climbing all the way down on the other side I hung upside down against the stall. It turned out to be a janitor's space behind the stall (judging by the mop-bucket and cleaning supplies I saw there). From my position hanging upside down I could see under the stall, but anyone looking under the stalls wouldn't be able to see me.

As expected, the bathroom door soon flew open, and I could see the high-heeled shoes and stockings of what was without doubt one of the investigators. She bent down to look under the stalls, then hurriedly left. But, before I could climb down a man came in. He entered the toilet stall just inches away from me and sat down to use it. I couldn't hold my position and the man heard me as I tried to adjust my grip to keep from falling on my head. The man made some comment under his breath that could have been, „Freakin' Fags", or something similar, then quickly pulled up his pants and left. Good riddance, I thought.

So, I climbed out from behind the stall and crept out of the bathroom. I knew there was still a chance that I would be spotted by the women who were earnestly looking for me nearby, but I had to get out of the mall before they got help (from mall security for example). So, walking as quickly as I could without drawing attention I exited the restaurant through the front then headed down the promenade looking for a mall exit.

Now, here's where things start to get interesting. I mentioned a moment ago that malls are a recurring theme in my dreams of late. But, I didn't realize until this dream (after I woke up and thought about it later) that the malls never have any exits! In the other mall dreams i never really realized the exits were missing because never before had I been so earnest to find one. But, this time I needed an exit, and fast.

After finding no exits from the promenade I began frantically entering the stores and looking for exits in the backs of them, with no luck of course. I just kept ending up back in the mall's promenade. Then suddenly I found myself at the end of a side corridor facing the entrances for three peculiar sideshows. Somehow I remembered from another dream (though because I was not lucid in this dream it just seemed like an ordinary remembrance to me, not from another dream at all) that in order to leave the mall I needed to watch all of the sideshows without getting drawn in and becoming a part of the entertainment, which it seemed, was a perilous task.

In the previous dreams I had already seen the first two shows, so I had only to sit through the third show and I would be free. But, I knew this third show presented the greatest challenge, and that there was a real danger that I would be trapped by it forever!

As I stood contemplating this obstacle I realized I wasn't alone. A small attractive and young woman stood next to me. With dreamlike understanding I knew that she was me too. We were to face the third sideshow together. But somehow I also knew that the real danger was for her. I was concerned, but we knew we had to take the chance so we could get out of the mall before being found again.

We both passed through the heavy dark curtains to enter the show. We found ourselves in a theater with enough seats for about 200 people. There were a couple dozen or so men scattered about in the seats making up the audience. After I woke up I realized this must have been a porno theater where men, and sometimes women, go to have sex. But, I didn't make that association at all the time in the dream.

Toward the front of the theater, in the first or second row of seats, a man stood facing toward me and she-me in the back where we had just come in. With a big jovial smile on his face he waved at us and hollered, „There you are! We've bee waiting for you!"

The dream abruptly shifted and I found myself standing alone in the parking lot outside of the mall. But, just before this transition I saw an image of she-me laying sideways in one of the theater seats wearing only a sheer and sexy nylon body-stocking. She seemed to be exposing herself to the men in the theater and was obviously in the throes of sexual passion, apparently in anticipation of her wildest sexual fantasies coming true.

The parking lot was empty, though the mall I knew was full of people. I stood for a moment and wondered what had just happened. How did I get out? What happened to she-me?

I'm not sure if the dream continued from there or not. But, when I finally woke up I didn't think much about the dream at first. It seemed fairly run-of-the-mill. But, a little while later its significance started to sink in.

After thinking about it some more, I remembered that in previous dreams I had already visited the other two side shows without getting trapped. The first was a party with lots of food, drugs and alcohol, and people. The second was a stage show of a battle with soldiers, guns and cannons, and such. I don't remember the party (first sideshow) too clearly. But, I remember that the staged battle ended up involving the audience (which was in a small theater with only 20 or 30 seats), and I was in a struggle for my life to keep from being shot by (or maybe from) a cannon. I managed to get control of the cannon, but when I fired it at the „enemy" only confetti came out. That made me realize that it was all just a play, that my life was never in danger at all. So, I left, with the „battle" raging on behind me.

Maybe these „sideshows" represented chemical/food addiction, power and control delusion, and sexual obsession. It seems likely. But, then what happened to she-me. Was some part of me still trapped in that mall? What did the mall represent anyway? Life? (Was it same kind of Hotel California?) What did it all mean, if anything?

According to the book on lucid dreaming, it was all just a product of a combination of my past experiences (memory), expectations and desires (motivation). The book says there is no „message" in dreams, though they can give us clues about ourselves, but that's all, like a Rorschach inkblot test, nothing more.

I like to think there's a lot more. I'm pretty sure that „higher consciousness" is involved. I think it's just plain silly to think that our consciousness is isolated. Frost said, „No man is an island." I don't think he meant socially (as most people assume). Perhaps he meant consciously, like I think.

It makes more sense for consciousness to exist on a spectrum, like all other forms of energy. In fact, I believe that someday, maybe soon, scientists will discover that all other forms of energy arise from pure consciousness itself (there are a lot of experiments already in Quantum Physics that strongly support this belief). So what I'm saying is, by my way of thinking, I'd be a fool to not consider the meaning of this dream, or any dream for that matter.

I think someday we will teach our children to dream lucidly, instead of to consume recklessly. And through dreams we will make a „real" world that is more conscious, and a world without limits of and kind (no social or physical „laws"). And, I believe that this new world will be in perfect harmony with the Universe. All because of dreams, like the one I just described.

P.S.: Here are some additional observations relating to the various aspects of this dream that have occurred to me since writing the above (one week ago).

The mall(s) in this dream and others seem to represent a „limited existence". This roughly corresponds to physical life itself. So, leaving the mall is synonymous to leaving this life. My attorneys, in the dream and in real life as well, are very concerned that I don't „leave the mall" because they think of that as death. I do not. I see death as a continuation of life, which I think this dream depicts well.

„She-me" is most likely my „Jazzi-Jet" alter ego (my transexual identity that was prominent for many years, especially while I was a „queen" in prison). The „sideshows" seem to have been some sort of „trap" designed specifically to separate me from my alter egos. I feel that the dream may have been a signal that it was time to let Jazzi-Jet go and leave her behind.

I actually felt bad when I realized that. Jazzi-Jet was like my own child. I brought her into this world, nourished her, and loved her. And she loved me. She looked up to me for guidance and protection, and she protected me too. And now I am to abandon her? But, I realized that she is probably better off left in that porno theater, which is essentially her element. She will be happy there, I think, where I could never be happy for very long. She is a much simpler creature than I am, with simpler wants and needs. So, maybe she is where she belongs (wherever that is) so I can move on to other realities without her.

The parking lot at the end of this dream then would represent the beginning of a whole new world, without limits. I have not been tempted to masturbate or otherwise engage in any sexual thoughts at all since this dream. Perhaps without the temptress there are no temptations. I am curious to see if I have become egoistically asexual at last. But, that will take time to tell.

Reflections

Sunday, July 1, 2012

Letting Go

“Let go; let God!” I have steered clear of these words in the past because they are badly tainted with Christian ideas of God. But, if you realize that God is no more, and certainly no less, than the unfathomable intelligence behind all that we experience (a.k.a. The Universe), then letting go, and letting God, becomes the very key that unlocks the door inside of us that opens to all of infinity. Heaven, salvation, bliss, ultimate truth, real power, true love, Nirvana and of course enlightenment are all references to what lies beyond that door. So why shouldn't we take this advice seriously? It is the key to our happiness, and to discovering and attaining our deepest need of all; the need to be (to know that we exist). You might think you already know that you exist, and no doubt on an intellectual level this knowledge seems plain to you. But if you still struggle against the illusion of death then it can only be because you have not yet accepted the knowledge of your existence in your heart. This is the well known “hole” inside of us that we perpetually and vainly seek to fill with all the delusional trappings of our experiential reality. We try to fill this hole with not just money, sex, drugs and power, but also with many other “fake gods”, such as righteousness, family values, and so-called morals. But ultimately what we attempt to do in all these cases is to establish our presence by exerting some form of control over our experience. It does not matter if the control we project is good or bad, just so long as it is control, and hense, evidence of our existence. But the truth that snaps at our heals and constantly threatens to rob us of our hard earned sense of existence (and purpose) is that nothing we do will last forever. In fact, the greatest influence possible by any one human (say, for example, a Christ, or Buddha) is clearly limited to several thousand years, perhaps tens of thousands at most. But even if one man could make a mark on the universe that lasted for over a billion years, when the mark is gone, so is all evidence that such a man ever existed. We can deny the inevitable erasure of such evidence in innumerable ways, and most religions focus almost all of their energy on exactly that. By imagining that what we do in this life will effect how we spend eternity is one way that religion attempts to dupe us into thinking we can escape that ultimate truth that seems to want nothing more than to destroy everything we have (our memories of our experiences). Yet, what we don't realize is that no finite experience will ever “live forever”. The very definition of finite demands that it has an end as well as beginning. Only something infinite, without end or beginning, can “live forever”. And that “something” exists inside of us, and all around us at the same time (anything infinite in time must also be infinite in space, since we know that space and time are all one and the same these days). It is the source of all finite experience, and whether we identify with it or not, it is ultimately who we are! But, we can't identify with our infinite selves if we turn to finite reality (and reason) for answers. This should be obvious, but for some reason such a self evident truth commonly eludes the most adamant soul searchers. Probably because the illusion of reality is so convincing. Yet, if it were not convincing then what would be the point? Seeking control, and hence confirmation of our existence (sometimes perceived as “love”) through finite experience is grasping the “golden sand” that can only seep through our fingers like in Poe's famous poem (A Dream Within A Dream). The only way to realize our true power (i.e. The Love of God) is to stop grasping at something that simple observation will tell us doesn't even exist! It seeps through our fingers no matter how tightly we clasp it, because it is only an illusion. We must let go of the illusion, or what Poe calls a dream within a dream, in order to realize the one true experience; which is who we are. That does not mean grabbing ahold of anything, or exchanging one idea of God for some other. It means letting go completely, just letting go, nothing else. Letting go is how we wake up from reality.

Reflections

Monday, July 2, 2012

Praise All-ah

I have said that I am God. But, after thinking about it some more (oops), I have decided that I am not God. To claim that I am God implies that I am singular, because the pronoun "I" is singular. But, in the sense that the term "God" is commonly used, it cannot be singular. "God" implies a separate (more powerful) being from the one using the term. And, if there are separate beings then there is more than one. So, in bowing to the convention of language I must capitulate my assertion that I am God, and admit that I am not. But, WE are! In every sense of the term "God" that I have just expounded on, WE are God! No, we are not gods. That would mean that each one of us as an individual is God. We are not God as individuals, WE are only God when WE are taken together as One. God is a WE, not a He or a She. WE created the Universe, WE are all powerful, WE are all knowing and all present. But, only in the sense that WE are connected as One, never in the sense that we are individuals, or in any way separated from each other. So, to experience God (i.e. enlightenment) is to recognize and embrace this connection with all other people, and things! In fact, in the truest sense, WE are not God either. Everything is! So, perhaps we should just say, All is God, and leave it at that. Praise All-Ah!

Chronicles

Thursday, July 5, 2012

Seatac or Bust

A little more than two weeks ago I had a court hearing in Boise Idaho. The only purpose of the hearing was to appoint counsel for the upcoming appellate court-ordered competency hearing. The lawyer that appeared at the hearing two weeks ago to be appointed told the judge that he had a scheduling conflict with the proposed date of the new competency hearing, which was scheduled for early November. So, he asked that it be pushed back to December.

The judge said he wanted no more delays (though he'd already pushed the hearing back several months for the prosecutor without even consulting the defense). Apparently a few more weeks was too much to ask. So he continued the appointment hearing for two weeks, to be reconvened then to give the public defenders a chance to find a different lawyer.

Monday (three days ago) was the continuation hearing. I was flown by private jet from Terre Haute to Boise on both occasions. For the first hearing, that lasted 15 minutes and accomplished nothing, I was gone from my cell in Terre Haute for just over 30 hours. They flew me to Boise the day before, then flew me right back to Terre Haute after the 9:30 am hearing. For the second hearing I was flown to Boise on Friday, spent the weekend in Ada County Jail, then, by complete surprise, flown to Seattle via twin engine Beachcraft and taken to the Seatac Federal Detention Center (FDC) where I now sit.

It seems I have been ordered to remain here until the competency hearing, which the judge finally pushed back to January 8th, 2013, before appointing the same lawyer that appeared at that first hearing. So, now I'm stuck here in Seatac in the SHU (Special Housing Unit, a.k.a. 'The Hole") for the next seven months, presumably so I can be more readily flown back and forth for pointless hearings like these last two (an hour and a half by Beachcraft instead of three hours by Lear-jet).

I don't mind. It gives me time to catch up on some reading, and work on the Fifthnail.

Reflections

Monday, July 9, 2012

Pure Language?

Why would a genuinely intelligent entity need to manipulate symbols? Even our most precise languages, of math and science, inevitably fail to truly represent the things they purport. They are, after all, only symbols, not the things themselves. I think that a truly intelligent being would understand, manipulate and communicate via reality itself, and not bother with symbols at all.

Reflections

Sunday, July 15, 2012

Pride and Shame

Pride and shame, shame and pride; where one takes root, the other will hide.

Reflections

Saturday, July 21, 2012

Intuition vs. Gut Instinct

There are those who say that intuition is overrated. But maybe it is not intuition that they are knocking. We also have a thing called “gut instinct” that is not the same as intuition. Our gut instinct comes from hardwired instincts. It tells us when to be afraid (often when there is nothing to be afraid of), as well as when to get aroused (even very young children will respond to adult sexual cues by becoming physically aroused, that is, by getting an erection, which is the cause of much confusion for both the adults and children who encounter this reaction). Clearly, gut reaction is not always rational. Our intuition can actually warn us when our gut reaction is inappropriate. For example, we intuitively know that a child's sexual response to adult sexual behavior, or an adults sexual arousal to a child's sexual qualities, is not an indication that adults should have sex with children. But because of our society's propensity for ignoring intuitive insight, many adults use their gut reaction to children (sexual arousal) to rationalize seeking out sexual relations with immature juveniles. This would be an example of how ignoring intuition can get us into a lot of trouble. But, it is only an example, not a model of intuitive deviancy. Gut instinct is more of a feeling, or emotional response, which explains why it is often called “gut feeling”. But intuition by contrast, is a kind of “inner voice”. Intuition can often invoke emotional responses, which are then mistaken for gut reactions. But intuition itself is not a feeling at all. It is important to be able to distinguish our "gut feelings" from intuition if we are to benefit at all from the later. Perhaps realizing that the only reason we end up confusing gut feeling with intuition is primarily because we have been conditioned to ignore intuition from a very young age. And ignoring our intuition requires constant effort, and hence energy expense. This makes it possible to "reverse engineer" the intellectual structures that we have installed inside our mind in order to block out our intuitive voice. We have only to focus on where our intellectual energy is going when we are at rest. This is something that happens, intuitively, when we meditate, thus leading to many personal "insights". Of course, when I say, "inner voice", I am not talking about psychotic voices in our head. However, I believe, based on personal and intimate experience with such "psychos", that such voices are often intuition trying desperately to be heard. But, this psychotic voices are filtered through the speech centers of the brain, and hense lose nearly all of their intuitive power. Human language, as I have explained in other blog posts, is not suited for conveying intuition. So what intuition actually "sounds" like is not something anyone can tell you. But, I can tell you that intuition is not a gut feeling, or psychotic voice. I call it an "inner voice", but even that description is desperately lacking. You must come to know intuition first hand. It is the only way.

Reflections

Monday, July 23, 2012

Can We?

Who am I? I am you, right now, reading these words written by someone you think is not you, but is. I know exactly what you are thinking this moment; And exactly what you are feeling. You are the one who wrote these words after all. If you think not, then you and I - we - are yet deceived. Eternity and infinity are one and the same. You cannot be eternal unless you are also infinite. A pure heart can see this plainly. Can you? Can we?

Reflections

Monday, July 30, 2012

Bane of Language

We greatly mistake our ability to manipulate symbols (human language) as the most telling sign of our intelligence. But what if it is our sickness instead? Perhaps words, symbols and language are the bane of mankind, not a boon at all! Many have said so before, but I don't think we really understand how much harm language could be causing. All life on Earth is at stake.

Reflections

Monday, July 30, 2012

Pardon Our Mess

We are in the process of changing this blog around so it might be easier for readers to find the type of information they are interested in. Many entries are not yet correctly categorized since it is a work in progress. We aim to have everything in some semblance of order by the date of this entry (which may change according to our progress). In the meantime, we appreciate your patience.

Dreams

Wednesday, August 1, 2012

The Incredible Hulk I Am

I have been having no luck with lucid dreams as of yet, but I did have a really "incredible" dream just this morning. I dreamed I was watching the Incredible Hulk fighting a team of supervillains who had stolen a powerful top secret weapon and was about to use it to destroy an entire mountain. The weapon was mounted on the top of a large truck trailer and the mastermind villain (a woman) was at the controls taking aim and preparing to fire the weapon. The Hulk came on the scene and began smashing through the villainous defenders, first a fifty-caliber machine gun that sent bullets pinging off the Hulks green skin before he smashed it. Then there was a large mass weapon that seemed especially designed to kill the Hulk. It fired a large wrecking ball sized projectile with spiked protrusions at a high velocity at the green meany. But, with a single punch of his giant fist the Hulk sent the projectile directly back where it came from completely obliterating the weapon that fired it and its wielder. Now nothing stood between the Hulk and the woman preparing to fire the weapon except time, of course. She was mere seconds away from setting off the secret weapon and destroying the mountain. But the Hulk stopped her just in the nick of time and saved the day. Now here is where the dream starts to get a bit incredible. The weapon turns out to be a smaller truck packed on top of the larger trailer, and all the Hulk had to do in order to claim his victory was get in the truck and drive it away. But, as soon as he touched the handle to the door of the cab a huge jolt of electricity (or some other super villain energy force) blasted the Hulk and knocked him out. Then the scene changed instantly to the inside of a pre-school classroom. The Hulk was now a small child with green skin, but otherwise no different than any other five year old. A man and woman couple were in the classroom with the child-Hulk asking him questions, but the Hulk could not remember who he was or where he came from. No one seemed to notice his green skin even though there were many other children in the classroom with normal skin. The couple seemed to be interested in adopting this mysterious but gentle and lovable boy. They held him and doted over him like any loving parents would. The pre-school teacher came over and motioned for the couple to join her at one of those child-sized tables with child-sized chairs in the back of the classroom while the child-Hulk joined the rest of the children engaged in other pre-school activities in the open carpeted area in the front of the classroom. At this point I became a participant in the dream and joined the teacher and couple at the little table. The teacher addressed me directly and said, "It's amazing what a sweet and gentle child you were". I knew she was alluding to the contrasting reality of my violent adult behavior (crimes) in real life. (I was the child-Hulk in the dream) I responded by telling her that yes, as a child I was in fact so adorable and sweet that I instantly became my kindergarten teacher's pet (favorite), which naturally caused the other children to resent me, which confused me greatly as a child because I did not understand why adults seemed to like me but other children did not. (I could not see my own "green skin") The teacher in my dream agreed that favoritism in the classroom causes problems and confusion for the child. Then she pondered, "At what point does the child WANT to behave (negatively?)?" At this point the dream was interrupted as I was woke up by the guards bring lunch to my cell, but the teacher's words were left echoing in my head the way dreams do when they are ended suddenly. I quickly ate my lunch then sat down to write this. There are two "incredible" things I'd like to point out about this dream. First, my statement to the pre-school teacher about being the teacher's pet when I was in kindergarten was completely true in real life. However, I had never in real life considered the negative impact being the teacher's pet had on my ability to get along with (and make friends with) the other children. In the dream I seemed to take these consequences for granted, as if they were obvious. But until now, in real life I'd never realized such things, even though now, because of this dream, the impact of being the teacher's pet on me as a child seems obvious and fits perfectly with my memories (and confusion) as a child. Secondly, the teacher's observation and question in the dream, "At what point does the child WANT to behave (negatively?)?" is a twist to the philosophical question of free will that I have never in real life encountered before. She was asking at what point does a child become responsible for their behavior, which I see now is an important question to most people and one that the System struggles with constantly. But, the question itself implies (assumes) that such a point exists, whereas I have long contended that it does not; i.e. free will and predestiny are both contradicting illusions caused by limited perspectives of reality. They are encompassed by the reality of infinite cause and consequence that I have attempted to expound upon elsewhere in the Fifth Nail blog. So, this dream has brought two "incredible" concepts to my attention that I may not have otherwise ever considered.

Reflections

Sunday, August 5, 2012

Quandary of Truth

This sentence is a lie. This sentence is the truth. The quandary that exist for the first sentence above is clear. What is not so clear is that the exact same quandary exist for the second sentence as well. To see this is to see the futility and utility of human language all at once.

Reflections

Sunday, August 12, 2012

The Truth Is What Fear Fears

It takes more courage to face the truth than it does to face your greatest fear.
The truth is what fear fears.

Reflections

Sunday, August 12, 2012

Shameless Humility

I have said in the past that I would wear my shame for everyone to see out in the open rather than try to hide or deny it. And I did this as sincerely as I could. But, as soon as I had exposed my shame to this light of conscious awareness it suddenly vanished!

It seems that shame does not like the light and prefers to hide like a shadow in the dark recesses of the mind as it invokes defaming emotions that have no substance or base in reality at all.

The truth is I have nothing to be ashamed of. And, I see this more clearly now that my shame has been exposed and expunged. Yes, I am perverted, but who isn't? Most men are sexually aroused by a woman's breasts. But, that is no less perverted than being aroused by another man's penis, or even a child's body for that matter. All of these perversions have been alternately embraced and scorned by different cultures throughout history, and equally so.

Perhaps nature herself is the greatest pervert of all! Is she wasn't then none of us would be here. Perversity is the prerequisite of diversity, which we all know is a crucial and vaunted element for the health and survival of all living organisms. Every species, in fact every entity on this planet, must tolerate perversion or die from an inability to adapt. Perversion lives at the heart of Darwin's brain child; evolution.

so, my mistakes and my perversions, are justified in this sense, but not excused! They are justified in the name of nature and humankind, but inexcusable in the face of higher truth and love. I guess what I'm saying is no different than what I have been trying to say all along, or at least since my arrest (in 2005) after I had somehow and unexpectedly woken up to the higher truth I speak of.

I'm saying simply that my real crime was not kidnapping, rape, or even murder. Those things are no more than natural perversions (i.e. variations) of human nature. My real crime was being fearful and ignorant (i.e. hateful) of the Living Truth! This is what caused my perverse behavior and perverted my mind. It is what causes all perversion.

But, being fearful and ignorant is nothing to be ashamed of either - though it certainly demands that we be humble in our estimations of our worth and importance. That is to say, I have come to realize that shame is a poor substitute for genuine humility!

Reflections

Thursday, August 16, 2012

No Regret

I have deep and genuine remorse for the things I have done ine the past, but no regret. For me regret ends up being just an excuse for what I did. It causes me to believe that I am a bad person, hence I have no choice but to do bad things. Genuine remorse does not allow such beliefs. Because of my remorse I know I'm not a bad person, so I have no excuse for doing bad things. I must accept full responsibility for what I have done (and for what I do). This doesn't make me a good person either; it simply says that I'm not bad, or evil, or unlovable – especially not unlovable.

I did the terrible things I did in the past (kidnapping, rape and murder) because of my regret, which had convinced me that I was a bad person. I didn't like believing I was bad of course, so I did everything I could to put responsibility for my misery and shame onto society, which perceived as the source of all my suffering for purely rational reasons. This would make my regret go away temporarily, but as soon as I stopped pushing my pain (and responsibility) away it would always came back again. I have since realized that responsibility can only be either accepted or rejected personally. It can never be put on someone else without their consent. (I now call the attempt to make others take responsibility for anything, the Blame Game.)

But, I don't believe I'm a bad person anymore. So I no longer have any reason to feel regret, or any need to blame other people for my pain and suffering, or behavior. Not even myself, since self blame is ultimately just another way to avoid responsibility (self blame leads to regret, not remorse, and hence more negative behavior, not responsibility). Now I have only remorse, and the forgiveness that comes with it (i. e. love), which is all I need.

The only reason I have remorse at all is because I found and accepted real forgiveness (not the Christian variety). What I mean is that someone essentially said to me (not necessarily with words, but certainly from the heart), „You are not the bad person you think you are." This, I now realize, is THE message of forgiveness, and my heart somehow managed to receive it, even though my eyes were blinded and my ears were defeated by deeply ingrained fear and ignorance (i. e. hate). And somehow I also believed it, even though it went against everything I had been told all my life.

I realized that I really wasn't a bad person after all. I had lived nearly my entire life believing a lie, and supporting that lie with many many other lies. So when that base lie fell to the light of the truth, all the other lies fell with it. My entire „world" (i. e. belief system) collapsed like a house of cards, and I literally bawled like a newborn infant from the sheer shock of being exposed to a whole new reality; a whole new truth; that I wasn't bad, and that I could in fact be loved for the person I was beneath the mask.

I don't suppose I'll ever be able to fully describe what a shock this realization was for me. I had believed for so long that no one would ever love the real me, so I had to fake who I was just to get people to accept me. But know I knew I didn't have to fake, or lie, anymore. I could remove the „bad man" mask, and if no one liked the real me it didn't matter anymore, because I was lovable, and I was loved.

At first I thought that „someone" was Shasta, the little girl who I had kidnapped in order to rape and murder (in my mind I was giving „society" a taste of its own sickness). But I quickly realized that she was only a conduit for the love I felt. The love I experienced through her came from an infinitely deep reservoir that her innocence and purity made her the perfect channel for. We worship a child's innocence because it allows us to glimpse this deeper love, but the love is not in the child, it's in all of us, and it's in the world.

This love was the cause of my remorse, and it was this love that compelled me to pick Shasta up and take her home. I let myself get „caught" because it was the only way I could be certain that I would not hurt anyone else. I did not confess out of guilt or shame, or because I wanted to be punished. I simply no longer feared the System, or even death. I knew I would probably be sentenced to die because of my crimes, I even told Shasta so on the way back to her home city. I told her that it didn't matter what they did to me; it only mattered that she was safe and with her father where she belonged.

I cried for days straight after I surrendered to the police. I spent many hours curled up in the fetal position on the floor of the jail cell I was put in, because the cold hard concrete gave me a comforting sense of contact with reality in an otherwise pain filled universe. I was loved! I was loved! And it hurt so much!

Only forgiveness and love can beget genuine remorse. Condemnation and punishment can only compel a person to feel regret, which is often mistaken for remorse. But regret is only concerned with ones own misery, and out punishment based justice system makes sure that's all anyone ever feels. We even reward regret, by giving criminals who „lawyer up" much lighter sentences, if they can be charged at all. A man who remorsefully turns himself in and freely confess will invariably have the book thrown at him. My own lawyers told me not to confess to my crimes in other states because of this, and because they wanted to use those crimes to bargain with. I told my attorneys that I would not allow such „bargaining" with the truth, and I confessed against their advice. I told my attorneys that the truth was not a commodity to be bargained with; it is a living and intelligent entity, that wants to be loved and acknowledged. My confession was an acknowledgement of the truth, nothing more, and I have been experiencing the consequences of my confession ever since, getting shipped from one jurisdiction to another to have the book thrown at me over and over again. If I had taken my attorney's advice I could have settled all my cases (crimes) at once and gotten life without parole instead of three death sentences (or more, if Washington State ever decides it wants to join in the Blame Game).

But, I still don't regret my confession, or my crimes. Because they are the Living Truth, that only wants us to know we are loved. Yes, my crimes are the truth too, as much as any other truth. They are an „ugly" truth, but if we deny the ugly truths then we deny all truths. Because in the end there is only One Truth, and no regret.

Reflections

Sunday, August 19, 2012

The Choice To Suffer

All emotional pain and suffering is self-inflicted. To believe otherwise is the gist of insanity. We choose to suffer in order to define ourselves against the threat of nothingness. We fear that if we do not suffer, then we would not exist. So, we invent all kinds of reasons to suffer and call it humanity.

Dreams

Saturday, August 25, 2012

Lucid With Whoopie

I haven't been having much success with my lucid dreaming attempts, so I decided to start following Dr. LaBerge's suggestions in his latest book, Exploring the World of Lucid Dreaming, more closely. I did an extended version of his „Prospective Memory Training" exercise, with good results, and I have also been keeping a fairly detailed dream log for the last several weeks. The log is meant to help me remember my dreams (which I don't seem to have any problem doing) and also so I can generate a catalog of „dreamsigns", as LaBerge suggests, to be used later for the „Mnemonic Induction of Lucid Dreams", or MILD for short. I'm hoping that by following LaBerge's research proven techniques I will eventually be able to have lucid dreams at will, which he says is perfectly possible.

So far I have had only one fully lucid dream since I've renewed my efforts to have them a couple months ago. But, I haven't completed the dream log yet (LaBerge suggests one full month at least), or the consequent catalog of dreamsigns. In other words, I had this lucid dream without really even trying yet, though I'm not sure what caused me to become lucid in the dream either. I just suddenly became aware that I was dreaming for no apparent reason.

I was having an ordinary dream where I was in a hotel, and unable to find my room. I asked the front desk clerk if she could look up my room for me and also give me a new card-key, but she told me she couldn't help me unless I had some identification, which I did not. So I walked away from the desk and entered a nearby stairwell. I climbed the stairs, for some reason struggling on my hands and knees, and at some points having to pull myself up the steps by grabbing a hold of the railings. I managed to climb about two or three flights before I couldn't go any further (though there seemed to be more flights above me). Then I saw a door that appeared to lead out to the roof, and I stood up without any problem and walked out the door. As soon as I stepped through the door I became fully lucid, but I don't know why or how. I just suddenly realized I was in a dream and that everything I was seeing wasn't real.

I was outside on the roof of the hotel and could see other buildings for miles into the distance. Everything was incredibly clear and real seeming (which is a well known characteristics of lucid dreams). I stood just outside the door I had just come through at the top of a kind of handicap ramp that lead down from the door along the wall to my right with a handrail on the outside. The camp extended only eight or ten feet as it dropped about two feet to the roof itself. I looked down at my feet and scuffled them on some loose gravel that was strewn over the tar paper roofing material that covered the ramp. I was totally amazed at how real and detailed everything seemed.

I started to walk down the ramp and noticed a broken window in the door (which was opened against the wall to my right). The window was dark and offered a good reflection, so I stepped close so I could see my face. Yep, it was my face. As far as I could tell it looked just like my face when I look in a real mirror. But before I could get a really good look something behind me caught my attention. I turned around and saw Whoopie Goldberg walking on the roof of the next building over about a hundred feet away from me. It was clear that she saw me and was coming in my direction. So I walked over toward the edge of the roof to greet her.

As she was walking I saw two identical Whoopies split off from each side of her, so now there were three of her walking, each with the same characteristic nonchalance that she does so well. When they were all close enough, the Whoopie in the center spoke to me, clearly and loud enough so I could hear her over the gap between roofs. She said something like, „Joe! Imagine YOU being in here! How did you get in?"

I wanted to ask her, „In where?" but I knew from other lucid dream experiences that I wouldn't get an answer to a question like that, so I just shrugged. But then I remembered that I wanted to recite Edgar Allen Poe's famous poem, „A Dream Within A Dream", while I was in a lucid dream, and now was my chance to do it. I also vainly thought that I might actually impress Whoopie with my ability to recite Poe. But I had a good reason for reciting the poem too.

LaBerge recommends setting goals to accomplish specific tasks in your lucid dreams, such as flying or meeting some famous or dead person (or both). According to LaBerge, these goals will not only make lucid dreams more likely to occur (by providing motivation for the dream), but tasks will also give the dreams direction and purpose (i. e. make them more interesting and exciting). Flying was too easy for me. I've done that many times in past lucid dreams, and while it's certainly always thrilling to do so, I had other interests in mind. I wanted to do something that would establish the level of my intellectual „presence of mind" during the dream. So I decided to recite a poem as one of my task goals in order to test the extent of my lucidity. I chose Poe's „Dream Within A Dream" for the irony, but also because it takes some effort for me to recall the lines to this poem, which is to say that I can't just spout them out without „intellectual effort" to remember the poem. But I certainly knew the poem well enough that I should be able to recite it in my dream at will, that is, assuming I have my normal waking intellectual facilities; and hence the nexus.

But, in this dream, as soon as I turned my attention to the task of remembering Poe's poem the dream itself began to fade out, and it was obviously a direct consequence of my effort to remember the poem! I realized instantly that I could remember the poem if I really wanted to, but it would cost me the dream in order to do so. In other words, remembering the poem would either cause me to wake up or at least loose lucidity somehow.

Naturally I wanted to stay in the dream so I could explore. So I abandoned my effort to remember the poem and returned my full attention to the dream at hand. But the dream had dissolved into a white featureless fog in which I was now adrift. I relaxed and began to concentrate without effort on the dream (a technique that I practice during meditation just for this reason) and soon the dream returned with the same clarity and detail as before, except now I was in an alley behind the hotel instead of on the roof, and Whoopie was nowhere in sight.

But there were plenty of other people walking around, even other famous actors who I recognized but could not name. There were props and stagehands moving busily about, and I could even see scenes from movies I didn't recognize being acted out around me (and presumably being filmed, though I never saw any cameras or film crews).

I started walking to explore my dream (I was still very much lucid), and entered a busy breezeway that boarded what seemed to be a staged city park. There I saw a group of adults and two young girls, all dressed in old-fashioned costumes, the little girls in frilly Victorian pink and yellow dresses. It seemed to me that the adults were buying a balloon from a vendor to give to the girls. But when I stepped closer I saw that the „balloon" was really a small parasol that lifted both girls into the air together as they clung to it desperately.

The girls were clearly distressed, and I considered dashing to their aid, but distinctly thought, „No, this is only a dream, so they wont get hurt." I didn't think they were in any real danger even though they were both screaming for their lives. (I also remember not wanting to ruin the dream by stiring up my perversion, sexual contact with children, which might happen if I came into physical contact with the girls, which of course I would have to in order to rescue them.) The other adults around did not seem concerned either. So I turned my attention back to the breezeway and suddenly woke up. Or so I thought.

Actually, I „woke up" into another dream, just as clear and real seeming as reality itself, or perhaps a lucid dream, though I was obviously no longer lucid, but I thought I was wide awake.

I „woke up" in an institutional dayroom, and thought nothing strange about it. I was sitting at a table that was empty, and a female psychologist had just sat down adjacent to me. She asked me to explain my thoughts and feelings regarding a piece of art that I had posted on the Internet. I didn't know what art she was referring to, so she told her (male) assistant, who was sitting on my other side, to pull it up on his laptop, which he had just placed and opened on the table so I could see the screen.

I didn't like the feeling of being interrogated, and I had to urinate. So I told her I needed to use the bathroom before we could continue. She and her assistant exchanged some kind of knowing look that I noticed, but ignored. I really didn't care what they thought.

I got up and walked over to a public mens room that was actually just fifteen or twenty feet away (the whole set up was similar to a prison visiting room, though I didn't think of it as such in the dream). I entered the bathroom and walked over to a small green facility on the wall that I thought must be the urinal, though it did not look right at all. As I stood there trying to figure out what was wrong with this bathroom I heard a couple of people talking to each other as they exited the bathroom behind me. One of them was clearly a woman.

I thought for a moment that maybe I had entered the women's bathroom by mistake. But then to my relief I saw the full size mens white urinals over a little ways on the wall. So I walked over to one of them and began fumbling with my pants.

Just as I extracted my penis to urinate a hand suddenly reached over and grabbed it. I now saw that the psychologist's male assistant had followed me into the bathroom and it was he who was molesting me. I pulled away from him by way of rebuffing his lewed advance, at which point he said something like, „Don't pretend you don't like it."

At this point I woke up for really real, in my cell here in Federal prison, and, of course, I had to pee.

I don't know what this dream means, if it means anything at all. But it has raised some questions in my mind about the nature of dreams in general. Why, for example, did Whoopie call me „Joe"? I always think of myself as „Jet" or sometimes „Duncan". But I consider „Joe" to be my father's name, not mine at all. (Though it was also the name of a very close friend I had in Fargo, and also the name of one of the attorneys working on my Federal appeal whom I talk to often and consider also to be a good friend.) I never think of myself as „Joe", and so when someone calls me by that name it lets me know that they don't know me at all, personally. So, if Whoopie was a construct of my personal unconscious mind (as many suppose), then why wouldn't she use my personal name?

Also, what did she mean by, „in here?" This is one of those questions that I have often and futilely tried to solicit an answer for in past lucid dreams, by asking everyone I could in the dream itself. Questions like, „Where is this place?" or „Are you real?" or „Where do you come from?" But the answers I got were almost always either vague or meaningless. I've since come to a kind of impasse, and suspect that maybe the questions themselves are meaningless in the dream context. But still, why would she make such an allusion?

Perhaps I will have a chance to find all these things out. But for now, the mysteries remain, and the dreams go on.

Note: (September 25, 2012) Since having the above dream (several weeks ago) I have realized a couple of things.

First, I had forgotten all about my "alter ego" Joe that used to help protect me when I was a kid in prison all those years ago. It could well have been this alter ego that Whoopie was addressing in this dream when she called me "Joe". That would imply a lot.

Second, I previously had assumed that when I tried to remember the "Dream Within A Dream" poem in order to recite it, that the reason the dream faded was because I was overtaxing my brain by expecting it to remember something little difficult to remember and maintain the dream at the same time. But that doesn't really make any sense. If my brain can't sustain a perception of the world while I'm taxing it, then it wouldn't be able to sustain its perception of reality either when I did so.

So, another more interesting and much better explanation has come to me. What if it wasn't my brain that couldn't keep up with the demands, but the connection to my brain that couldn't keep up? In other words, suppose that the dream was actually a kind of "out of body" experience in which I was only "tethered" to my physical body (and brain) through a restricted communication channel? Of course I'm thinking of the "silver cord" that mystics commonly refer to when speaking of their own out of body experiences. Though I have never seen such a cord, in my dreams or otherwise, it could explain why my dream faded when I tried to remember Poe's poem. I figure that maybe by trying to access my physical brain so heavily I was in effect "pulling" on that cord and hence causing my "mind" to "return to my body" and hense "wake up".

It's just a thought for now, but one I will certainly be exploring in future dreams.

P.S. I think it is best to think of the "silver cord" as a symbolic metaphor rather than a form of reality the way some mystics pretend. The important aspect of this metaphor is the connection that is sustained between mind and body in a dream. So the fact that I have personally never "seen" this connection is not significant to its possible presence.

Confessions

Sunday, August 26, 2012

About Jeff, Who Was Not Very Polite

When I was 15 years old, and my brother, Bruce, was 13, we lived in a suburb in Tacoma, Washington, called Lakewood (which has since been incorporated and is now its own city).

One day, while my brother and I were out terrorizing the world together on our 10-speeds, we saw a black man flying a line-controlled model airplane in an empty parking lot of the local high school. It was the weekend, so there were no students around.

Being the boys that we were, my brother and I were of course drawn to the scene like flies to well, you know. The man quickly befriended us and even offered to let us try to fly the plane. My brother and I had similar planes of our own, so we had no trouble getting the model into the air.

The man said his name was Jeff Polite, and he soon asked us boys if we wanted to go to his room to see his other model airplanes. He was obviously retarded and still lived at home with his parents though he was in his mid 20's.

Because he acted so much like a kid – like one of us – my brother and I accepted the invitation without apprehension. Jeff seemed a little weird, definitely not dangerous.

Jeff's parents were not home, of course. But, he invited us into his bedroom anyway, of course. The room was almost a typical of what you would expect of any teenager's room – there was nothing „adult" about it all. There was a made bed in the middle, a few plastic Revel model airplanes hung from the ceiling with fishing line, and more plastic models on some book shelves.

At the end of the bed was a desk that might have had a model airplane in the process of being assembled. The desk did have various implements and gadgets used for building model planes, which my brother and I took an interest in.

Then for some mysterious reason Jeff became agitated with me and asked me to leave. But my brother was welcome to stay so Jeff could „show him something". My brother and I were still completely unsuspicious of Jeff, so I just thought he'd decided he didn't like me, and my brother wanted to stay to look at the models and stuff some more.

So, I left, and my brother stayed. But, not for very long.

Before I got even halfway home on my bike (about a mile) I heard my brother calling from behind for me to stop so he could catch up.

When he caught up he just said, „Jeff's a weirdo". Then we continued on together.

I asked him what Jeff wanted to show him, and my brother said he didn't know. He told me that Jeff just asked him to hold onto a two or three foot length of wire that went „inside his pants".

This didn't make sense to either of us. But apparently Jeff made my brother nervous enough that Bruce quickly decided to leave and try to catch up with me after all. When I pressed my brother for more information he repeated what he'd already said, and we both shrugged it off as some „retardo" thing.

Less than two years later I was convicted for raping a 14 year old boy in the same neighborhood. I guess things change pretty quickly at that age.

Some fifteen years or so after that, while I was still on parole for the rape, my brother came to visit me at my Seattle apartment, and gave me an interesting update on the Jeff Polite saga.

Bruce told me that he had run into Jeff recently at a fast food restaurant, and decided to confront him about the incident back in 1978, when we were boys.

It seems that my brother had decided over the intervening years that Jeff was masturbating that day in his bedroom while he held onto the wire. It wasn't just a „retardo" thing; it was a „perverto" thing! So my brother asked Jeff for an apology right there in the restaurant.

My brother told me that Jeff very nervously denied even recognizing him. But Bruce was certain that Jeff not only recognized him, but was guilty as hell too, because of the way he was acting. „Scared shitless", was the way my brother put it.

Bruce, unlike me, had grown into a fairly imposing man. He was over six feet and easily more than 200 pounds. He liked to keep scruff on his face (which made him look macho) and carried a concealed 38 automatic of some impressive sort, because he could. He was the type of person who would „accidentally" let people see he was packing heat, just for the fun of it.

But when I suggested to my brother that perhaps Jeff was just scared over being so rudely confronted by a scary man in public, my brother insisted again, „No, he's a perve, and he knew I knew it! I wanted to blow his stinkin' head off right there!"

That was just the way my brother talked, which after 15 years in prison didn't impress me very much. I suggested again that maybe Jeff genuinely did not recognize him, and even if he was masturbating back then, so what?

Big mistake on my part that, „so what?" bit. My brother got angry at once (which he tried to hide as usual, but I could tell as easy as I could when we were kids that he was about to be rash). So, I tried to clean it up by asking him to tell me again what actually happened back in '78 in Jeff's bedroom. What he told me was pretty much the same thing he told me back then, except now with a little more insight to Jeff's motives.

Bruce said that Jeff „molested" him, even though he kept his privates in his pants, and never touched my brother on his.

I tried to question my brother about what he meant by „molested", but he could only tell me the rote responses that someone might get from a book, or magazine article.

„He used me", my brother said.

„He asked you to hold a wire. You didn't even know what he was doing then, even if you do now", I retorted.

„It doesn't matter if I didn't know. I was just a kid and he molested me!"

We clearly weren't communicating. To me my brother was just spouting off all the classic „victim" expressions but saying nothing about the reality of what happened at all.

What I wanted to do, but sensed danger so I didn't, was remind my brother of the times he himself „molested" younger children even before we ever met Jeff. (By my brother's own definition of course. As far as I know, my brother has never really molested anyone. But, as kids we sometimes „played doctor" or „spin the bottle" with other children, which involved a bit more explicitly sexual behavior that what Jeff had done with the wire. Jeff was, after all, mentally only a kid himself even though he lived in a man's body.)

So, instead I reminded my brother about the time he was „molested" by George Worley, who pumped air up his butt with a bicycle pump. George was 15, and Bruce was 10 at the time. George became an „Eagle" in the boyscouts, which is how my brother and I knew him, he was in our troop 462, and at least I heard George was some sort of commander in the U.S. Navy stationed in Hawaii.

I asked, „How come you don't go demand an apology from George?"

That was enough to send my brother storming out the door of my apartment. I guess I'm lucky he didn't „blow my stinkin' head off".

(No disrespect, bro'! I just never could take you seriously; you were my younger brother after all! I love you and miss you dearly!!)

My brother died from a sudden heart attack in 2006. I learned after his death that he believed I „molested" him too, and was even going to write a book about it. I wish people could see how victim hysteria creates more victims than it will ever help. My brother's emotional trauma was real. The reason for his trauma was a fabrication of the worst kind, and not real at all.

Reflections

Sunday, August 26, 2012

Lots To Tell

I've probably said this many times already, but it bears repeating; I am an ignorant man, so I realize that my judgment and opinions aren't worth squat. If anything I say (or write) appears judgmental then it is only because our language has evolved primarily to express judgment, not reality or even truth. So it is hard, nearly impossible at times, to express anything using words that does not sound judgmental. In most cases it is judgmental, but not here. Everything I write for this blog is intended to express either past views - which were certainly judgmental at times, but are expressed here for the record and for understanding - or my current views that reflect not just how I see others, but also how I see, or rather, perceive myself at the same time.

For example, when I harp on Christians for being so ignorant, in words and deeds, of Christ's message, I am expressing my own ignorance as well. I may think I understand the message of Christ better than a typical Christian - better even than the pope himself - but I fully realize at the same time that their ignorance is my ignorance too. The contradiction and duality that appears here is due only to the limitations of human language. Words were not meant to express the true nature of things, and in fact serve only to obscure it, as it does here. But if you understand the true meaning of "One God", then you know there is no contradiction when I say, "There BY the grace of God go I!" (The Christian priest who famously said, "There BUT FOR the grace of God go I", as he watched condemned men being paraded past his house, was expressing the duel view of God that Jesus himself spoke so often against.) There is no us and them, no you and me; there is only God, "... so that they may all be one, as you, Father, are in me and I in you, that they also may be in us, (and us in them)" (John 17:21, excuse me for quoting the Bible here, I really try not to, but this time it seemed so pertinent, and there just happened to be an old tore up Bible in this cell that someone left. I don't keep a Bible around personally anymore because it's too tempting to use it to support what I say, and I prefer to let what I say stand on its own if it can, or fall on its face if it can't).

So anyway, please try to read past the limitations and syntactical bias of human language as you read this blog. It is important that you try to take all my words in the broadest context possible, so you can see the real meaning BEHIND the words rather than the superficial meaning IN them. This is why I sometimes say, if you have come here in order to pass judgment, then you should leave now, before you get hurt (i.e. "offended" by your own judgment). But, if you have come seeking to understand yourself, then stick around; I have lots to tell you! :)

Reflections

Saturday, September 1, 2012

The Sound of One Hand Clapping

The answer to life's "Big Question" is: there is no answer.

That does not mean that the Big Question has no answer. It simply means that the answer is found in "no answer". This only seems enigmatic because words cannot properly express what "no answer" really means. The meaning must be realized through direct experience, which usually comes when all sensual experience is exposed as an illusion.

"No answer" does not mean there is no solution to life's struggles. It means that the solution can only be found by letting go of the question itself. The question only arises because of the illusion, and without the illusion there would be no question. Any answer other than "no answer" is just another part of the illusion as well, and hence not really an answer to anything. So if you think you know the answer, then you have bought into a lie and are still suffering from delusion.

When you finally realize that there is no answer, and truly believe it, then you will have found the answer in the "nothingness that is everything". To know you know nothing is to know everything you need to know. And to think you know anything is simply not knowing that you know nothing, which is another definition of ignorance.

If you have trouble comprehending what it is I am trying to say, it is likely because you are still clinging to the illusion of knowing something, and attempting to determine the illusory value of my words rather than experiencing them - and me - as the truth always intends, directly.

It might help (if you are interested in the truth at all) to meditate on the enigma of not knowing. This has at times been referred to as, "the sound of one hand clapping". You could begin by questioning what it means to know anything, and thus turn the illusion - with all its questions - against itself.

Dreams

Sunday, September 2, 2012

Gap Chasm Dream

Last night I dreamed I was in a wheelchair and a man offered to help by pushing it for me. But I told him it was okay because I really didn't need the wheelchair, I just used it to help carry my "stuff". Then I go up out of the chair to show him, and he left.

I got back in the chair and continued wheeling toward a lake that I intended to go scuba diving in (I was just returning after retrieving a scuba mask and a towel so I could do so). Suddenly there was a drop-off and I jump out of the chair just before the chair itself went over the edge. I could see the chair had fallen about twenty feet into a chasm that was about fifteen feet wide with dirt walls. I knew I had to cross the chasm to get to the lake, so I found a spot that I was somehow familiar with and started to climb down.

But, I lost my footing and started to fall. Instead of panicking though I pushed away from the wall just enough so I could see the vines and grab them to slow my fall. Thus I reached the bottom safely. When I went to retrieve the chair though it was gone! Now I panicked. I thought, how could it be gone? It was only out of my sight for a moment and there was no one else around. Or was there?

I suddenly remembered that a wise friend had told me that Gremlins could steal things and take them back to their lairs without anyone seeing them. He also showed me how to find a gremlins lair, but I had to move fast, as soon as the item went missing.

So I ran off down the bottom of the chasm which soon opened up into a rocky valley. I knew what direction I needed to go in hopes of retrieving the wheelchair, but then I saw a large tyrannosaur-like creature prowling nearby - much to near for comfort. So I thought, well, I can live without that wheelchair, and I turned to continue my journey to the lake; a much safer place than this strange valley.

But no sooner did I turn around and I realize that now my scuba-mask and towel were missing too! I was carrying these things on me, and somehow the gremlin took them! These I could NOT live without. So I turned right back around and continued my pursuit of the gremlin in spite of any danger.

The dream continued a bit after that, but the important parts are here. Later today I picked up the book I have been reading about Carl Jung's life (Memories, Dreams, Reflections), and shortly came across this passage:

"These victims of the psychic dichotomy of our times are merely optional neurotics; their apparent morbidity drops away the moment the gulf between the ego and the unconscious is closed."

I realized instantly that the "gulf" Jung spoke of was possible what the chasm in my dream represented. The lake I was trying to get to then would have represented my unconscious mind according to this theory.

I typically read books like this with a pencil (or some other marker) in hand, and I employed my pencil to underline Jung's reference to the "gulf between the ego and the unconscious", and continued reading.

A little later I picked up another book that I'm also reading to help with my meditation (Tulku's, Openness Mind), and shortly ran into this:

"The shadow of fear is always hiding in the gap between our subjective and objective worlds."

Again, I instantly recognized the possible relationship this could have to my dream (assuming that "subjective" refers to the unconscious, and "objective" to the conscious "ego" that Jung spoke of). I thought it was strange that both books I was reading would mention the same concept in the section I read on the same day of this dream. It was a perfect example of what Jung calls "synchronicity" (coincidences that are really coincidences at all).

But Tulku's book went even further. The very next sentence reads:

"We have the fear of losing ourselves, of losing out identity."

Wow" Did I really just read that? I thought about it for a moment and quickly realized that it was explaining the dream yet again, perfectly!

The wheelchair symbolized how I saw myself as a damaged (mentally handicapped), an important part of my self image. In the dream of course I denied any handicap at all, and proved it by getting up and walking. But that fits my "identy" perfectly. I am constantly trying to prove I am not "mentally handicapped", even though I secretly think I am (I rationalize this contradiction by telling myself that my "handicap" is not important as far as others are concerned - in other words, I think I should be the only one who can "see" it).

The scuba mask represents my "adventurer" identity, and the towel stood for my "swimmer" identity (i.e. someone who "swims" in the "unconscious"). I realized after making these connections with my dream that these are three of my most "cherished" identities (or at least, most important to me). And the gremlin stole them! No wonder I wanted them back so bad.

Wow. This has given me much to think about. Is there more to the dream message? Perhaps some indication of the direction I should go? Both books suggest eliminating the gap, but I'm not sure what that means in practical terms. I will certainly be increasing my diligence in meditation and keeping a sharp eye out for any further clues in my dreams or otherwise.

(Note: I've long suspected that dreams hold important clues to lifes mysteries, especially our personal ones. But I'm only just now becoming really convinced!)

Reflections

Sunday, September 2, 2012

Obsession

Psychologists frequently mischaracterize a person who has admitted to committing as sex crime as overly „obsessed with sex".

Well, I have known many such men, and am one myself, but we aren't „obsessed" with sex any more than an avid SCUBA diver is „obsessed" with water.

Sure, many men who want to please the psych doctors readily admit to being obsessed with sex, but only in so far as they really do think about sex far more than most „normal" people do. But that doesn't necessarily mean they are obsessed with it.

Obsession implies a constant preoccupation with something; which means you cannot think of anything without thinking about whatever obsesses you. Few sex offenders actually rise to this level of sexual obsession.

For example, a SCUBA diver may think about water for more than most „normal" people do. But as long as his aquatic thoughts do not impose upon his routine thoughts then he is not obsessed. Every time he sees anything that reminds him of water, or his diving gear, he relates it to diving and may even briefly fantasize „what it would be like" in that context. But he is not „obsessed", he is just „interested".

But a man who is „interested" in sex instead of SCUBA diving (or sports, or clothes, or food, etc...) is considered to be obsessed for having a similar perponderance of thoughts about what is interesting to him throughout the day.

This mischaracterization accounts for a lot of misunderstanding and consequently misdiagnosis and mistreatment for „sex offenders" who are really just misguided and simply need to be educated about their own sexual nature.

I'm not suggesting that this analysis is the magic bullet cure for all sex offenders, but I am certain that it could help a lot of men re-think their problem, perhaps in terms of an ordinary addiction, rather than a debilitating obsession.

If a man is told he is obsessed there is a good chance he may actually become obsessed. I would even assert that most serious obsessions are the result of the person at some point being told (or otherwise coming to believe) that they are obsessed. I say this because I have never met an obsessed person who did not know they were obsessed (perhaps such people exist, but I would imagine them to be confined in the very bowels of some mental institution – which would explain why I have never met one).

Obsession is only one of many mischaracterizations of so-called „sex offenders" that contributes markedly the „sex offender" phenomenon (and hence allowing sex crimes to proliferate).

Reflections

Monday, September 3, 2012

Electroshock Criminology

Trying to solve the problem of crime with punishment is a lot like trying to treat mental illness with electroshock therapy. In theory it should work, and sometimes it actually does work. But, for the most part, it only makes things worse.

We know this today in regards to electroshock therapy, but how much more suffering must we inflict (and endure) before we realize it is true for crime and punishment as well?

Reflections

Sunday, September 9, 2012

Horizon of Volition

I have intentionally contradicted myself on occasion regarding my views of free will. One moment I state that it is important for us to recognize our choices and to accept responsibility for them. In fact, it was this realization that allowed me to „choose" to bring Shasta home and surrender myself to the police in Cour d'Alene in 2005. Then the next moment I strongly implied that I had no choice but to bring that little girl home and turn myself in, once I „saw the truth". So how can I have choice and no choice at the same time? To understand we must try to realize that the concept of choice (also free will, volition, etc...) is an illusion, very much akin to the illusion of „the edge of the world" one sees when peering out at the horizon on the ocean. It's only because few of us have yet dared to venture out beyond that „horizon of volition" that this world still imagined that we live on flat intellectual surfaces, where right is always right and wrong is wrong, just as up was once always up, and down was down. The real nature of free will (i. e. the ability to choose right over wrong for instance) is as circular (or globular) as the world; perhaps even more so.

No choice we make is ever personal. First, as soon as the choice is made the entire universe is forever changed! Even the simplest choice, to step over a sidewalk crack on the way to school, for example, will cause unimaginable changes in this world alone in a relatively very short time.

Such a trivial choice, when properly extrapolated, will invariable change the entire course of history and dramatically effect every living thing on the planet in a very short order of time. The choice is not trivial at all!

Second, no personal choice is ever made in a vacuum. Whether or not you step over that crack in the sidewalk depends on your mood, which depends on the weather, and how things are for you at home, and at school, and even the color of a car parked nearby can influence your choice on a subconscious level. And all of those things depend on other choices made by you and other people.

So your choice is really no choice at all, unless! Unless you have the ability to consider every other choice that goes into your choice, and every outcome of your choice for all eternity. And only one being (by definition) has that ability.

God.

Or, „the universe", in its known and unknowable entirety. So you see, our choices only appear limited by a horizon of volition, but the horizon is only an illusion.

Reflections

Sunday, September 16, 2012

When The Music Dies: The Systematic Attack On An Offender's Social Structure

The single most common element of all antisocial and criminal behavior is a lack of appropriate social support structures. Conversely, the single most common element of all rehabilitated criminal offenders is the development of appropriate and substantial social support structures. A meta-analysis of studies on the effects of social support structures in relation to antisocial and criminal behavior shows a clear and conclusive direct relationship between the lack of social support structure and criminal behavior. This relationship is so strong that it is demonstratably possible to trigger criminal behavior by simply causing a person to experience the loss of appropriate social support. This works with even "law-abiding" and socially "well adjusted" persons, though in such cases the loss of social support must be pronounced in order to overcome the persons residually perceived social support.

In cases when a person is already susceptible to antisocial behavior (due to a clearly lacking social support structure) the opposite is true. In this case, a very small almost insignificant perceived loss of social support will cause a severe relapse.

Clearly, social support is the key to social control of antisocial and criminal behavior.

So will someone please tell me why we insist on passing laws and creating institutions that seem to have no other goal than to undermine the social support structures of people who have demonstrated a clear lack of said appropriate social support in the first place?

Systematic efforts to use social support for rehabilitation are blatantly superficial. You can't just tell an offender, "I support your positive social behavior" and expect that to fix anything. (Actually, studies show that even such superficial efforts have an effect on criminal behavior. But only superficially, which should be expected.)

(A perfect example of the difference between substantial and superficial efforts to develpoe social support structures for x-convicts can be found in the history of the Interaction Transition House in Seattle, Washington.)

Chronicles

Thursday, September 20, 2012

The Smell of Seattle

Today I took a little trip into downtown Seattle for the first time in almost ten years. The thing that struck me first was the pleasant smell. When I live in downtown Seattle I never realized it even had a distinct smell. But now, after having been gone for so long, the smell was so distinct and identifiable to me that as soon as I smelled it I knew I would have known where I was even with my eyes closed.

I was in chains on a Federal Marshal's Service bus, of course, but I sat next to a large window on the bus that afforded a good view of the city as we drove in from the south and then through downtown to the new Federal courthouse. There were several other prisoners on the bus, being transported from FDC (in Seatac) to the courthouse for their court hearings. I was kept separate in the front caged off portion of the bus along with one overweight but pretty female prisoner. We didn't talk though, since we were told to sit in opposite corners of the cage and I was preoccupied with looking out the window at what I have long considered the most beautiful city in the US of America.

The distinct smell was like coffee and donuts, but subtle, and mixed with the aroma of evergreens and the slightly musky smell of decomposing pine needles. Imagine a coffee shop in the forest, but in the distance so you know it's there but aren't overwhelmed by the odor. That's what Seattle smells like.

I was being transported there not for a court hearing (my hearings are currently all in Boise, Idaho), but for a court ordered four hour long video taped psych-evaluation. The evaluation was being performed by a Canadian college professor who was hired by the prosecutor as an expert on legal competency (he'd apparently written two books on the subject). In other words, yet another "hired gun", as the lawyers say. My own "defense" attorney was watching, along with the prosecutor from Boise, via the video feed from an adjacent room. Afterwards my attorney told me that he thought the interview, "went well", which I think means that I sounded crazy. Oh well.

Besides the smell of downtown Seattle, the other thing that struck me was the number of images (buildings, stretches of woods next to the road, unique over passes, etc...) that seemed to come straight out of dreams I have had recently. T don't think there is really anything "synchronicitous" (as Jung might say) about this, as much as just my own brain recalling long forgotten details from when I lived in Seattle many years ago. It's still a very interesting phenomenon though.

And now I'm back in the SHU (single cell) in Seatac, reflecting on a rather enjoyable day; and relishing the memory of the smell of Seattle.

Dreams

Sunday, September 23, 2012

1-800 HELL

Shortly after my arrest in 2005 I had a disturbing dream that I am only now able to understand at all. I may have written it down in a journal I was keeping at the time, but I don't recall ever talking to anyone about it.

The dream had an obvious interpretation that did not make any sense to me. I was afraid that if I told anyone about it that they would draw the only conclusion that the dream seemed to offer: that I belonged in Hell!

It was a lucid dream, which is to say that it was vivid, with clear details, and I was fully conscious of the fact that I was in a dream and that in "reality" I was asleep in a jail cell awaiting prosecution for capital murder and kidnapping.

At the time of this dream I was still struggling consciously (while awake and asleep) to sort out what had happened, and why I had surrendered to the police. A strong feeling that pervaded my thoughts and feelings at the time was a sense of having joined some mystical community that as yet remained a mystery to me. While I could distinctly feel a sense of belonging to this community, I could not otherwise identify its existence. I thought maybe that the community was purely "spiritual" with little or no real counterpart in the "physical" world.

The dream I had seemed to be yet another manifestation of that sense of belonging to some mystical community. In the dream I found myself standing in the foyer of a congregation hall, like a church, but not a church. I approached the main entrance to the hall, large double doors that were wide open and through which I could see a large gathering of people apparently waiting for some ceremony to begin.

I thought maybe they were waiting for me. But as I approached the entrance, two large male porters who were standing there turned and took notice of me.

They seemed to recognize me immediately, but not in any positive way at all. In fact, one of them exclaimed, "How did you get here?" implying by his tone that I definitely did not belong.

Then, without waiting for me to answer (I tried to explain to them that I was having a lucid dream and that I wanted to be a part of their congregation, but I never got the chance) they quickly took me by the arms and shuffled me toward a coatroom, where an attendant was waiting.

The same porter who spoke the first time indicated to the coatroom attendant that he should retain me, and then told him (and this part I remember clearly), "Call 1-800 HELL"

Then I woke up (or, rather, found myself suddenly back in my jail cell) with the clear impression that I was not wanted in that congregation.

What confused me was that these men clearly judged me, apparently without cause. Even then I understood that such judgment was not conducive to an enlightened body of people. I should have been accepted and loved, especially since I had sincerely repented my ignorance (and my "crimes"). So why was I so harshly and brashly judged?

Well, I think I have finally come to an understanding. I think that perhaps because I was still alive (i.e. had a physical body) that the condemnation to “hell” did not have to be eternal. In other words, I was being “sent back” for more work.

Actually, I'm still not sure what the dream meant. But at least I now have a plausible explanation. Maybe hell is no more than some kind of soul smetter, and my soul was yet to be fired. Or maybe that's just one definition, or purpose, of hell. I'm not going to pretend I know what hell or heaven is. But if they exist at all then they must have some reason to exist beside simple reward and punishment.

Chronicles

Monday, September 24, 2012

The Hard Way

Over the last couple of weeks I have been interviewed by four different psych doctors, two psychiatrists, and two psychologists, three I have seen before, one not, and two I have seen many times over the years since my arrest in July of 2005. They have all been asked to shed their professional opinion on the question of whether or not I was "competent to waive my appeal" back in 2008 when I did so.

I told them all the same thing I've been telling them for the last eight years; my "competency" is the wrong question they should be asking. It has no meaning (according to the so-called legal definition) for me, and would have no meaning to them either if they only understood, which is to say, experienced, what I experienced in 2005 that caused me to bring Shasta home and turned myself in. It is the same thing I have been trying to convey with this blog as well.

I don't expect anyone to accept my word on faith about what happened back then. My only hope is that they will simply question the basic assumptions that are preventing them - preventing all of us - from discovering and experiencing the truth for ourselves.

Today's visitor, a professor and brain researcher from Penn State, asked me to sign a release form allowing him to use my case and information in a study designed to determine if the minds (brains, specifically) are any different in "Capital Case defendants" than other "average" (a research pseudonym for "normal") people.

I agreed to sign the release, but only after taking at least ten minutes to try to explain why the study was asking the wrong question as well (see "Serial Killer Fence" entry). I signed even though I strongly disagree with the direction such studies are trying to go. My rational for this (if you can call it rational at all) is that they must learn for themselves, as I did, the hard way. The easy way is a path that can only be seen in hindsight, but never traversed methinks.

Dreams

Tuesday, September 25, 2012

Dream Comments

One of the reasons I keep this dream blog, and the primary reason I am so fascinated by all dreams (mine, or anyone else's), is because I believe dreams are the best clue we have into the nature of consciousness itself. I'm not as interested in the interpretations of dreams as I am in the mechanical aspects. That is, what can and cannot be done in dreams? Or, what precisely is the difference between dream experience and "real" experience? And, how exactly are they the same?

Just now I awoke from my morning siesta in which I was having a typical dream as I woke up. I somehow managed to retain the thread of consciousness as my mind slid from the dream state back to reality (or rather, what we call reality). As I did this I noticed the dream experience transitioned into a narrative that I myself was dictating or "making up" as the dream went along. In other words, it was like I had caught the man behind the curtain, and that man was me! One minute I was talking to someone on the phone in the dream world, and the next I was merely imagining the conversation I was having and inventing the words of the other person I was talking to as well as my own. The dream went from dream experience to simple and ordinary imagination without skipping a beat.

If this type of transition had only occurred once or twice then I would register it as interesting, but not give it much significance. Perhaps it could be just some sort of trick of the dream consciousness, or even just an anomaly. But, I have experienced these types of transitions, where I "catch" myself imaging the dream as it goes along, several times (though they are rare). That makes me wonder, is a dream no more than an unconsciously imagined or invented story that our brain then translates for us into an actual experience? And if so, then might "reality" be no more than a similarly imagined story that some superconscious being is narrating, and inventing as He goes along, as well?

I realize of course that I'm not the first person to ever propose such a question about the nature of reality. But, i only do so now because of the experience I had this morning of that exact thing seeming to happen, at least on a personal level. So why shouldn't it happen on a cosmic level?

Chronicles

Thursday, September 27, 2012

Psychological Rape

What is rape? My Webster dictionary defines rape as, 1: a carrying away by force. When someone breaks into your home and takes what they want, you feel raped. when someone puts a gun to your head and demands your wallet, you feel raped. And when the guards handcuff me, enter my cell, and take my extra books, I feel raped.

I realize that most people think I have no right to complain, and I'm not complaining, at least not about loosing my books. My only complaint is against my own ignorant feeling of being raped. I shouldn't feel that way, but I do. If I thought it would help I would gladly let them have all my books, and paper, and even personal pictures and pens, everything, if it would prevent me from having to feel so violated the next time they decide to come take something from me. But I've tried this in the past (getting rid of everything they could possibly find an excuse for "confiscating") and no matter what I surrender, the system always manages to find something to take away; it has to, because that's all it knows how to do.

In fact, experienced prisoners have learned that the best defense against these "shake downs" is to keep some sort of nuisance contraband in your cell for them to take when they come to take something. This usually works, because they don't feel like they're doing their job unless they take something. So if you leave them nothing to take they'll take something you don't want them to take. Technically, everything is contraband for one reason or another, which means they can always find something to take, and usually do (some guards, the more mature and experienced guards, don't feel so gung ho about "doing their job", but these types are the exception, not the rule). So, I leave little "gifts" for the guards to take, but sometimes they take things I don't want them to take anyway; things that having meaning to me, like a good book that was hard to come by, even one I was two-thirds of the way through reading (like today).

It was this kind of psychological rape that drove me insane with rage all those years ago the last time I was in prison. Getting violently raped up my ass on numerous occasions by other inmates when I was still just a kid all those years ago ended up seeming like a pleasurable experience by comparison (though it certainly didn't seem pleasurable at the time). The persistent psychological violations that the system calls "rehabilitation" and "corrections" ends up becoming a deep emotional sore that is extremely slow to heal; if it ever gets the chance!

I told my attorneys shortly after my arrest this time (in 2005) that they'd be doing me a huge favor if they just let the system kill me (by death sentence) since the prospect of spending the 30 or so years remaining of my life as a prisoner waiting every day to be violated at the guards which was a nightmare I had no desire to relive all over again. And yet here I am. It's hard for me not to be mad at my attorneys for putting me through this personal hell, but I know they're not to blame; nobody is, not even the guards. But that doesn't make it feel any less like rape.

Reflections

Sunday, September 30, 2012

Having Faith Is Enlightenment

What I will tell you now is ancient wisdom that has been told in all the great writings of truth, but seldom understood, since it can only be understood through contemplation of what is inside of you, not inside of some book.

To know the truth one must have faith in the truth. But it is not possible to have faith by any mortal effort. Faith comes only when it is desired but not sought.

By seeking faith you lose your faith. You may pray for faith, or meditate for enlightenment. But as soon as your goal becomes faith or enlightenment then your prayer or meditation becomes useless.

Let me be clear. You can have faith by praying for it. But, if the goal of your prayer is to have faith then you have already lost faith and the prayer does you no good.

Also, you can have enlightenment by meditating. But if the goal of your meditation is to attain enlightenment then you have already lost faith and enlightenment will ellude you.

This appears as a dilemma only when you look outwards for understanding. In truth there is no dilemma. The solution is simple; have faith, be enlightened. To try is to fail. One must learn to be, and to do, without effort. This is the only way. Yet, it cannot be learned.

You must unlearn instead.

You must stop trying.

You must simply, believe, without believing in something; do, without doing, without purpose or intent. This is having faith.

Having faith is enlightenment.

Reflections

Sunday, October 7, 2012

Penultimate Prison Break

The boy opened his eyes. Where am I? He saw the ceiling in front of him. He hurt. I hurt? He hurt all over his body. My body? What am I doing in a body? I hate bodies! The boy hated being in a body. So, he tried to leave it. He tried to fly to the ceiling.

I can't move! He stayed on his back, and then rolled his head to the side. Oh, god! I have a head! He saw a wall. Why is there a wall? He told the body to get up. The body complained severely. It groaned. I hate groaning bodies!

He tried to leave the body again, but the body had a brain, a large brain. And, the brain latched onto the boy, like a clamp. I hate brains! The brain spoke to the boy. The brain said, “I am a boy.”
Great!
The brain said, “I am a boy.”
I heard you the first time!
The brain said, “I hurt.”
Brilliant!
The boy told the body to at least roll over. The body started to move and painfully it rolled over.
Why can't I leave?
The brain said, “I'm scared.”
Of course you are, you're a brain!
The brain said, “Help me!”
I hate brains.
He looked in front of him. His eyes hurt. Oh, god! I have eyes! He saw a door. A door? The door was closed. So?
The brain said, “I'm scared.”
The boy looked down. The body was laying on a bed.
The brain said, “A hospital bed.”
I hate brains.
The boy looked at his body. I hate bodies.
The brain said, “I'm in the hospital.”
I really hate brains.
The body gracelessly rolled back over onto its back on the bed. The boy looked at the ceiling.
He tried again to leave the body, but the brain clung on tight, not letting him go.
The boy closed his eyes.
The body closed its eyes.

The brain went to sleep.
And the boy flew away.

Reflections

Sunday, October 14, 2012

Justice Eternal

They say that justice delayed is justice denied. This is more true than perhaps it was intended. If justice is not immediate then it simply cannot be justice. There is, fortunately, immediate justice for all infractions in the universe. In fact, you can use this truth as a touchstone to determine what infractions are real and which are mere fabrications (imagined). If justice is not invoked by the act, then the act is not universally criminal, but is rather superficial and unimportant. True consequences are eternal, in fact, as the Bible concurs, a sin (i.e. "universal crimes") is already "paid for" by the very existence of "God in man" (i.e. "the Christ"). This means that real justice has already occurred and will continue to occur both before and after any "sin" is ever committed. A philosophical consideration of the term "instantaneous" reveals that in order for something to be instantaneous then it must also be eternal (occurring both before and after any given event eternally).

There ultimately is only one possible eternal consequence. This consequence goes by as many different names as the One Eternal Being Itself. For convenience here I will call it "separation from the One Eternal Being" (or more correctly, perhaps, the illusion of said separation). All suffering comes from this illusion. Time itself is perhaps the most powerful form that this illusion portrays. Timeless existence is enlightenment, also known as heaven, or eternal life. And it is also known as knowing the will of God, or being one with the universe (or God).

Reflections

Sunday, October 21, 2012

Hebrews

The thing I like about the book of Hebrews in the Christian bible, is the way that it emphasizes the humanity of the Christ.

To me, and apparently to the author of Hebrews, if Christ wère not human then he simply would not have the authority, or even the ability to „save mankind".

This implies that his human nature is an integral part of his ability to unite us with „God the Father". Which means – and this is clearly stated in Hebrews – if Christ were not 100% human, then he would not be able to fulfill the role of „high priest" and intermediary between man and God.

So, his humanness is not just a central feature, it is the Key feature of his role on Earth. Even being God, or the Son of God, is secondary to this aspect of Christ. And this is true for preternatural reasons, not mere theological theories. Which is to say that Christ must be human in the same sense that the flesh must receive physical nourishment in order to survive.

And what is that reason? Hebrews tells us it is because unless Christ were human he could not know human temptation and suffering. So, he must know „temptation" in order to be the savior. Why?

Because temptation defines man's enslavement to the flesh and separation from God. Christ must not just know temptation, he must overcome it. By overcoming temptation he sets men free to return to the source of their being. If he were not human then men who seek salvation in Christ would not be able to have faith in his ability to overcome temptation. And it is man's faith in Christ's ability to overcome temptation that gives the man the ability to overcome his own temptation, or in other words, let Christ lead the way.

This is critical. Because if Christ had any advantage to overcoming temptation that other men did not have then men could not look to Christ for salvation. Because he would be „cheating" temptation, not overcoming it.

So far few Christian's would argue, but now lets follow this reasoning to its only conclusion, one that Hebrews attempts to reach: In order for Christ to know temptation as a man knows it, then he must also be a sinner, like man! If Christ were not „born in sin" then he could not know temptation. Sin and temptation can not be separated, as even St. Paul tells us in his letter to the Roman's.

And Hebrews itself confirms this conclusion by telling us that Christ, like any other man, had to be taught obedience to the Will of God. He was not born obedient.

And that's why I like Hebrews, because it says plainly what no modern Christian likes to admit: that Christ was born into sin, and was a sinner, before he was „purified on the cross". It is only in death that Christ overcame sin, and only by dying did He become our savior – not by How He Lived.

Reflections

Sunday, October 28, 2012

Breath of Life; Breath of Death

Buddha teaches that all life is suffering. We most suffer in order to live. "Enlightenment" is not an escape from suffering, it is an understanding and acceptance of it. We "end suffering" by becoming (or being) one with it.

Of course, that is all a bunch of cryptic gobbledygook that essentially means nothing to most people. But what if we put it like this:

Nature learns by making mistakes; lots and lots of mistakes. This process is sometimes called evolution. But it is much more than a way for genetic information to be manipulated for some survival benefit. It is the fundamental method of all intelligence, genetic information being just one form of intelligent "thought".

But every mistake results in "death", and hense a loss of "information", which causes the being that experiences this loss to suffer. Thus, we have a system in order to live. Or, more correctly, a system of life that is itself a process of suffering.

Every thought you have and every experience is only possible because of a continues cycle of birth and death that occurs on all levels of life and in all forms; genetic, physiological, psychological, mystical and others we have yet to even intellectualize.

This is the suffering we must embrace to have peace. It is the suffering that Christ spoke of as well as the Buddha. To seek pleasure is an attempt to escape the suffering of life (but so is seeking suffering). The object is to accept, by not seeking pain or pleasure. In this way, pleasure and pain both become infinitely enjoyable gifts, not something ever to be gained (born) or lost (die).

Birth and death become like breathing for us, on all levels. And likewise, we come to see breathing as a form of birth and death.

Dreams

Thursday, November 1, 2012

Whose Dream Is This Anyway?

I dreamed this morning that I was back in Summit House (a preferred prisoner housing unit without bars or concrete walls at the McNeil Island prison in the 1980's). I had some dirty laundry and was trying to find my way downstairs to the laundry room but the stairs had been moved. When I found them, on the wrong side of the stairwell, I went down and discovered that all the halls and doorways - including the main entrance and exit - were walled up with bricks! But, there was one small door that looked like a utility or maintenance closet. When I opened it and looked inside, sure enough, I saw a dimly lit room that had a dirt floor with various pipes, ducts and conduits running through it mostly along the walls. But, I also saw a long and wide tunnel in place of one wall that looked like it extended out far beyond the prison perimeter security fences then opened up to the outside. It was a way out of prison.

At first I thought it must be a trap. But, then I realized it didn't make any sense for there to be a trap like that, in fact, the whole situation, I suddenly realized, didn't make any sense. At that point I thought I must be dreaming, though I wasn't 100% certain. But, I decided if it was a dream then no harm could come from exploring the tunnel. So I did.

I went through the tunnel and exited on a paved area next to a warehouse. I seemed to be in some sort of warehouse district. There was a six-foot high chain link fence that ran along one side of the roadway I was on and a warehouse on the other. I walked the length of the warehouse hoping to find something interesting, but the fence curved around then end of the warehouse and forced me back toward the tunnel I had come through, but only on the other side of the warehouse.

At one point I saw a very interesting looking all glass house on the other side of the six-foot fence that hemmed me in, about two-hundred yards away across an overgrown grass field. The house was brightly lit from the inside (it was dark out in my dream) which made it stand out beautifully. I wanted to take a closer look, so I began to climb the fence.

But, I couldn't get over the top, and I somehow started sliding down the fence as I hung onto it trying to get over. I was moving away from my goal of reaching the glass house, so I let go and fell back on the paved warehouse-side of the fence.

Then I got mad and thought, whose dream is this anyway? This is my dream! I should be able to go where I want! So I redoubled my determination to get over the fence as I grabbed it to pull myself up. This time when I got to the top I saw another fence, just like the one I was on, not twenty-feet away. That other fence wasn't there before. I realized that someone or something was deliberately trying to discourage me from going where I wanted to go.

That only made me even more determined than ever. So, I stood up on top of the fence and leaped into the air, trusting from dream experience that such a leap would result in my becoming airborne. And indeed I flew! I flew up about fifty-feet and easily cleared the second fence, though I was much higher in the air than I needed to be and promptly began to fall!

But, I also knew that I would not hit the ground. Experience told me to just relax; my dream would not let me get hurt, and once I was down I could continue to the house. So I just turned over on my back as I fell, expecting to be levitated again before hitting the ground. But, instead - and very much to my surprise - I hit the ground hard, flat on my back, with enough force to knock the wind out of me.

I was stunned, to say the least. Especially since at that exact moment of impact the dream ended, and I physically raised my arm - threw it into the air actually - as I woke to try to compensate for the impact I had just felt.

Wow! It seems clear that I was forcefully ejected from my own dream, and clearly because I refused to accept my containment. That was the firs time I'd ever hit the ground from a fall in a dream that I can remember. Here is the question I am now forced to ask: Is there an intelligent force, other than my own, somehow preventing me from exploring my own dreams? I have had other lucid dreams recently that were similar to the one just described, though until now I had not been so forcefully ejected, but in every case I have been clearly discouraged and prevented from exploring my own dream. None of the books I have been reading recently on lucid dreaming have mentioned this problem. In fact, they all express unrestricted freedom once lucid state is achieved. Could this also be the reason I have been having so few lucid dreams despite so much effort which in the past resulted in many lucid dreams?

It is a mystery I fully intend to pursue. I don't know, but I'm inclined to believe that some other intelligence than my own is involved, and hopefully I will be able to find a way to converse with it, or maybe learn how to listen to what it's trying to tell me.

Reflections

Thursday, November 8, 2012

Faith Alone

„Faith alone will save our souls", so say the Bible. But „faith alone" does not mean faith in one particular belief of other.

Faith alone means just that; faith, all by itself. We do not need to have „faith in Christ" or „faith in the Bible" in order to know the saving grace of „God". In fact, having faith in anything that you can define, or even just imagine, is what the Bible warns us not to do, over and over.

This is called idol worship. Any time that you put your faith in something imagined, which can be (and usually is) an Intellectual construct sometimes represented by a physical form (e.g. golden calf), then you are idol worshiping. It does not matter if the image you are worshiping has a physical form or not, if it is an idea, then it is an image, and it is a „false god."

Now, I'm not saying „faith in God" or even „faith in Christ" is always a form of idol worship. As long as „God" or „Christ" are not imagined to be something (i. e. a man from Nazareth, or an „old man in heaven") then you have the kind of faith that saves. That is, formless or imageless faith, which is faith alone.

Chronicles

Friday, November 16, 2012

America's Most Wanted

This morning a woman came to my cell door and told me that America's Most Wanted (the TV show) wanted to interview me. She then asked me to sign a form saying whether I agreed to be interviewed, or refused. I automatically refused, of course, like I always have to such requests. I also told her I would not sign anything - there was no reason I should sign. She responded by repeating my statements back to me, "So, you refuse the interview, and you won't sign the form", as confirmation, presumably (I think she was surprised that I would refuse at all). After I reaffirmed what I had just told her she said, "okay", and the guard with her closed the bean-slot and then they both left. So I climbed back under my covers and tried to go back to sleep. I was having an interesting dream about a nontraditional Santa Claus before she woke me up.

A few moments later, as I laid there curled on my side beneath the blankets trying to get warm so I could go back to sleep and maybe finishing my dream, I overheard one of the guards mocking my refusal to agree to the interview. The woman who had come to my door and asked me to sign her form (some admin-type) laughed along. Then I heard the guard key the door to the SHU to let her out.

But why did they mock me? I don't understand.

Chronicles

Saturday, December 29, 2012

What Happened In Prison – Part V: The Merry-go-round

In early 1993, after thirteen years of imprisonment for a crime (rape) that I was supposed to serve only five years for, I was found paroleable (again) by the ISRB (the defunct parole board now called the Indeterminate Sentencing Review Board). But, this time they set conditions that I had to meet before my release.

These conditions were a part of their newly invented MAP requirements. The ISRB came up with these requirements ostensibly to help inmates prepare for the supposed „shock" of being set free after so many years in prison. The real reason of course had nothing to do with helping inmates at all. It was just another one of their ruses to delay the parole-release process as long as possible so the ISRB could keep their jobs. You see, they only had a fixed number of old guideline inmates (with indeterminate sentences) left in their charge after the SRA (sentencing reform act) laws went into effect. Once those inmates were gone (released or deceased) then so was the ISRB, along with all of its support staff and lawyers. They would loose millions of dollars that they raked in annually from the state coffers to pay their ridiculous salaries so they could continue flying around the state going from prison to prison playing God.

It took nearly two years after I was found paroleable for me to meet all their MAP requirements so I could be released. It was only supposed to take nine months at the most. The system made it literally impossible for me to complete the requirements. It took an attorney working on my behalf just to get the ISRB to make the necessary arrangements that would allow their requirements to be met. Without the attorney I would have been stuck indefinitely.

The MAP requirements stipulated amongst other things that I had to complete a five week Victim Awareness class and spend six months at a minimum security institution. The minimum security stipulation was supposedly so I could acclimate to the fewer restrictions on my freedom in preparation for my release.

So, in the middle of the last semester of school at Walla Walla, which I needed to complete an associates degree, I was abruptly transferred to the Olympic/Clearwater Corrections Center (OCC), a work camp in the middle of the Olympic rain forest on the Washington state peninsula. The transfer of course kept me from finishing the last three humanities credits I needed for my degree. I don't have to tell you what a negative impact that was on my ability to get a job or even to continue my education after my release, not to mention what a huge let down it was for me not to get the degree after working so hard and so long on it. My g.p.a. was over 3.8, which would have easily gotten me accepted at a four-year University, if I had an A.A. degree. But, it seemed the ISRB thought cleaning bathrooms at a minimum security work camp and listening to victim sob stories for five weeks was more conducive to my success on parole. Yah, right. They consequently ignored my requests to delay the transfer for the few weeks it would have taken to complete the degree.

The reason I ended up at the OCC work camp specifically was because the Victim Awareness class was supposed to be there. Of course as it turned out wasn't there anymore. Apparently either someone didn't think to inform the ISRB (not likely), or the ISRB just wasn't doing the job they were so eager to keep (i. e. by reading the program status memos that are routinely posted on the DOC computer network bulletin board), which was almost likely the case.

Of course it seemed to me at the time that the real reason for this fiasco was that the ISRB was stalling again. I believed that they had deliberately sent me to OCC knowing full well that the Victim Awareness class wasn't there, just to piss me off even more than I already was. It was like kicking a mad dog for good measure before releasing it on an unsuspecting neighborhood. I was the mad dog, and it seemed the „kicks" came more and more the closer I got to that release gate.

As it turned out the Victim Awareness class was only available at two different institutions in the state. One was the Spokane Pre-Release, which did not accept sex offenders, and the other was at McNeil Island Corrections Center (MICC), the same medium security prison where I'd met my man, Big Al, and where I had previously served six years before going to Walla Walla. But, the MAP requirements stipulated that I remain at camp for six months. So, I was stuck cleaning bathrooms and „acclimating to the fewer restrictions on my freedom," so I could later be sent back to a medium security prison with more restrictions again to take the Victim

Awareness class. And all this was going to make me more suitable to be paroled. Yah, right.

The acting CUS (Custody Unit Supervisor) at OCC was a haughty and overly ambitious middle aged female counselor. As soon as I arrived she took me into her office for a little „girl chat". Apparently she was expecting me and had a speech all prepared. This made me very uncomfortable right from the git. She told me that if I had any problems with any of the inmates because of my sexual disposition (I'm paraphrasing here) that I could confide in her and she'd put an end to it. I took this as an insult of course. The idea of asking for her help dealing with other inmates was as repulsive to me as asking a rapist for a back rub when he was done. I just smiled and nodded politely so she would continue. She told me that she was considering placing me in the medical room which was rarely used and would afford me some privacy. Translation; she wanted to separate me from the other inmates, which I actually didn't mind. I still just smiled and let her continue. Then she told me that she was the head honcho at OCC and as long as I respected her (i. e. her rules) then she would respect me. Translation; don't mess with her and she won't mess with me. I think she was starting to detect my disdain. I bit my tongue and said nothing. But then she blurted out that, „Some of the inmates here call me mom..." and I couldn't help but laugh a little. Since the cat was now out of the bag I told her that I didn't need her help dealing with other inmates and by virtue of her „authority" alone I would never respect her; but the private medical room would be nice. Her reaction was predictable and she did exactly what she said she'd do; started messing with me every chance she got.

The first really mean thing she did was to have me assigned to an open bunk in the middle of the main dormitory right in front of a large picture window that gave anyone on the back porch a direct view of the bunk where I slept and especially the area in front of the bunk between it and the locker where I had to stand to get dressed (or undressed). The back porch area was where all the inmates congregated to play cards, smoke their cigarettes, or just hang out. It seems my privacy wasn't such a big concern for that acting CUS after all. She must have thought that staking me out for the wolves would make me regret snubbing the offer of her personal protection. But, wolves (predatory inmates) didn't bother me. My man, Big Al, and years as a queen in the penitentiary (i. e. real prison) had taught me how to handle them. It was her blatant renege on my privacy that pissed me off. I thought if that dominatrix bitch wants to play games, well then I would certainly oblige. I still wanted to get moved to the private medical room, which by now I had seen. It was spacious and comfortable looking with a read bed and even a private shower! I had an idea of how I still might get moved there, or at least have some fun trying.

On the very next workday morning I came from the shower wearing just all my white bathrobe with nothing on underneath (most of my personal clothes were white, which I considered Jazzi's signature color). I stood directly in front of the picture window between my assigned bunk and locker. Outside on the porch were about 30 or 40 inmates talking and smoking cigarettes as they waited for the DNR busses that would take them to work (planting trees). I couldn't see them very well because it was still dark outside and only a few relatively dim lights illuminated the porch area. All I could see was mostly my own reflection which i pretended to ignore as if the window weren't even there. I knew full well of course that all those inmates were out there and that they could see me as plainly as a mannequin in a brightly lit display window at night. I proceeded by opening the locker door so it would block the view from the dorm area. I didn't want anyone to see my privates from the front. That would have been embarrassing. Then I doffed the robe and stood completely naked with my backside to the window, reached into the locker and took out a bottle of lotion and began applying it all over my body with my hands, starting with my shoulders, arms, torso and working my way very deliberately down around my waist to my butt and legs. I was careful to keep my legs together so no one could see anything I didn't want them to see dangling between them. I might have spent a little more time than necessary applying the lotion and rubbing it in on the lower portions of my body (especially my ass) and bending over (of course) to do my legs, but I do that anyway, even when I'm alone and in private, just for the fun of it.

I didn't need to look out the window to know I had everyone's attention. The usual commotion that came from the back porch had ceased. I had a very sexy and effeminate looking body that I was proud of. From the back, my slender shoulders thin chest and narrow waist going to a pear shaped ass and long smooth legs, made me indistinguishable from a real genny (genetic female). I had actually expected some cat calls and whistles, but the silence from outside was even better. Those mostly short-timer inmates were completely stunned (or so I at least imagined). They didn't know what to think or how to react to such a blazon display of sociosexual contradiction. But, at least a few of them knew how to snitch, which I was counting on.

After finishing with the lotion I put it away and slipped into a pair of my panties (men's white bikini briefs) and, as discretely as I could, tucked my "embarrassment" between my legs, turning sideways to make adjustments so it would look like I was fondling my vagina (assuming I had one). I made sure right there in front of everybody that everything was securely in place, penis pulled back to the crack of my ass and testicles pushed up inside my body where they'd stay out of harms way. This arrangement allowed me to wear super tight pants pulled all the way up in the crotch comfortably with no bulge at all between my legs. I quickly finished getting dressed for work in tight fitting state khakies. It was eight o'clock sharp, time to go clean bathrooms.

Before I even get to the janitor's closet so I could start work I heard my name called over the camp's PA system, „Inmate Duncan, report to the front office". I put on my best what'd-I-do? Face and walked into the front office (a.k.a. Segeant's office).

The acting CUS was sitting at the sergeant's desk. The sergeant and another unit officer were standing on either side. Their presence, positions, and postures (not to mention facial expressions) told me that they were prepared to physically restrain me at any moment.

She told me to sit down (they never ask you to sit, they just tell you to), then she played her cards without further delay. „We have several reports from inmates and staff that you were seen exposing yourself to the work crews this morning." she said.

My jaw dropped in feigned indignation. So that's what she was in the sergeant's office with her goons. She thought she had me on a major rule infraction, for exposing myself no less. In all my years in prison I had been infracted for just about everything, but never for anything sexual like this. Considering the sexual nature of my original charges and my subjection to the ISRB's arbitrary rule, this could be very serious. I would at least loose my minimum security custody and be sent back to a medium security prison on the next chain bus. So much for paroling in six months. The ISRB could add years for something like this; they'd certainly already done so for much less.

But, I knew i had done nothing wrong (as if that would really make any difference). So, I told her, „I have no idea why anyone would think I was exposing myself, unless they were peeping in the window next to my assigned bunk where I was getting dressed this morning after my shower. I opened the locker door to try to block the view as best as I could, but I couldn't block that window."

She frowned. Apparently she didn't expect a ready excuse. Most likely she expected to see me squirm the way most duck inmates do when they've been caught. But, I wasn't squirming at all and that seemed to make her unhappy. She still had more cards to play though, so she followed suit with, „Two staff members said they saw you fondling yourself in front of the window."

I had to assume that her statement was another authoritarian doublespeak question, so I answered her by explaining that I was in fact just putting on my body lotion and then adjusting my „privates" the same way I always do after a shower and while getting dressed. I told her that I didn't like having to get dressed in front of that window, but I had little choice. „You were the one who had me assigned to that bunk." I said, letting the implication hang there. Then, in case the implication was not enough, I said, „If any other inmate had been getting dressed in front of that window no one would have paid any attention."

She just looked at me for a moment, then frowned again and looked at the sergeant and raised her eyebrows. The sergeant just shrugged. It seems my cards played, but she still had her trump, so she laid it down, „From now on you will get dressed and undressed in the shower only. Is that clear?"

I had to concede of course. So, that was that. No medical room for me. But, I had managed to announce my arrival at camp in a way that now everyone knew who I was and, more importantly, that I was no snitch or anyone's punk. But, now „Mom" was out to get me more than ever. Someone like her would never let me undermine her „authority" (i. e. power trip) without retaliation. She did eventually manage to hang me in a paper noose, but it took her a few months to do it. And, in the meantime I had the run of the camp with certain liberties I hadn't had in a very long time.

As I've said, my job was cleaning the bathrooms and showers, twice each work day, once in the morning and again afternoon. I didn't mind the job at all, even though the bathrooms and showers were really disgusting, especially in the morning. I'd just put on a pair of thick rubber gloves and scrub practically every inch then hose it all down afterwards. At least I knew the bathroom was clean when I used it, and it was a lot better than having to trudge up and down muddy hills all day planting trees.

Some of the Mexicans would literally stand on the toilets then squat over them to take a dump. They frequently ended up getting more shit on the toilet than in it, and I had to clean that too. But, in the afternoons all I needed to do was just check the bathrooms to make sure they were still clean, which they usually were since nearly everyone was out of camp with one of the DNR work crews. So I had lots of time to myself in the afternoons.

I liked to go up to the „yard" behind the camp that was up on a hill and out of sight of the main buildings. There was no fence or any other kind of perimeter around the camp, not even the yard. If I wanted to I could easily walk off into the woods that surrounded the camp and bordered the yard, but I never did. Just knowing I could was exciting enough for me.

I almost always had the yard to myself, even in the evenings, and I enjoyed it thus even more immensely. I would just sit and watch the ravens, which were so numerous at times I felt like I was in a Hitchcock movie. I tried jogging around the mud track too, but my knees still couldn't take much of that. So, I'd walk for miles just in circles, frequently fantasizing that I was really free, walking in the forest. The yard was by far my greatest pleasure at camp. I never understood why no other inmates felt the same way about it (but in hindsight I realize that after working all day in the woods planting trees, the „yard" probably seemed like just another muddy trail to them).

From the yard I also had an excellent view of the surrounding hills, which would have been something beautiful to behold except that nearly all of them had been stripped by the logging operation called clear cutting. The only thing left were the ugly dead stumps of the trees that once dressed the hills in luscious green. The saplings planted in their stead didn't even begin to cover up the black and brown nakedness of the soil exposed by the violence I came to think of as the brutal rape of mother nature.

One day I found an editorial cartoon in the newspaper that ridiculed such logging operations, and I hung it up on the camp bulletin board near the front office. The cartoon showed a doe and her fawn standing in a natural forest looking out across a field at a tree farm with uniformly spaced trees and no undergrowth. The fawn was asking its mother in the caption, „Mom, what's wrong with that forest?" I made no effort to conceal what I did, but it was a good thing no one saw me putting up the cartoon because the next day it was gone, and in its place was a memo from the acting CUS („mom"), „ANYONE CAUGHT POSTING SUBVERSIVE MATERIAL ON THIS BOARD WILL RECEIVE A MAJOR INFRACTION FOR INCITING". So much for free speech in that neck of the woods.

Another thing I liked about OCC was the kitchen and dining hall, which doubled for the visiting room on weekends. It was a modern building that stood separate from all the other barracks-like camp buildings (dorms and rooms). It was like a campus cafeteria, not a prison chow hall at all. They even had a self-serve salad bar and all the peanut butter and jelly sandwiches you could make yourself and eat. The good food was considered the main perk for being at a work camp, and the DNR crews claimed they ate even better out in the field, but I wouldn't know. For me the biggest perk was being able to sit alone in the yard area completely out of sight of everyone else with only trees around me.

During the few months I was at OCC I got visits from my mom, who drove from Tacoma over the Narrows Bridge, and from Dave, who came from Seattle across the Puget Sound on the ferry. Dave was the friend I had met in Walla Walla through a Gay newspaper (SGN) ad. He was also the one who hired the attorney that made the ISRB obey the law and find me paroleable, which is what got me sent to camp and which I was about to find out was really just a merry-go-round ride designed to get rid of Dave and the attorney.

I can't say that I was ever in love with Dave, but I certainly came to love him as a friend and eventually even as a lover. I respected him in ways that I don't think he ever really understood. To this day he thinks I used him from the start, which is what the ISRB and acting CUS and OCC wanted him to think back then, but try as they might, they only made him love me even more by attacking me and screwing me around the way they did.

The acting CUS knew of course that Dave was the one who hired the attorney that got me sent to camp (this information was communicated to her through my central file and flagged „confidential" so I would never see it). So, unbeknownst to me she started reading every letter that Dave and I exchanged as soon as I got to OCC. Her intent of course was to look for her chance to drive a wedge between us, or, in her mind, to „warn" Dave that he was being used.

I had written to Dave and asked him to make a copy of a computer printout (dot-matrix) hat I had changed so it would appear to say my original offense was assault, not rape. The document was an unofficial Earned time/Good time report that was essentially meaningless in my case since I was so far past my ETRD (Earned Time Release Date) that the numbers on the report made no sense. But, it did show my original charge, and by making the change I'd be able to show other inmates „proof" that I was in for assault. I had asked Dave to make a copy so the place where I made the modification would not be visible (I had used a razor to literally cut and paste the new information in place of the old).

I knew my mail was routinely scanned (i. e. read), but I didn't know the acting CUS was personally reading all my mail looking for anything she could use to screw me over. So, I thought nothing of asking Dave to make the copy, since I honestly did not think I was doing anything untoward. But, the acting CUS decided to arbitrarily call it an official document so she could then infract me for forgery! Forgery is a major infraction that would cause me to lose minimum custody and get kicked out of camp. She also took it upon herself to contact Dave to let him know how I had tried to involve him in a criminal act, and warn him about how inmates use people.

But, Dave took my side, especially once I explained to him what she was calling an „official document". It was by now clear to him how the system was trying to screw me over every chance it get, all in the name of „Justice", of course.

The acting CUS presided over the hearing and she completely ignored my observation that the printout I had modified was in no way marked „official" and even said, „unofficial" right on it. I pointed out that making a modified copy of a page from a book is not forgery, and neither was this. She reiterated that it was an official document (with no evidence) and found me guilty. I was on the next chain bus back to Clallum Bay Corrections Center (CBCC), which was the closest medium security state prison to OCC.

When I got to Clallum Bay I cried, literally. As soon as I arrived I went straight to the sergeant's office for the unit I was assigned and cried like a lost little girl and asked the sergeant to put me in protective custody. I didn't really need protection, but I was devastated by the sudden turn of events. One minute I was at a camp on my way to freedom, and the next I was back inside another cold concrete prison surrounded once more by posturing apes seeking precious status within the dregs of human society. The razor-wire and steel doors with shatterproof glass all reminded me of how hated and feared I was yet again. And if all that weren't enough, I was being punished again for something I didn't even know was terribly wrong. It felt like the nightmare of my incarceration was being revived all over again; and my fear that it would never end (i. e. that I would never get out of prison alive) was just too much for my poor lonely little girl heart.

In other words, I had let down my emotional defenses while I was at camp, thinking I'd never need them again, only to find myself right back in hell.

I desperately missed Big Al. When I got to the SHU (Special Housing Unit for PC inmates) I could see black prisoners playing basketball outside of the window from the solitary cell I was in. Seeing them play reminded me of the times Big Al and I had play HORSE while we were in adseg together at MICC. We'd talk as we played and tease each other over missed snots, letting each other win in turns because the score didn't really matter to either of us; the company was all that mattered.

In the SHU I cried off and on for a few days, then after I'd calmed down (and reinstalled my defenses) they let me back out into population. I stayed to myself and pretty much didn't talk to anyone except to let the convicts know who I was and who my representation was (i. e. Big Al). That was enough to keep the wolves and other predators off my back (literally), so I didn't have any problems in that regard, mostly thanks to Big Al's reputation, not my own so much. I wasn't interested in sex at all, I suppose my longing for Big Al pretty much squashed that need, not to mention that since I was throwing his name around as representation I had to honor our relationship even though technically we had already agreed hat all ties, other than our continuing friendship, were officially severed. I ate at a neutral table in the chow hall, and didn't make any friends that I remember (not that I tried not to, but I didn't try either).

Within a few weeks (as I remember) I got my minimum custody status back. It normally takes at least six months to get enough points back after a major infraction, but they had just opened a brand new minimum custody housing unit inside Clallum Bay and needed to fill beds. So they gave me an administrative override and moved me to the new unit.

It was exceptionally clean, and I had more so-called privileges, like a key to my cell, and no toilet in the cell. So the move was a step in the right direction, I suppose. But it was still inside the double razor-wire fence and didn't make me feel any closer to getting out. I still ate in the same chow hall and went to the same recreation yard to walk around the track with the medium security inmates. So why they called it „minimum security" didn't make any sense to me (I found out later that it was technically called „closed minimum", as if that made any difference).

I passed the time mostly on the yard walking the track by myself or just sitting someplace looking out at the trees. At least I could see the trees, even if I could not be amongst them. I'd also go to the library and spend quiet time there reading. I checked the school offerings, but they had no college level courses (except vocational).

Because the housing unit I was in was considered minimum security, the time I spent there counted toward the six months minimum custody requirement for the MAP conditions of my parole release. That meant that after a few months the only requirement I had left before I could be paroled was the illusive Victim Awareness class. So I was chained up and put on yet another prison bus to be transferred back to McNeil Island (MICC) where the class I need was supposedly being offered. But, of course, once again no one bothered to check the current status of the program before I was shipped off. So I didn't find out until after I had arrived, just like last time, that the class had been discontinued at MICC as well. Oh, they had an active class just a couple of months before, while I was completing the six months of minimum security in a medium security prison, but that had been the last one before the class was canceled. This of course was just another kick in the ribs of that already starved and mistreated dog; my soul, if you will. (I found out later that the counselors and ISRB were in fact conspiring to keep me locked up as long as possible, as if delaying the inevitable was somehow going to help anything more than their job security – if a mad dog bites a child, then the dog catchers get a pay raise, even is they're the ones who beat and starved the dog in the first place – it's what we call the justice system in this great country of ours).

The only place in the state that still offered the stupid class was Spokane Pre-release. But they refused to accept sex offenders (nothing like a little state sanctioned discrimination to make things even worse than they already are). So now I was stuck at MICC with no possible way of completing the last MAP requirement for my release. The counselor at MICC was no help of course. He literally shrugged his shoulders and told me there was nothing he could do (the proverbial „my hands are tied" excuse for injustice). I wouldn't be the first inmate forced to max-out (serve the full 20 year sentence for a crime I was only supposed to serve five years at most for according to the so-called SRA Laws) because the system set impossible to reach requirements for release. It was a trick that worked well under the old-guidelines (pre-SRA). But lucky for me there were new laws that the ISRB were still somewhat inexperienced at circumventing (my case was an early attempt to bypass laws requiring the ISRB to release inmates under specific conditions, but it ultimately failed only because I had a lawyer and they made mistakes, like keeping computer records of their communications regarding my case. But they've since gotten a lot better. My friend, Big Al, was found paroleable over nine years ago, and is still sitting at a so-called minimum security camp in Monroe, Washington, waiting to complete the very same last MAP requirement that I had; the Victim Awareness class. He has been waiting for years, because, guess what? The only place that has the class is still Spokane Pre-release, and Big Al is considered too violent for them too. He has lawyers trying to help him too, in fact MY lawyers, from my death penalty case, who are helping him pro-bono, out of the kindness of their hearts. My attorneys met and interviewed Big Al while preparing my case for trial. They were so impressed by him – one person said that out of the hundreds of people she has interviewed over the years for her cases, Big Al was one that impressed her the most, for his intelligence, and sincere compassion, and humble outlook – so they took it upon themselves to help him as they could. But so far, apparently, they haven't been having much luck.)

The lawyer that my friend, Dave, had hired for me back then filed a PRP (Personal Restraint Petition – which is a standard legal remedy for prisoners), and within a couple of months the Spokane Pre-release was somehow persuaded to accept at least one „sex offender", namely me. It seems that the ISRB decided to quickly fix the problem rather than allow the PRP to go through the courts, since it contained evidence of their conspiracy to keep me locked up way past my legally sanctioned release date. So the PRP became moot and was dismissed, but not before it had served its purpose; to make the ISRB, and DOC, at least pretend to obey the law. I found out later that there was another reason why the ISRB wanted this PRP squashed quickly; because it would have set a legal precedent that other prisoners (like Big Al) could take advantage of. Those board members are devious as hell when it comes to legal maneuvering, they manipulate the law more than they obey it, just to keep their jobs.

But, before I was chained up and shipped off one last time, I had a couple of months to get reacquainted with MICC. It had changed quite a bit in the four years I was gone, and was still changing quite drastically right before my eyes!

Summit House, the preferred housing unit that was nicknamed the Hotel, had been torn down and replaced by a modern SHU (thus replacing the most open living unit I ever know of in prison, with the most closed and restricted). They had also closed the main cellblocks and moved all the prisoners to brand new „medium security" units that had been built right next to where the old cellblocks stood. These new „medium security" units had all the same amenities and privileges as the so-called „minimum security" units I was in at Clallum Bay. In fact, the only difference I could see was that the actual shapes of the buildings and floor plans were triangular instead of square. Everything else was the same (i. e. dry cells, inmate keys, etc...).

I had arrived just in time to watch them tear down the old cellblocks with a wrecking ball and giant tractor mounted jack hammers and hydrolic pinchers for grabbing and tearing out all the steel bars and cutting the rebar. I couldn't help but feel that somehow fate was involved with allowing me to witness the destruction of such an icon from my past just before I expected to be released. I suppose I could have even taken it as an omen, but I didn't. My rational mind insisted it was pure coincidence, and I left it at that.

They were still using the old chow hall though, but i knew they had plans to build a new one in place of the cellblocks being torn down. I had actually seen the plans for the new chow hall, complete with a whole new kitchen, back before I'd left MICC four years ago. While I was working as an aide to the Food Services Manager (the last job I had at MICC before being sent to Walla Walla) he showed the plans for the new kitchen to me like a proud father. He explained how efficient the new serving line would be, telling me that each inmate will be served a tray through a slot in the wall, so everyone gets exactly the same amount of food. The servers never see who they are serving and the inmates never get to see who is serving them. „So there'll be no favoritism", he boasted. I asked, „Doesn't that strike you as inhumane at all?" He just shrugged. This was the same man who liked to put prune juice in the juice machines when the menu from Olympia (his headquarters) called for orange juice. When I asked him about that he told me, „The inmates drink less prune juice than they do orange juice, so it saves money". So I asked if he got some sort of an award or other incentive for saving money, and he said, „No. It's just my job to save money." He also claimed that he knew for a fact that the WWF wrestling matches were real, because he used to be a professional wrestler (apparently back before it became a popular form of commercial entertainment for children and idiots).

Anyway, since I basically grew up at MICC I knew a lot of people there still. So I got to talk to a lot more people than I did at Clallum Bay, mostly old acquaintances I met on the yard or in the chow hall. Though most of them didn't want to be seen hanging out with a queen, so they wouldn't talk for very long, usually just long enough to say hi and exchange a little news (i. e. gossip mostly).

I ate a neutral table in the chow hall like at Clallum Bay (at OCC camp, all the tables were „neutral" as far as I was concerned, in other words, no one was liable to smash you in the face for sitting where you weren't supposed to). But I usually took my time eating so people who knew me would have a chance to come over and say hi, and gossip if they wanted.

There were a lot of new faces too. I'd guess that there was about a seventy to eighty percent turn over in the time I was gone. For the most part all the ducks (newbies) left me alone because, like at Clallum Bay, they just didn't know me. But it was clear by the company I kept (or at least by the people I talked to, even if briefly) that I had been around for awhile and was known by all the old-timers. Only once did anyone try to mess with me. Some idiot duck in the chow hall scrape room (only ducks worked in the scrape room) apparently thought it would be funny to spray me with water as I dropped off my tray. Without even thinking about it I just threw my tray as hard as I could through the window, and was shortly rewarded by a huge crash as I had apparently struck a large stack of trays (and they were metal trays, so you can imagine how much noise they made). The whole chow hall seemed to just stop and everyone looked in my direction to see what happened. But, I just walked away calmly as if I had nothing to do with it. Everyone, even the guards apparently, just assumed some klutz must have knocked over a stack of trays in the scrape room. But word eventually got out (maybe I helped a little) and I never had anymore trouble from any ducks after that. (By the way, yes, I was aiming for the inmate, but the stack of trays was just as well).

There was only one staff member that I was interested in seeing while I was back on the island, and that was the vocational electronics instructor, Glen Backman. When I'd left four years before I was angry at him for letting the guards find me guilty for „stealing" items from the electronics shop where I worked at the time. This was the infraction that got me kicked out of Summit House, so it really hurt. Glen was supposed to testify at my hearing that he'd given me permission to have the items in question (some wire and miscellaneous jacks and resistors that I used to fix – usually quick patch jobs – other inmates radios and such). But he never showed up at my hearing and I was consequently found guilty for stealing (I had actually even paid money to the electronics shop for some of these items, and I would never have stolen from the shop out of respect for Glen and the other inmates who worked there. So to be accused of and found guilty for stealing from the shop was a blow to my pride as well). It was because of this infraction that I had quit my job (as lead technician with the most seniority at the time) and took the job for Institutional Industries as a computer programmer, which had been offered several months before but I had turned down, even though it paid four times more than what I made in the shop, out of respect and loyalty to the electronics shop.

But, over the years my steam cooled and when I thought through everything that happened back then it dawned on me that Glen had most likely been threatened with the loss of his job if he testified at my infraction hearing. So I forgave him and wanted to see him now so I could formally apologize.

So, I signed up for an electronics class in computer programming (even though I already had an AS degree in electronics from the last time I was at MICC). But the class was in the evenings and I found out that Glen only worked during the day now (he used to work evenings too) and a part-timer filled in the evenings. At least I got to snoop around the electronics shop, which actually wasn't a shop anymore, just a classroom in the basement of the building where the shop used to be. They no longer allowed inmates to repair other inmate's radios and such, so the shop was closed down, and much of the old equipment was just sitting off to one side of the classroom in stacks of boxes.

It was some of these boxes that I was rooting through one day when I found the actual very first book I learned to program computers from. It was the Apple_IIe_Programmer's_Manual that was like a bible to me when I had it back in the 80's. It was just laying by itself in a box of probes and other junk (the only book in the box) as if it was put there for me to find someday. This book had tremendous sentimental value for me and I could hardly believe I'd found it. So I commandeered it of course, which was easy enough to do, and I still had that book with me when I was eventually released many months later.

I don't remember if I ever got a chance to apologize to Glen, but I'm sure I did. I do know that as of just a few years ago my attorneys confirmed that he was still working as an instructor on the Island and had even spoken to him about me. Surprisingly he had nothing but good things to say about me, despite knowing that what I had done after I got out of prison. That's what I always liked about Glen, he was honest and treated everyone fairly. I should never have gotten mad at him.

I don't recall exactly how long I was at McNeil Island this time, but it seems like it was six months or less before I was finally shipped off to the Pre-release in Spokane, clear on the other side of the state.

Spokane Pre-release was the least restrictive custody, between a minimum security camp and work release. The prison was located in an annex of Eastern State (mental) Hospital, comprised of an old hospital building surrounded by several portables that served as kitchen, chow hall, recreation center (gym), as well as administration offices and classrooms, and one extra dormitory unit. The entire complex (about two acres all together) was surrounded by a ten foot high chain link fence topped with razor wire. Behind the main building there was a yard big enough for playing softball, with the obligatory track going around it. The even had an outdoor basketball court, though, strangely, no one ever seemed interested in it (I guess they preferred to play basketball inside the air-conditioned gym).

It seemed to me like I was the only prisoner there who'd ever seen the inside of a real prison. Almost everyone else had either been sent directly from Shelton (the state receiving and classification center), or from one of the minimum security camps. They were mostly serving less than two years for class „C" felonies.

I had no problem „adjusting” to this new social genre at all. I even befriended a few people I'd met with common intellectual interests. After the fiasco at OCC camp I'd toned down my flamboyant queen act, and though I made no deliberate attempt to conceal my sexual orientation, I was better at fitting in, even if as a „gay”. So nobody bothered me and seemed to think I belonged even (i. e. didn't stand out). I signed up for yoga and meditation classes, and of course, enrolled in the required Victim Awareness class.

The Victim Awareness class was just as pointless as I suspected it would be. We cut up pictures out of old magazines and made „victim” collages that were supposed to express how victims feel (or something dumb like that). Then we'd watch videos about victim impact (or something dumb like that). And occasionally a „guest” would come in to tell us what it feels like to be a victim (or something dumb like that). We weren't allowed to ask questions. The principles of the class were taught like a dogma; criminals are insensitive, and victims are innocent. I guess whoever thought up the class didn't think „criminals” knew what it felt like to be a victim. Imagine that.

After I finished the class, my counselor notified the ISRB and submitted updated parole plans. Everything went extremely well in this regard, especially considering that the counselor rarely ever had to deal with the ISRB or submit formal parole plans for most pre-release inmates. I suspect the pre-release staff wanted me out of their hair as quickly as possible, so they weren't about to play the ISRB's games.

My plans were to parole to Seattle. The Interaction Transition program House had already accepted me many years ago and their policy was that once someone is accepted (a process that can take years) then that person is always accepted, even if they don't have a room, they'll let the person sleep on a couch is necessary, until a room opens up. Fortunately for me they had a room available, and my friend Dave (who had become a regular face at the IT House on my behalf) had already paid the first months rent (about 300 dollar).

Surprisingly, my parole plans were quickly approved. I suspect that the ISRB had to call in some favors to get me accepted at Spokane Pre-Release in the first place in order to get themselves out of the legal bind my attorney had put them in. And my speedy release now was one of the conditions of their bailout imposed by the Pre-release officials, who I'm certain did not like having a „violent sex-offender” in their charge one bit. Within a matter of days I had an actual release date – my god, I get emotional even now just remembering that. A real honest-to-god release date! And I found out what the actual date was just weeks before it came, so I didn't have long to wait biting my nails.

Needless to say, those past few weeks passed by very quickly. In fact, I have no memories at all of the time even passing. The next thing I knew I was walking out the prison gate carrying a brown paper grocery bag with a few belongings in it (I had already sent most of my stuff, personal property, including the Apple IIe book I'd commandeered from the electronics shop at McNeil, by mail to the IT House in Seattle a few days before so it wouldn't be a burden on my release day). A couple of prison staff (guards) were waiting in a state owned sedan to take me to the airport. My friend, Dave, had paid for the cost of a plane ticket ahead of time in order to spare me the long bus ride to Seattle. Dave himself would be waiting, with my mother, for my arrival at the Seatac airport.

At the Spokane airport, the guards handed me an envelope that contained my ticket and 20 dollar in cash (I was to get the rest of my 100 dollar „release money” when I checked in with the parole officer in Seattle). Then they let me out in front of the main entrance to the airport and drove off without any further instructions and without even saying good-bye. I suppose they were „just doing their job".

I entered the airport terminal wearing all white, 505 jeans and shirt, with my hair pulled back and tied into what I'd hoped was an inconspicuous ponytail. I wasn't worried about people thinking I was gay, I just didn't want them to think I'd just gotten out of prison. So I tried to act as casual as I could as I found my way to the airport coffee shop. I desperately wanted a good shot of caffeine to calm my nerves.

When I asked the young woman behind the counter for a coffee she said, „Americano or Laté?" At the time I had no idea what an Americano was, so I ordered a Laté, and chose vanilla, thinking that would be the safest choice (I'd never had a Laté before, but had heard of them from TV and visitors in prison). After paying the shocking cost of the drink, I found my way to a tall coffee shop table so I could set down my bag and try the drink. A moment later the entire drink was in the trash and I was off to find someplace where I could sit and watch the planes on the tarmac; maybe that could calm my nerves, since I didn't know how to order a regular coffee and was too embarrassed to ask.

I eventually found my gate, and managed to board the plane for Seattle without any difficulty.

I was fortunate enough to end up with a window seat on the plane. I was looking out the window as the plane taxied to its runway for take off, and I remember thinking, it's not over yet. I knew that I wasn't going home, nor would I ever be able to. My mother had lost the house in Tacoma where I lived when I arrested as a kid. So couldn't pay the mortgage, so the bank took the house shortly after my parole plans were denied for the first time many years ago. If I had been paroled back then I would have been going home, and I could have helped my mom keep the house. But not now. Somehow that lost home epitomized everything else the system had taken from me over the years, my youth, my future, even my innocence. So no, it wasn't over, because I could never go home again. And I thought too that I would never be free either, until the score was settled, and perhaps, even probably, not even then.

Inside, buried deep, I was one very mad dog, starved and beaten for years, both psychologically and spiritually. But outside, and on the surface of my mind, I was perfectly serene. I was biding my time as I wore the two-faced mask I had learned to wear, happy side out, just so I could have this day at all; my release day.

When the pilot throttled up the engines and released the brakes I leaned forward in my seat and pushed my face even closer to the window. Not so much so I could enjoy the view during take off, which I certainly did, but more so no one could see my face at that particular moment. I was afraid if they did that they might ask why I was crying.

2013

Chronicles

Friday, January 18, 2013

"Child Porn" Found In My Cell

Amongst the very few papers I brought with me from the Federal Detention Center in Seatac, Washington, as I was transferred via private jet to the Ada County Jail in Boise, was a document that discussed historical Jewish Law (the Talmud) in relationship to sex with children. I used this document to support an assertion I made in an affidavit to the court in which I pointed out that, like me, Jesus was a criminal of the most foul sort, as judged by the society in which he lived. I bolstered my argument to this effect by pointing out that in Jesus' day, sex with children, even child rape of both sexes, was not only legal, but ordained in some circumstances (such as the consummation of a marriage to girls as young as three by coitus, and an explicit exception to the law against laying with another man as a woman for boys under the age of nine, amongst other laws in the Talmud). I gave this affidavit, which directly cited the document I mention above, to my attorneys so they would know my current views in regard to the question of my competency, and how it related to my decision to waive the appeal of the three death sentences imposed upon me in Federal court back in 2008.

The other day I found this document missing from my jail cell, and realized it had been confiscated. So, I told my attorney, and he told me that he had been informed by the marshals that they had found and removed "child porn" from my cell. They did not tell him what the document was, just that it was "child porn".

So I submitted a written request to the jail to have the document returned, as it was a legitimate part of my case. The response I got was, "Sex with children is illegal in Idaho". So, I was not allowed to have the document.

since I had already written the affidavit, and the document itself is freely available on the Internet (Google: "Talmud Law Sex With Children") I was not too concerned about getting the document back. I was concerned, however, with the fact that once again a misleading record has been established of my attempts to keep "child porn" in my cell that can later be used in court as an "aggravating factor" (i.e. proof that I'm a "bad" person). And, it's not the first time either. In fact, this kind of slanted record keeping is pretty much par-for-course. I could give a dozen more explicit examples just off the top of my head, some I have already attempted to counter-document in this blog (e.g. the "assault on a guard" infraction I got in prison for accidentally hitting a guard with a small plastic lid, to mention just one).

It's just another way that the system promotes its view that there are "good people" and "bad people", a view that the system depends on to justify doing bad things (like crucifying the Truth and killing the innocent children of God).

Chronicles

Saturday, February 9, 2013

Back in Boise

I'm back in Boise, Idaho, for yet another "competency hearing". It's expected to run until the end of January, maybe a little into February. Check the news in Boise for updates.

Chronicles

Thursday, February 14, 2013

Without Question

After a very expensive and prolonged "retrospective" competency hearing (one of the marshals told me that they estimated the court at around two-million dollars), the attorneys for both sides, government and defense, gave their closing arguments today. The government argues, in the interest of seeing me killed in the name of justice (truth be damned), that the defendant (me) has consistently demonstrated his competence, and was in fact fully competent when he (the "defendant") waived his appeal of three death sentences, and has never demonstrated the overt incompetence that the defense lawyers assert. The "defense" argues, in the interest of saving my life (truth be damned), that Mr. Duncan (me) has a severe psychotic brain impairment that causes him to make all his decisions (legal and otherwise) in the erroneous context of a complex delusional belief system that is completely removed from reality. Hence, the decision to waive his appeals was made non-volitionally and incompetently. I would argue if given the chance, in the interest of the Truth (my life, or death, be damned), that the question of my so-called "competence" or even "sanity" should not be a part of the process of determining what society should do in response to my clearly criminal (i.e. socially destructive) behavior. The only question should be, "What happened?" If we ask ourselves that question honestly, instead of seeking blame, retribution, or even forgiveness, then we would know what to do, without question.

Reflections

Thursday, February 14, 2013

Am I A Nut?

My lawyers claim that I'm psychotically delusional. The government says I'm not. I think they're both right and wrong at the same time. There is definitely something seriously wrong with the way I think, perhaps even psychotic (whatever that means). It was only because I realized this that I was able to turn myself in and stop killing.

But I also think that most people suffer from the exact same "sickness" that I do; except that it manifests itself in different (i.e. more "socially acceptable") forms.

For example, I thought that I had the right to rape and kill because of tremendous pain and loss that I suffered when I was virtually a child and as a direct result of the systematic betrayal I experienced as a trusting teen. And, of course, "society" (most other people) see ME as the "betrayer", and they think THEY have the right to persecute and kill me because of the pain and loss I caused.

Just as I once completely ignored or minimized my own role in causing the pain and suffering I experienced, so "society" (in general) now completely ignores and minimizes its role in the carnage that has been (and is still being) wrought. In both cases the roles we played (society and myself) were directly responsible for the "evil" that ensued. So, we are both (all) directly responsible for what I did, but no one is to blame!

That's what I realized the night before I turned myself in. I realized that I was wrong to blame society, or anyone, even myself, for what I was doing (or had done). This realization opened the way for the greater realization I had the next day that caused me to throw down the rock I was about to kill eight year old Shasta with, take her home (back to Cour d'Alene, Idaho), and turn myself in. But, I didn't actually think, "I'm wrong". I actually thought, "There's something wrong with me". In a sense, I realized I was a nut.

So, when this so-called competency hearing began, I told my attorneys this. I've known I'm a nut since I turned myself in. But I also think we are all nuts. So, it seems pretty nutty to me that a bunch of nuts are calling me a nut. And even nuttier still that a bunch of nuts are claiming that I'm not a nut.

Reflections

Thursday, February 28, 2013

I'm Baaaack!

I'm back on Federal death row in the Terre Haute, Indiana US Penitentiary. I was gone for about ten months for the court ordered "retrospective" competency hearing in Boise, Idaho. Because of all the moving around for the hearing, not to mention apparent interference by BOP authorities, I have not been able to make updates to this blog as often as I would have liked. But, now that I'm back in Terre Haute I hope to be able to continue posting and improving this blog.

Reflections

Tuesday, March 12, 2013

The Color of your Soul

A person cannot change their psychological makeup any easier than they can change the color of their hair or skin. They can dye their hair, and tattoo their skin, but that doesn't change the nature of these things any more than behavior therapy or changing a habit changes the nature of the person.

So to judge someone for the way they think, i.e. the color of their soul, is no better than judging them for the color of their skin, or other physical attribute. In many ways it is the ultimate form of prejudice, and incidentally one that literally defines most religious institutions and that causes most of the misery in this world.

Reflections

Wednesday, March 13, 2013

The System's Dilemma, As I See It

During the competency hearing last month some twelve or so doctors testified on the question of my sanity. All of them, both for the defense (who claimed I was insane) and for the government (who claimed I was sane), concluded that I was not malingering (faking symptoms or being dishonest), and all of them also agreed that all of my decisions, both legal and otherwise, were inextricably intertwined with and based upon, my unique belief system. But the defense doctors said my belief system was psychotic and delusional, while the government doctors all claimed it was idiosyncratic, but perfectly rational.

While my full "belief system", as they call it, is complex and admittedly difficult for me to articulate, there are certain aspects of it that clearly and directly effect the so-called "choices" I have made in regard to my case, and hence directly relate to the question of my so-called "legal competence". For example, the decision to represent myself and to waive the appeal of the several death sentences ordered against me.

Unlike most defendants who make such choices, I did not imagine that I could do a better job representing myself than my attorneys, nor did I desire to die, or otherwise seek some personal objective in any regard. I only wanted to "let the Truth speak for itself" and not "interfere with the process". It was consequently this Truth - with a capital "T" - as I see it, that became a focal point of the competency hearing.

The question the court must answer is: Is Mr Duncan's understanding of "the Truth" delusional or rational? And therein lies the Systems dilemma. If my understanding of "the Truth" is rational (which a finding of competence would assert) then it is rational to view the System as "an evil entity with an intelligence and will of its own" that cannot be "outsmarted on its own terms" and can only be overcome by submission to an even higher "intelligence" which I encountered directly "on the mountain" just hours before I turned myself in. This was the "epiphany" that I have often spoken of since my arrest in 2005, which also became a major focus of the competency hearing.

Was my "epiphany" a rational choice, or a psychotic event? If the court decides that it was rational, then it also admits that the System itself can be rationally perceived as "evil". And if the system can be rationally perceived as evil, then shouldn't we be questioning the system's competence, instead of mine?

I can only hope that the significance and importance of this question, as derived above, is realized by those who would pretend to judge. It is a question that strikes at the lying heart of the System, and has the potential, if asked and answered honestly, of exposing the true nature of the Beast, and bringing about a revolution in the way we all think about ourselves, and our roles in this world. And that is what my "belief system" is all about!

Reflections

Monday, April 15, 2013

Me After All

I have attempted to say this before, but I have yet to be satisfied with my words; as usual. So, I will try it again and hope I can be at least a little more clear.

The reason I stopped murdering and raping to get revenge on what I perceived to be (and still perceive to be) a morally corrupt social system, was not because I realized that what I was doing was wrong. It was because I realized that what I was doing was pointless, and futile.

I wanted revenge before I had this "epiphany" (as it has been dubbed in recent court proceedings concerning my crimes, and the reason I stopped killing even though I could have easily continued). But something made me change my mind. I no longer wanted revenge, or forgiveness. In fact, I suddenly no longer wanted anything at all, except for the Truth to be known.

But, unlike most who want the "Truth" to be known, I realized that it was not a truth that only I knew, or one that I had to convey somehow. Instead, I realized to the core of my being that The Living Truth - as I have since often referred to it - can, and does, reveal itself to everyone, at all times.

In other words, I realized that the Truth was infinitely greater than me, my life, or anything I could possibly think, much less convey with words. I also realized that my entire life's experience was only an infinitesimally small part of that greater Truth. And yet, as a part, my life was no less, and no more important than anyone else's life. Suddenly, the naked little girl standing in front of me, whose skull I was about to crush with a large rock that I was holding over my head in preparation for the killing blow when this "epiphany" came to me... suddenly her life was equal to my own, even superior in certain ways.

But, not equal in the mathematical sense. Her life, and my life, were equal in the absolute sense. I suddenly saw, or realized, that she and I were one and the same in the "eyes" of the infinite Truth. That is why what I was doing - killing her to "send a message" to those who had so unjustly hurt me when I was yet just a child (i.e. society) - became a pointless and futile jest. I could no longer send my "message" because I could now see through this understanding - through "the eyes of the child before me" (Shasta, as I have oft poetically claimed) - that the intended recipient of my "message" was ultimately me!

I saw not only that I and Shasta were one, but that we are all One. So killing her in order to hurt society no longer made any sense to me at all. And killing me now, in the name of justice, makes no sense to me either. I can see how it makes sense to someone who cannot see the Oneness, though. And that's why I don't blame them for wanting to kill me. They are me after all! And the message they are trying to send is for their own ears to hear someday, hopefully.

Reflections

Thursday, April 25, 2013

The Bad Guy Affirmation

"I am bad, and that's good.

will never be good, and that's not bad.

There's no one I'd rather be than me."

Wreck It Ralph

Reflections

Thursday, April 25, 2013

If I Could...

would rather worship the devil created by God, than a god that created the devil.

(Fortunately, I know better than to worship either.)

Reflections

Sunday, April 28, 2013

Evolving Crime

Crime evolves, like a living thing. It adapts, and changes in order to survive, and propagate. Modern crime would not survive in the past any more than a modern human could survive with the dinosaurs. Neither could past criminal behavior survive in our modern world. Imagine a cattle rustler attempting to rustle a herd today. He'd never get past the first fence.

And so crime evolves. Someone like Jack the Ripper would never have gotten past their first victim in today's world, not with even the most basic forensic techniques. Even Ted Bundy would not have gotten very far before he was made just another anonymous crime statistic rotting in a prison cell somewhere.

But rotting criminals don't solve the problem of crime. It only forces criminals to evolve. As laws get tougher, and detection gets more sophisticated, so do criminals. If criminals didn't evolve there'd be almost no crime at all these days. The so-called war on crime follows the pattern of escalation that precedes war, not the destructive chaos that defines war. Real wars only come AFTER the escalation (and is unfortunately all we have to look forward to if we allow the escalation to continue).

Soon, criminals will be compelled (by "tough on crime" laws) to commit crimes so heinous and sophisticated that what I did will look almost innocent (I raped and killed four children, and killed three other people, an entire family, that I perceived as, "in my way"). Soon men will attack adults with children right out in the open in order to fulfill fantasies that are shaped by the very social mechanisms purported to stop such crimes. Attacking the means of crime while ignoring the motivation only compels the criminal to find some other means. Where there is a will there is always a way.

Reflections

Sunday, May 12, 2013

Dukha: A Sure Road To Hell

According to my understanding, Buddhism teaches that all suffering stems from our craving for pleasure. This causes an attachment to the unreal self; or tamba, that prevents us from being able to perceive what is real (i.e. nothingness, or nirvana).

Buddhist's tell us of the eight fold-path that helps us break away from tamba, and achieve enlightenment (i.e. direct awareness of nirvana). This path seems to essentially consist of denying oneself pleasure, much like the Christian path of virtue. But, like the Christian path, I think the eight-fold path is often misunderstood and incorrectly followed.

The idea, as I see it, is not to deprive ourselves of pleasure, but rather to disconnect ourselves from it. Indeed, it may be useful to deny ourselves our every desire, but only as a tool for helping us recognize desire, and pleasure, for what it is, dukha. Dukha is the life of suffering that attachment to the unreal causes. But it is not necessary and in fact can be very harmful to deny ourselves pleasurable experiences if we only do so with the aim of enlightenment or salvation. To seek enlightenment for its own sake is a deceptive form of seeking pleasure. And hence, seeking salvation (in the Christian sense) is a sure road to hell, and only ends up leading to more suffering.

The idea of Buddhism, and Christianity when correctly understood, is fundamentally about balance; balance between desire and apathy, between that that is, and that that is not. It is a matter of seeking without effort, which is not something the intellectual mind can ever accomplish, though it can certainly interfere.

So, the idea of meditation, and/or prayer, is not to control our minds, or desires. But, it is to surrender control instead. And attempting to deny ourselves every pleasure, and suppress every desire, only ends up being another form of control that will lead to more dukha, and straight to hell.

(PS: Surrendering control over desire is not the same as surrendering TO desire - so be careful to make this important distinction.)

Reflections

Sunday, May 12, 2013

A No Brainer

I'm not sure if I had said this before or not, but it is a fundamental and important truth with regard to the achievement of ultimate understanding; so I will state it here as plainly as I can, and hope it will perhaps provide a passage for someone to find their way around the class of deception it has the power to dispel.

The ultimate truth - regardless of what it is understood to be - must be attainable (i.e. capable of being experienced, or understood) in the complete absence of intellectual capacity.

In fact, the only function intellect has in regard to the Truth is that it provides a false means of communication of the truth. This is why it is often said that the Truth can never be told, and that words can do little more than obscure it (unless those words aim to defeat words themselves, as these words, hopefully, do).

Again the ultimate Truth does not demand higher intellect to be experienced or appreciated. It just takes honesty, and perhaps a little faith (not in some fantasy or idea of the truth, but in Truth itself as an "unknowable", i.e. non-intellectual, experience). But, whatever it takes, it can't be had by any effort - only by grace.

(PS: Someone might ask, "If this is true, then what should I do?" The answer is, no matter what you are doing, you are already doing exactly what you need to do in order to ultimately experience higher truth. That's what "having faith" in the Truth (a.k.a. "God") really means - and it is what allows us to truly love (hence, understand) our neighbor, no matter how much they seem to harm us.)

Reflections

Sunday, May 19, 2013

The Devil's Twisted Logic

I just heard a man (supposedly educated with a doctorate in theology) preaching on TV that, "... if God were in control of everything we do then we wouldn't be able to convict a rapist, or a child molester". This caught my attention even though the ignorance of a such a statement seems obvious to me. So, I turned back to the offending channel (I was flipping channels when I heard the statement and had flipped past the channel as soon as I saw a man preaching; what he was actually saying didn't register until a second later), and I listened for a moment more to what he was saying.

I'd heard this kind of half-reasoned logic before coming from Christians and other self-righteous zealots, but never applied directly to child molesters and rapists - a subject most preachers seem to have enough sense to steer clear of; but not this guy.

He continued his argument in the classic and extremely predictable way of using Christian scripture, taken completely out of context and interpreted to mean what it doesn't even begin to say in a context, to support his erroneous logic. Specifically, he asserted that the Bible says "if... if... if... only IF we obey God, are we saved.". But the Bible, in context, says that if we obey God, then we will know we are saved - obedience to God is an indicator of salvation, not a method of obtaining it (by context I mean the repeated message throughout the Bible, and especially emphasized in the new testament by Paul and John, that salvation is by grace alone; the Bible states clearly and plainly that no one can choose to be saved, God chooses us). I'm just saying what the Bible says directly (see Romans 11:6, Ephesians 2:8, Titus 2:11 and 3:7, just for starters), not necessarily that I agree with it (I do, and I don't, but that's a different matter).

It just amazes me that people accept such garbage without stopping or even trying to think for themselves. You'd think that in matters concerning their "eternal soul" they'd make some effort to think through the logic. If God is in control of everything we do, then he's the one "convicting" the rapists and child molesters too! It makes no sense to just go half way with the logic, and then use twisted Bible scripture to back it up. But that's exactly what I saw this "doctor" doing, and it only took me about 30 seconds to confirm it, and continue flipping channels.

I found nothing else worth watching either, so I wrote this instead.

PS: If you consider the Bible to be an authority on such matters then you might be interested in reading Romans Chapter 9, where St. Paul discusses and defends the absolute sovereignty of God over every choice we make. See especially verse 16-20, Paul couldn't have been any clearer, and yet amazingly so many people still buy into the Devil's Twisted logic, and believe we have the ability to defy God's will!

Reflections

Saturday, May 25, 2013

Experience vs Understanding

Everyone has heard stories from people who claim to have visited other worlds not at all like our own and apparently not limited by physical laws. Some claim that they visited heaven after they died then came back to life (and back to the physical world) after meeting Jesus, God, angels or dead people. We have also heard stories about visits to our world from angels or other beings as well. Most of these stories involve some sort of message being conveyed from this other world, or worlds, to our own world.

Our history is permeated with such stories, and most of our religions are based upon them. So clearly they are important. But given that no two independent sources ever tell truly coinciding stories - they are consistently inconsistent - what are we to believe? Should we pick and choose? Or just ignore them all? Well, here is a solution that I think makes perfect sense, and yet is seldom considered simply because it might be too obvious.

Instead of looking to what we experience - either personally or vicariously - for insight into the nature and source of our existence, we should look at our personal and innermost understanding of things instead. This is commonly called intuition (though emotional experience is often confused with intuition. Especially when it is consiquetly *(sic)* rationalized, it is not the same thing).

I am speaking about genuine intuition; the kind we typically ignore in the face of our experiences, emotions, and reason. It is impossible to define this in terms of experience, and yet experience itself is defined by it.

There is no easy way to say what intuition is, but I can - and often do - say what it is not. My only point here though is not to harp on what intuition is, or isn't; but, rather to just point out that the big mysteries in life don't seem so mysterious at all, when you stop relying on experience, and hence judgment, to try to understand. Looking to experience, whether they are "real", "emotional" or "spiritual" (e.g. dreams too) only confuses things, because all experiences are mere emanations (as proven by science and romanticized by poets), or dreamlike. So experience, not even so-called "reality", cannot be relied upon to inform us of our true nature, or the true nature of our existence or origin.

I hope this makes sense, because it is an important and fundamental concept that relates directly to the source of all confusion and, hence, suffering. the more we look to our experiences for understanding the more we suffer from confusion. The more we trust the source of all experience, the more we grow toward peace and understanding. I'm not saying anything different here than what our sages (Jesus, Buddha, etc...) have been saying all along. I'm just repeating an age old message, in hopes that you will hear.

Reflections

Saturday, May 25, 2013

Breath and Listen

Every thought, or feeling, or any experience that a person has is as unique to that individual as their body. Even though we have many thoughts, feelings, and experiences that seem the same for us as they are for other people - the so-called, "common experiences" - in truth, our experiences are as uncommon as the pattern of blood vessels inside our eyes. And this is no small or unimportant distinction. In fact, the presumption of common experience is a major cause of misunderstanding and conflict in our world. Only when we learn to see each other as wholly unique from each other will we ever be able to see the single common factor that binds us as One. Only then will there be true peace and harmony. Only then will all suffering, injustice and fear come to an end. Only then will death be defeated (i.e. not by any medical or scientific breakthrough!).

Everything that I've asserted in the above paragraph must be perceived directly. You will not understand by taking any word for it. That's what faulty religions all have in common; they want you to take their word for the truth. But the one true religion (which can be found, surprisingly, at the core of the faulty ones) never demands that you believe anything that you don't already experience directly for yourself. This is the common experience of Life itself, which comes before all other experiences, and is in fact the source of all experiences.

It was this prime (or primal) experience that I recognized for the first time in my life literally seconds before I was about to commit my eight murder. It caused me to atop killing and turn myself in. And even though every aspect of my experience with this "Living Truth" is perfectly consistent with historical records - especially religious writings - it is still so alien to our ability to grasp with our "logical" or "rational" minds that the so-called "Justice System" - which desperately pretends to be logical and rational - cannot comprehend why I stopped killing and surrendered to the faulty authorities of this world.

What they could not see, and will never comprehend, is that it was not man's faulty authority that I surrendered to. It only appears as though I have surrendered to man's authority to those who cannot see the One True Authority of which I have since so often written.

I do not fear death because I know, through direct and personal experience, that my last breath will be no less miraculous, and no less alive, than my next breath today, or even my first some 50 years ago. I die with every breath I take, and am reborn each time. I know this, not because it is written by men (which it is in nearly every religious and philosophical text), but because I am experiencing it right now. And so can you. You have only to look past your thoughts, your feelings, and even your physical experiences, and experience the experiencer just once to know what I'm trying to say; to know what men have been saying for thousands of years; to know what any child can tell you with a look, and a smile - if only we listen.

Reflections

Tuesday, June 25, 2013

Love Discriminates

Unconditional love is not the same as indiscriminate love. True love - unconditional love - DOES discriminate. But, not against race, religion or psychological profile. It discriminates against fear, hate and ignorance; that is all, and that is enough.

Reflections

Saturday, July 6, 2013

The Good Fight

It doesn't bother me, or even surprise me, that some people see me as something less than human. I completely understand the need to try to separate ourselves from things we don't understand. It's much easier to deny our connection to reality, and to each other, than it is to face the truth; that we are not only just connected, but inextricably intertwined.

Denying our intimate relationship with anyone we meet is a survival mechanism. In nature it provides the premise for evolution. It establishes a boundary of conflict necessary for a struggle that results in adaption and growth as a species.

So when someone insists that I am an "evil monster" (because of the things I did in the past) and I don't deserve to live, all they are really doing is establishing a basis for conflict that will, I believe, ultimately result in our growth, together.

I'm not saying they are right. But, neither are they wrong. So long as one person sees me as a monster, then for that one person that is exactly what I am. It's not up to them, of course, to resolve the conflict they create; nature will take care of that all by its self, one way or another. That's what I genuinely believe, and it is why I can find peace even in the midst of extreme conflict. I know that in the end we are all fighting the same fight, and I like to think it's a good one.

Reflections

Friday, July 12, 2013

Faith In The Mystery

Fear and ignorance go hand in hand. One will never be found without the other. Fear causes ignorance, and ignorance causes fear. Together they are the parents of hate, all hate. This is a key principle that can help us unlock so much understanding inside of ourselves. It gives us a means to overcome all our fears, and our ignorance at the same time.

Well, "means" might not be the right word. It's more like a hint that can lead us to the means. The means itself is a mystery - in fact, it is THE Mystery that the Christian Bible calls "God in man", but also goes by many other names around the world and throughout history. It implies faith and understanding the same way that certainty implies fear and ignorance. But, even though it is by definition, a mystery, it is 100% available to everyone at all times. The hint tells us which direction we must look to find it (i.e. inward), that is all. But, it can be found - or, rather, it will find us, if we only have faith in the Mystery.

Reflections

Sunday, July 21, 2013

Understanding Shame

I have said in the past that I am not ashamed of the terrible things I have done in the past. I later realized, and blogged, that as much as I wish I had no shame I could not upon honest introspection deny that it was there.

So, I decided to "wear my shame openly" in the hopes that it would help me become a better person by teaching me whatever it was given to me to teach. This decision has helped me by way of finding new levels of genuine inner peace that had always alluded me in the past. It was as though it wasn't the shame that disturbed me deep down, but only the denial of it.

I'm only realizing now why this would be so. After all these years of living with my shame out in the open, where I could keep a constant eye of consciousness (or "light") on it, I have come to know and understand my shame as never before possible. And I see clearly now that shame is no more than a learned response to the very natural fear of social rejection. In fact, the fear of social rejection and shame are almost one and the same thing, and in effect very difficult to distinguish from each other once this level of understanding (i.e. self honesty) has been achieved. But the difference is an important one, and one that only becomes apparent when we finally learn to accept our shame.

In fact, accepting our shame is what makes our fear of social rejection - shame's true cause - become apparent, because we only experience said fear as shame when we deny it and run from it!

Yes, I'm saying now that shame is no more than the fear of social rejection, denied. As soon as I brought my own shame into the light of consciousness and no longer denied it, it became no more than the natural fear of social rejection. And though I felt this change in understanding at the time, I did not have the words for it until now. But, now that I do have the words, and have put them down here, they "feel" right.

Reflections

Saturday, July 27, 2013

Simple Logic

The question of free will can be indisputably answered with direct and simple logic.

Let us agree that if an event (i.e. behavior, thought, speech, etc...) has a cause other than "free will", then said event is determined by said cause, and is hence said to be "predetermined", and not "free willed".

Now let's extend this understand directly to a given sequence of events. If in a given sequence of events each event is directly determined by its predecessor, then the entire sequence is predetermined. Inversely, and more significantly, if any event in the sequence is not determined directly by some preceding event then the entire sequence that follows this "free event" is no longer predetermined, but is in fact determined by the so-called "free event".

This "free event" could easily then be called "free will", but I'm not going to argue nomenclature here. Instead I will simply point out that if an event has no determinable cause, then it is technically a random event.

If you take the time to openly reflect on this simple and irrefutable logic then you will no doubt get yourself quickly tied up in all kinds of logic loops and contradictions. For example, if every event has a cause, then what was the first cause? Or, if a "free event" is really random, then what is "free will"? But, if you reflect long enough the one, and only possible, solution should become apparent.

"Free Will" is neither random, nor predetermined. Instead, it must be determined by an INFINITE sequence of causes. In other words, there is no "first cause", nor will there ever be a "last event". Any other conclusion is not only irrational, but, in my view, completely insane.

I have been contemplating this philosophy of infinite cause for a long time, and a lot of dissallusion and new understanding has resulted, which tells me it's worth hanging onto and contemplating even more. It may very well be the "keystone of understanding that completes my bridge to enlightenment... but, then maybe not.

Methinks, the key to knowing God is simply finding a way of comprehending infinity - and logic will always fail in this quest. But, what you do when it fails is what determines your progress. Do you give up, like most people, or start over, and over, and over again, each time changing one small thing. Like evolution itself, we may fail a thousand, even a billion times, but as long as we are willing to keep failing then we will never be a failure.

Reflections

Sunday, August 4, 2013

Social Amnesia

We forget. And, when we forget it is easy to substitute alternate truths in place of the ones we have forgotten - not just easy, but necessary. Because the one thing we rarely forget is that we once knew. And that leaves the door open for pride to work its twisted logic. We can't bear to admit that we lost control over something so directly and intimately linked to our sense of self; our memory.

Our sense of pride is, of course, derived from our sense of self. Or, at least, it is derived from our FALSE sense of self, the same self we associate with and that depends upon our memories, and other intellectual experiences.

So, when we forget, our ego panics. And before we even consciously realize what has happened, it fills in the memory gap with something false. Numerous published scientific experiments bear this out. But, science barely paints complete pictures. So, let me add some interesting details.

In 19th century America, it was a common practice for entire families to sleep together in one room, and even share the same bed. White Americans, collectively, have not forgotten this, what we have forgotten, and filled in with false perceptions that pass for morality, is what sleeping together as a family means.

It means that is was once common and unquestioned for bodies of all ages and relationships to be snuggled up with each other in extremely intimate proximity under the cover of complete darkness. Do we really suppose then that when fathers, or brothers, or uncles, awoke, in the dark, with a sleep induced erection, and found a warm body pressing against their groin, that they didn't let nature take over?

Of course they did. But, did they talk about it the next day? Of course not. And did little Sussie, or Tommy, or uncle Joe, complain about the wet spot on their jammies the next day? Or that they dreamily half woke in the night to the sensation of someone dry humping their leg? It is more likely that they themselves enjoyed the intimacy and reassurance that such contact naturally engenders, especially between loved ones, not just lovers.

The children would not have understood enough to even realize what was going on, and absent all the "good touch, bad touch" lessons of today, they would have had no reason to question something that would have seemed completely natural to them. And the adults and older children (i.e. young adults) would have either pushed away from the "offender", or snuggled closer, and thought nothing further of it. It would have been something that happened a lot.

If you imagine homosexual behavior to be something that depends on intellectual intentions, then you have no understanding of sex at all. This is what we have forgotten as a culture. They are the kinds of things that don't get routinely conveyed with words, written or otherwise. They become lost to our cultural identity. And our cultural pride compels us to fill in the details with invented ideas of morality and so-called decency that end up being completely detached from reality. And from the truth we have forgotten.

This is just one example of how we substitute memory with distortions of the truth. The result is that today we must battle against a growing tide of violent perversions that are really the result of the truth's attempts to reassert itself. We are sexual beings. Our children are sexual, and our brothers, sisters, mothers, fathers, aunts, and uncles are sexual too. The only reason we see so many women and children getting violently raped and murdered today is because we have forgotten these truths. And, out of pride, we try to supplant the truths with laws and moral inventions that cannot replace them, and certainly never suppress them. Our children suffer, and we all suffer, because of our pride, and our arrogance. The road to hell should be call Amnesia.

(P.S. I'm not trying to suggest that we should teach our children that they are sexual by nature. That probably wouldn't be any better than telling them that they're not. But, I do think that if we just stopped lying to our children, and ourselves, about our true nature - sexual and otherwise - that nature itself would remind us of everything we need to know when we need to know it.)

(Originally written by Joseph E. Duncan III on May 14, 2013)

P.S. If you doubt that humans naturally enjoy all kinds of sex, homosexual, pedophilia, etc... then study history - not the history they teach in high school - but the REAL history of sex. And again, I'm not trying to justify anything... the Truth needs no justification, and will speak for itself no matter how much we try to forget it.

Reflections

Sunday, August 11, 2013

Zimmerman's Justice

People who protest the Zimmerman trial verdict seem to forget that our justice system was never designed to protect citizens from the injustice of other citizens (i.e. crime). It was primarily intended to protect citizens from the injustices of the state.

If a man goes free due to a lack of evidence against him, that does not in any way mean that justice has not been served. In fact, it only epitomizes what American Justice is supposed to be about, and what it should be about; protecting the citizens from the government, not necessarily from each other!

If we rely on the government for protection from each other, the we give it the power and control over our lives that the American Revolutionary War was fought to take back. They called it Freedom in 1776, but the protests we see today, are a clear sign that we have completely forgotten what Freedom means. In fact, the protesters are in essence demanding that the government take over their lives, their responsibility, and their freedom, all in the new name of their so-called justice.

Reflections

Sunday, August 18, 2013

Criminal Mentality

Cops routinely lie to criminal suspects in order to gain their trust and trick them into confessing. Thy system then uses any information thus dishonestly obtained in order to "punish" the "criminal". If you doubt this, or don't realize the routine prevalence of this systematic deception, then all you need to do is watch some reality police show like "COPS" (to see how they lie to criminals on the streets), or "The First 48" (to see how it's done at the police station interviews), or "Jail" (to see how they use deception to manage inmates). And if that's not enough to convince you, then consider the reason behind the Federally required Miranda warning.

The lies are part of a police officers training, so it's not some sort of covert conspiracy that only a select few know about. But what few people do realize is the way this systematic deception ends up instilling a strong sense of betrayal and distrust in the people who are directly and grievously injured by it; the so-called "criminals". To see this you have only to imagine what it must be like, to be a naive and trusting young person, caught stealing, or with drugs, and some cop tells you that "things will be much worse if you're not honest". So you tell him the truth, only to learn later that everything you say is in fact used against you, and things were not "easier" because you were honest at all, but much much worse! Only a completely retarded moron wouldn't learn quickly and painfully not to trust the police. And that is the defining characteristic of the so-called "criminal mentality" that directly leads to and supports all the other sub-characteristics and traits of said same mentality!

It's just one more example of how our so-called "criminal justice system" promotes the very crime it purports to protect us all from. Everyone knows the direct relationship that "criminal mentality" (distrust of authority) has on crime. It is a well publicized and oft quoted relationship that the police themselves use perversely to explain the necessity of their authority in the first place. They claim that because of such "anti-social" people, a "police force" is required to keep order in modern society (though they usually associate said "order" with "law" by calling it "law and order" in order to promote the concept and status of "law" as well, implying that without law there would be only dis-order - i.e. chaos - a claim that natural history belies by the way).

This should all come as no surprise. It is, after all, the exact same mechanism of social control that the Catholic church has used since Rome turned to religion as a means of social control via control of "the Truth" (i.e. deception).

Chronicles

Saturday, August 24, 2013

Spoiled Baloney For Lunch, Again

Today is Thursday, July 4th. Over this last weekend a guard was attacked in some other part of this prison (USP), or so the memo everyone here in the SCU (pronounced, "skew") received on Sunday informed me.

The nature and extent of the "attack" was left to our imaginations. But, our punishment was spelled out clearly. The entire prison would remain locked down for a week.

For the SCU prisoners, that means no "recreation" (outdoor cages surrounded by concrete walls), and sack lunches (baloney, cheese, or peanut butter sandwiches with a piece of fruit) for every meal. And since I personally never go to "recreation", my only punishment is the sack lunches for every meal. That in itself wouldn't be all that bad (I lived on sack lunches for two years in the Indio Jail in California, so I'm used to worse) except that the single slice of baloney they've given us each meal for the last two days was spoiled around the edges, and the bananas were too green to eat without getting sick.

Of course, I could save the bananas for a few days until they are edible, but the green baloney had to go in the toilet. And when the prisoners complained to the guards, and the guards complained to the kitchen, they were told, "the baloney isn't spoiled". They said that it was just, "exposed to the air".

Apparently nobody ever taught them what causes food to spoil (hint: exposure to air!).

So, we were all supposed to ignore the foul smell and ensuring stomach cramps and eat the food we all deserve for being bad inmates and "attacking" a guard.

Oh, wait. Officially, of course, we're not being punished at all. The lockdown is merely imposed to give staff time to "investigate the incident" and "evaluate policy". At least, that's what the memo said.

But, every prisoner and guard alike all understand that the lockdown is really just our punishment. Punishment is all the prison officials understand. It is their only means of control, or at least that's what they think. When inmates behave badly, take something away - it's the only logic they seem capable of.

Of course, historically, punishment has never been shown to curb negative behavior, except in the most superficial ways. The one thing that does solicit positive behavior is simply treating people as fellow human beings (commonly referred to as, "respectfully"). It's a truth that the system doesn't seem capable of comprehending. No surprise there.

Reflections

Sunday, August 25, 2013

Crime Fantasy Vs. Crime Fiction

There should be a clear distinction between fantasy and fiction. I know that literally they are the same thing, but in spirit I think they are completely different.

Fiction should be something that COULD be real, even if it isn't. And fantasy should be used for anything that completely defies reality as we know it, and could never be real.

If we distinguish between fantasy and fiction in this way, then it would be easier to separate the BS from good fiction in books and on TV.

For example, so-called crime fiction shows on TV, that depict impossibly intuitive cops against ridiculously psychotic criminals, could be readably identified as FANTASY crime shows instead. Then maybe there'd be a lot of fewer people who actually believe that some people are born without emotions, and others with an innate need to "serve and protect".

What I'm saying is that most crime fiction is as close to reality as dragons and unicorns. The "monsters" are no less impossible, and the "heroes" no more likely. Of course there are real monsters in this world, even human monsters (I certainly was one, in a careful sense), and real heroes as well, (I was just as certainly a hero too). But, the only monsters real heroes fight are the ones within themselves. I'll admit that some crime shows, and books, (more books than shows) endeavor to depict this, but few can even be said to approach reality in their attempts. The characters they create invariably end up being as impossible as winged horses, and they are usually constructed in the same way; by imagining various real things, such as wings and horses, then combining them in very unreal and impossible ways.

So, the next time you see some impossibly emotionless "psychopath" on TV being hunted and captured by ridiculously intuitive cops, just try to remember that it is pure fantasy, and in the real world the worst monsters and greatest heroes are the ones inside of all of us.

Reflections

Monday, September 2, 2013

Proof That Smoking Doesn't Cause Cancer

It is only obvious that smoking does not cause cancer, because a lot of people who smoke never get cancer. And, I know this first hand because I used to smoke and I don't have cancer. Also, my father smoked all his life, and he doesn't have cancer either.

So, all the science that associates smoking with cancer is a bunch of hype generated by a bunch of sympathy seeking wackos that don't know what they're talking about. Obviously, there are completely detached from the real world.

And it's not just smoking and cancer that they know nothing about. It's just as obvious that an abusive childhood has nothing to do with adult criminal behavior. Like cancer, crime is the result of sinful thoughts and choices. Smoking is not a sin, so it has nothing to do with cancer. Only people who sin get cancer, and only people who choose a life of sin commit crimes. It's as simple as that. Really.

Chronicles

Wednesday, September 4, 2013

Remiss Misgivings

Yes, I have been remiss in updating this sub-blog (Chronicles). My intention was to post the day-to-day stuff here so anyone interested could get a feel for what it's like for me to be on death row in Federal prison. But most of what happens around here ends up being stuff I can't write publicly about without risking getting someone in trouble, guards and prisoners. So many rules are broken everyday that I couldn't even report what it's like to get chow without exposing violations that any other prison (or jail) I have been in would consider "serious". I dare not even say what the violations are for fear of getting someone in trouble.

So, you'll just have to imagine what it's like for now. I'll post what I can, but it won't be much. But generally I am comfortable - nobody harasses me, not even the other prisoners. People for the most part speak to me respectfully; though I keep to myself and seldom speak to anyone. I rarely leave my cell, by choice. In fact I've only been out of my cell once since my dental appointment two months ago, and that was for a mandatory six-month administrative review (they took me to the counselor's office, ask me if I had any concerns or questions, I said no; then they took me back to my cell).

Life is better for me than even I think it should be, but I still look forward to my "release day"

Dreams

Saturday, September 7, 2013

A Dream Within A Dream

I dreamed this afternoon that I was working for a consulting company like the one I worked for a while I was living and attending college in Fargo. Except instead of factory automation software, this dream company designed and built portable inflatable business complexes that included offices, living quarters, and dining halls.

In the dream I was flying over some of our buildings, watching as they were being inflated into fully equipped utilities. I thought nothing of the fact that I was flying, it seemed natural.

I soon landed near the chow hall, where I met a couple of my coworkers and went inside. I was given a prefabricated meal tray, and we sat down together to eat. But, the food I was given, eggs and oatmeal, was not enough to satisfy me. So, I got up to get in line for more food.

I was able to find to serving line with no problem, but I was confused over which end to start. I eventually discovered the correct location, where I could get a tray, a plate, and utensils, then begin my way through the serving line. But a very rude woman prevented me from getting a tray so I could join the line by standing directly in front of the trays and refusing to move.

So I decided to return later, and went outside. Actually, I flew over to the entrance, and this time I felt special for being able to fly. When I got outside I realized that I should not be able to fly unless I was dreaming. At first the "realness" of the experience seemed to contradict this conclusion. But, I soon overcame the impression of reality by flying up to the roof.

I realized now that I was in a dream. But - and this is interesting - I assumed my "reality" was the world in which I was a consultant, not an inmate on death row. I was dreaming a lucid dream within a non lucid dream. And just like any lucid dream, I became impressed by the incredible detail and realness of it all.

I flew off the roof and up over a medium sized city with beautiful buildings in the distance. It was evening, and the city lights were intricate and mesmerizing. I remember thinking that I wanted to fly down and explore the detail of it all. But, as often occurs in my lucid dreams, some mysterious force began pulling me in a direction I did not want to go.

I was pulled away from the city, and then down into a steep walled valley. It seemed the more I resisted the less detailed and intricate the dream became. Then there were three bird-like things flitting around my face, and I thought they were intrusions into my dream from "reality". But, the "reality" I supposed they were from was the one where I was a consultant.

I didn't like being pulled down. So, I decided to wake up. After a moment, I awoke and found myself, unexpectedly, in this prison cell. I thought, how strange it was to dream that I was lucid from within another dream.

Chronicles

Saturday, September 21, 2013

Dental Work

I just got back from the small dental office in the SCU downstairs after having my teeth cleaned for the first time in over nine years (since before my arrest in 2005).

The hygienist who cleaned my teeth and examined them was very nice, and had kind friendly eyes. She was also very experienced and professional about her work. I was able to ask all the questions I had about taking care at my teeth in prison (e.g. how and when to request an appointment if I have a problem with my teeth - no easy task considering how intricate policies and strained resources determine if and when a given request is responded to - many of my requests have been ignored in the past due to a simple lack of correct wording it seems).

The exam and cleaning went well. She found only one problem area where an old filling appeared to be giving out and needs replacement. Other than that my teeth are in good shape. The filling I got two years ago, to fix what the jail dentist in Riverside, California said needed a root canal (so he wouldn't have to fix it with a filling) is holding up well (surprise, surprise). So now, with this cleaning, my teeth are in good shape, all 28 of them (sans the wisdom teeth), with a lot of fillings in the molars but no caps, root canals, or anything else wrong with them. Not bad, methinks, for a fifty year old man who's spent more than half his life imprisoned.

(Originally written by Joseph E. Duncan III on June 7, 2013)

P.S. A week after the above dental visit I got called out for another dental appointment to actually have my one ailing tooth repaired. The dentist fixed it quickly with a few taps of his drill and a dot of amalgam, without even numbing me up first (per my request - the shot to kill the pain would have been more painful, by far, then the entire procedure!). So, now my teeth are in tip top shape, oh happy me! (It's seems my teeth have caused me more worry and concern these last several years - because I could not get routine dental care - than all the death penalty cases against me, and I'm not even exaggerating!)

Chronicles

Saturday, September 21, 2013

Broken Toe Blues

The night before last I got woke up again by my neighbor, Marvin Gabrion, at two-thirty in the morning. He is an obnoxious old man of low intelligence who nobody likes. Do in order to punish everyone for not liking him he likes to moan and wail all night and most of the day. And if that's not enough to bother everyone he'll clap his hands loudly once in a while just to wake up as many people as he can to hear his "singing", which, of course, is exactly the kind of thinking and behavior that makes him so unpopular to start with.

Anyway, the night before last was the umpteenth time he kept me awake at night, so I got up and stupidly kicked my door, hard enough to break my big toe again (the last time I broke it was in junior high gym class while playing soccer). So now I not only have to put up with his ignorant shenanigans, but I must suffer in silence for my own.

There is no point reporting my broken toe on sick call since the best they can do is confirm it's broken with an x-ray then put a splint on it. And, since I don't have to walk around at all (being confined to my cell 24/7) there's really no need for an elaborate splint. I've just been keeping my shoes on, even while I sleep, which seems to provide plenty of support. Luckily I have aspirin to help get through the first 48 hours or so, which was the most painful. But now the pain has subsided and I just have to be careful not to put any weight on it.

As for Gabrion, the stupid old man who instigated my folly, even as I jot these words he is wailing away in the cell across the hall from me, oblivious to the guards banging on his door to give him his "meds" (anti-depressants for sure, but he needs anti-psychotics). I don't feel bad mentioning his name openly in this blog because I'm not saying anything that can get him in trouble. "Singing", as he calls it, isn't against the rules, which he knows well and frequently insist on his "right' to do it when guards or other prisoners complain. He himself is notoriously the biggest "rat" on the tier, frequently telling on other prisoners out loud and in front of everyone. Then he turns right around and accuses solid convicts of being "rats, fags, child molesters, and cowards", to name a few of his favorite insults.

Marvin Gabrion is one man who really challenges my belief that everyone has merit and deserves to live. The only merit I can find in him is that he really challenges and hence strengthens my ability to be patient, which my broken toe painfully attests.

Reflections

Saturday, September 28, 2013

Personal Sovereignty

In the natural order of the universe our greatest weakness is the very thing we believe to be our greatest strength. It is our blind and ignorant belief in personal sovereignty (or, what modern

Christians call, "limited free will", though such a concept appears nowhere in the Bible and in fact is strongly contradicted by it). You don't need to be religious or even philosophical in order to be caught up by this lie. If you think for a moment that you are solely responsible for what you do, then you believe in personal sovereignty; and you are deceived.

There is a difference, of course, between personal sovereignty, and the divine sovereignty that Jesus gave his life attempting to disclose. While personal sovereignty is an impossible delusion that no one can ever have, divine sovereignty is very real, immediately present, and experienced by everyone and everything in the universe. It is our divine birthright that the Christ (and Buddha, and others) often spoke of. It says we are not responsible for just what we do; we are responsible for everything that happens - Everything!

When we realize this beyond intellectual understanding then we find the true meaning and infinite power of unconditional love that all men of Truth throughout history have spoken of. With just an ounce of faith in this Truth, mountains, even stars, will move. I've seen it happen within my own heart, and so will anyone who has the faith to believe.

Reflections

Sunday, October 13, 2013

Real Freedom For Everyone, Even Me

Freedom from judgment is freedom from human law, freedom from hypocrisy, and freedom from suffering. it is also freedom from hate, and freedom from hell. Real freedom is the very salvation that Jesus promised, and the nirvana of Eastern enlightenment at the same time.

The teachings of Jesus were never meant to enslave us all over again with a bunch of new laws and ceremonies. The man from Nazareth told us as plainly as he could that he came with the news of a new law that freed us from human law, and human judgment, and human hypocrisy, and from hate and hell.

This new law was extremely simple to obey; in fact it is impossible to disobey once it was understood. It is a law that is directly "written" in every heart and every mind - though those who put their faith in human laws, and human beliefs, and human judgment (i.e. their own, or anyone else's), would be blinded to it.

Jesus sometimes called the law "charity", or as it is more commonly translated, "love" (though technically the word love, as defined and used in modern language, did not exist in any language until the spawning of the so called "romantic languages" long after Christianity was born). He also told us that the law was essentially ineffable (could not be properly expressed with mere human words), but could be expressed by what we do, and by what HE did. This is why what he did, i.e. "die for our sins", was so important. It was not some divinely magical event (a.k.a. "miracle") that set us free. It was a simple law of nature, hidden to us by our own vain faith in human intellect and human judgment, that spawns so many human laws that only serve to enslave us to a life of eternally repetitious and self inflicted pain and suffering.

Freedom from hell is freedom from judgment, and from human law. I took my first step toward that freedom when I surrendered to the authorities of this world. I did not surrender so I could be judged - I surrendered because I knew beyond any more doubt that I would never be judged by men again. I became more free than I had ever been. And, I become freer and freer the longer I sit in this prison cell and meditate on the true meaning of freedom.

No matter how I am judged by men; no matter what punishment is imposed upon me (either life in prison or death); I will always be more free than the people who impose their judgment - this I sincerely believe; and proves my faith valid again and again. Real freedom is for everyone and anyone, perhaps even especially for me!

Reflections

Sunday, October 20, 2013

Pedophile Hypocrisy

Why do women shave their body hair? Why do they use make up to make their eyes look big, cheeks flush, and lips red? And when a woman wants to appeal to a man, why does she revert to a girlishly high voice including childish lilts and inflections complete with demure looks?

All of these things have one common factor; they all mimic the characteristics of sexually immature children. And yet in our culture we accept a woman's attempt to deduce men with immature traits as though it were perfectly natural, while at the same time we condemn the men who dare admit that they are sexually aroused by real children and call them pedophiles.

I'm not suggesting anything here about whether this is right or wrong. I'm only asking why it is - because it is.

Reflections

Saturday, November 9, 2013

Creepy Commercials

Okay, I can't suppress this any more, and I can only hope I'm not the only one who feels this way.

The commercials on TV for eHarmony.com are creepier than an old man in the kiddy-pool at a public park. And I'm talking about all of their commercials, not just one or two of them.

That old man, Dr. Warren, who founded eHarmony and insists on being in all the commercials, is the quintessential creepy old man. And the way he interjects himself into the middle of supposedly ideal romantic relationships makes me cringe every time I'm forced to see it (when flipping channels for example). Not to mention how he slides like a genuine sleazeball into the seat across from that hopelessly pathetic woman at the speed dating table. I always imagine him saying, "Do you have young children?" I love women with children." every time I see the way he sits down and hear that sleazy tone of voice he no doubt imagines to be sooting (as any true sleazeball would).

But then, maybe I'm just being biased (or outright prejudice) since I learned how eHarmony only caters to "upstanding" (i.e. Christian-like) people. It "filters out" the "undesirables" with its questionnaires and only allows "acceptable" people to use their service. How creepy is that?

Reflections

Tuesday, November 12, 2013

A Question For Christians

I have a question I'd like to ask any Christian who believes I am condemned for not believing what they believe. If you are such a person, then please post your answer to my question as a comment for this blog entry, or mail an answer to me personally (my current mailing address can be found by searching for my name, Joseph Duncan, at BOP.com).

This is no simple question, so a little foundations is in order. Please bear with me.

First, it is important to remember from your Sunday school lessons that Jesus, the Son of God, as a man, was in the eyes of society at the time he walked the earth some two thousand years ago, not only a known criminal, but also a pariah of the lowest sorts. He may have entered Jerusalem triumphantly, but by the time of the Passover he was being pursued and hated by mobs of people who threatened those who merely admitted knowing Jesus with punishment, or worse. And after Jesus was condemned by the dominant religious order of his day, he was spit upon, cursed, and openly scorned as a blasphemer, the lowest of the low.

And that brings me to my second point of foundation. It is a well documented but little understood historical fact that in Jesus' day the crime of blasphemy was the most despicable crime of all; worse than stealing, worse than kidnapping, worse than rape, and even worse than serial murder, as the release of Barabbas clearly attests. But, what few people realize is that blasphemy was even worse than child rape, a lot worse. In fact, child rape was not even a crime, and in special circumstances it was explicitly sanctioned by Jewish law, THE Law of that day.

The Talmud, only a part of which appears in the Christian Bible, explicitly demands that a man have intercourse with a girl he takes as his wife, who can be as young as three years old, in order to consummate the marriage. It also decrees that if a man dies and his brother wishes to adopt his wives, he must again copulate with them, regardless of their age, young or old. And if a small girl is raped before the age of three, the Talmud states only that as long as she heals so that her genitalia remains intact she is to be still considered a virgin for the purpose of marriage. No penalty what-so-ever is mentioned for the rapist, except that he must marry the girl if she "loses her virginity" to him.

And if you think that's shocking, it gets worse (or maybe better, if you're a "deviant" like me). Remember the oft-cited old-testament law against homosexuality, the one that explicitly forbids a man to "lay with another man as a woman"? Well, the Talmud goes on to clarify, just as explicitly, that a boy under the age of nine years, is not considered a "man" for the purpose of this law, and therefore it is perfectly acceptable to lie with a boy, "as a woman", and even preferable since there is then no risk of obligating yourself to a wedding afterwards!

Now, like I said, all this is well documented, unjustified, and unexcused even by modern Orthodox Jews. I haven't mentioned what Jewish law permits in regard to slave girls, but I hope that by now you can start to imagine (or perhaps, fantasize). If you don't believe me then Google it for yourself. It was printed documentation of this kind of information that was once confiscated from my jail cell in Ada County (Boise, Idaho) during my competency hearing. The U.S. Marshals who found it called it "child porn", and refused to return it to me even though there was nothing pornographic about it. It was strictly an unbiased and academic discussion of "Child sex in the Talmud" (a good Google quote). Apparently the subject alone was enough to be considered by them as, "pornographic". (They incidentally reported to my attorneys that they had found "child porn" in my cell, without telling them what they meant by "child porn"; a clear - but failed - attempt to foster attorney-client bias.)

Are you still with me? If you're like most Christians you'll be rationalizing at this point, making up excuses and reasons to explain away or justify the raw information I have exposed you to here. You will remind yourself that I am after all a "child killer", and subject to the devil, so anything I say that causes you to doubt what you believe in regard to Jesus or God is just the devil using me to get to you, to "take your soul" I suppose. But, if every time that you question or doubt what you believe you blame the devil, then how will you ever learn the truth if what you believe is wrong?

Wait, that's not my question. Before we get to that let's go back one more time and take another look at the heinous crime of blasphemy that "our Lord and Savior" (by his own admission) was guilty of.

What's so bad about blasphemy that it was once spat from the mouths of common citizens with the same hateful vehemence that we now cry "child molester!?" You might think that Jesus' crime was only played up by the Pharisees in order to justify killing him out of their own self-centered ignorance of the truth. But that's not the case at all. The truth is that blasphemy was a very real and serious threat to social order and not just the authority of the Pharisaic lawmen.

In those days religious beliefs were the glue that held society together; and it was the only glue. Without its authority there could be no cities or towns or even villages. The Romans knew this, and that's why they never interfered with the religious beliefs or authority of the regions they conquered. Instead they simply imposed a separate authority - the authority of the state - over religious authority. But, they let the religious authorities practice and enforce their beliefs with very little to no interference. The Romans understood from experiences that to interfere with local religion invariably resulted in the dissolution of community and the loss of the conquered town or city as a resource.

A blasphemer could, and often did, cause people to question the ruling class' right to make laws and enforce them. This inevitably resulted in violent riots and uprisings that could and did destroy entire cities, even whole regions. The insoluble instability in and around Jerusalem even today is no doubt the result of blasphemers. So the fears of the Pharisees were well justified, and the crime of blasphemy a very real and serious one. The crowd spat on Jesus not without good reason. He threatened not just what they believed, but everything they had; their land, their families, and all their possessions. Blasphemy was the worst possible crime against society.

Of course the message of Christ was meant to free people from such dependence on human law and human authority. But clearly they - society in general, then and arguably now - were not ready for that message. So they cursed Jesus, and punished him in the worst way they knew how. They sought to send a clear message of their own to any other would-be blasphemers out there thinking about challenging their faith in their law and authority.

Now comes my question: Am I, Joseph E. Duncan III, not if anything else, a blasphemer of our age? Was what I did not a direct challenge to the authority, laws, and beliefs of our modern society? Did I not defile our societies most sacred symbol of purity and innocence as Jesus defiled his by entering God's temple and violently desecrating what he found there? Christians say he was, "righteously indignant" and not "angry" (which would be sinful). I too believe I had the right to do what I had done. By attacking children so brazenly and vilely I was overturning the tables where modern lawmakers trade coin for beliefs (i.e. by selling false idols; ideas such as "justice" and "liberty" that have no value or even definition outside of human intellect) in order to hypocritically line their own pockets with gold.

Let me be more specific: They make laws against physically loving children (i.e. pedophilia) then raise taxes to "enforce" their laws. But where does that money go? Nearly all of it goes into the pockets of lawmakers, law enforcers, and lawyers - the Pharisees of our day. Of course they genuinely believe in the importance of what they do, as did the Pharisees. And I am and had every intention of being as much of a threat to the authorities of this world as Jesus did to his. Now here's my question to all you so-called Christians out there who think you know the Will of God and the mind (or Message) of Christ just because of what you read in a barely decipherable "holy book", or, more likely, because of what somebody else read and told you about: Isn't spitting on me, the same as spitting on Christ?

I'll wait for your answers, and welcome all attempts to do so. Just please try to keep in mind that everything I wrote above was (is) intended to solicit thoughts, and questions (yes, doubt) about what you believe. So if your answer is some rote quotation or paraphrasing of what you learned in church, then don't bother answering at all. I want to hear from your heart and soul what you really think about all this. There are some Christians out there who can do this, though they are rare, and only mistakenly identify with other Christians. The ones of which I speak might be called True Christians, and I have discovered evidence of their existence in things I have read from various variations (denominations) of Christian beliefs. Ninety-nine point nine percent of Christian literature is garbage, but if point-one percent of what Christians write shows evidence of real understanding of Christ's real message (a message that I nor any man is worthy to convey - not even those who knew Jesus personally) then there must be hundreds of thousands of Christians out there who understand what I'm asking. And if only one of those sends me an honest answer (not an answer that I already think I know; I don't have one) then I will consider the last six hours I spent writing this (after months of contemplating it on and off) well worth the time God gave me to do it. And if you can honestly tell me why I am not "like Jesus", then hell, maybe I'll actually learn something - I'd really like that!

Reflections

Sunday, November 17, 2013

Lost Love

I believe that no matter what you think you love, if it can be taken away, ever, then it is not true love you feel, only a kind of conditioned familiar attachment. In this world it is a common confusion, and a severely detrimental one, to say the least.

As I've written here before, I think true love is not an emotion, at least not in any conventional or contemporary sense. It can certainly stir up emotions, but not just the pleasant ones. True love is behind rage as much as infatuation. Yet both rage and infatuation, as well as most other "human feelings", are merely distortions of true love's real intent.

Reflections

Sunday, November 24, 2013

Just You

When someone you thought you knew well does something completely unexpected and something completely contrary to the person you thought you knew, it leaves you with an intensely bewildering sense of not knowing that person at all. But, it's never really that person whom you don't know, it's always just you.

If you doubt this truth, as many will, then you ask yourself honestly how it is that you know anyone at all. We say we "know" someone when our experience with that person forms a consistent pattern. We then typically lean on our experience with that person and expect them to remain consistent, to not change.

If a person we meet is unpredictable or inconsistent, then we never get the sense of knowing them. It is like predictability that allows us the sense of knowing anyone, or anything for that matter.

But ultimately, nothing (and no one) is ever truly predictable. Of course I'm saying only that things change, people change. Nothing remains the same, or behaves the same, through time. Not even molecules. Atomic particles change their behavior according to their proximity and relationship to other particles. So do people.

So the next time someone does something you don't expect, ask yourself who YOU really are, not them.

Reflections

Sunday, December 1, 2013

Welcome To Your Eternal Life

To suppose, as many do, that this life is some sort of precursor to another eternal life of idealized perfection (e.g. heaven) is not just ignorant, it is contrary to the reality of perfection, and the reality of eternal life; it is contrary to heaven itself.

This life is your eternal life, and it is already perfect. If it wasn't perfect (in the absolute sense) then you simply would not exist. Think about it. In order for you to exist, circumstances going all the way back to the Big Bang had to be exactly what they were, i.e. perfect. You are the product of perfection! If one single atom had spun up instead of down ten billion years ago, our solar system wouldn't exist today, and of course neither would you.

But, that atom did spin down, and in combination with trillions upon trillions upon trillions of other profound events, equally significant, we came into being. If just one of those events of the tiniest impact had been any different, any less perfect, then the universe, our world, and you, would simply not be.

This is not some mystical idea that requires blind faith to believe. It is a fundamental and self-evident truth that takes only a little honest introspection, and courage to challenge your established beliefs, for you to see it, and comprehend it for yourself. You needn't take my word or anyone's word for it. The universe was created perfect, for all with eyes to see and bear witness too. And it will remain perfect throughout all of eternity.

James T. Kirk once said (in a Star Trek book that I don't remember the title of off hand), "The doors to truth are guarded by paradox and confusion. If we turn our back to these, they will remain closed behind us." So, if we are to know truth, we must accept confusion and paradox, but only because we look at eternity through mortal eyes; we see infinity through the finite, and it makes no sense.

Chronicles

Tuesday, December 3, 2013

A Day In The Life...

I wake up at approximately 4:30 a.m. I lay still for several minutes thinking about the dream I just woke up from. I always seem to wake up from dreams these days, but I usually forget them within ten or twenty minutes. Today I've forgotten. It's Tuesday, December 3, 2013.

4:44 a.m. I sit up and punch the light button on my clear plastic battery powered alarm clock. It's fairly dark in these cells when the lights are off at night, which is a real blessing most prisoners don't get. I'm not sleepy, so I decide to get up. I urinate, throw some warm water on my face to rinse the sleep away, and brush my hair just enough so the guards won't think I'm a nut case when they look in my cell. I haven't cut my hair in over a year, and amazingly it's still only hinting about turning gray.

4:45 a.m. I put on the cheap but amazingly accurate Casio watch that I bought while I was in Idaho Maximum Security several years ago. I haven't actually worn this or any other watch since before my arrest in 2005, but I wear it today as a reminded to write this.

5:05 a.m. I finish up these first few paragraphs and since it is all quiet on the tier I decide to pull out my book about Chaology and read until breakfast. First I put some water on to heat for coffee using the stinger I made by clipping two pairs of stainless steal "safety" trimming scissors to the prongs of my T.V. plug. I just set a cup on a makeshift shelf so the scissors are immersed and in about seven to fifteen minutes the water will boil, depending on how hot the tap water is to start with.

5:19 a.m. The water's ready, so I pour it into an insulated mug with a water bottle of clean water in it. I use the stung water, which tastes like rust, to heat clean water this way indirectly. It takes a lot longer, but everyone knows you can't drink stung water unless you like getting sick. In the morning, because the top water isn't very hot to begin with, it takes two zaps to get the water in the bottle hot enough for a decent cup of coffee.

5:27 a.m. Second zap is complete. It only takes about 90 seconds to transfer the maximum amount of heat from the stung water to the bottled water; I know because I once jerry-rigged a thermometer out of an empty pen ink-tube and timed it.

5:32 a.m. Coffee is served, nice and hot the way I like it (freeze-dried of course). I turn on the T.V. and flip it to VH1, but I'm disappointed to see that the morning music videos aren't on yet. So I watch "Black Ink" (a tattoo reality show) with no sound while I enjoy my coffee.

5:39 a.m. Finish my coffee, turn off T.V., jot this down, and pick up my "Chaos" book, kick back on my bunk and read.

5:59 a.m. I hear a guard come on the tier and start opening bean-slots to pick up laundry. I get up and wait by the door for my bean-slot to open then push out the three partly filled mesh laundry bags I had prepared (i.e. tied shut securely) last night. Laundry is picked up on Tuesday and Fridays in the morning and usually returned clean on the same afternoon.

6:11 a.m. I finish updating this and go back to reading.

6:27 a.m. I hear guards come on tier and start passing out breakfast trays.

6:31 a.m. The bean-slot in the cell-door opens and I am handed two eight-ounce fat-free milks, and two 2x8x10 inch plastic trays with lids (I just now measured them), one "hot", and one "cold". The "cold" tray has a halved apple, two packs of saccharin based sweetener, a pack of dried coffee, and a spork utensil pack that contains a small napkin and a little salt and pepper that I never bother with. The "hot" tray today is my favorite; two biscuits, a serving of chopped up boiled potatoes, oat meal, and gravy with hamburger meat in it. If I'm hungry, I'll eat the oat meal with about eight packs of my own store-bought aspartame based sweetener (saccharin is only good with tea as far as I'm concerned because tea hides the bitter aftertaste). But, today I'm not that hungry, so I just eat the biscuits and gravy and drink one milk. I put the other milk in an insulated pitcher of ice that I save each day for this very purpose by wrapping the pitcher in some sheets to keep the ice from melting overnight. They usually pass out ice around dinner time (4 p.m.), and I can keep it from completely melting this way for about one day.

6:50 a.m. Trays are picked up, bean-slot is closed, I write this, then go back to reading about Chaology, chapter 13: "Evolution and Order without Design". Fascinating stuff!

7:48 a.m. Finished chapter 13. I feel empowered when I read books like this, that help me articulate my own experience and understanding better. I get up, remove the jacket I'd been wearing since I got up this morning and lay it on the top of the ice pitcher where I keep it when I'm not wearing it, then I cover the door window with a towel that I keep hanging on the door for that purpose. Being able to cover the window like this is another luxury that most prisoners don't have. I've never been in a prison or jail before where you could get away with covering the door window, or any window for that matter, even temporarily, without getting in trouble for it. Here, they not only allow it, generally, but I suspect they even appreciate it since I'm sure they don't like looking at a man sitting on the toilet or taking a shower any more than we like being looked at while we do so. I covered the window in this case so I can sit privately and relive my bowels a bit on the stainless steal 3000$ toilet provided kindly for such purpose. When I finish, I wash my hands thoroughly and dry them on the same towels as I uncover the window again. I put on some more water for coffee and then sit to write this while I wait for it to heat.

8:13 a.m. I put my jacket back on. I was a bit warm when I took it off a moment ago, but now I'm cold again. I usually wear a personal (i.e. store-bought) thermal undershirt with long sleeves, on top of my state issued T-shirt, which generally keeps me warm enough. But today my one and only thermal shirt is in the laundry, so I'll have to make do with this jacket.

8:14 a.m. Water is hot and ready. I make my coffee and enjoy it while watching music videos and commercials on VH1 without sound. If I see a video I like or haven't heard before come on then I'll pick up the earphones and put them in one or both ears, otherwise I prefer not to subject my brain to so much unnecessary noise.

8:30 a.m. I finish my coffee and making the above entry, then get out my copy of "The New York Review of Books", which came in the mail yesterday, and I start combing through its pages and making a list of interesting books that I'll send to one of my "defense team" friends and ask her to print off and send me the Amazon.com information for the books. This is how I find good books to read, and it's how I found that book on Chaology that I was reading earlier. If I find a book I really like then I'll ask one of my lawyers to order it for me, which they are always happy to do much to my deeply felt appreciation.

8:49 a.m. A guard taps on my door. I look up and see his face in the window. He asks, "Rec?" I shake my head, no. He continues on to the next cell. I have not been to "rec" (i.e. recreation) in over a year. I see no point in it. Some of the guards don't even bother asking me if I want rec anymore, which I appreciate. If I ever decide to go to "rec" (i.e. a walled in cage outside, or room with an exercise bike inside) then I'm sure I can find a way to let them know. I return to making my list of books.

10:10 a.m. Lunch is served, interrupting my perusal of the Book Review (I also read any interesting articles I find, and this morning I found several; one about Norman Rockwell, another about Mike Tyson, and a third especially interesting one about the paradigm shift in sexual views that occurred when Christians took over Rome, or in my opinion, when Rome took over Christianity.) For lunch we get two covered trays again. On the "cold" tray is a pasta salad, two slices of wheat bread, and some lettuce, tomato slice, and onions, along with a small packet of "Miracle Whip" like salad dressing, and a spork. On the "hot" tray (which is never hot at all by the time we get it) we get a "chicken patty" (imagine a single chicken McNugget smashed thin so it's the size of a patty, then overly peppered - probably to cover up the fact that there's not enough chicken in it to taste) and a lemon pie, and some plain white rice. I eat the pie with the milk I saved from breakfast, then put the rice in the empty milk carton and put it back in the ice pitcher in case commissary (store) doesn't show up today - it should be here by now but is late - and I get hungry. I leave everything else on the trays untouched (except the salad dressing pack, which I squirrel away); I'm not THAT hungry (the smell of onions on the "cold" tray ruined everything on it for me, and the pepper on the "chicken patty" ruins that (I've tried scrapping the peppered breading off in the past, but there's just not enough meat underneath it to scrape anything off of).

10:44 a.m. Trays are picked up and I go back to perusing my magazine for books.

10:50 a.m. My hands get cold, so I put on the jersey gloves I bought on store a few weeks ago.

10:56 a.m. I find another interesting article I'd like to read, about sea monsters of map legends, but now my eyes and back are a little tired from reading all morning. So, I mark the page for later, and kill the light by tapping on the touch sensitive button near my door. Then I lay down, still wearing my jacket and gloves, and meditate in the prone position for a while. Hopefully commissary will come before long.

12:40 p.m. I fell asleep. Just woke up by "fire alarm" buzzer. It goes off about twice a day lately, and is very loud and annoying. So loud in fact, that the guards have ear protection they can wear when it happens. Fortunately this cell I am in is about twenty feet from the buzzer. The cells directly under the buzzers are much worse. I often wonder if they intentionally set the alarm off as some form of psychological torture. It sure seems like it.

12:42 p.m. Fire alarms finally stops. I turn on the T.V. and flip through the channels. I'm lucky and find a documentary playing on History Channel ("How The Earth Was Made", and awfully pretentious title methinks, but at least it's something to watch that won't numb my brain). I put on water for coffee, then put an earphone in my ear and enjoy the program.

1:02 p.m. I hear the guard/counselor ("Mr. Edwards") in the hall answering the "legal phone" and passing the receiver to another prisoner. I get his attention (he's one of only three staff here that I recognize and know by name) and ask him if the "regular phone" (a.k.a. "cell phone") is being used. He goes and gets it from the end of the tier and passes it to me through the bean-slot with the cord running out through a notch when the slot is closed. The "cell phone" is an old black traditional push button phone that you'd expect to see on a typical government desk. There is frequently a line of prisoners waiting to use it, so I was lucky it was free.

1:07 p.m. I call the Federal Defender's Office in Boise, Idaho and ask for Tom, one of the attorneys who was on my "defense team" during my trial in Boise, and a friend. The receptionist says he's not in. I'm fixing my coffee while I'm on the phone since I don't like to waste the hot water, and I ask for Nancy, and investigator for the "defense team", and also a friend. A moment later she picks up and I thank her for the cute pictures of her dogs dressed up for Halloween that she sent recently because she knows how much I like animals, and then ask her if she knows when Tom will be in the office. She says maybe Thursday would be a good time to try him. I thank her again for the pictures, remind her to send Christmas pictures (of her dogs of course) and say good-bye. I have another call to make but must wait 30 minutes before I can make another call. I check my account balance using the phone. I have $99.45, which means the money for the store this week (about $22) has been withdrawn, a good indicator that we should get our commissary orders soon, hopefully today. I finish my coffee then I write this, then go back to watch the History Channel while I wait for my next call.

1:40 p.m. I call the Federal Defender's Office in Sacramento, California and ask for Erika, and investigator and friend, but she is not in. I ask for Joe, another lawyer/friend working on my case and he's busy. I talk to Joe a lot, and was just calling to say, hi.

1:47 p.m. I go back to watching the documentary about the formation of the Hawaiian islands on the History Channel.

2:11 p.m. I hear a guard on the tier, and another prisoner requesting the "cell phone", so I pass it back out through the bean-slot and then go back to watching the Earth documentary, now on Yellowstone National Park geology. I've seen it before, but I don't mind watching it again to help me learn.

3:37 p.m. My laundry is returned. I open the bags and start folding clothes.

3:45 p.m. Dinner is served, very early today. I haven't even finished putting away my laundry. The "cold" tray is just two slices of bread, a pat of butter (or more likely margarine, but I don't know the difference) and a spork. The "hot" tray contains sweet potatoes, green beans, and a mess of something that I think is supposed to be beef stew, but I can hardly tell because it looks like someone put it in a blender. I taste it and I don't gag, so I decide to give it a shot, but it'll need some work first. I chow down the potatoes and green beans, then retrieve the rice I saved from lunch in the ice pitcher and I dump it in the "stew". Much better, but now it was too cold to enjoy. So, on goes the water, and out comes the water bottle with the top cut off that I use for heating up concoctions like this. It'll take at least three cups of stung water to heat it sufficiently, but I think it'll be worth it, especially since I'm pretty hungry after not eating much all day, and it doesn't look like commissary is going to make it (which means we probably won't get commissary until Thursday; bummer).

4:10 p.m. While I wait for my "stew" to heat up I write the above and then finish putting away my laundry, which includes taking off the jacket I've been wearing all day and putting on my thermal undershirt.

4:25 p.m. I just finished washing my "dishes" (plastic soup bowl that followed me from Idaho Max, the cut off water bottle, and a personal plastic spoon that is much nicer to eat with than a spork) after enjoying my "stew", which turned out pretty good after heating it up and adding a little "seasoned salt" from store. I just put some water on for my after dinner coffee and life is good - too good after all the hell I've wrought in this world - all the more reason I should enjoy what I have; to not appreciate what I've been given to enjoy would be to dishonor divine grace.

4:45 p.m. Trays picked up and mail passed out at the same time. I got a letter from a friend in Europe, which helps make up for not getting any commissary today.

5:15 p.m. Finish reading my mail, and watch end of "O' Brother, Where Art Thou?" the only George Clooney movie I actually like George Clooney in.

5:23 p.m. C/O Joslin, one of the three staff here who's name I know, and the only C/O (guard) I actually like (because she's always fair and considerate with all the prisoners, even the asswipes), brings around the ice, a little late, but always appreciated (by me at least). So now I can have a cold milk with my lunch tomorrow, a good sign that tomorrow will be another good day.

5:44 p.m. I cover my door window and uncover the air vent then get naked and step in the shower. The water is nice and hot, the way I like it, and quickly steams up the entire cell even with the air vent wide open. I brush my teeth thoroughly in the shower as usual, and wash all over with state soap, but don't use any shampoo (I have two different kinds of shampoo, one with conditioner and one without, but save it for visits, if I ever get one). I have no "social life" so no reason to use shampoo, which I consider a cosmetic (no, I don't have dandruff or itchy scalp either, and my hair is dry not oily). After my shower I dry off and admire my body in the mirror over the sink for a moment. Not narcissistically, I'm too old for that, but I do appreciate how my body is aging slowly. I could stand to loose about five pounds or so off my waist, but I still have a full head of mostly brown hair, a mouth full of 28 teeth (sans four wisdom teeth that I paid good money to have pulled while I lived in Fargo, North Dakota) and no health issues at all. Not bad for a 50-year-old man facing death for the last eight years. I honestly think masturbating a lot helps, which I'll probably do later tonight but won't write about it here, sorry.

6:30 p.m. Well, that's about all for my day. I'll probably read a little more, watch some T.V. ("Naked Vegas" comes on later, which I enjoy watching for different reason. ;)), and write a letter. I'll also floss later (probably while watching T.V.) and then hit the hay sometime after 11 p.m., or whenever I get tired.

This has been a fairly typical day. Other than some prisoners yelling angrily at each other on occasion, which I typically ignore so didn't bother writing about it. Nobody yells at me and they generally all treat me respectfully when I have any dealings with them at all. I treat them respectfully too, except for inmate Gabrion, who wouldn't know respect if it hit him in the face and whom nobody respects because he respects nobody. Gabrion was fairly quiet today though, which added to the day's pleasantness. The noise from other prisoners is typical, especially in the evening, but if I'm ever bothered by it, which is rarely, I just put in my earplugs, or put on my headphones and the problem is solved.

Chronicles

Sunday, December 15, 2013

Noisy Neighbor

The only other prisoner here in Federal Death row who seems willing to talk to me beyond just being polite is my current next door neighbor. He is a tall sixty-something unshaven and scraggly gray-haired man who only talks to me when he thinks he can get something from me; a magazine, extra food, or some sort of favor.

I suppose he thinks that because most of the prisoners here shun me he should be able to win favors from me by being nice. I only suppose this because he is rarely nice to anyone else and talks trash about homosexuals, child molesters, and niggers, openly and frequently. But, I treat him kindly and politely all the same. I figure it's not his fault that he is so transparently self obsessed. To top it all off, he fancies himself a brilliant amateur scientist with ideas for trapping unlimited energy from the earth's core that can solve the entire world's energy crisis, if only President Obama didn't personally have it out for him. (According to my neighbor, the reason he is on death row is because of secret presidential orders to keep his revolutionary energy ideas from being taken seriously.)

This might seem comical, but I don't laugh and try to ask interesting questions when he talks about such things, though it is extremely difficult to get a word in at all, much less a question, when he's on such subjects – when he's on ANY subject, really. I try not to just humor him the way most of the guards and other prisoners do, and maybe that's why he talks to me – it's another theory at least.

The other day he yelled out my name to get my attention, „Hey, Duncan! Joseph Duncan!" I answered by yelling from my bunk without getting up, „Yeah?!"

He asked, „Do you want to use the phone?"

I honestly did not understand why he would ask me such a question out of the blue like that. So, I replied with a question that seemed natural to me, „Why would I want to use the phone?"

When I asked that I heard someone further down the tier (or „range", ad they like to call it here) laugh out loud. My neighbor reacted by lashing out at me.

„Fuck you, you piece of shit coward!"

He made sure to yell it loud enough so the person down the tier (or „range") could hear. I didn't know if he was yelling at me or the other prisoner. So I asked as bemusedly as I could, „Are you talking to me?"

Well, he said he was talking to me and then over the course of the next few minutes he accused me of showing my asshole to other inmates through the cell door window, talking about fag sex with other inmates through the air vents, being the most self-centered person he ever met, and a liar to boot.

I didn't bother telling him what I thought about him, and neither did I bother attempting to defend myself by refuting his accusations. Instead I just asked why he was attacking me just because I'd asked him why he asked me if I wanted to use the phone. I also asked him why he thought I was self-centered, which he couldn't answer but I assume it is because I refused to buy things on commissary for him when he tried to get me to in the past, not to mention other „favors" I refused to do for him (he seemed to forget about all the things I did for him without ever asking so much as a thank you in return, like loaning him books and magazines, and giving him coffee, sweetener, and extra food when he asked for it, and that I've never asked him for so much as a conversation in all the time I've been here).

From his responses to my questions, and other evidence, I was able to discern that the reason he asked me if I wanted to use the phone was because he was trying to involve me in an overt attempt to keep another prisoner from getting the phone. It was this other prisoner who laughed when I didn't go along with the plan, which my neighbor thought was a conspiracy between me and the other prisoner (who, according to my neighbor, I was having a homosexual relationship with through the vents and windows), all to make him look bad.

So, after assuring my neighbor that I'd never spoken to any other prisoners at all through the vent, and that I didn't even know the inmate who laughed at him (nor did I know anything about any other inmate's homosexual proclivities) and that I'd only asked why he asked me about the phone because I genuinely was perplexed by the sudden unexplained question, my neighbor „accepted" MY apology (which I took to be the closest thing to an actual apology from him) and was then quiet for the rest of the day (for him to be quiet at all is a gift in itself, and I suspect he actually believes he's doing me a favor when he is quiet – and to tell you the truth, so do I).

I had also asked him when he thought I had ever been dishonest, and hence, a liar. His answer surprised me. He told me that he didn't believe that I killed all those children, and I lied to protect someone else.

Why would he think that? Actually, I didn't bother to ask because I doubt if he would tell me the real reason. Ever since I first met him, or, more specifically, since he first started talking to me, I have strongly suspected that he was after any information that he could report to the Federal authorities. I even sent several affidavits to my attorneys in the past detailing every conversation I had with him at first, because I was concerned he would happily lie under oath and say I said things I would never have said.

This is not paranoia on my part. In the past, several inmates have reported conversations I had with them that never even happened. One inmate at IMSI (in Idaho) got so mad because I ignored all his attempts to get me to talk to him (from several cells away) that he started banging on his walls and door (it actually wasn't until he started banging that I even realized he was trying to get my attention). And, even though I just continued to ignore him, and never even said, hi, I found out later that he reported all kinds of conversations I supposedly had with him where I told him things like, that I hated myself and wanted to die, and that I hate children and talked about all the „sick" things I liked doing to them. I know about this only because the Riverside (California) investigators asked me about it during an interview they held with me in the Indio jail. They admitted it didn't sound like something I'd say, and I told them I was shocked that such statements would even make it into their files.

So when my neighbor here started talking to me for no reason, and asking questions about my case (that I carefully never answered), I made sure to at least document my side of the story. And when he told me that he didn't think I killed those children, and that I lied to protect someone, I knew exactly where he got that idea, from the FBI. I happen to know that this is a theory of theirs that they've been investigating for some time, mostly (and I'm assuming here) because I don't fit their profiles for a person who rapes and kills children. (I'm assuming this to be the reason for their suspicion that I lied to protect someone, but the fact that I don't fit their profiles for a child killer is formally established in their own official reports – which state in plain language that I deviate from their profiles in extremely unusual degrees and regards).

My neighbor hasn't spoken to me since, and I can only hope he won't, for a while at least. I call him „my neighbor" because for some reason he keeps ending up in the cell next to me or across the hall from me, even after the „random" cell moves that take place every three months.

I'll continue to be polite, and speak to him when he speaks to me. But, I'll never trust him. Not because I'm worried he'll find out the truth, but because I'm worried he'll help the authorities of this world cover it up.

(Originally written by Joseph E. Duncan III on June 20, 2013)

P.S. I doubt that my „neighbor" above will ever see or learn about this entry. But, just in case he ever does, then I hope he will understand that I am really saying nothing about him at all, only about me (i. e. my own doubtlessly deluded perceptions). I also hope that the readers of this blog already understand this.

Reflections

Tuesday, December 17, 2013

Being In The Now

Being in the Now does not mean ignoring or otherwise disregarding the past and/or the future. It means incorporating and embracing the past and the future as part of the Now.

It makes no sense to ignore the lessons of the past, and even less sense to ignore the possibilities of the future. Some say that the future and the past do not exist, only the Now is real. But that is like saying China does not exist simply because you are not there and cannot see it. Of course we ultimately don't know if China exists unless we are actually there, and even then the reality of it is debatable. But, to assume that China does not exist simply because we can't see it is more foolish than assuming it does. And so assuming that the future or past does not exist only because we are not there now is more foolish than assuming they do exist. It is better to assume they do.

It is better still to assume nothing, not even that you exist. In this way we can focus on our experience "in the Now" without the confusion of pointless philosophical questions. The past and the future in this sense become as much a part of our experience in the Now as anything else. Our memories become our experience in the now of the past, and our imagination becomes our experience of the future. Is not memory and imagination just as real as what you see, touch, taste, smell, or feel? Of course it is, and science even confirms this to be so. Numerous studies show that what our mind "sees" is not the same as what our eyes "see". Everything we experience is filtered and interpreted before we ever become aware of it. So to assume that what you imagine the future to be is any less real than what you see the Now to be is just another way of deceiving yourself, and ultimately only deprives you of truly experiencing the Now at all!

We must embrace the future in the Now, and bring the past along too. That doesn't mean letting the past determine the Now, or even the future. It means only remembering the past in the Now, but not mistaking it for the Now. If we are not in China then we do not need to speak Chinese. But, if we know how to speak Chinese we do not pretend we do not. I hope I'm making my point - the past is the past, and is best left in the past, but not forgotten.

Likewise, the future is the future, and while it is good to prepare for what we imagine the future may bring, it is not good to try to force the future (i.e. via the present) to be something it is not. In other words, if the future does not bring what we expect or what we hoped, then we must accept what it does bring, learn and adapt. That is all part of being in the Now.

Chronicles

Tuesday, December 24, 2013

Bald For X-Mas, But Legally Sane

My attorney, Joe, called last week and told me that the judge in Idaho has finally issued his ruling on the six-week multi-million dollar "competency" hearing that took place at the beginning of this year (2013). Not unexpectedly the ruling is that I was, in fact, "competent" when I waived my death sentence appeals, and "competent" when I opted to represent myself (and consequently provide no legal defense - i.e. no witnesses, evidence, or arguments against any sentence of death - the news reporters claimed that I wanted to die, but hopefully, if you've been reading this blog, you already know that's not true at all). So, I am officially now legally sane; what a relief, LOL. They had me worried for a while there, LMOL!

I haven't actually read the judge's 60 page decision yet, but Joe is sending it to me and once I have looked it over I'll write what I think here (for those who care). In the meantime, I shaved off all my hair. It was getting too long to manage easily, and signing up to be chained up and taken downstairs to get it cut was too much trouble in my book. Besides, it was fun cutting it all off myself with a single razor in the shower, and it gave me something to do that was out of routine, which helps to break up the monotony. I've been waiting for the judge's decision before I shaved my head because I didn't want any reports of "unstable behavior" reaching him and possibly influencing his thinking. I have no plans on keeping it shaved clean. I just wanted to be rid of the mess for awhile, at least until it grows back.

This decision (competency) also means that I can start being a little more honest again about some of my thoughts and feelings that I was worried the "defense" attorneys (who are all great people) and doctors would use to convince the courts that I am not competent. It's not that I've been dishonest, I've just been avoiding certain forms of expressing myself that could be misunderstood or even misrepresented. Now that the district court judge has made his ruling I don't need to worry about this so much because all subsequent rulings (appellate) are supposedly made "from the existing record", and not from anything I say or do now. In other words, I'm free to be as "crazy" as I want again. LMOL LMOL! LMOL!!

Reflections

Sunday, December 29, 2013

Politics and Religion

History tells us that organized religion has always been about politics - i.e. a means of manipulating the consent and consensus of a group of people in order to consolidate power and control over them. But, since all history is written by those currently in power it is not so easy to read in it the fact that all political organizations - i.e. governments - are systems of religious belief, used as the means of manipulating the consent and consensus of a group of people in order to consolidate power and control over them. If one but only looks briefly however, this becomes apparent; which is why all governments spend so much time and effort distracting the people so they won't think about looking behind the curtain of politics, or a question what they have been systematically taught to believe.

Made in the USA
Columbia, SC
12 April 2024

f6615189-b800-4fd2-8de9-3bc9bd07355aR01